ANN FLEMING'S FAMILY TREE

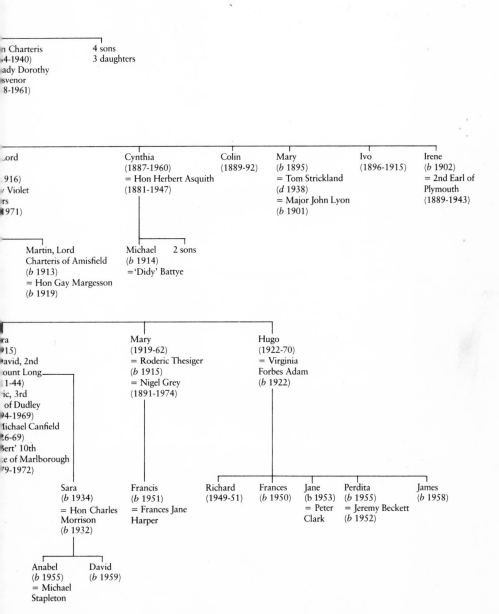

n Charteris
4-1940)
ady Dorothy
svenor
8-1961)

4 sons
3 daughters

_ord

916)
Violet
rs
971)

Cynthia
(1887-1960)
= Hon Herbert Asquith
(1881-1947)

Colin
(1889-92)

Mary
(b 1895)
= Tom Strickland
(d 1938)
= Major John Lyon
(b 1901)

Ivo
(1896-1915)

Irene
(b 1902)
= 2nd Earl of
Plymouth
(1889-1943)

Martin, Lord
Charteris of Amisfield
(b 1913)
= Hon Gay Margesson
(b 1919)

Michael   2 sons
(b 1914)
= 'Didy' Battye

ra
15)
avid, 2nd
ount Long
1-44)
ic, 3rd
of Dudley
4-1969)
lichael Canfield
6-69)
ert' 10th
e of Marlborough
79-1972)

Mary
(1919-62)
= Roderic Thesiger
(b 1915)
= Nigel Grey
(1891-1974)

Hugo
(1922-70)
= Virginia
Forbes Adam
(b 1922)

Sara
(b 1934)
= Hon Charles
Morrison
(b 1932)

Francis
(b 1951)
= Frances Jane
Harper

Richard
(1949-51)

Frances
(b 1950)

Jane
(b 1953)
= Peter
Clark

Perdita
(b 1955)
= Jeremy Beckett
(b 1952)

James
(b 1958)

Anabel
(b 1955)
= Michael
Stapleton

David
(b 1959)

THE LETTERS OF
ANN FLEMING

By the same author

Lord Dunsany
The Letters of Evelyn Waugh (Ed.)

THE LETTERS OF

ANN FLEMING

edited by

MARK AMORY

COLLINS HARVILL
8 Grafton Street London W1
1985

William Collins Sons and Co Ltd
London · Glasgow · Sydney · Auckland
Toronto · Johannesburg

Photograph Acknowledgements

Permission is gratefully acknowledged to the following for the reproduction of photographs: the estate of Ann Fleming for nos. 1, 2, 3, 4, 5, 13, 14; the estate of Cecil Beaton for nos. 9, 10, 15 and 20; Judy Astor for nos. 6, 7, 11, 12, 18, 19 and 21; Virginia Charteris for no. 8; Sir Nicholas Henderson for no. 16; Mark Bonham Carter for no. 17.

First published 1985 by Collins Harvill
Copyright © in the Introduction and compilation Mark Amory 1985
ISBN 0 00217059 0
Photoset in Linotron Sabon by Wyvern Typesetting Ltd, Bristol
Made and printed in Great Britain
by Mackays of Chatham

CONTENTS

ILLUSTRATIONS

FOREWORD

Some months before her death in 1981 Ann Fleming was turning over in her mind the idea of writing an autobiography. Mark Boxer, then a publisher, had suggested it. Her sister, Laura, Duchess of Marlborough, had written one that naturally described their parents and childhood and Ann felt that she could, almost should, write a complementary account. At least once in her life she had started a novel. She feared however that her inexperience and shaky grammar might need assistance and I was standing by to see if a supporting role emerged. During two or three country walks we spoke lightly of which bits of her life, which friends and which places should appear. No word was written.

When I was approached as her literary executor, I therefore knew her mind more precisely than can usually be the case; not that any special knowledge was required to be confident that she was in favour of frankness, even of stirring things up – certainly of letting the chips fall where they might. This book tries to be true to her wishes but bears little resemblance to the one she would have written. That would have dwelt on Stanway and her childhood, whereas the surviving letters begin during her second marriage. She would have drawn character sketches of many friends – Lucian Freud, Francis Bacon, Frederick Ashton, Arnold Goodman – who scarcely appear. Nor is it the book I originally imagined. By chance and because it appeals to me it was first planned as a portrait drawn from several different sources and viewpoints. Her friend and my publisher, Mark Bonham Carter, agreed that a conventional biography would be a mistake. I was familiar with her letters to and from Evelyn Waugh, which recounted her social life in crisp and high-spirited detail. Among her papers were schoolgirl diaries, fragments of a novel set in the late 1940s, a libellous review she wrote of Kingsley Amis's pastiche James Bond novel and some notes she had made for Ian Fleming's biographer. Patrick Leigh Fermor generously volunteered to put down his thoughts and recollections in a free-associating memoir. There must be newspaper cuttings. By incredible luck an unpublished novel by her brother Hugo Charteris contained a striking if critical portrait of her when she was still married to Lord Rothermere but in love with Fleming. Perhaps a passage in some Bond story would prove relevant. I might even fabricate a few scenes myself.

If the sources were varied, the plot was to be simple, even reminiscent of the most hackneyed romantic fiction. A beautiful aristocratic girl, effectively an orphan, falls in love with a fascinating but faithless charmer. Circumstances keep them apart. Unfortunately she had rushed into an early marriage before she met him; then, when she is free, he hesitates and, bitterly hurt, she marries another. However she loves him still and forsakes a life of ease and glamour for her penniless journalist. In the nick of time his books are a success and he becomes the most famous author in the world. All this to be set in the most elegant drawing-rooms and expensive hotel suites of London, Paris, New York and Kitzbühel, with frequent visits to the lush tropics of Jamaica.

I abandoned this approach for two reasons. It did not suit the subject. Ann was not a figure of vast importance, the tiniest details of whose life command attention, nor was she particularly complex. Her character was clear and unusually consistent. As a result much of the material, unremarkable in itself, threw no new light. Too many demands would have been made on the reader continually to change gear, sometimes simply accepting, sometimes evaluating, sometimes mistrusting what was put before him. The second and simpler reason was that the letters to and from Evelyn Waugh overwhelmed me. It had long been decided that this should not be a massive book but their sheer bulk refused to be diminished or assimilated.

The story also changed under closer examination. Ann was not in fact an orphan; her father lived to be over eighty and she was immensely fond of him. Her childhood was scarcely pathetic; the marriage to Lord O'Neill which lasted twelve years and produced two children who remained a great part of her life cannot be brushed aside so lightly. Similarly she was passionately in love with Lord Rothermere for years and much enjoyed the trappings, the parties and the ability to meet anyone who interested her. The 'happy ending' with Fleming was in fact the collision of two strongly independent characters and became a struggle that exhausted them both – 'if we were younger we would get a divorce'. She outlived him by more than fifteen years, years which were dominated by the deaths of her brother, many friends and, particularly, their son. Nevertheless the romantic line holds. Ann herself considered Fleming the centre of her life.

My view of her character, on the other hand, altered less than I expected. I admired Ann for, among other qualities, her sharpness, determination and lack of pretence. It seemed possible that as I probed further back I might find that these had once combined to form a ruthlessness that was less attractive. Some of her contemporaries, particularly friends of Ian Fleming, implied as much. All I can say is that that is not the impression I received. Not all people reveal themselves in their letters; Ann to a great extent does so, but inevitably there are aspects that do not appear. You would not realize from these pages the great pleasure she always took in nature – birds and fish, flowers and trees were an important part of her life. The fortitude she showed during her last decade is under-emphasized, nor is it clear how very often she was ill. The letters begin too late to show how much she developed; how, by seeking out intelligent and gifted friends and allowing them to add to her, she grew, without sacrificing a scrap of her own character, steadily more interesting and remarkable. For when we start she is already thirty-two and in her prime.

So this has become a conventional collection of letters, printed in chronological order, including some written to as well as by Ann but trailing a few pieces of decoration left over from the earlier plan, which I hope and trust will not prove distracting. It has moved no nearer to being a biography, indeed it has taken a step further away. What appears depends on what letters happen to have been written and to survive. It is accepted that the telephone has destroyed old habits of correspondence and Ann was a busy telephoner. Nevertheless she wrote to those who were kept at a considerable geographical distance. Ian Fleming was often abroad, particularly in Jamaica. Hugo and Virginia Charteris and Evelyn Waugh lived for the most part deep in the country, making only occasional raids on London. Lady Diana Cooper lived in France at first, the Countess of Avon moved to the West Indies, Patrick and Joan Leigh Fermor built a house in Greece, Somerset Maugham remained by the Mediterranean, the Foreign Office kept sending Nicholas Henderson to foreign countries. These were her main correspondents and each preserved at least some of her letters.

For her part Ann kept files of the most interesting ones she received. This suggests an intention and order that never really came to exist. Letters from Somerset Maugham, fifty of them, brief and dull, were respectfully preserved and some others found their way into the appropriate niches. The rest, the vast majority, which included Waugh's, had to take their chance in the rough and tumble outside. Her own to Ian Fleming she had presumably gathered together after his death but they too were in disorder. On the surface lay a froth of unremarkable thank-you letters. A mass of information from her children about their progress at various schools survives. Otherwise it seems to have been a hit-and-miss affair with several important letters missing. A sad gap is made by the disappearance of almost everything from her brother Hugo Charteris. Much of their relationship can be inferred from hers to him but he would have supplied an intimate, critical commentary unlike any other. There were nine years between them; she married when he was ten and was living with Lord Rothermere before he left Eton. Their sister Laura was soon to marry another extremely rich and prominent peer, the Earl of Dudley. Charteris disapproved of the friends and behaviour of his elder sisters and demonstrated his sincerity by exiling himself in poverty to Scotland to work on his novels. Nor is there any hint of sour grapes about this. Many who decry the hollow glitter of the metropolis were not asked to the party in the first place. Charteris was immensely attractive and charming and with his talents, let alone his sisters, could have found the money to sustain such a life had he wanted to do so. The difficulty was not envy or resentment at the good time they were having so much as an underlying assumption that as a result of their gold-plated frivolity and his poverty-stricken integrity, they should continue to look after him indefinitely. His novels were praised and read but he never quite broke into the first rank. Ann did get him a job on the *Daily Mail* and helped in several ways, often financial, but sometimes reacted sharply when her hand was nipped yet again. This was not unreasonable. On the other hand it is rash for an amateur, even a sister, to advise a struggling novelist on where he is going wrong.

Ann had been attracted by Ian Fleming's looks, moodiness and authority when they met socially before the war and he became a friend of her husband Lord O'Neill. However soon afterwards she fell passionately in love with Lord Rothermere, though her friendship with Fleming continued to grow. After an undistinguished career as a stockbroker, Fleming both enjoyed himself and impressed others in Naval Intelligence during the war and when peace came was rewarded with an interesting job improving the foreign news coverage of *The Sunday Times*. It was not until Ann was safely married to Lord Rothermere that he said he loved her, though she does not seem to have thought this significant. It is not chance that other people's love letters often make unsatisfactory reading. All letters should be adapted to their intended reader, but love letters are an extreme case; they are for one person only and are meant to convey unique emotions. If we discover that, for example, an amusing account of a dinner-party has been written to several people, we have small grounds for complaint. The most severe reaction would be that invention was running low in the writer. If we find a batch of similar love letters sent to different people we think less not only of the fickle writer but of the letters themselves. They are not what they claimed to be. Also, particularly in a clandestine affair, the mere existence of the letter may be more important than what it says, clumsy reassurance more to the point than delicate expression. Later other people can enjoy ardour, elegance or wit; those may not have been the qualities required. So it is not really a criticism of Fleming to say that his early letters to Ann are, to us, repetitive, sometimes dull, even embarrassing. She did not think so, which is their justification. Many have been left out.

At first neither thought of marriage. Some say Fleming wanted to marry a girl who was killed in the war. He appears to have remained what he had long been, a formidable womanizer determined to stay a bachelor. It seems to me that, after Ann lost his child and Rothermere issued an ultimatum that they were no longer to meet, they found that they were bound more closely than they had realized; but the uncertainty of dates makes the detail of their emotions hard to follow. Many of Fleming's friends consider that she forced him into marriage. Naturally after they are living together there are few letters. Those that exist are usually written by Fleming from abroad and contain innocuous travelogue. However the Flemings in general and Ian in particular are exceptionally uncommunicative in person and later on there are occasional explosive exchanges which seem to be fuelled by months of pent-up emotion. Rare though these are they at least hint at, and sometimes recount directly, the central drama of Ann's life during these years.

Evelyn Waugh was a famous and best-selling writer living for the most in Somerset by the time Ann got to know him. The two women with whom he came closest to falling in love after his second marriage – Lady Diana Cooper and Clarissa Churchill, later Countess of Avon – were Ann's closest friends. He was attracted to women who moved in society, were quick-witted and stylish and above all were not intimidated by him. Ann's self-confidence was not in doubt. Each had the leisure and inclination to sustain a correspondence, indeed Waugh sustained several. His last letter (to Lady Mosley) begins 'Beware of writing to me. I always answer.' Ann wrote far more often to him than to anyone else and after his death warned Sir Nicholas Henderson rather in the same manner, 'Deserted by Evelyn and permitted a sip of whisky, you may hear much more from me . . . now all my correspondents are dead except you.' And indeed Sir Nicholas did take Waugh's place in so far as anyone did.

Waugh and Ann wrote to each other mostly to amuse but sometimes to sympathize or support. The main topic is the comedy to be found in the behaviour of their friends and acquaintances. Politics are mentioned rarely; writing, except for simple praise from Ann, never. They are capable of discussing serious topics but on the whole choose not to. Waugh does suggest that Ann attempt to pray after the death of her sister while she can openly admit that she is unhappy. Far more often she makes light of emotional difficulties or, without denying them, leaves them out altogether. This was true with everyone she wrote to except Lady Diana Cooper (Waugh too wrote his most personal letters to her) and the same intimate note is sometimes struck with Lady Avon. The few surviving letters to Peter Quennell suggest that with him too she held nothing back, which, while Fleming was alive, often meant confessing that things were not entirely well with their marriage.

Her remaining correspondent was Patrick Leigh Fermor, with whom she is less personal but completely at ease. The keynote of his character, as any passing acquaintance could confirm, is energetic enthusiasm. He was born in 1915, two years after Ann, and the educational system of England, in this case King's School, Canterbury, could only manage to contain him until 1933, when he set off to walk to Constantinople on a pound a week. He travelled, often in the Balkans, for several more years and managed to turn the war into a continuation of his dashing and romantic existence. His most conspicuous adventure was to kidnap the German Commander of Crete. For two years he lived in the mountains, 'black-turbaned, booted and sashed and appropriately silver-and-ivory daggered and cloaked in white goats' hair and deep in grime'. With great chunks of poetry known by heart and voluble in many languages, he would sometimes combine his gifts by singing 'D'you Ken John Peel' in Italian. His letters to Ann are what you would most like to receive on a dank February morning in England, full of warmth and high spirits with perhaps a description of some exotic landscape, two or three words you have to look up, some historical conjecture that has just occurred to him and a comic account of a recent personal disaster. They are necessarily about his life not hers and, though I struggled, a place in this book could not be found for more than one of them. Ann writes back much the same content that she writes to Waugh but catches something of Leigh Fermor's generosity and lack of malice.

So the dominant tone is set by Waugh, and Ann's response to him. A friend has suggested that it came a little falsely from her; I think this harsh. Certainly she adapts to him, even takes on some of his comic exaggeration. Her style remains her own but is sometimes heightened. Nor is it inappropriate to her subject. The centre of this book is set in the 1950s when Ann married the unsociable Fleming and then tried to construct a life that included their friends. Few of hers got on with him; she liked almost none of his. Each of Ann's husbands complained about the people with whom she surrounded herself and they did take up the forefront of her life. Waugh might dismiss most of them as 'fuddy-duddies' but there could be no one sharper with whom to discuss their goings-on. As in life, the social surface is what is seen at a glance but there are occasional reminders of other things behind.

Fleming became ill and died in 1964. An enfeebled Waugh followed him in 1966. Charteris succumbed to cancer in 1970, when only forty-eight. Worries about her son Caspar dominated the early 1970s and were shown to be justified when he committed suicide in 1975. Some thought she would not recover from this blow. It took time and she was perhaps never quite so forcefully herself again. The gaps left her with fewer people to write to and the sadness made her less inclined to write at all. So there are not so many letters and those there are become less vivid. The last years pass at great, I hope not bewildering, speed.

What appears here is about half of the letters that I have seen; still more exist. My impression is that the vast majority of those not shown to me are of minor importance but naturally I cannot be sure. Many letters have had to be excluded, many have been cut internally. The customary dots to mark omission have themselves been omitted; it became absurd to put so many, particularly towards the end. Repetition, social arrangements, conventional gratitude and good wishes, comments on her children and sympathy about illness account for the bulk of what has been removed. All cuts tend to distort. Ann may appear too brusque or a less thoughtful mother than she was; the astonishing amount of time when she was less than well does not emerge clearly. Of course readers suspect that scandalous stories have been removed and of course they have, but not often. Ann was not promiscuous; there was no string of lovers to suppress.

Ann Fleming was surrounded by professional writers but she was not one herself. She could not spell. The difference between 'where' and 'were' eluded her, she never spotted the first 'a' in Isaiah, her apostrophes were scattered in the most unlikely places. All this we have endeavoured to correct. Dates have been made uniform with square brackets around any contribution from me and a question mark where I am still uncertain. No letter has been published before. The nearest to an exception are a very few by Waugh which have had a beginning or an end added, so that some part has already appeared. Also two letters which I had wrongly made into one in *The Letters of Evelyn Waugh* have been split apart once more by the scholarly Alan Bell, added to and now stand separately (see pages 313–4). Some new letters by Waugh are from a cache that Ann simply neglected to show me when I was editing his letters, some are interesting in the context of Ann's life rather than his, some repeat information that Waugh also wrote to others (usually Nancy Mitford) and were excluded from the earlier book on these grounds. Often a letter cannot be used precisely because it has already been published and there is a lack of continuity as a result. In such a case I have usually quoted from the original letter in a footnote. It is exceptionally generous of Auberon Waugh, representing his family, to allow this amount of quotation and the use of his father's letters.

Naturally I am most grateful to those (or their heirs) who received letters from Ann and allowed me to see and use them. Those who refused through idleness, caution or good taste made me appreciate even more the bold and helpful. The extent of my debt to them is clear -- without their cooperation there could have been no book. I therefore thank particularly Lord and Lady Annan, Judy Astor for letters to Michael Astor and photographs from his album, the Countess of Avon, Mrs John Bailey (Iris Murdoch), Hugo Vickers for letters to Sir Cecil Beaton, Sir Isaiah and Lady Berlin, Mark Boxer, Lord Campbell, Virginia Charteris for letters to Hugo Charteris, Bruce Chatwin, Lady Diana Cooper, the Duchess of Devonshire, Lord and Lady Donaldson, Nicholas Fleming for letters to Peter Fleming, Patrick and Joan Leigh Fermor, Milton Gendel, John Gere, Alistair Horne, Virginia Ironside, Robert Kee, Viscount Lambton, Lady Mary Lyon, John Morgan, Lord Neidpath, Sir John Pope-Hennessy for letters to James Pope-Hennessy, Peter Quennell, Jacob Rothschild, John Sparrow and Sir Angus Wilson.

The books on which I have drawn most heavily are *The Life of Ian Fleming* by John Pearson, 1966, *Laughter from a Cloud* by Laura, Duchess of Marlborough, 1980, *Maugham* by Ted Morgan, 1980 and *The Letters of Evelyn Waugh*, 1980.

I must also thank Lords Charteris, Goodman and O'Neill for permission to quote Ian Fleming's letters and for much further help; John Sparrow for permission to quote those of Sir Maurice Bowra and some lines of his verse; Deirdre Levi for permission to quote a letter from Cyril Connolly; Alan Searle for permission to quote two from Somerset Maugham; Patrick Leigh Fermor, Lucian Freud and Peter Quennell for permission to quote from letters by themselves; Charles Ritchie for permission to quote from *Storm Signals*, 1983; and Weidenfeld and Nicolson for permission to quote from *The Strenuous Years* by Cecil Beaton, 1973.

Into one category which ranges from a formal nod to those who answered a letter or placed a quotation, to deep gratitude to those who gave much time and took great trouble are all the above and also Gillon Aitken; Joseph Alsop; Hardy Amies; Kingsley Amis; Fiona, Countess of Arran; Sir Frederick Ashton; Sir John Jacob Astor; David Attlee; Sir Alfred Ayer; Francis Bacon; Noël Barber; Sheila, Countess of Birkenhead; Mark Blackett-Ord; Blanche Blackwell; Nancy, Lady Blakenham; Philip Brownrigg; Edgar Crickmere; Lord Dacre; Madame Jacques de Beaumarchais; Edwina, Lady d'Erlanger; Nigel Douglas; Maureen, Marchioness of Dufferin and Ava; Alastair Forbes; Stephanie Gaitskell; Mary Gascoigne; Martha Gellhorn; Barbara Ghika; Sir Ian and Lady

Caroline Gilmour; Francis Grey; Lord and Lady Grimond; Robert Harling; Robert Heber-Percy; Robin Holland-Martin; Peter Janson-Smith; Roy Jenkins; Susanna Johnston; Charlotte Joll; James Kirkman; Speed Lamkin; Loelia, Lady Lindsay; Margueritte Littman; Lady Caroline Lowell; Lady Dorothy Lygon; Laura, Duchess of Marlborough; Katherine, Viscountess Mersey; Fionn Morgan; Sheridan Morley; Malcolm and Kitty Muggeridge; John Murray; Sir Edward Pickering; Lady Antonia Pinter; John Perry; Anne Pitt; Tom Pocock; John Pringle; Alan Ross; Margaret (Nin) Ryan; Lord and Lady George Scott; John Stoye; Patrick Trevor-Roper; Dame Margaret, Lady Wakehurst; Alice Windsor-Clive; Anne Wyndham and Francis Wyndham. I cannot resist picking out Laura, Duchess of Marlborough, Peter Quennell, Fionn Morgan and Virginia Charteris as those who have been most patient with my questions. Particular thanks are also due to Alan Bell for his industry and generosity with the Waugh papers, to my mother, Gaenor Amory, for typing and fielding general knowledge queries and to Mark Bonham Carter and Ariane Goodman who have shaped, advised and encouraged.

PRINCIPAL DATES

1913   Ann Geraldine Mary Charteris born
1915   Laura Charteris born
1919   Mary Rose Charteris born
1922   Hugo Charteris born
1925   Ann's mother, Frances Charteris, dies
1931   Ann comes out
1932   Ann marries Lord O'Neill
1933   Laura marries Viscount Long
        Raymond O'Neill born
1936   Fionn O'Neill born
        Ann meets and falls in love with Esmond Harmsworth
1938   Ann meets Ian Fleming
1940   Mary Rose marries Captain Roderick Thesiger
        Ann takes a house at Buscot, near Faringdon
1943   Laura divorces Lord Long and marries the Earl of Dudley
1944   Lord O'Neill killed in action
1945   Ann marries Viscount Rothermere
        Ann's father, Guy Charteris, marries Violet Porter
1946   Mary Rose divorces Captain Thesiger
        Ann visits Fleming's house, Goldeneye, in Jamaica
1948   Hugo Charteris marries Virginia Forbes Adam
        Ann's baby daughter dies in Edinburgh
1949   Mary Rose marries Nigel Grey
1952   Ann and Lord Rothermere divorce
        Ann marries Ian Fleming
        Caspar is born
        James Bond is created
        The Flemings buy No. 16 Victoria Square
1953   The first James Bond story, *Casino Royale*, is published
1954   Lord Dudley divorces Laura
1957   The Flemings move to The Old Palace, Canterbury
1959   The Flemings buy Sevenhampton

1960   Laura Charteris marries Michael Canfield
1962   The film of *Dr No* comes out
        Mary Rose dies
1964   Ian Fleming dies
1966   Evelyn Waugh dies
1967   Guy Charteris dies
1969   Michael Canfield dies
1970   Hugo Charteris dies
1972   Laura marries the Duke of Marlborough
1975   Caspar dies
1981   Ann dies

INTRODUCTION

When Ann Charteris was born during the last of the long hot summers before the First World War, she seemed destined for a life of the utmost security and ease. Her parents were children of a set – the Souls – whose gaiety, charm and intelligence seemed to some, not least themselves, to have evolved into the most agreeable and civilized existence yet devised. But it was 1913, her mother was to die young and Ann grew up an aristocratic waif, cared for by grandmothers and aunts, passed from one to another, so that some holidays were more welcome than others. It was her uncles rather than her brothers who were killed at the front and it was the depressed 1930s rather than the gay 1920s that saw her exchange the schoolroom for the dance floor. Nevertheless her model of how life should be derived from before the war and really from an echo of the 1890s. She thought of her grandparents' house, Stanway, as her home and her affection for it never wavered.

All descriptions of Stanway use one of the favourite words of the Souls, 'golden', to describe the local stone from which it was built; usually it is remembered glowing in the sunlight amid peaceful lawns bounded by yew trees with the village church beyond. At the foot of the Cotswolds, the house had originally been intended as a retreat for the Bishop of Tewkesbury. When the monasteries were dissolved, it was given to the Tracy family and passed through the female line to the Charterises in the late seventeenth century. The fine gatehouse, which has been optimistically attributed to Inigo Jones, leads to the western front with its four wide gables, mullioned windows and the great oriel window through which the light filters in different hues into the hall. Behind, the ground rises steeply to a plateau where there is a folly, the Pyramid, a suitable destination for short if tiring walks. The many fires crackling indoors did not succeed in banishing the cold. Into the great hall, the setting for the Christmas tree, cricket lunches, private theatricals and other forms of entertainment, came not only softened light but chill winds. One small bedroom had five doors said to be so ill-fitting that the converging draughts 'were like five spears'. The atmosphere of this rambling house was imposing but informal.

Six families have been named as central to the Souls: the Wyndhams, Charterises, Tennants, Custs, Windsor-Clives and Grenfells.[1] So when Mary Wyndham, one of the Graces in 'The Wyndham Sisters' by Sargent, married a Charteris in 1883, Stanway could hardly avoid becoming a meeting place for the group. Mary Wyndham was Ann's grandmother and her husband is most often referred to as Viscount Elcho, since his father lived to be ninety-seven and he did not succeed as Earl of Wemyss until 1914. Of their five children who lived to marry, four married the children of Souls.[2] Arthur Balfour, known as King Arthur in recognition of his dominating status among them, had known Lady Elcho before she married; indeed she had expected him to propose and would have accepted him. Instead, he became her lifelong devoted friend and conceivably lover, though when this was suggested in print the family denied it. It is more probable that he died a virgin. In any case he was constantly at Stanway and her children called him not King Arthur but Mr Rabbit.

The Souls found each other in the 1880s and were defined in 1889 by the guest list of a dinner given by Lord Curzon for fifty-three friends. They were in conscious revolt against the philistines who surrounded them and it was said in praise that they made it 'no longer fashionable to be dull' and in criticism that one of them was 'lightly skimming the cream from the surface of life'. They were an upper-class élite who delighted in each other's company. Something of their erudite high spirits was shown one evening at Stanway when George Wyndham turned somersaults on the floor while reciting Virgil and then went on to serenade Balfour with 'The lark now leaves his wat'ry nest'. When justification for them is sought, it is true that after the Prime Minister and the Viceroy, Lord Curzon, have been mentioned, there is a dearth of spectacular achievement. But why should justification be required? Only because some of them, and some of their admirers, seemed to be claiming too much. There was an inclination to go on about one another's charm and brilliance. The nicknames and private language of any circle (and circles exist for the purpose, if not quite of making others feel 'out',

1 The Souls, Jane Abdy and Charlotte Gere, 1984.
2 Hugo, Lord Elcho married Lady Violet Manners, Guy Charteris married Frances Tennant, Lady Cynthia Charteris married Herbert Asquith and Lady Irene Charteris married the Earl of Plymouth, a Windsor-Clive.

then at least to remind the members that they are indeed 'in') tend to sound affected. Some of the Souls may indeed have felt superior and exclusive. Among these was not Lady Elcho, who was accused of being too undiscriminating a hostess and whose own charm rested on her great and genuine interest in everyone she met. Her husband was an MP for over ten years but remained best known in the House of Commons for his speeches suggesting it should adjourn on Derby Day. He had an agreeably dry wit, as when he commented, 'My hair preferred death to dishonour', a reference to his own bald dome and the strands wound like a turban to conceal the bald patches on his brother's head.[3] He was entirely open about having a mistress and when she died found another. He is also said to have been given to depression and lived in constant fear of being bored, not least by the guests imported by his wife. In his wild youth the family fortune had been lost on the Stock Exchange and now he had to live on the income of a trust of £100,000 so that, for instance, only Lord Elcho himself travelled first class while the rest of the family went third. Nevertheless a variety of guests poured into Stanway, among them many connected with the arts such as Mrs Patrick Campbell, H. G. Wells, Henry James, Edith Wharton and, in particular, Sir James Barrie. More surprisingly Sidney and Beatrice Webb were frequent visitors.

Guy Charteris, Ann's father, was born in 1886, the second son. He was the least shy of the children, made cheeky remarks to his intimidating father and so became his favourite. Lady Cynthia Asquith, his sister, recalls how, when he had been caught smoking with the footman and as a punishment was forced to tackle a huge and powerful cigar which it was thought would put him off the habit for life, he puffed it with apparent enjoyment and asked for another.[4] His passion for birds became apparent in childhood, lasted the whole of his life and was passed on to Ann. Untidiness also stayed with him; a son-in-law was to say 'We can't have that scruffy bastard in the house again.' Universally liked, he had no wish or obvious ability to make a mark in the world. His second daughter, Laura, comments 'I believe he had some kind of work at a place called the Investment Registry, but I would say that he was an

3 *A Family Record* by the Countess of Wemyss, 1932, and Lord Charteris to the Editor.
4 *Haply I May Remember*, Cynthia Asquith, 1950. The commas in this book were supplied by Edward Marsh.

inefficient and uninterested man of business.'[5] He married at twenty-six; Ann, born before war broke out, was the eldest child. Charteris joined the Shropshire Infantry, which took him to lodgings in Edinburgh but not to the front. He turned down an offer to be ADC to General French because that would not get him there either. Then he transferred to the Scots Guards and was at the Somme in 1916 before being invalided out of the army. His brother Ivo had been killed the year before, his brother Hugo ('Ego') was killed in Egypt that year. Laura was born in 1915, Mary Rose in 1919[6] and Hugo in 1922.[7]

Their mother was Frances Tennant and although the Tennants were Souls too, they were rather different. For one thing they were rich. For another, Tennants may get a mention in the late thirteenth century but they are not comparable in lineage. John Tennant made a fortune manufacturing chemicals in Glasgow and left a million pounds when he died in 1878. His son, Sir Charles Tennant, born in 1823, put the family on the map socially and politically. He entered the family business, immediately displayed his talents and was soon speculating on the Stock Exchange, building the Forth Bridge, which opened in a hurricane but stood firm, and mining for gold with new techniques which later became universal. A great capitalist in the great age of capitalism, Tennant showed a profit on the mining shares alone which allowed a manager to invest £7.10s and eighteen years later sell for £2905. He became a Liberal MP and a baronet, collected pictures and had sixteen children. One of these was Margot, whose husband Herbert Asquith became Prime Minister in 1908. Another was Frank, Frances's father and Ann's grandfather. Though Frank and his wife Anne Redmayne had six children only two of the others married (one to Sir Iain Colquhoun, the other to the Duke of Rutland). All the same Ann had a large number of cousins, about twenty, while her more distant relations were innumerable and sometimes seemed to connect her to the whole British aristocracy.

5 In her autobiography, *Laughter from a Cloud*, 1980. Laura Charteris (1915–   ). Married 1933–43 to Viscount Long, 1943–54 to the Earl of Dudley, 1960–9 to Michael Canfield and in 1972 to the Duke of Marlborough, who died that year. *See* Appendix of Names.

6 Mary Rose Charteris (1919–62). Married 1940–6 to Captain Roderick Thesiger and in 1949 to Nigel Grey.

7 Hugo Charteris (1922–70). Novelist. Married in 1948 Virginia Forbes Adam. *See* Appendix of Names.

Frances Tennant had been given a house in Westminster, 26 Catherine Street, as a wedding present by her parents, and there her growing family lived in winter. They had comparatively little money so no butler or housekeeper, but there were some maids and a cook. In 1915 Frances went to a family wedding and Margot Asquith recorded in her diary, 'My brother Frank's little girl of two [in fact his grand-daughter] Ann was the sweetest thing in the church. She relieved the congregation by wandering up and down the aisle trying to put on a large white silk glove. She looks to me as if she is going to be wonderfully full of character and vitality. A Darling.' Ann's own comment on her early childhood was that she vividly remembered the horrors of Christmas in London, but this was meant to contrast with other, happier times. When Hugo was one, Laura reports that a wicked nanny, aptly named Oger, kicked the little boy across the room on his china pot which broke and 'he always said he would carry the scars until the day he died'. Ann was Oger's favourite and was therefore never kicked. In the summer holidays houses were taken, sometimes by the sea. Inept governesses came and went. Later a term spent by Ann at Cheltenham Ladies' College was not a success.

In 1925 Frances Charteris went into hospital for a gynaecological operation. During the war Cynthia Asquith had recorded in her diary an instance of Margot Asquith's ability to get things wrong: 'She said – to Frances, who has as nearly as possible died at the birth of each of her children – "You are the strongest woman in the world for having babies, you ought to have one every year!"' Now at the age of only thirty-eight she did suddenly die. Ann wrote years later in a letter to her aunt, Lady Mary Lyon, 'I was too old not to remember it well and remember minding very much when she went to the nursing home – curiously much.' She was twelve. In later life Ann felt so strongly that children should not be exposed to the ordeal of a parent's funeral that it seemed likely that she had suffered this herself, though Laura remembers that they did not in fact go to Aberlady in Scotland for their mother's funeral.

Guy Charteris was bereft. 'I never had much heart,' he said, 'but all the heart I had died with her.' Everyone, including Charteris himself, seems to have realized that he could not cope with his young family. He managed to have them for a brief stay at his new house in Oxford Square during the winters, but their time was now mainly divided between Granny Tennant in Scotland and 'Grumps'

(Now Lady Wemyss) at Stanway. Laura once overheard the arrangements being made: 'You can't have Laura for Easter. I shall be away. You can have Ann.' Charteris became more like a favourite uncle than a father.

Ann remembered the homes of her grandmothers in sharp contrast. Tennant life at North Berwick was physical to the point of heartiness – golf, tennis, picnics on the beach, occasional riding. Ann took a reasonably active part in the games and sports but she never excelled and looked back on them with loathing. When asked how she knew so much English poetry by heart, she said that at least there had been a good library in which she had spent long adolescent afternoons alone. Laura on the other hand thrived in this strenuous atmosphere. Hugo was too small to count and Mary Rose was already set apart from them. When it was remarked later that, if some people have a skin too few, the Charterises had a skin too many, the reference left out Mary Rose as she was so often left out. Ann, Laura and particularly Hugo, when he took to writing novels in which his closest friends and relations appeared in highly recognizable and unflattering roles, were often in the position of saying that they were sorry if someone was upset but that they had not meant to do any harm and, anyway, what was all the fuss about? Mary Rose was made of less stern stuff, more trampled on than trampling.

At Stanway Laura preferred her grandfather, who in turn preferred her. Ann loved her grandmother but Lady Wemyss was the centre of a large household and perhaps Ann was a little left out. It was now, while Lady Colefax vied with Lady Cunard in London, that Ann saw the last of an earlier style of entertaining. The atmosphere to be created was gaiety this side of boisterousness, of wit but not self-conscious exhibitionism. Games after dinner at Stanway were more hilarious but less erudite than those with other Souls. Serious topics were treated lightly, light matters given serious consideration, solemnity barred. Politicians of importance might be present but they would not discourse on politics. Lack of money, by now acute, was not allowed to influence the scale of hospitality, though there was no ostentation. Lady Wemyss, her daughter Cynthia Asquith reports, 'used to bemoan the deplorably growing (now surely fully-grown?) habit of guests whispering together in couples'.[8] Conversation should be general and sparkling. All this

8 *Haply I May Remember.*

could be said of Ann's later entertaining, though she possessed a delight in stirring things up, almost an aggression, that Lady Wemyss lacked.

In 1926 there was an event sufficiently unusual to be noted by all those recording life at Stanway. Family plays were frequently performed but here was one on a more ambitious scale: *The Wheel*, created by Sir James Barrie especially for them, as he notes in the subtitle, *A play written for eight children and their Grandpapa*. A battered copy with her name underlined in red on the cover was among Ann's papers when she died. The eight children were all first cousins: Guy Charteris's four children – though Hugo had only one syllable to declaim – David Elcho[9] and Martin Charteris[10] (the sons of Guy's elder brother Ego, who had been killed in the war), and Michael[11] and Simon Asquith,[12] sons of Lady Cynthia and Herbert Asquith. Lady Cynthia recalled: 'In untellable tension two plays were quiveringly produced . . . from the strain of which I have not yet, twenty years later, quite recovered.' Lady Wemyss says more ambiguously that those that saw them could never forget them, that 'that magician' Barrie coached the children himself and that Mary Rose, in a surprising stroke of casting, was a chilling Lady Macbeth.[13] Laura remembers the seriousness and hard work on which Barrie insisted, also a tricky performance as Juliet when she threw open the top half of a door but remained outside perched on a ladder held by a groom. Barrie used to sit on one leg and cry 'Don't say "Wheel", say "Hwheel", can ye no say "HWHEEL"?' and once at least he stormed out of rehearsal in a rage.

The play starts with the children in the nursery at Stanway into which the magical wheel intrudes. Those that step through it are not only transported into the past or future but somehow transformed into more or less Shakespearian characters. Thus we meet the children as themselves, see them in imagined later life and are

9 David Elcho (1912–   ). Succeeded as Earl of Wemyss in 1937.

10 Martin Charteris (1913–   ). Went to Sandhurst and became a lieutenant-colonel in 1944. Private Secretary to Princess Elizabeth in 1950, Assistant Private Secretary to the Queen 1952–72 and Private Secretary 1972–8, when he was made Provost of Eton and Lord Charteris of Amisfield. Married Gay Margesson in 1944.

11 Michael Asquith (1914–   ). Married 1938–52 to Diana Battye and in 1953 to Helga Ritter.

12 Simon Asquith (b. 1919). Married Vivien Jones in 1942.

13 *A Family Record.*

treated to a series of pastiche scenes from Shakespeare before they are brought back to the present. Barrie, who knew the family well and was later to employ Lady Cynthia as his secretary, shaped the parts to fit their characters. Ann, as a child, cries prophetically, 'I shall be snapped up by a nobleman in my first season', and, when the others are frightened of the Wheel, says 'Pooh' and later 'You cowards' as she is the first to step through. Her sister is labelled 'Name Laura – Profession Vamp'. They share a scene which is at first *As You Like It* but turns into *A Midsummer Night's Dream*. Ann is a boisterous back-slapping Orlando to Laura's plotting Rosalind. After the balcony scene from *Romeo and Juliet* ('O Simon, Simon, wherefore art thou Simon?') and a more extended section of *Macbeth*, Act III finds them all at home and children once more. Grandpapa, now Lord Wemyss, who like Bottom had been wearing an ass's head for a time, and even Lady Wemyss appear in *tableaux vivants* of themselves when young. In all, an elaborate production.

All this comes from impressions Ann gave to her friends of her childhood and accounts by the family, and there is no reason to doubt it. There is however some evidence that does not confirm the simple division of happy days at Stanway, grim ones in Scotland. It was at Stanway, not North Berwick, that Laura remembers finding Ann composing poems on a tombstone and commented, 'What a melancholy waste of time.' It was the Stanway groom Ann quotes as saying, 'Very white and spiteful aren't we this morning, Miss?' Mademoiselle Angerhoff, a governess who lasted quite a while, wrote to Guy Charteris of Ann complaining that she did not have time to do all the things she wanted to do in Scotland, so at least there were some things she wanted to do. Though Ann was herself to write later, 'None of us had any affection in our tempestuous childhood and I have only seen its necessity very late', this would not be guessed from letters to her father about pet rabbits and learning to draw. Fierce Granny Tennant so liked her version of *My Blue Heaven* on the piano that she was eager to buy more foxtrots. Something of the impression her granddaughters made on Lady Wemyss may be gleaned from a mock reproof she typed out, hoping that they would correct their ultra-modernity, play the organ rather than the gramophone, dress plainly, seldom go out in society but be content to make infrequent appearances at garden parties and their best friends' weddings, and paint ('I don't mean their lips, but learn to sketch'). This was written in 1930 when they were a pair of forceful, flamboyant girls, poised to take on the world.

From the beginning of that year Ann kept a diary in the large schoolgirl hand that never altered. It shows a certain characteristic verve but is for the most part surprisingly conventional, even dull. Nevertheless, detail helps to convey what her life was like. She starts the year at Gosford, a great house belonging to the Earls of Wemyss, confusingly close to North Berwick where the Tennant grandparents lived. There is a ball, but Ann does not find the young Scottish soldiers who attend amusing to talk to, still less to dance with. David Elcho went to bed at eleven o'clock but, with Laura, she hoicked him out, commenting unfavourably upon his lemon and pink pyjamas. If she could not yet banish or transform dull guests, she could find some entertainment in stirring up a member of her family who only wanted a little sleep.

Two weeks in St Moritz are reported neutrally. Lord Long is a funny sight with bandages and his whole face scraped after shooting fifteen feet into the air off the Cresta Run. Three years later he will marry Laura. Sir Samuel Hoare[14] teaches Ann to skate but, even after professional help, she can only manage the outer edge with one leg. The town looks lovely by moonlight. Skiing is exhausting and includes more than one terrific toss. Curling, on the other hand, is tame and she is almost sent off for dropping a stone. As in Scotland, she seems to be bringing her characteristic zest to sports for which she has little natural skill or enthusiasm; but she never complains.

By the end of January Ann is back at Stanway, playing tennis already, falling off her bicycle very violently, which was entirely Laura's fault, and taking painting lessons. In London she goes to Burlington House, admires a Mantegna and is not disappointed by the Botticellis. Laura is mentioned often, as in 'Laura has had her hair waived [sic], fancies herself lovely'; Mary Rose only to say that she is ill; Hugo scarcely at all. Relations, particularly her grandmother Lady Wemyss and Lady Cynthia Asquith, often come to lunch or tea and on at least one occasion a whole group of grownups, with only little Simon Asquith for excuse, play hide and seek. Some plays and lots of films are reported. Ann enjoyed *Bitter Sweet*, 'the dresses were so gay and the music lovely', Laura adored Ivor Novello in *The Rat*.

14 Sir Samuel Hoare (1880–1959). Represented Oxford at skating. Conservative MP 1910–44, Foreign Secretary 1935. Created Viscount Templewood in 1944.

On 28 March Ann, then sixteen, was confirmed, but makes no comment. Earlier Mademoiselle had been worried as to whether her religious knowledge was up to it. Ann never bothered about detail in such matters, retaining a firm but vague faith in an after-life. She told her grandchildren to think about eternity rather than ask themselves exactly what they believed. Some weeks of April were spent with her father at Stanway finding birds' eggs and once a viper and going on treasure hunts; at Easter she 'dined down and acted most amusing sherads [sic]'.

Then she was packed off to a finishing school at the Villa Marie Antoinette in Versailles. She is suitably enthusiastic about most of the French culture with which she is presented, particularly the palace itself and Corneille. On 19 June, her birthday, she borrowed a man's breeches, went riding at Fontainebleau, looked a ghastly sight and had a wonderful time. Ann does not seem to have thought of herself as unusually pretty; certainly she did not mind appearing in unbecoming clothes, but she did enjoy dressing for an occasion. References to men are few and innocent and, though she says which ones she thinks are attractive, she notes more often and in greater detail which girls are well-dressed or beautiful. Towards the end of her second term, however, after a dull summer in Scotland where day after day the only entry is 'Golf', she meets Jean. He is six foot six and has an English sense of humour. At a dance they discuss the fall of the Cabinet but then move on to the more dangerous topic of the expressions of the eyes. On the way home she falls asleep and when she wakes her hand is being held. Alas, in less than a week she is leaving, but Jean arrives at the Gare du Nord with three pink carnations and says 'Au revoir, Enchantereuse, au revoir, ma petite darling.' Ann may add 'Ah, chèr petit Jean et chère Paris, j'ai beaucoup de tristesse à vous quitter,' but any sadness is momentary. A fur coat Aunt Kakoo[15] gives her for Christmas inspires as much, perhaps more, emotion; and there are games of 'murder' and 'sherads'. Jean writes but it is not clear that his letters are answered. Ann's first hunt ball is wonderful. At New Year there are no bellringers at Stanway so Ann and Laura, in spite of being swung off their feet and nearly concussed, ring the New Year in. It was quite the most amusing New Year's Eve of her life.

15 Kathleen Tennant (1894–   ). Married 1916–40 to the Duke of Rutland.

The diary for 1931 opens, 'So another year begins and I am out.'
It continues with parties and boys, interesting only when the names
are going to crop up again later in her life. David Cecil[16] waltzes
beautifully, Boofy Gore[17] in spite of his effeminate manner makes
dinner seem a short meal with his quaint ideas and fictitious gossip.
In the summer Duff Cooper[18] stands at a by-election and Ann
supports him with the slogan 'Down with the Press, Beaverbrook,
Rothermere and Empire Crusaders!' She remains by modern
standards astonishingly innocent. Admirers are flattering but can
become a bore: 'John was irritatingly in love with me, I had to keep
on saying "Cuckoo" to cheer him up.' Possibly it was the same John
who proposed with such confidence that he went into detail as to
which side of his park they should live. When he discovered that he
had been refused, he went round looking as if a bucket of cold water
had been thrown over him. Ann's own feelings do not seem to have
been much involved and even when she confesses that she has done
things she shouldn't, and enjoyed them, it seems fairly innocuous.
After being kissed on the shoulder by a bounder she felt sick for ten
minutes.

In London Ann has as many bases as ever, speaking of staying
with both her grandmothers and her father, and constantly seeing
aunts, but really being under the wing of Aunt Letty.[19] The Duchess
of Rutland actually gave her coming-out party:

> Thursday night my dance which began badly and ended
> perfectly . . . I got back and found I had half an hour to
> dress; I enjoyed wearing my new dress very much, a cloud

16 Lord David Cecil (1902–   ). Historian, biographer and Oxford don. His
books include *The Stricken Deer*, 1929, *Lord M*, 1954, and *Max*, 1964.

17 Arthur ('Boofy') Gore (1910–83). Journalist, who was to marry in 1937 Ann's
cousin Fiona Colquhoun. He remained a lifelong friend. Succeeded his brother as
Earl of Arran in 1958. *See* Appendix of Names.

18 Alfred Duff Cooper (1890–1954). Politician and writer. Married Lady Diana
Manners in 1919. Minister of Information 1941–2, Ambassador to France 1944–
7, created Viscount Norwich 1952.

19 Lady Violet Manners (1888–1971). Sister of Lady Diana Cooper and sister-in-
law of Ann's Aunt Kakoo. She married in 1911 Lord Elcho, Ann's uncle who was
killed in 1916. In 1921 she married Guy Benson. Ann was fond of her but years
later when the Bensons were living at Stanway she was delighted to be told that the
local people remembered and preferred the Charterises, and wrote in 1949, 'Letty's
taste though good is hygienic and overpure, the murder of the yew hedge and the
planned murder of some other trees which obscure views are distressing.' Stanway
is now lived in by Lord Neidpath, eldest surviving son of the Earl of Wemyss.

of white with silver and green leaves on it, unfortunately I had a spot on my nose that would shine through the powder! ... The greatest scandal of the evening was Ronnie [Worthington] who arrived quite drunk with Aunt Mary's[20] dinner party. Aunt Dinah[21] and Kakoo had heard of but not seen Ronnie drunk before and were not favourably impressed and said 'Ann has the wrong kind of friends'! I enjoyed the whole evening quite enormously; all of London's most beautiful women, Clare Beck,[22] Aunt Mary, Lady Hoare,[23] Aunt Kakoo; all the most interesting men, Duff Cooper, Winston,[24] Lord Salisbury,[25] and Douglas Fairbanks![26] All my old friends were there and all my new friends; of new friends I like Anthony Chaplin,[27] and Sim Feversham.[28] I had dinner with Ronnie, Michael Duff[29] and Thurstan Holland-Martin;[30] Thurstan hissed 'Come and dance with me and not with that drunkard Worthington'! I approved more of Thurstan but preferred Ronnie, alas! Why do I like cads and bounders.

Friday I was a wreck ...

20 Lady Mary Charteris (1895–   ). Married to Algernon ('Tom') Strickland 1915–38 and in 1943 to Major John Lyon.

21 Dinah Tennant (1889–1974). Married Sir Ian Colquhoun in 1915.

22 Clarissa ('Clare') Tennant (b. 1896). A cousin, married 1915–18 to Captain William Bethell, 1918–28 to Lionel Tennyson, who succeeded as Lord Tennyson in 1928, and 1928–43 to James Beck.

23 Lady Maud Lygon (1882–1962). Married in 1909 Samuel Hoare, who that year became Secretary of State for India.

24 Winston Churchill (1874–1965). Though he had held many positions including Chancellor of the Exchequer 1924–9, he had this year resigned from the Conservative Shadow Cabinet and started his period in the political wilderness.

25 Marquess of Salisbury (1861–1947). Son of the Prime Minister. ADC to Edward VII and George V, Leader of the House of Lords 1925–31.

26 Douglas Fairbanks Senior (1883–1939). Swashbuckling film star nearing the end of his career but with *The Private Life of Don Juan*, 1934, yet to come.

27 The Hon. Anthony Chaplin, later Viscount Chaplin. Zoologist and composer, Hon. Secretary of the Zoological Society 1952–5.

28 Earl of Feversham (1906–63). Lord-in-Waiting to the King, Parliamentary Secretary to the Minister of Agriculture and Fisheries 1936–9. Earldom extinct.

29 Sir Michael Duff (1907–80). In 1955 Ann wrote from the *Queen Mary*, 'I have become very fond of Michael Duff.' Lord-Lieutenant of Caernarvonshire 1960–74.

30 Thurstan Holland-Martin (1908–68). Farmer and horse-breeder.

At the end of the season Ann sums up: 'I seem somehow to have avoided losing my heart at all, except to Ronnie and it returned very quickly when I saw him drunk! Perhaps my five favourite men are John Hare,[31] Thurstan Holland-Martin, Shane O'Neill,[32] Maurice Bridgeman[33] and one other.' But the coyly anonymous one other was not her next proposal: 'Maurice Bridgeman picked me up and we started for Apperley; he proposed to me which I had expected for some time but not when I was looking supremely unattractive with a cold in the head! Anyhow he told me how he adored me, how much money we would have (sensible unromantic man) and I replied by telling him to wait three years and ask again. I shall probably marry him in the end, I am all for love being on the man's side.'

After a summer of dancing, the convention was an autumn of shooting in Scotland. Ann went to the Hebrides with Aunt Letty and enjoyed the peace but could not quite agree that she would like to spend the rest of her life there. The diary becomes sporadic. Ann says that she has done something very stupid, allowed herself to fall in love with someone young and inexperienced and, coming home from Oxford, 'I stopped the car on the Burford road, turned the lights off and opened the windows and sat with the wind blowing in and his head on my shoulder, alone on the top of the Cotswolds.' No more is heard of that and the diary ends, 'Shane [O'Neill] does not make up for Ronnie and my thoughts kept wandering to Overbury . . .'

Lord O'Neill had moved from a sporadic mention into her list of five best friends and now, albeit in an inadequate way, became the man in her life. There is a characteristic story in which Ann is positively enthusiastic for his company. At a dance she heard him ask his partner to sit out on the stairs. 'I don't want to do that,' objected the girl, 'I'll ruin my dress.' 'I don't mind ruining my dress,' said Ann and plonked herself down beside him.[34] At another dance in 1932 he proposed and Ann accepted. It has been suggested that

---

31 John Hare (1911–82). Conservative MP 1945–63, Minister of Labour 1960–3, Chairman of the Conservative Party 1963–5. Created Viscount Blakenham 1963.

32 Lord O'Neill (1907–44). Married Ann in 1932.

33 Maurice Bridgeman (1904–80). Married Diana Wilson in 1933. Chairman of BP 1960–9. Knighted in 1964.

34 Quoted by Lord Annan in his address at Ann's memorial service.

Ann (and Laura) married the first respectable man who asked them because they had neither home nor money and were in search of stability. We have seen that this was not strictly true, that O'Neill was at least the third man to propose to Ann. What is more difficult to gauge is how serious these proposals were on either side. In that circle at that time they seem to have come about swiftly and often, by no means always ending in marriage. This one was not the result of simple passion. O'Neill was on the rebound, Ann seems to have felt little more than she had before and went to Ascot the next day with no precise thoughts of marriage. But O'Neill was a man of action and on her return she found that he had seen her father and all was formally arranged. It is, however, possible to overstress the passivity of her feelings. Ann was not one to allow herself to be carried along by events against her will. They were married on 6 October.

It was a match welcomed on both sides. The O'Neills had been in County Antrim in Northern Ireland for over six hundred years and indeed stem from the most ancient family in Europe that it has been possible to tabulate. Their house, Shane's Castle, had been badly burned in the 1920s. The third baron was a popular, tall young man of twenty-five, well off and with a respectable job in the city. His mother pronounced Ann's surname in two syllables to rhyme with 'Tartars', which showed that she was old-fashioned and possibly out of touch, but there was no question of her being anything other than utterly acceptable. Ann may have been thought by the most staid of the elder generation to be a little wild but her lack of money was of no importance, her family was impeccable and she was one of the prettiest and most popular girls around. Her cousin Martin Charteris is not alone in thinking that she became steadily more interesting and unusual throughout her life. Her diary, letters and friends all support this, suggesting that at nineteen she was a conventional, attractive, uneducated upper-class girl, remarkable only for a certain dash and energy and even in these not unique.

The young couple moved into Montagu Square and entertained frequently but not flamboyantly. There were small dinner parties, followed perhaps by bridge. At weekends they would often stay at the grandest country houses and O'Neill in particular enjoyed the chance to see their treasures. Their son Raymond[35] was born eleven

35 Raymond O'Neill (1933–). Succeeded as Lord O'Neill in 1944, Major in the

months after they married, a daughter, Fionn,[36] not until 1936. Though Ann was a fond mother, the children did not interfere with their social life. Ann wrote later, 'Meditating on entertaining I realized with a start that I was but twenty-two when I was "collected" by Emerald [Cunard] and Sybil [Colefax].' Some contemporaries remember Ann as restless, liable to suggest going out to a night club and likely to receive some dampening answer about the necessity of getting up in the morning. O'Neill's parents were formal and well-mannered rather than demonstrative and spontaneous and he naturally took them for a model. While he was at work Ann would sometimes write letters alone, but she was scarcely a captive housewife. Friends seem to have felt simultaneously that the O'Neills were happy enough and that it was inevitable that Ann would meet someone else.

Much later Ann recorded her first encounter with Ian Fleming at Le Touquet in August 1935. She was with John and Nancy Hare and saw him by the swimming pool, 'a handsome, moody creature'. Fleming was then twenty-seven and when Loelia, Duchess of Westminster[37] saw him arriving late for dinner at Warwick House that autumn, she thought, 'That's the most attractive man I've ever seen.' With his long, thin face and a nose that had been broken on the football pitch he was not however as classically handsome as his elder brother Peter; nor was he as clever, popular, rich, serious, or virtuous. Ian had grown up in the shadow of just about the most promising young man in the country and one on whom the elder generation beamed approval. Strongly competitive but doomed to lose on every score to this paragon, he had little alternative to becoming a black sheep.

After not quite being sacked from Eton, he dropped out of Sandhurst. What was to be done with him? His forceful mother considered a one-way ticket to Australia. In fact he was sent only as far as Kitzbühel, where he learnt to speak German perfectly, later adding excellent French and competent Russian. He also had, according to John Pearson, his biographer, three regular girl friends

North Irish Horse, AVR, Lieutenant-Colonel RARO. Married Georgina Scott in 1963. Chairman of the Northern Irish Tourist Board 1975–80 and of the Northern Irish National Trust Committee since 1981.

36 Fionn O'Neill (1936–   ). Married 1961–75 to John Morgan.

37 Loelia Ponsonby (1902–   ). Married 1930–47 to the Duke of Westminster and in 1969 to Sir Martin Lindsay. See Appendix of Names (Loelia Westminster).

and any number of incidental affairs. 'He was quite ruthless about girls,' says a woman who knew him at this time, 'or perhaps absent-minded is a better word.' The wildness and melancholy combined with his charm were irresistible. Later he often seemed to prefer older women; in Kitzbühel he took on all comers. An external student at the universities of Munich and Geneva, he planned to write a novel but did not do so. In 1931 he failed to get into the Foreign Office and his fragile self-confidence took another beating. An engagement was broken off. He was becoming bitter, obstinate and solitary. Reuters was the next solution and seemed a good one. Fleming enjoyed devising ways of getting the news home first and was a success in Russia. Unfortunately, his respectable Scottish banking family left the Fleming money to his mother and he decided to enter banking himself. Like Scott Fitzgerald he thought the rich were different and perhaps glamorous, though Pearson maintains that he was not a money snob but a financial romantic. This did not make him particularly good at his new job and soon he moved to a solid stockbroking firm, Rowe and Pitman, where he remained a junior partner, at least in theory, until 1945. So the man whom Ann met by the swimming pool was not very successful and, if he was not ordinary either, the framework of his life at least had become conventional. Writing had been forgotten.

In the meantime it was Esmond Harmsworth who had the more immediate impact on Ann's life. He was a younger son of the first Viscount Rothermere, but his two elder brothers had been killed in the war. His career was thus thrust upon him and he always gave the impression that he would have been happier without it. He accompanied Lloyd George to the Peace Conference of 1919, he had been the youngest MP of the 1920s and now at thirty-eight was chairman of Associated Newspapers and proprietor of the *Daily Mail* – a reluctant press tycoon. He was also devastatingly good-looking, athletic and a sophisticated lover with a wife and three teenage children. When asked about him much later, Ann said on several occasions that their affair was a physical passion, and she was exceptionally honest. She would however have been aware that people thought she had made a worldly conquest, and may have been redressing the balance a little when she did not mention his great wealth nor the powerful world into which he introduced her; she relished these things too. Certainly O'Neill minded the Rothermere riches, with which he felt he could not compete. Ann was not discreet then or ever, but Harmsworth was cautious and reluctant to get divorced (Ann despised this caution as she despised his hypochondria and later his fear of bombs).

Fleming was meanwhile being moody in the background. Ann later described the growing part that he played in her life:

> In August 1936 I went to Austria and met Esmond Harmsworth. I had by then given up all hope of falling in love, but we fell in love with each other (cannot think of any more original expression!) and remained in love till early war years, though from 1939 onwards I grew more and more attracted to Ian and very curious about him. From 1936 onwards, though he [Fleming] became a frequent visitor to Montagu Square, his life remained a mystery, he simply telephoned if he felt like bridge or wanted to play golf with Shane at weekends. My marriage had become very difficult, and when I could not see Esmond I found Ian the best antidote among the friends. Ian 'got off with women because he could not get on with them'. This was said about him by Rosamond Lehmann; I repeated it to Elizabeth Bowen, who said Rosamond had not invented the expression, that it was in *Death of a Heart*! [It is used to describe the character based on Goronwy Rees.] Anyway it was certainly true of Ian. Most women found him attractive. One of his gambits was 'I might marry you if you had a broken leg', or 'If you want a husband you should go to the Baltic Exchange.' I never discovered why the Baltic Exchange was an endless source of bachelors!

Ann dined with him in early 1939: 'He had migraine, was unable to speak for an hour, gave me a book to read and told me to "keep quiet till I am ready for you". Considering the slightness of our acquaintance, very odd behaviour.' It is unclear how things might have turned out if there had been no war.

Ann's diary resumes as the war starts, the style, if not pedantically correct, much matured in seven years. She remains light-hearted, sometimes frivolous, but the events and characters she has to report are often weightier. On 4 September 1939 Ann lunched at the Ritz with an old friend, Anthony Winn.[38] They saw the situation in terms of Noël Coward's patriotic spectacular *Cavalcade*, or said they did for cheerful conversational purposes. She bought tinned foods of all sorts and O'Neill told her to keep £100 in notes against emergencies. That afternoon he rang to say he was bringing Ian over and that she was not to laugh at his new blue uniform as he was sensitive about it. Fleming had in fact organized himself most efficiently and was already in the Royal Naval Volunteer Reserve; he was a lieutenant (Special Branch) which meant Naval Intelligence. Laura came, also in uniform as she was on her way to Birmingham where she was a nurse; Ed Stanley[39] looked in and they had a gay evening making jokes about air raids and gas masks. If Ian's uniform was not openly mocked, he was christened the Chocolate Sailor by Winn.

So first the phoney and then the real war began. O'Neill joined the North Irish Horse Guards and began training over there. He was to see action in Tunisia and rise to command his regiment. Harmsworth meanwhile had a house at Ascot and sometimes stayed with Ann at the Dorchester. There was a theory, quite untrue, that that hotel was particularly safe and many fashionable figures spent much of the war there, among them Lady Cunard, Phyllis de Janzé, Duff and Lady Diana Cooper, Mr and Mrs Charles Sweeney and Mrs Ronnie Greville. Ann said that there was 'a mass of cabinet ministers and Mayfair remnants milling around' and later described it as 'that gilded refuge of the rich. Lord Halifax prays for guidance in the Turkish bath [no longer in use], Duff Cooper indulges in bridge and brandy upstairs. Beauties of various ages and ladies of varied reputation rub shoulders in the lounge.'

38 Anthony Winn (1909–42). Admirer of Ann and of Lady Margaret Douglas-Home. He had been lobby correspondent of *The Times* but left when his description of Duff Cooper's resignation speech being well received was suppressed. That month he described Ann as 'quite unaffected by Armageddon, which was all to the good'.

39 Lord Stanley of Alderley (1907–71). A man of considerable charm, married four times, who wrote about sailing and towards the end of his life neglected his clothes. In 1950 over lunch with Maurice Collis at White's he 'gradually revealed his buccaneering character. He related how he lived on a ship of 250 tons and went about the world looking for adventure . . . and taking out a bank note lit it and lit his cigarette with it, taking care however only to burn a fraction of the edge.' *Diaries 1949–69* by Maurice Collis, 1977.

Soon she took a house at Buscot near Faringdon, to be near her sister-in-law, Midi Gascoigne, with her children Bamber and Veronica[40] and a friend, Lady Margaret Douglas-Home, with her children Robin, Fiona and Charles.[41] Those who were old enough did lessons together. Ann shuttled between these centres, sustaining the roles of wife, mother and mistress, sometimes throwing in bridge partner or guest. Following Scottish custom on New Year's Eve, Fleming, as the darkest man present, came over the threshold and embraced everyone except Duff Cooper, who refused to start the year being kissed by a man. A piper appeared and Ann and Lady Diana[42] danced a Scottische together, 'undignified but fun'.

Ann portrays herself as terrified by the air raids, which is hard to believe. Her first bomb fell when she was at Ascot in the spring of 1940: 'Went to bed early, was woken by ear-splitting crash and opened my eyes to a sea of flame and broken glass. I lay speechless with terror but thank God only one bomb fell near, the rest several hundred yards away in the wood. I tiptoed over debris to the landing and met the hysterical pantry boy, flashing his torch. "Mr 'Armsworth's buried," he said. "Put the torch out," I shouted, "we must find him in the dark." Luckily he was alright, only a bit of the ceiling had fallen on him. He appeared covered in plaster and most annoyed having heard my cowardly speech.' Another entry has her trembling with fear as she makes her way from the Dorchester to the Lansdowne to dine with Fleming and, later, is too frightened to return.

Harmsworth's father died at the end of 1940 and he succeeded as Viscount Rothermere. Ann said later that she had been brought

---

40 Mary O'Neill (1905–). Married Colonel Gascoigne in 1934. Remained a friend of Ann's all her life. Bamber Gascoigne (1935–), author, broadcaster and publisher. Veronica Gascoigne (1938–), married in 1960 William Plowden. James Lees-Milne wrote in 1942, 'Midi's younger child Veronica is undeniably beautiful with copper-coloured hair and a fair skin but she tries to be funny and is strikingly unfunny. Bamber is a sensitive, delicate and adventuresome little boy.' *Ancestral Voices*, 1975.

41 Lady Margaret Spencer (1906–). Married 1931–47 to Henry Douglas-Home, brother of the Prime Minister. Robin Douglas-Home (1932–68), novelist, pianist and playboy. Fiona Douglas-Home (1936–) married Gregory Martin in 1962. Charles Douglas-Home (1937–), Defence Correspondent of *The Times* 1965–70, Editor since 1982.

42 Lady Diana Manners (1892–). Actress, hostess and indestructible beauty. Married Duff Cooper in 1919 but retained the style Lady Diana Cooper when he became Viscount Norwich. *See* Appendix of Names.

up to believe that the royal family was the top of the social pyramid and that press lords were beneath contempt, but that she never really met the first until she consorted with the second. Through Rothermere she also met other press lords and politicians. Soon after she has referred to Lord Beaverbrook[43] as 'the Canadian mountebank' she went to stay with him at Cherkley for the first time and found it an amazing mixture of bad taste and discomfort. The guests were varied, some social, some Labour cabinet ministers, and Roosevelt's special envoy, Harry Hopkins,[44] was there. Beaverbrook's attitude to the women was like that of a gangster towards his molls. 'Lady Brownlow[45] is well fitted for that part and indeed appeared eager to play it. I found myself becoming pompous, which is an extraordinarily rare experience.' She liked Hopkins ('detached, cynical charm') and whisked him off to a night club, The 400, the following week. Beaverbrook became a friend or at least someone she enjoyed seeing.

Voluntary work in a canteen is not mentioned often but that may be because there is little to say about it. For the same reason references to the children are brief and usually about some mishap or illness, as when Ann feared that her heavy pancakes would harm Raymond or, much later, when Fiona Douglas-Home fell off a carthorse and broke her wrist.

In spite of all this, Ann sometimes managed to get to Ireland, where O'Neill had taken a dark Victorian house. She was grateful for the extra meat and cream, but always pleased to return. Fleming went to America to establish closer links with his counterparts there, but this was made more difficult by the fact that they did not yet exist. He wrote a memorandum for 'Big Bill' Donovan, which may have influenced the structure of the CIA. He was also allowed to watch the safe of the Japanese Consul being opened at three in the morning and his code book being photographed. It was the most

43 Lord Beaverbrook (1879–1964). Minister of Information 1918, Minister of Supply 1941–2, owner of the *Daily Express, Sunday Express* and *Evening Standard*. Created a peer 1917.

44 Henry ('Harry') Hopkins had been sent on an exploratory mission by the President. On his return 'dozing on the couch of the President's oval study, Henry suddenly opened one eye and said to the President, 'You know, Winston is much more left than you.' *Eleanor and Franklin* by Joseph P. Lash.

45 Katherine Kinloch married Lord Brownlow in 1927.

thrilling year of his life. On his return he and Nigel Birch[46] gave Ann dinner and told her she would be mad to marry Rothermere but that they would despise her if she did not get an enormous settlement. There was an incident when Lord Rothermere got into a state bordering on hysteria because his wife was arriving on a train into which he was seeing Ann. She reports this with cool amusement but it cannot have impressed her favourably. A note written later runs:

> In the spring of 1941 Esmond was persuaded by me that we must marry or part, so we went through the rigmarole of giving evidence at Bournemouth (Esmond went back on this two months later).[47] The evidence coincided with one of Ian's forty-eight hour leaves, and he persuaded me to continue from Bournemouth to Cornwall for a day's golf. Ian met us at Bournemouth and we motored (press lords had plenty of petrol). I was being sick every twenty minutes from nerves and guilt. Ian told Esmond I was not to be indulged. We were to stop at no more inns and I could damn well be sick in the hedge. This had a curative effect!
>
> When we arrived I went to bed. Ian came to my room, told me I was behaving very badly and must return to Shane. I burst into tears.
>
> The rest of the forty-eight hours was spent quarrelling with Ian, and Esmond getting him back to the Admiralty on time – in fact we only went to Cornwall to please Ian, he had a *very* dominant personality.

Another note written later by Ann shows the shift in their relationship: 'Shane was abroad. Ian by then spent all his leaves wherever I was. I never showed Ian I was in love with him. I knew instinctively it would be fatal, but I did know he was becoming more and more dependent on me. He said I had the heart of a drum-majorette which offset his melancholy.' Her diary ceases so it is

46 Nigel Birch (1906–81). Conservative MP 1945–70. He resigned over economic policy in 1958 and was made a life peer, Lord Rhyl, in 1970.

47 According to another version Lord Rothermere did not exactly go back on his decision. The crucial evidence in those days of contrived adultery came from the hotel maid who served breakfast in bed to the man and his hired stranger. In this case, possibly because there had recently been a well-publicized divorce with witnesses from the same premises, she said she had no recollection of ever having seen him before and the case collapsed; but he could have tried again.

impossible to know any further detail before October 1944 when O'Neill was killed in action in Italy. Ann wrote:

> I was with Esmond and Ian at Esmond's house at Ascot when the telegram arrived to say that Shane had been killed in action in Italy. I was extremely distressed and went immediately to Ian, asked him to tell Esmond, asked him to arrange for my two children to be sent to me, one from home, one from school.' [Soon after hearing the news she was heard saying to herself, 'Death is the best revenge.'] 'I was thirty-one when Shane was killed and all my family expected me to marry Esmond. Esmond was very anxious to marry me, I was fond of him – very – but no longer in love. I knew he had not wanted the divorce because he thought Shane might be killed – he had always wanted to wait until the end of the war before we took any legal steps. The night before I married Esmond [28 June 1945] I dined with Ian, and we walked and walked in the park. He said several times 'I want to leave some kind of mark on you'; if he had suggested marriage I would have accepted.

With the end of the war and her emergence as Lady Rothermere, Ann's life entered its most spectacular phase. She was thirty-two. She had the money, the style and the energy to brighten the drabness that had descended on London, and set about doing so. Warwick House, where they lived, was a magnificently imposing and central base from which to operate. James Lees-Milne allows it 'little architectural character, but its site with terrace over park and proximity to St James's Palace is enchanting'.[48]

Soon it was filled with the sound of the rich, powerful and amusing at play. Ann has been called a political hostess, sometimes the last of the political hostesses, but this was true only in the simple sense that she was often a hostess to politicians. She had no axe to grind, was not plotting to further one man's career or destroy another's. Policy was not altered under her roof, suitable allies were not subtly thrown together. Power attracted her but she did not want it for herself. When a new figure rose to prominence, she would be intrigued to meet him; but if he turned out to be pompous

48 *Caves of Ice*, 1983.

or banal, boring in any way, the interest evaporated. Lions were not hunted. Her own politics were instinctive. Near the end of her life Ann wrote to a friend who had become Ambassador in Poland, 'How interesting that you have lurched to the right; why do very clever people have to actually live in a communist regime before they see the light? I don't like the proletariat at all, and only believe in oligarchy, a ruling class employing contented craftsmen, cooks, charcoal burners, ladies' maids and laundry maids, all bobbing and curtseying and taking pride in their work.' More revealing because entirely free from self-mockery was a complaint about the tedium of neighbours 'that fall into that category of person which is ever increasing and neither "landed" nor "peasantry"'; most people would place the rise of the middle classes rather earlier. Ann knew that she was an aristocrat and that some of her values – approval of fortitude, scorn for any form of ingratiation – and most of her political opinions sprang from an outmoded tradition, but she did not change them. Nevertheless, it was from the Labour front bench that she drew many friends, particularly in later years. This was partly because the Labour Party was in power through much of the 1960s and 1970s, partly because she enjoyed conflict and would stir up her guests with bold attacks, but also because she found them more intelligent and interesting than their Conservative counter-parts. Those who were not used to being teased were often the most enchanted. In this she was perhaps less influenced by the example of her gentle grandmother than by that of her great-aunt, Margot Asquith. She was also particularly good with men who were not good with women and, by extension, with homosexuals (though she remained naive on the subject, asking when a distinguished novelist well into middle age, 'Why are you homosexual?').

People came to Warwick House not for the flowing champagne or the food, which Ann kept at a suitable standard simply by spending the readily available money, for she had no great knowledge or flair for catering; nor for the importance of the other guests, though this was likely to be considerable; but simply for the fun and the stimulation. It was here that Ann was supreme. She has been compared to an actress, by herself among others, and it is true that a glittering display was expected from her, whatever her mood, and that she would often gear herself up for the evening performance. But a better comparison might be with a conductor: a quiet voice would sometimes have to be drawn out at the right moment to be heard above the din; an instant decision taken as to whether a theme was exhausted or might be allowed a variation. All this with no score and with instrumentalists who, far from keeping an eye on their leader, had wills and egos of their own. Ann's knowledge might sometimes be limited but she did not try to impress others; her gift was to grasp with formidable speed such essentials of a topic as would enable her to ask the right, the interesting, question. She provided the energy, the daring and so the opportunity for others to sparkle. Occasionally she would demand a solo but there always lay a risk of failure, embarrassing to others and humiliating to the performer (who would then feel like the understudy for Ophelia, met at her exit by Lilian Baylis with 'Well dear, you had your chance. And you missed it.') More often the spirited hubbub of general conversation would give way to someone already in full spate. Guests might arrive keyed up, even apprehensive, but they would leave elated not only by how interesting others had been but by how interesting they had been themselves. Ann made people wittier and more clever than they had been in any other drawing-room, indeed than they had thought themselves capable of being.

During those years at Warwick House her interests shifted a little and the emphasis moved from politicians and journalists to painters and writers. Lucian Freud,[49] Frederick Ashton[50] and Francis Bacon[51] appeared, Peter Quennell[52] earned the nickname 'Lady Rothermere's Fan'. Lord Rothermere may not have welcomed the change ('Esmond was hardly allowed to speak as they roared rude remarks past him') but he was a passive man and put up with it, just as he put up with Ann's considerable interference in the running of the *Daily Mail*. Her friends were hired and her advice taken, to the consternation and fear of professional journalists not in her circle. Rothermere tolerated also a certain wildness. A party where girls were auctioned off got into the papers, the treasure

---

49 Lucian Freud (1922–). Painter; grandson of Sigmund Freud. *See* Appendix of Names.

50 Frederick Ashton (1904–). Founder-choreographer of the Royal Ballet. *See* Appendix of Names.

51 Francis Bacon (1909–). Painter. First one-man exhibition in London at the Hanover Gallery in 1949. *See* Appendix of Names.

52 Peter Quennell (1905–). Writer and one of Ann's closest and most enduring friends. Edited *The Cornhill Magazine* 1944–51, *History Today* 1951–79. *See* Appendix of Names.

hunts in the style of the 1920s were noisy and attracted disapproval as well as attention. At a house party a game involving forfeits was played and both Ann's and Laura's dress became skimpy; that was all right, but when Lord Dudley[53] had to kiss Cecil Beaton[54] on the lips his lordship did so but became, as so often, apoplectic with rage.

Rothermere allowed all this to continue; perhaps he enjoyed it, perhaps he could do little about it. He was a kind man, an excellent stepfather (though Fionn always preferred Fleming) and he gave Ann opportunities she exploited to the full. Sometime in the first half of 1949 Ann wrote a series of portraits of press barons, including her husband. She praised his financial acumen; she also said the paper had much improved under him. However, 'Esmond Rothermere is a much less colourful personality than the first generation; he has not the drive, the fire or the conviction, but these are difficult times and he has the same qualities as the reed in the fable for weathering storms. He owns ... a wife [herself] who inclines to Company so he can seldom indulge his penchant for solitude . . .' There was, as we have seen, a threat to their marriage from the moment it began. 'Something seems to go wrong in the taxi from the registry office', said a friend of Ann's marriages, and she admitted herself that there was some truth in this. During the first Christmas after the war, Fleming, who was staying with a spectacularly rich and flamboyant mistress, sent Ann a letter saying that he loved her. 'A damned inconvenient moment', Ann commented.

53 Earl of Dudley (1894–1969). Ann's brother-in-law. He was married to Lady Rosemary Sutherland-Leveson-Gower 1919–30, to Laura Charteris 1943–54 and to Grace Kolin, who had been married to Prince Stanislas Radziwill, 1961–9.
54 Cecil Beaton (1904–80). Photographer, theatrical designer, diarist and socialite. Knighted 1972. *See* Appendix of Names.

LADY ROTHERMERE

1946-52

Almost all of the earliest surviving letters are between Ann and Ian Fleming. It is in the nature of things that you write to a lover and not to a husband. Many have been omitted as they are repetitious and some have been hard to date. Nevertheless the course of the affair is charted from difficult meetings in London to snatched holidays in Ireland and the paradise of Jamaica. After a glimpse of that island during the war, Fleming had decided that he must return there, and as soon as he could he built Goldeneye, not everybody's dream house with its lack of baths and window-panes, but the scene of many of Ann's happiest days with him. In spite of the chaperoning of Loelia, Duchess of Westminster, there was much gossip.

In 1948 Ann went through the shattering experience of giving birth to a daughter who lived for only a few hours. Her health never entirely recovered. Lord Rothermere came to know that the child had been Fleming's and decreed that they must not meet for six months. They considered obeying this ultimatum but found themselves unable to do so.

At this stage there are letters to Ann's brother Hugo, who is in Paris working for Lord Rothermere on the *Daily Mail*. They fill in other sides of her life, and in particular show the great interest she took in that newspaper and the considerable influence she had there despite the fact that she often bewails her inability to change things. She also writes to her brother of her family and the splendid social life at Warwick House, which she rarely mentions to the ungregarious Fleming. This provides a permanent background to her life and inevitably takes up most of her time; when she sends a heartfelt letter of sympathy to her sister-in-law who has lost a child she opens with apologies for being slow to do so, explaining that there have been plans to be made and parties to be given.

Finally Ann goes against the advice of her more cynical friends, gets a divorce and marries the more-or-less penniless Fleming in Jamaica on 24 March 1952, confident that she is doing the right thing but nevertheless a little apprehensive as to what people will say.

From Ian Fleming to Ann Rothermere

New York   [Early January 1946]

sweetheart,
i shall have to write this like james joyce because the machinery for
making capitals has broken on the typewriter and i shall also not be
able to make question-marks or any of the exciting things which
happen on the top half of a typewriter. you will also observe a
certain rainbow effect which is all to do with the same trouble. i am
afraid it will affect my style but i know you wont mind.

everybody here talks about their health and about the russians
and how long are you staying and what part of england do you
come from and thats absolutely all, except the most intelligent ones
talk about soandsos quote machine unquote and about shadowy
figures called marsh and prendergast etc who are supposed to be
running the president – much that i care. i keep on explaining to
these intelligent people that i am not interested in english politics let
alone american. this is not to say that i dont enjoy the orange juice
and fried eggs and so on but i am submerged beneath a deep
gloomth at the fabulous limitations of these people and their total
unpreparedness to rule the world which is now theirs with the
exception of you and peter[1] and cyril[2] and ed [Stanley] and a few
more prickly ones – on a list of whom you and i would disagree. . .
so i am sitting here sloshing down three roses like in the advertise-
ments and writing to you as if i were one of your other and better
lovers in the burma jungle or otherwise engaged with an enemy. i
think it will be all right when i get to jamaica because i shall sweat it
out of me and dig a hole in the ground and be away. i have spoilt
myself for too long to stand the fencing in which goes on here and
which god knows is worse than the very worst i have ever suffered at
your dear hands.

however, there has been plenty of work to do during the day and
the mighty kemsley foreign service[3] is thrusting out deep and
enduring roots into the lush soil. i took iddon[4] and alastair cook
[*sic*][5] out to lunch at toots shaws, and told him you all love him

[Iddon] which worries him all the time. he has much ambition but i explained with that blunt camaraderie which a. forbes[6] appreciates so much that all columnists like all great editors reached a point where they thought they were making the chancelries tremble but that since northcliffe this had been a pipedream and that he would be wise to stick to his last and relax. i did suggest to him that any question of an iddon london diary was littlehampton madness[7] and that the most promising alternative was an iddon world diary. this sunk in, so if the idea comes home you will know that i never cease to cosset my competitors particularly when i love their wives. he is a very good lad with the highest regard for you and reverence for es [Lord Rothermere] and he will do the mail very well till he dies. if he doesnt it will be your fault – but dont make him do serious stuff because he doesnt understand what its all about, though he wishes he did. cook is strictly third rate, though i must say i have always enjoyed his column in the standard. i much admire your overseas edition which is very well done. all this is in the best traditions of journalism, namely that one says how wonderful everyone elses stuff is – waiting for them to say how wonderful they think you are. you neednt say it to me because i should only ever work for gomer[8] – not even for the times – and you wouldnt understand that and i am the only person in the world who knows whether what i do is good or not. bracket im afraid the four roses is beginning to work and that it is nearly time for me to go to bed bracket.

i wish you were here as i would like to walk out with you very much and go to 123 which is a late night club where nothing happens except that a man plays the piano when he feels like it. its always the wrong time and place with us but never mind.

there should be an awful lot of interesting gossip for me to tell you but i have been in the wrong hands all the time. someone cut the cards wrong at the beginning and its been like that all along. i havent fought for a redeal because i havent and thats why my last letter and this sound so awry. frinstance i spent last weekend with the morgans on long island which really was quelquechose as you would say. rather like glenborrodaile castle where i spent some of the unhappiest years of my youth[9] and there have been several other bits like that which have all added up – to the point where i had to take to the four roses and write to you. so far as women are concerned i am sorry to say i have been corralled and that it all couldnt be wronger or more confused and my face is getting out of hand and its time i was away before i carve a chip out of anglo-american relations. and its not what you might imagine any kind of affair to be like but just something out of juan in america[10] where everything starts wrong and goes on wrong and getting wronger – and god knows what she thinks its all about and it really isnt all one persons fault but just that both our sets of rules are wrong – like baseball and rounders, which is really what happens between most english and american people. but i find it very galling and very uninteresting and very difficult to straighten out and altogether unsatisfactory. one day i will tell you all the affairs i have ever got into and you will tell me what i have done wrong and why they have been such mazes. but you will have to be very wise and concentrate and sit quiet or i shall get impatient because i have thought over all the obvious answers and none of them quite fit.

well my darling it has been nice writing to you and you are a fine girl and one day i shall write you my first love letter since i was 22.

ian

1 Peter Quennell was book critic on the *Daily Mail* 1943–56, and has described how as the result of her influence on the paper Ann 'acquired the status of a legendary monster, with whose name journalists in far off suburbs were believed to frighten naughty children. But reforms took place.' *The Wanton Chase*, 1980.

2 Cyril Connolly (1903–74). Writer and critic. A friend about whom Ann constantly changed her mind. Then editing *Horizon. See* Appendix of Names.

3 Fleming had been put in charge of starting a foreign news service to be shared by the papers belonging to Lord Kemsley, notably *The Sunday Times*. He was paid £5000 a year with two months' holiday.

4 Don Iddon wrote a breezy column which tended to show the Americans as ridiculous and extravagant. He was perhaps the most successful British columnist of the time.

5 Alistair Cooke (1908–). Journalist and broadcaster commenting largely on American affairs. UN correspondent of the *Guardian* 1945–8.

6 Alastair Forbes (1918–). American journalist educated in Europe. He became political commentator on the *Sunday Dispatch*, a Rothermere paper. Good-looking, a brilliant talker and sometimes vitriolic letter writer, he was not always on easy terms with Ann, and occasionally in a state of open warfare. *See* Appendix of Names.

7 Littlehampton in Sussex is the seaside town near Bailiff's Court, the house belonging to Lord Moyne that Ann took after the war. Though in fact modern, everything was in Elizabethan style, which meant, according to Ann's sister Laura, that you ate with buttonhooks and according to Ann's nanny, Joan Sillick, that there were weeds rather than garden flowers on the dining-room table. The maids wore something close to mob caps.

8 Lord Kemsley (1883–1968). Chairman of Kemsley Newspapers Ltd and Editor in Chief of *The Sunday Times* 1937–59. Fleming was the only one of his employees

who called him by his unusual christian name. Ann had written during the war 'The vulgarity of the Kemsleys is quite amazing: Lord K is arch, coy and common. He talked incessantly about the power of the press which in his case I trust is nil.'

9 The castle was taken for family holidays by Valentine Fleming. Ian was not enthusiastic about sport and is recorded as having said when asked what he wanted to do, 'Well, if I have to make a choice I would rather catch no salmon than shoot no grouse.'

10 Novel by Eric Linklater, 1931.

From Ian Fleming

Hotel Dorset, New York   Monday [January 1946]

My love, my love, my love,

Your letters take me by the heart and hold me so close that I choke. They are so warm and gentle and sweet. Don't ask me if I like them like they are, because they are bits of you and I like them because of that and that is as much as I can like. Today I got one which was very long and there wasn't a word which didn't make my heart ache – and that's how I like your letters, so don't ask any more stupid questions. By now you will have had *my* letters and you will know all this. Anyway I am still carrying yours around like a GI bride and it's a pest but still I simply love it and I love watching for each post and being an idiot and moping for you and it all serves me right.

My address in Jamaica is

> Goldeneye
> Oracabessa
> Jamaica BWI

and please remember it and get it right because I can't do without letters from you because talking to you has maddeningly become part of the day.

But listen, listen, listen, have you got something to lock up? Please fix it. I know how you leave things around like a jackdaw and I expect every day that it will be the end. I do wish you'd take trouble and not leave my letters among your brassières and your pants. *Do* please try. I know perfectly well that you are going to come along one day with a tragic face and say that all is discovered, fly – and all that is going to be for the sake of taking a tiny bit of trouble. Please darling, keep my letters locked up or I shan't think you care enough to take the trouble. Or else tear them up and burn them. I shall write you enough and they will be all the same – don't be a goose . . .[1]

Hells, bells. Write at once or telegraph and say that you understand and won't go on treating my letters like cracker mottoes. I've now worked myself into a state and it's too silly and it's all your fault and mine for loving you so much that I write you all these letters for you to leave about in your bag so that we shall never see each other again.

Now you see what you've done.

Blast, blast, blast, and I do love you so.

Ian

1 Fleming was accurate in saying that his letters would be alike. Ann kept many and in spite of his plea it is unlikely that she was discreet. As a friend comments of her telephoning, 'It never seemed to occur to her that Esmond was listening on the extension.' A few of Fleming's letters convey the style of them all.

Fleming had been to Jamaica during the war and had asked a friend to take any opportunity to buy a plot of land on the north coast. Patrick Leigh Fermor[1] wrote in *The Traveller's Tree*, 1950:

Here, on a headland, Ian Fleming has built a house called Goldeneye that might serve as a model for new houses in the tropics. Trees surround it on all sides except the sea, which it almost overhangs. Great windows capture every breeze, to cool, even on the hottest day, the large white rooms. The windows that look towards the sea are glassless but equipped with outside shutters against rain: enormous quadrilaterals surrounded by dark wooden frames which enclose a prospect of sea and cloud and sky, and tame the elements, as it were, into an overhanging fresco of which one could never tire.

1 Patrick Leigh Fermor (1915–   ). Traveller, writer, close and lasting friend of Ann's. *See* Appendix of Names.

Noël Coward[1] later took Goldeneye for what he considered the extortionate rate of £50 a week and found that after a while 'the comfortable beds were then more accurately described as "bed and board", the delicious dinners became a monotonous succession of either salt fish and ackee or curried goat followed by stewed guavas with coconut cream, all of them tasting of armpits, and so dreaded by Noël that he used to cross himself before each morsel. As for the spacious sitting-room, the long window-sills had been so cunningly designed that they entirely cut off the view as you sank into the sofa upholstered with iron shavings . . . "All you Flemings revel in discomfort." [2] Coward used to give directions: 'Straight on for miles and it is the nearest ear, nose and throat clinic on the right.' Hence 'Goldeneye, nose and throat'.

1 Noël Coward (1899–1973) also had a house on the north coast of Jamaica, was much admired by Fleming and was to be godfather to his son, Caspar. *See* Appendix of Names.
2 *The Life of Noël Coward* by Cole Lesley, 1976.

From Ian Fleming

Goldeneye, Jamaica   26 January 1947

My dear darling,
    My love, I miss you too much and I think of you too much of the time. There are so many things which would make you giggle here and you would love it anyway. Aimée and Roddy are my next door neighbours and live a mile or two away at the most lovely house which they have rented. The weather is beautiful and you would feel a different person and you would get small freckles under your eyes which would annoy you but which I would like. And you wouldn't be able to dance about like a dragon-fly because there is no point in it here. And there are plenty of butterflies and when you bathe in the dark there is a lot of phosphorous in the water and fireflies which drift about and disappear. We never wear any clothes when we bathe and it is just a question of walking out of bed and down the steps into the warm sea. There is a great deal to do what with the garden and what we are going to eat and the small blackamore troubles which arise the whole time like the Methodist parson coming to call and whether the ruined cathedral is full of 'guppies' which are the local ghosts.

The night before last Ivar[1] and John[2] and I went over to the opening of the famous Sunset Lodge Club[3] at Montego Bay. A huge bonfire on the beach, a lot of expensive people and two superb local bands playing the sort of Rum and Cocacola tunes you like. Miss Ernst came up to me in an ingenuous way and said 'We were talking about you the other night and I was trying to remember which paper you were mixed up with. I was certain your boss was a woman, but the only woman who seemed possible was Lady Rothermere which was impossible of course. Silly, wasn't it?' I made an appropriate non-committal grunt (I think) and I still can't make out whether it was a clever crack inspired by Pam[4] or the Beaver [Lord Beaverbrook] or whether she was tight. I think the former. She has a hard central European eye and I should guess is a wily customer.

[unfinished]

1 Ivar Bryce (1906–). Life-long friend of Fleming's, was married to Vera de Sã Sottomaior of Brazil 1930–8 and to Sheila Taylor-Pearse Byrne, 1939–50. It was he who bought for £2000 the rough grassland overlooking a magnificent view where Fleming had built his house. Before the greenery grew Bryce thought it 'a cubist arrangement of concrete surfaces . . . a masterpiece of striking ugliness'. *See* Appendix of Names.

2 John Fox-Strangways (b.1908). Son of the Earl of Ilchester, Eton friend of Fleming's. Badly wounded in the war, he became notorious in 1951 for kicking Aneurin Bevan on the steps of White's.

3 Carmen Pringle, a resident Jamaican, turned a house of hers into a hotel with fourteen bedrooms soon after the war. It swiftly became a centre for the Europeans who discovered the island during the following years. For a brief spell, which ended in 1960, certain very rich and certain rather poor upper-class English people drank, idled and committed adultery in the sunshine, creating an atmosphere reminiscent of that of Happy Valley in Kenya.

4 Lady Pamela Smith, daughter of the first Earl of Birkenhead, married in 1936 Michael Berry who was created Lord Hartwell in 1968. A political hostess after the war and so, in a sense, a rival of Ann's.

To Ian Fleming

South Wraxall Manor, Bradford-on-Avon[1]   [6 August 1947]

Darling – the misery of telephoning; I have to listen and LISTEN so that all thoughts go out of my head – either Esmond walks into the room or else the children walk in the window. Alas, alas I think tomorrow is a dream, because Papa has plenty of room and my fertile imagination to find an unanswerable reason for spending tomorrow night at the Lygon Arms proved barren. I could lunch with you in Oxford on Saturday, it would be a magnificent way to celebrate the petrol cuts, at a guess we should use half the population's basic ration for one year to exchange a kiss in the High Street.

My Uncle H. Asquith[2] died in Bath yesterday which means a funeral on Monday and a wake tea party here for the family; but I shall come to London on Tuesday at dawn and try and squeak Wednesday as well. So please, my love, don't get entangled with a bunch of spivs.

I will bring a tent to Dublin and we will find a Connemara cave and live in it, and if anyone asks impertinent questions we shall say we are digging for a leprechaun's gold.

E. [Lord Rothermere] sails on Wednesday the 20th so kindly write 'A' in your book in red letters. We shall come to London on the 18th but the nights of the 18th and 19th I shall have to stay home, so if you have any Quoits or Liesels or Irmas on your tawdry mind kindly dispose of them on those dates; and as I have taken the trouble to write all this down, please get it straight, any errors will be attributed to sloth, negligence and heartlessness and I shall start our longest honeymoon by hurting you where it hurts most so that you will only be able to write letters to me like Abelard did to Héloïse; and I shan't really mind because I shall have been your last woman, which will give me enormous satisfaction because I have such an unpleasant character. I should be writing to other people but I would rather write to you.

I love you,

Ann

1 South Wraxall Manor, Lord Long's house, had been inherited by Sara Long, Ann's neice, and was taken for the summer by the Rothermeres.
2 Herbert 'Beb' Asquith (1881–1947). Writer, editor, wounded in the First World War.

To Ian Fleming

[Shane's Castle][1]   Wednesday evening 9.30
                                                              [undated]

My darling Ian,

I arrived here at 7.30 dazed and sad, and was thrust with horrific speed into both my other lives. Terence arrived with the children five minutes later and cross-questioned me about who I had seen in the south, and then the telephone rang and it was Esmond from Montreal, and whatever I asked him he said haven't you had my letters and of course they had arrived while I was away and I could see them on the mantelpiece but I hadn't had time to read them – oh dear! and then we had supper and Fionn told me an extraordinary story which meant I had to tell her the facts of life before she went to sleep because I could see she was worried – and I have just done that and now I must write to you and then take *The Dubliners* to bed.

Darling, I can't write this evening about our days together. They were the nicest days of my life and I enjoyed it so much that it must have made me dull, because it was so short and so full of happiness and I am afraid I loved cooking for you and sleeping beside you and ... I don't think I have ever loved like this before; and I only hope I bring you some joy because there are a lot of little empty places in your life that ought to be filled and I never like to say that to you because you are such an independent person and I don't like to believe that you love me in case it isn't true. Your letter to me was very very sweet and I'll tell you why when I see you – Please find us a bed for Saturday night.

Darling, I wish you had felt well all the time, thank you for it all – it is too close to me tonight to say much about it, and I am in too emotional a mood to write at all but I somehow feel we do love each other and it no longer matters if I am just myself with you.

I long for Saturday. Goodnight my darling one.

A

1 The effect of the burning of Shane's Castle, Lord O'Neill's house in Northern Ireland, during the Troubles had been to remove the grander rooms and leave the nursery and those of the servants. Compensation was paid and Ann's son Raymond was to rebuild in 1958 but meanwhile it was less than elegant. John Martin Robinson in *The Latest Country Houses*, 1982, describes the present

version as 'a good and convincing Regency design'. Ann referred to it as 'Raymond's Georgian nook'.

To Evelyn Waugh[1]

SS *Mauretania*   4 January [1948]

Dear Evelyn

I was flattered when the greatest author *de nos jours* sent me his latest book,[2] and my intention was to immediately send respectful thanks; but flu, Christmas and Laura's latest caprice in preferring Mr Koch de Gooreynd to Lord Dudley have occupied a great deal of time.[3]

The ship has been rolling considerably and I think longingly of the healthy heroine of 'Brideshead' who was able to consummate her great love at the height of a storm; but I have no great love, only seasickness and my unslender loins have remained unmolested; however on arrival in New York I hope to emulate your Swedish gym instructress and become wholly carnivorous.[4] It is redundant to say how much I enjoyed your book and how much I look forward to the February *Horizon*.[5]

With best wishes for the New Year to you, cousin Laura and the little ones.

Ann

1 Although Evelyn Waugh (1903–66) became one of Ann's closest friends, references to her in letters and diary up to this time show that he saw her only as an acquaintance and a hostess. He knew Lady Pamela Berry better. *See* Appendix of Names.

2 *Scott-King's Modern Europe*, 1947.

3 Late in 1947 Ann's sister Laura had flown with her husband the Earl of Dudley to Paris for the first lavish ball after the war, given at the British Embassy by Duff and Lady Diana Cooper. They quarrelled and Laura stayed on, alone and tearful in the Ritz. She was still dressed in 'a mass of pale tulle, no shoulder straps, just a broad band of real leopard skin making a bodice finishing under the arms'. By chance she ran into Gerry Koch de Gooreynd, an old acquaintance, who, over lunch at Maxim's, asked her to run away and marry him. When she returned to London, Laura stayed at Warwick House and though she was expecting Koch de Gooreynd's child, there was a reconciliation with Lord Dudley in the spring. Koch de Gooreynd continued to write unhappy letters.

4 Miss Sveningen, who 'towered some six inches above the heads of the crowd', ate beefsteak for breakfast in *Scott-King's Modern Europe*.

5 *The Loved One* was to be printed entire in that issue.

Ann contrived to stay with Fleming in Jamaica in early 1948 and she wrote:

[no date]

Arrived at Goldeneye at typical tropical sunset hour. Violet, Ian's housekeeper, two other maids and the gardener all lined up to welcome 'Commander' with much grinning.

Grinning over, immediate dark and noisy with frogs and crickets. Felt suddenly depressed, hid it from Ian who was ecstatically excited.

The house is scarcely furnished, a dining alcove with hard upright benches, a vast long well-proportioned room, more window than wall, the jalousies not closed; a desk, but nowhere to sit in comfort and nothing to sit on but two planters' chairs – a gift from an admiring sugar planter's daughter – and a canasta table from Lady Huggins.[1] Ian said that he expected me and Loelia [Westminster][2] to help with furnishing. I suggested curtains which appalled him. Ian sat at dinner facing the long rectangular window and staring at the night. (He always sat at the end of the bench with guests on his right, and later when we married put me on his right and guests beyond, so he could stare or talk as he wished; occasionally I would persuade him to sit in the centre for good manners.)

Woke at six because of light. Ian asleep. Black maids asleep. Beach is semicircle white coral sand with arms of rock each side and a cave on the left full of sand martins. Water warm transparent shallow, then rocks emerge here and there, and far beyond a white line of waves where the reef ends and the depths begin. Walked all round property, sea grapes hanging over cliff and inland orange, lemon and grapefruit trees and a good deal of unidentifiable scrub. Palms etc. Sun came over mountains at seven thirty, Ian still asleep, so went swimming. Depression totally gone, only Ian could devise this manner of life. Climbed steep steps up cliff to find Ian awake and fearfully sulky that I had not waited for him to explore. Too full of well-being to be troubled over this. Breakfast of paw paw, black mountain coffee, scrambled eggs and bacon.

Vultures arrived; protected by law to feast on carrion, they are easy to approach. I found them as exciting as the long-tailed humming birds. Ian ceased sulking, and it has been a wonderful day of birds, flowers and above all fish. We have Italian Pirelli masks that inflate at the back of the head, quite easy. Tropical underwater is more beautiful than land, strange alarming canyons of coral rock.

Ian has devised a halcyon way of life. He bathes at sunrise, then Violet brings his shaving water and he tells her what manner of way his eggs should be cooked for breakfast. After breakfast he reads in the sunken garden, then he rows in the India rubber dinghy or does some planning with the gardener. Little will come of this as it is clear no work will be done in Ian's absence. Each rose has a large black beetle eating its heart out. More flowers are to be planted round the sunken garden to attract hummingbirds.

Much morning swimming. There are long trident forks with which to spear lobsters. They are the clawless *langoustes* of the Mediterranean who peer nervously from under rocks; if they emerge too far one can thrust the spear into the horny head. So far I have failed, but Ian has shot one or two and they are delicious to eat.

We have a martini before lunch and then local fare, or if it is not local Ian tells the smiling Violet that he did not come to the tropics to eat beef roll. All vegetables are called chaw-chaw or some name that rhymes with chaw-chaw. Silk fish or snapper is grilled in butter and served with a great deal of rice – the staff and their many relations eat what is left. The national dish is curried goat, or sucking pig. Steak, kidneys or liver grilled on charcoal are best.

The living room is lighted high in each corner, funeral pyres for moths and beetles. I wait hopefully for a praying mantis or some specially beautiful moth to capture and paint.

After dinner it is a ritual that we lean over the cliff railing, and as our eyes grow accustomed to the dark watch the spray of the reef or the high bright large stars of that region. The air is so clear of dirt or dust there is an illusion of vast universe and the sea horizon is very round. Ian remains longer than us, smoking and wallowing in the melancholy.

Loelia and I have been consulted about interior decoration. Where to place the prints of the Vienna riding school. But when the carpenter arrived we were sent to the garden and our advice was not heeded.

Neighbours are not inspiring. Ian says it would be better without our Mayfair talk. We reluctantly go to dine with a military man and agree to say nothing. The conversation totally dull, but Ian insists that he learned of local matters and hopes we will continue to be silent.

Ian consulted all his friends these past years for suggestions to name the house. Alastair Forbes suggested 'Rum Cove', a totally appropriate description of the owner. Another suggestion was 'Shame Lady', the local name for the sensitive plant which grows everywhere. Ian decided on 'Goldeneye' because the village is Oracabessa, the Spanish for Goldenhead.

1 Molly Green was married 1929–58 to Sir John Huggins, who was Governor of Jamaica 1943–50.
2 Their friend Loelia, Duchess of Westminster, had come as a chaperone. She comments, 'What a wet worm I was. They were madly in love, used to go out in the boat snorkling and spearing from ten in the morning to seven at night. I was left on this stick of coral to wander about among the blackamores in the village.'

From Ian Fleming

Goldeneye   [undated]

Darling A

I followed your plane in the car as far as I could but you went too fast. Sheila [Bryce] said you passed straight over the house but I expect you were holding your head in your hands. I'm sure you passed directly over Goldeneye too. I HOPE you looked out. Dinner yesterday was awful and I'm afraid I shouted at Sheila. I apologised to Ivar at breakfast this morning and he said he had to face the same sort of thing twice a day. I suppose that is what it's like to be married to her! Ivar is the soft-answer-champion of the Caribbean and wouldn't help at all. He's quite right of course if he has to live with her, but all the same I think their marriage would have been much happier if he had given her a bit of roughage!

I left the house at 9.30. It was too full of a small black ghost with a spot on its chin and all the answers. I decided to motor all the way round the Blue Mountain home along the coast. I didn't get home till five. I called on a wonderful lighthouse keeper who said that my house used to be called Rock Edge and before that Rotten Egg Bay. You would have liked him. When the birds migrate they come and commit suicide on his light which is very tall and bright and built in 1840. He picks them up and eats them and doesn't know what sort they are. Bodies and fish and wrecks get washed up on him and it's clearly the place for you and me. It's called Morant Point and is opposite Mexico.

All these things will seem very small to you now. I expect it's like hearing from someone you met on a cruise or on winter sports. (That's fishen!)

I got home and fell into the sea and it was wonderful and lots more of the seaweed had been cut away. There was a deputation of lobsters to thank me for sending you off home but the general feeling in the sea was that you were more of a tease than a danger. I said that teasing with you meant love and that one ought to be very pleased. A small but intelligent lobster said that you had teased him so much that he could never make love again and was that really fair? I said it was a great privilege to have one's antennae torn off by you because you did it in such a well-born manner. After a lot of grumbling the lobsters went off, but I don't expect I've heard the last of it. They seemed to think you were old enough to know better. I said I would speak to you about it...
Goodnight my precious
xxxx I.

Lord Rothermere met Ann and the Duchess of Westminster in Miami.

To Ian Fleming

Miami Beach, Florida   9 February [1948]

My darling,

It's all very bewildering, and a little Miami goes a long long way. We went to a Gala at the Surf Club – fabulously decorated to represent Reno; it was a fortunate choice for me as the abyss of boredom was redeemed by fruit machines and a vast illuminated roulette wheel. I shot my way out of our party and clinging to Alex Clifford[1] I spent the evening gambling and letting my tongue scorch the natives. The impenetrable respectability, lack of taste, misplaced wealth, old age and ugliness of our fellow guests consternated me. I think the only hope for the world is for America to slump into oblivion and start all over again – I am not sure I have not become pro-Russian. Yesterday we spent a long day in the small select millionairedom of Palm Beach. We started with lunch at the Seminole Golf Club where Loelia and Esmond ate for Great Britain, they started by tearing up stone crabs with nutcrackers and continued with roast beef, avocado pears, Roquefort cheese, strawberries and cream and chocolate layer cake. Esmond ended by putting pepper in his iced coffee and spluttering it all over his pale grey Nassau suit and a good dollop over Mrs Laddie Sanford's white beach dress. We then drove to the garden of Eden home of Mr and Mrs Duplaix, friends of the Cliffords and quite amusing, he is an artist who thinks he is Picasso: dissected women on all the walls but a lovely swimming pool. Johnny Ryan took pictures and a lot of light talk. No time for a siesta. We then tidied chez Loelia and went to cocktails with the Windsors, they were also entertaining Dock Holden, Eric [Dudley], Princess Karpurthla and two specimens of USA manhood, one of whom proved capable of a reasonable speed of conversation. I was mostly left with the Duke, who now calls me sweetheart and treats me as a fount of wisdom on British politics. Eric did his best to draw me aside but I was obdurate. Finally the entire collection bubbling with martinis retired to Dolly O'Brien's for dinner. We had a very good and quite gay dinner, the Duke being quite surprisingly funny, unfortunately towards its close Eric retold the story of the Lady Stanley[2] party in New York, maintaining he had had to force his way in to please Laura. Such flagrant lying provoked me to a flow of invective which shattered the social froth, reduced the Earl to silence and sulks, and caused temporary embarrassment to all.

I am only writing you all this because I can see so clearly the snarky sneers you will be able to indulge in and also to give you a vignette of my life.

Today has been spent with the local newspaper owners, and a passable man called General Johnson of Johnson baby powder, bandages, etc. Tomorrow local senators and Thursday, *Dieu merci*,

New York.

This conventional letter is partly explained by the fact [that] I am not alone in the room.

Oh, my love love, are you still alone? Have you been faithful to me? Are you sad or have you forgotten all the fun we had? I'm sorry I pulled the lobster's paws off and I wish wish I was still with you. Please write lots to New York and London. The *Queen Mary* sails on the 19th but may be delayed a day. You are a great big piece of my life and I feel amputated without you. Come back soon, don't put it off for a day.

I do hope the remoteness of Goldeneye won't force you to collect some sordid female to replace me and I hope you enjoyed all of it as much as I did, from the day we left London to last Thursday.

Don't have headaches or drink too much, and be careful fishing.

Bless you my darling

A.

P.S. I can't get a copy of the Knickerbocker column to send you. How lucky he gets his facts so wrong.[3]

1 Alexander Clifford, journalist with Reuters and the *Daily Mail*. He married Jenny Nicholson, daughter of Robert Graves, and they had a house at Portofino.
2 Edith Hawkes, who had been married to Lord Ashley and Douglas Fairbanks, was married to Lord Stanley 1944–8.
3 Cholly Knickerbocker wrote a social column in Sunday's *Journal-American*. An item had concerned Loelia, Duchess of Westminster staying with Fleming: 'Fleming is a sort of Beau Brummel of the islands. At one time he was rumoured to be Millicent Huddleston Rogers' hottest romance. But the Standard Oil million-heiress, who owns a dreamy little house on the bay, showed that it couldn't be that serious, because she left Jamaica shortly afterwards to join Clark Gable in Hollywood. [There is then a detour about Clark Gable and Lady Stanley.] But to get back to the Duchess of Westminster and Captain Fleming. How serious this flirtation might be is hard to tell. Only future history will record the happenings.' In her next letter Ann reports that 'Cecil Beaton congratulated me on giving Knickerbocker the dope on you and Loelia, he thought it a very funny joke and refused to believe it was fortuitous (to borrow one of your affected words).'

To Ian Fleming

The Plaza, New York   Friday the 13th! [February 1948]

My darling,

I can't find my pen, and the Plaza pens and pencils don't write. I loved your letters, and thank God they were here because the journey back on our train meant that I couldn't think of anything but you for 24 hrs; I think of you most of the time anyway but the train is exclusively yours. I have never travelled with nymphos in it like you have and it has no other memories for me, it just said Ian-Ian-Ian the whole way to New York. So you see I remember you more than someone I just met on a cruise! I hate to think of you driving alone to Goldeneye and going to lighthouses without me, it seems so silly. Dinner with the Bryces sounds disagreeable; there seems some mental comparison going on in your nasty mind between a possible marriage of ours and their sad relationship. May I say at once that I should play Ivar's role and you Sheila's! If there is any shouting it will *always* be you who starts it – we can continue this in March, it's dull in a letter because I can't pinch you.

I do hope I shall get *lots* more letters from you while I am here – please don't stop writing and please mean it when you say you will be good. It would be an interesting feat to be faithful to someone for three weeks, you have never done it before and it might make you feel very happy. I couldn't be unfaithful (much!) to someone I was in love with, and it would be impossible for me to be unfaithful to you. I have done what had to be done and luckily it called for no effort on my part because it has been the most difficult thing since I left you, and I don't feel very happy about it. I don't feel very unhappy about it either because fate seems to have played a large part in it, and I have a happy-go-lucky faith in things that just happen. Please write all about Pam and if you see Elsa[1] and all the other bitches who have earned you the name of 'Don Juan of the Islands' in the American press, wait till I tell London that!

New York is cold and I foresee a round of dull entertainments. We were met at the station by Frank Owen[2] in the Mayor of New York's car. The Mayor has placed it at his disposal; Frank is having a great success here and I should think doing well. He is off to Pittsburgh and Chicago today, staying with publishers and lecturing. We dined with the Owens and Iddons last night which was hideous for Esmond. I didn't mind as I clung to Frank (you needn't be jealous). I am going to lunch with Nin[3] in a few minutes, and tomorrow Elsa is taking us to a ball given by Helen Hayes;[4] as it is writers and theatre it may be bearable.

Esmond has no dollars, and is appalled at my extravagance, he refuses to eat anywhere but the Ritz grill and says '21' is out of the question. Loelia is ensconced at the Stephensons[5] and sounds happy, I am going there on Sunday.

I shall *never* go to Miami again except en route to Jamaica, the last days were spent with the governor, a senator from Virginia and the owners of the *Miami Herald* and *Evening News*. I got off with the senator from Virginia, he is 72 and a great admirer in the old days of Margot [Asquith], so he was prepared to finance the great-niece at roulette which added thirty dollars to lend lease.

I think of you going into the sea in the mornings. I think of you talking to Violet and shouting at poor Holmes, and I think of you finding things without me.

Tell the lobsters from me that I love them because they are your lobsters, and they were very silly to leave their homes because I teased them; and tell the lobster who said he couldn't make love any more that if teasing stops him making love, he doesn't know anything about love and that he had better learn fast or I shall pull his other antennae off.

Bless you my darling, darling

A.

<hr />

1 Elsa Maxwell (1883–1963). Ugly energetic gossip columnist who liked Fleming.

2 Frank Owen (1906–79). Son of a Welsh pub-owner, the youngest MP in the House 1929–31 (Liberal), he had been taken up by Beaverbrook and was Editor of the *Evening Standard* 1938–41. During the War he was Lord Mountbatten's press agent, became a lieutenant-colonel and received an OBE. His buccaneering dash appealed to Ann and she was not dismayed by his radical views. He was made Editor of the *Daily Mail* in March 1947. '*Mail*men gossiped that Owen's promotion was plotted by Ann Rothermere, who keeps a bright and calculating eye on her easy-going husband's affairs', *Time*, 17 March. Owen remained there until 1950 and improved the standard of the paper and the morale of its staff. He was however erratic and often absent.

3 Margaret ('Nin') Ryan, the daughter of Otto Kahn, and wife of Johnny Ryan.

4 Helen Hayes (1900–   ). Actress. Appeared in London for the first time later that year in *The Glass Menagerie* by Tennessee Williams.

5 Mary Simmons, who died in 1978, married in 1924 William Stephenson, Director of British Security Co-ordination in the Western Hemisphere 1940–6. Known as 'Little Bill' or 'the Quiet Canadian', he was a hero to Fleming.

To Ian Fleming

RMS *Queen Mary*   Monday afternoon

Darling,

There are 200 1st class passengers instead of 800. Sir Samuel Hoare, Lord Brownlow,[1] a charming American Jew film director – George Cukor[2] – Polly[3] in cabin class and B. Baxter.[4] Es. plays gin rummy with Baxter all night, pretends he doesn't watch the score and interferes at the last minute – result he has taken £20 off poor Baxter. I have not dined down except the first night, but on that night I produced Polly who is looking very pretty and takes my place more than adequately. I was amused at the rapidity with which she found Es's cabin (long before we sailed). She had been told in Nassau we were parted and as her Frenchman has left her I presume she thought it was a reasonable future. I was in the bathroom when she appeared and was so amused at the conversation that I remained with an ear glued to the door; finally she asked him to dine with her and he came out of the vague mood with which he had replied to her questions and said 'I must ask Ann, where is she?' 'Here,' I replied, stepping out of the loo – a most enjoyable moment for a horrid bitch like me. We fell on each others necks and I told her to dine with us and now she is fixed for a gay voyage. My spelling, writing and punctuation is worse than usual but all circumstances have combined to make me feel very ill; and it is will power that I am holding a pen at all.

I have lots to tell but not in a letter – one funny *very* bad taste joke.

Darling, you sound as if you were leading an innocent life with your animals and bathing; everything you say makes me homesick. I did love it all and please take me back next year. I shall like it even better because I shall have tiny roots there and I always like that. I hate new places. I suppose you are hating the thought of leaving – you beast, but please remember how much I want you.

love

A.

1 Lord Brownlow (1899–1978). Personal Lord-in-Waiting to Edward VIII at the time of the abdication, he drove Mrs Simpson across France, pursued by the press, a week before the final announcement. Suffering comparative social eclipse afterwards, he was among those referred to as 'Gone With the Windsors'.

2 George Cukor (1899–1983). Distinguished Hollywood director, particularly noted for his direction of Garbo in *Camille*, 1938, Katharine Hepburn in *The Philadelphia Story*, 1940, and Judy Garland in *A Star is Born*, 1954.

3 Polleen Peabody (1917–   ). American correspondent in England during the war, and daughter of Caresse Jacob whose second husband was Harry Crosby, the poet and creator of the Black Sun Press.

4 Beverley Baxter (1891–1964). Editor of the *Daily Express* 1929–33, Conservative MP 1935–64. Knighted 1954.

To Evelyn Waugh

Warwick House, Stable Yard,
St. James's Palace, SW1   18 July [1948]

Dear Evelyn

I am full of sympathy, but I presume nettle rash cannot last nine months, and tho' temporarily wrecking the complexion does not deform the figure; but I realise this is the point of view of a heathen woman and not a good Catholic who has to rely on an uncertain margin of safety not to be permanently in my sad condition,[1] and probably becomes resigned and accepts her duties cheerfully. I did not mean to be taken seriously re Quennell and the Beefsteak,[2] I thought it might be an opportunity for you to show compassion, which according to *Time* magazine is the only quality you lack, but perhaps there are better opportunities, such as calling at Warwick House when the nettle rash permits and taking my mind off my sorry state by being brilliantly nasty about my friends.

I trust the itch is abating

Love

Ann

1 Ann was pregnant.

2 Ann had suggested that Waugh put up Peter Quennell for the Beefsteak though he was struggling unsuccessfully to keep him out of White's.

Ann went for a golfing holiday with Lord Rothermere, Ian Fleming, the Duchess of Westminster and the children to Gleneagles in Perthshire. Suddenly it became clear that her child would be born a month prematurely. She was rushed to Edinburgh, where a daughter survived only a few hours. Ann was ill, Lord Rothermere at her side, Fleming writing almost daily from hotels. Later she said that it was Fleming's understanding at this time that made her truly love him.

To Ian Fleming

[Edinburgh]   Monday evening [undated]

My darling,

There was morphia and pain and then you were here and now you've gone and there's nothing except the grim realisation of what happened in the last ten days. This is a selfish letter but I have cried all day, it may make me feel better to write it. I am very bruised and bewildered, this afternoon I forced myself to ask Esmond where she had been buried, I have been haunted by the thought for days. They christened her after me and put her next to my mother in the family churchyard at the edge of the sea at Aberlady – Esmond, Laura, my hated Grandmother [Anne Tennant] – while I was lying in a haze of morphia and you were playing golf – Oh my darling I must grow up soon but I do love you; please help me over this. I am muddled and distressed and in danger of losing all sense of proportion about it. I feel full of remorse towards Esmond and yet my grief and loss is entirely bound up with you; and both are too feminine for you to understand; the loss of a baby of 8 hours' age cannot be a grief to a father, so I mustn't get ideas about Esmond's feelings, or get hysterical about it all. My love, please forgive all this but we are too close for me to hide things from you. I hope you are playing wonderfully and feeling well, it is the greatest comfort to know you are near me, and thankyou for your sweetness all this year and for your letters. I am *longing* for Saturday and will know about your journey tomorrow and send you a telegram and a more cheerful letter. Goodnight my sweet

Ann

Ann wrote the next day beginning, 'Forgive the letter I wrote to you yesterday, it was self-indulgent to let the waves close over me for a day and a night, but it was cruel to take it out on you during your golf week . . .'

To Ian Fleming

[Edinburgh?]   Tuesday evening [undated]

My darling,

I am alone in a room with a wireless and books, a setting you are more conditioned to than me; it makes me feel sentimental or mad but perhaps it is time I learnt about it. Tonight I feel remote, caused by aches and sleepiness, but I want to write to you before I go to bed. Thankyou for the magazines, thankyou for the cutting and the one coming tomorrow – I like to see your writing and I LOVE you making a fuss of me, I want to purr.

Tomorrow I shall start preparing a flower-strewn path for you – a room with a view, three-minute eggs, buckets of martinis and bunting, and a brass band to meet you at the station, so I hope you won't arrive with your ears folded back like a wicked horse.

I think any other man would be a frightful bore after you. I should miss the infinite variety of wall gazing, pointless bullying so harsh and then so gentle if I cry. Wonderful ideas and wrong-headed arguments, tremendous charm and occasional shocking manners; a very good mind which I fear will never expand to capacity owing to an unfortunate adroitness at short cuts and an unusual gift for well-organised leisure – but you beast, you *must* write your book, even if I have to sit in an upright chair knitting beside you, which was how Mrs Galsworthy made Mr Galsworthy give birth to *The Forsyte Saga*; and after all the aids you have given me in creation I think it would be an appropriate *quid pro quo*, however much badgering it may mean.

Goodnight, goodnight, and no pains in your neck or chest and no elephants or nightmares my love,

love

A.

When Ann was better Lord Rothermere took her to Paris and then to Portofino in Italy. He knew by then that the child had been Fleming's, not his.

Lord Caernarvon had bought some land at Portofino and in 1874 built a house of Portland stone, which was imported from England. Some of the peninsular had since been sold and the house in which Ann stayed belonged to Alexander and Jenny Clifford.

To Ian Fleming

[Postcard of Portofino]

My love,
   More letters please. The hero of *Crime Passionel*[1] is staying here, wearing clothes and hair like on the stage, he is good company but I am not flirting with him.
   Yesterday I did my nails in the blazing sun and thought of you and felt happy, when suddenly I felt a burning pain in my fingers, and realised I had used the ascetic [*sic*] acid you gave me for my warts instead of acetone, so when we meet in Paris I shall have no fingertips to caress you with! Darling, I want to know what you are doing *every* moment. It won't be very long now.

xxxxxxxxxx

A.

1 Michael Gough (1917–   ). Actor, who played Hugo in *Crime Passionel* by Jean-Paul Sartre in 1948.

To Ian Fleming

Il Castelletto, Portofino   Tuesday

My darling
   Letters seldom reach here, the postman sits on an old boat in the middle of the piazza and waits for people to collect their mail from him. Yesterday there were two ENORMOUS envelopes from you but not nearly enough writing; you're a *damned idle beast* to stuff my letters with lumps of *Time* and *Life* magazine instead of your thoughts (if you have any) or your actions (if you do anything); but I admit what you did scribble pleased me, because I could see you sitting in your or our nest nursing your cold and I love it when you talk about us being a long long time together. I thought I was free from your social gaffes here, but not at all, for during lunch at Rapallo yesterday I produced your lump of *Time* magazine and brightly showed it to the Cliffords. Jenny glanced at it, put her head in her hands and burst into tears occasionally uttering imprecations and curses against Alan Moorehead,[1] while Alex sat scarlet and shamefaced. Apparently they lent this house to the Mooreheads,

foregoing a large rent from rich Italians, and Jenny before leaving them in possession had confided that she was writing a book on Portofino and was foolish enough to read them her manuscript, most of which is embodied in the offending article. It cast a great shadow over the day for whenever we passed a post office Jenny sent abusive telegrams to Alan while Alex was dumb and miserable but unable to save the Clifford-Moorehead axis from becoming an Italian vendetta – so thankyou, darling, for my happy day to which Esmond added the *coup de grace* by becoming absorbed in the article and pronouncing it interesting and excellently written.

This long letter comes to you by courtesy of having my monthly troubles for the first time, which means one has them very badly so I am in bed while the others pick olives and E. has gone to the village to collect telegrams for him (no doubt *DM* troubles) and the post which I hope he won't read in case there is something from you. My bedroom is so so romantic. On one side a large window through which an umbrella pine pushes its head, and in front a larger window with a pretty curved top and a view of miles and miles of blue Mediterranean and fishing boats. I am lying on a double bed with wrought iron head and thin wrought iron barley sugar posts draped with a large white bridal mosquito net, and I can hear the sea so there is really only one essential missing which is you.

Did you play golf at Huntercombe this weekend? Have you been brave about the dentist? I want to know so many things.

Yesterday at Rapallo I bought you a gun and mask; all the guns are loaded with Neptune's tridents so I presume that is correct; I have bought an extra one, with which if all goes well I shall wage an unceasing warfare against the seapricks! I hope you are courting the Connollys and not leaving all the work to me.

Find out in London what time my train reaches Paris – I know all about yours, you should arrive (full of a good breakfast on the train) at the Ritz about 10 o'clock. I shall not be able to send a telegram but hope to be in the Vendôme side, Room 72.

No headaches or colds I hope, and no women either.

My love my darling

A. xxxxxxx

---

1 Alan Moorehead (1910–83), the Australian writer, was a close friend of Alex Clifford. Moorehead's *The Villa Diana*, which includes a description of a strike in Portofino, was not published until 1951 but separate chapters appeared earlier in various magazines.

From Ian Fleming

Goldeneye, Jamaica   30 September [1948]

Dearest baby, I haven't written for 3 whole days and you will think that a Cleopatra has gripped me. In fact I have had to use both hands on my modest life and could only have written with a toe. Everyone has gone sick on me and my department is melting like snow in sunshine. My own cold has needed a firm hand and now that I am a grass widow my social existence has executed a modest whirl. Elsa Maxwell tonight for instance with your old friends the Bensons, and various more modest other occasions. With all this I think of you all the time and a small blackhaired ghost waits for me at home every evening and walks with me to the Etoile and sits with me among the falling leaves in the small square.

Your letters are heaven, particularly the long first one from Portofino, although I am concerned at Es's pronouncements. I knew it would come and I know our weekends are going to be difficult. Don't force an ultimatum or I shall get too embarrassed ever to see him.

I will write a good letter tomorrow and this is only to keep you from squawking and snarking. Tell me about Portofino and the bathing dresses you buy and *mind* they are the right ones.
All my love and kisses my dearest
I

                                                              Friday

My love, its the first of October and the end of the week and you are away and I am full of the old goose and white wine and exhausted after 2 hours of Edith Sitwell[1] with no William P[2] or Rosamond L[3] to help and only some miscellaneous frousts. Moreover I am staying with Peter [Fleming] and Celia[4] tonight with Joyce and Reggie Grenfell[5] and so all this makes me love and miss you more than ever so I am using the 'Chief's' time to send you this thin wail. Your letters are sweet and warm and please go on sending them when you can. I shall have to change the writing on my envelopes to you or the Cliffords will smell a loving rat. I hope they arrive. I can't spell Castelletto I don't think.
                    Dear Baby with all my love
                                I.

1 Edith Sitwell (1887–1964). Poet. Fleming had offended Miss Sitwell at a lunch in honour of her brother Osbert and she claimed to have mistaken him for Lady Cunard's social secretary. However they became friends and even thought of writing a book on Paracelsus together.

2 William Plomer (1903–73). South African writer. Discovered and edited Kilvert's Diary, 1938–40. Served at the Admiralty 1940–5. Wrote libretti of Gloriana and Curlew River for Benjamin Britten. Fleming's first literary friend and midwife to James Bond.

3 Rosamond Lehmann. (1901–). Novelist and old friend of Fleming, into whose bedroom she is said once to have thrown a dead octopus when annoyed. Later, when married to Ann, Fleming asked her to Goldeneye and it swiftly became clear that it had been a mistake. Fleming appealed to Noël Coward to persuade her to stay with him instead and he agreed at a price, saying in front of her, 'I'll settle for the Polaroid camera.' Fleming handed it over, there was a pause and Coward added 'And the tripod.' He got that, too.

4 Celia Johnson (1908–82). Already a distinguished actress when she married Peter Fleming in 1935. She had recently achieved her most lasting success in Coward's film Brief Encounter, 1945. Made Dame of the British Empire, 1981.

5 Joyce Phipps (1910–79). Actress, particularly in revues. Married Reggie Grenfell in 1929.

To Ian Fleming

Shane's Castle   Tuesday evening [late 1948]

My darling,

I miss you all the time and I wish we were at St Margaret's in our nest;[1] but we are so lucky that I must be good for a fortnight. The children very much feel this is their home and background as opposed to Warwick and Wraxall; feelings which must be respected and helped; and as for me you have become my background and I don't like being without it, I have never cooked or unpacked for anyone else and it makes me feel close and affectionate.

This letter will make little sense, the boys are playing the gramophone loudly and Cyril Connolly says in Enemies of Promise that no one with Irish blood should write after twilight because of the danger of mawkish sentimentality. I am thinking too much of Jamaica, you must tell me to stop; but it would be such anguish not to come with you and how HOW can I do it without wrecking you with Gomer[2] – I started fussing about it all ten days ago and I can't stop, if you have any views other than the hazy optimism with which we run our love, you might scribble them on the first chunk of magazine you send me – the piece in the E. Standard on Boodle's would do, I should like to see it anyway, it may provide ammunition for snark; I don't really feel anything but affection for the solid stolid old place because it is nice knowing you are there now and not 'dipping your wick' in some horrid harlot.

Is my love becoming claustrophobic yet? I feel the only thing that prevents it is my natural instinct for using the loved one as part of the social furniture – oh I enjoy so much your anger on those occasions!

Bless you and goodnight.

A.

1 Noël Coward had bought the lease of a house called White Cliffs at St Margaret's Bay near Dover in 1945. This he often lent to Ann and Ian Fleming. In *The Life of Noël Coward* Cole Lesley describes it as 'an elegant little house in a dramatic position at the very end of the beach . . . depending on the weather the waves either lapped against or lashed the end wall of the house and this was to become the wall of his [Coward's] bedroom, against which was the head of his bed. The drama of the situation of course appealed strongly to him, the drama intensified by the White Cliffs of Dover rising steeply to his right.' Fleming later took over the lease.

2 'The least he [Ian Fleming] had hoped for was a directorship. It never came. The editorship of *The Sunday Times* would have been acceptable. It was never offered . . . Gradually it dawned on him that there was a reason – a private reason – for this absence of recognition. In one respect, he was made to feel, he had failed to preserve the high moral tone of Kemsley House: it was the delicate matter of his friendship with a married woman. At any rate by 1949 there were enough straws in the wind to tell him that his great hopes of an important career in newspapers were over.' *The Life of Ian Fleming* by John Pearson, 1966.

Ann went to Goldeneye early in 1949 but left before Fleming.

From Ian Fleming

Goldeneye   Tuesday evening [20 February 1949]

My precious, it's too extraordinary being without you. It's made everything go suddenly uninteresting. There was no point in looking for conches and things on the beach when I got back and I'm afraid the point won't come back until you do. It was odd being in the car alone and it's queer in the house. I went sentimentally into your room and looked at the little bits you had left and I've wandered about in an empty gloom ever since, expecting to hear you or see you all the time. It's very melancholy and I'm thankful I'm going to Mo Bay and also that there is no one else here so that I can have your ghost to myself.

It was horrible seeing your plane go away. I knew as well that I ought to have been with you but I funked it. I funked the longer goodbye and the waiting with you in Miami, I've funked everything these last few days and almost purposely tried to squabble with you and vex you so that the melancholy should keep away. I'm sorry I was so bad and I'm sorry I didn't come with you at any rate part of the way but really I should have hated it too much. Please forgive, my darling love.

I.

To Ian Fleming

[February 1949]

My dearest love,

I'm sorry I was so unbrave about the inevitable end of such complete happiness. I'm very ashamed of myself. It is bad that at 35 years old one should cry and cry – I have never done such a thing for anyone before and it would be more appropriate at 17. My only consolation is that I think you minded very much and will miss me and miss me. Colonel Clarke's zany son met me and I insisted on trying to force my way onto the 5 p.m. Constellation, this has failed and it is too late to go to the Clarke home so I have bought available writing paper and stamp and am writing to you – but not too sentimentally in case I cry again, I'm trying to make myself cross instead about your not being more efficient about my journey! Not really.

Two nuns are sitting opposite telling their beads, and I wish there was somewhere more comfortable to sit; I have another two hours to wait.

You and Ed [Stanley] looked small and pathetic as the aeroplane swept by and I was almost as sad for you as me – for we are happy together and, thank God, you did mind me leaving.

Please till we meet again think about both of us very carefully; I cannot contemplate life without you but I am a frustrated romantic and you must decide. I know it must be done with wisdom, conviction and commonsense – also fairly soon because the new difficult days will destroy and irritate the very happy relationship we have now, and if it starts doing this I can only hope I have the courage for the sake of us all three to go with you or give you up. None of this need be immediate but we will have to be brave one way or the other before the end of this year. I think it is you who must determine it because you have had a comfortable life and to share a few pennies with a snarky girl accustomed to money is a frightening undertaking. I can only promise to try to make you happy and if we had enough money for gin and cigarettes I think it might be very happy. I know Jamaica was not the place to face up to it, but I am nearly home and it is bound to worry me a little bit.

Love
and all love
Ann

From Ian Fleming

[London?]   [February 1949]

Darling baby,

I agree with all you say about us and I will try and be sensible and have all the answers ready by the time I get back. It's terribly difficult to be sensible while our love is in mid flight with no sign, I think, that we are tiring of each other. At the same time I know it can't just go happily on and that we must both be grown up and quickly. I would love to nest with you for ever and you are absolutely the only person I have ever contemplated saying this to. But apart from the money side we must be absolutely sure that we should be happy or it would be a real crime for me to drag you out of a basically happy life into one that would be far more difficult in a thousand ways.

Having never been married I cannot weigh the odds with any certainty and you must realise that. My difficultness may seem all right while you are in love with me, but it would be quite different if the love turned to the usual married friendship and you might get too irritated. I don't know. Both your other husbands have been more lethargic and also more self-disciplined than I am and I'm afraid I shall never settle down until I settle into the earth! Anyway, my dearest love, I am completely devoted to you and would like to look after you for ever and make a nest with you in the way we both like and you should know this when talking to Esmond. When you have got the facts and I have found out what I can from Gomer we shall have to agree a course of action and carry it out as definitely and as cleanly as we can. Above all, let's do everything courageously and not let any slime get on our lives or it will always be between us. It works out like that always.

Forever

Ian

To Ian Fleming

New York   Thursday [February 1950?]

My darling.

I think I have a cold, probably because New York is hotter than Jamaica; also I am very tired. It was a great emotional strain to leave you and your lobsters and I'm afraid I was very 'unenglish' about it, do you know that when you said that to me if I'd had a revolver I should have shot you? Damn you, I am going to complain about it for MONTHS. Oh I was angry, angry; and you were too obtuse to see it. I am also fairly cross, considering the number of times you have flown from Kingston to New York that you couldn't be more competent about it. There is a world of difference between being alluringly sentimental in London and saying 'darling, I will come to New York with you and see you off' and being so vague that I am left in the Miami airport from 4 to 8.30. You're a selfish thoughtless bastard, but as we love each other and have been as happy together as is possible and if I may continue to tell you what hell you are, I don't really mind. This was meant to be a tremendous love letter and it is really but the words are not quite the ones I intended to write.

I got to bed at 2 a.m. on Tuesday and 2.30 a.m. last night. I wished you had been with me at *Kiss Me Kate*[1] – great fun. I sat in the stalls with the answer to one of the question in Noël's Quiz Book – Who is Known as Princess Alice in America? Ans: Alice Mary Roosevelt (Teddy's daughter), a bright old lady who must have been very pretty. Afterwards an interminable supper party at the Stork Club, I sat between Rex Harrison[2] and Charles Boyer[3] and was too tired to flirt much, and am wondering how to avoid going to see the former's play this afternoon. To make conversation I pretended enormous interest in *Anne of a Thousand Days* and he offered me the house seats.

Always love

Ann

1 Cole Porter's version of *The Taming of the Shrew* had come on at the end of 1948.
2 Rex Harrison (1908–). Actor, famous for slightly caddish charm. He was appearing as Henry VIII in *Anne of a Thousand Days*.
3 Charles Boyer (1899–1978). Actor who built a durable career out of flirtation. In 1948 he had played Hoederer in *Red Gloves* (Sartre's *Les Mains Sales*).

From Ian Fleming

[London?]   Friday [February 1950?]

My darling love

My headache is nagging at me and making me say a lot of things which I expect I only half mean. But they are things which have been in my head all along and which you know about and which I suppose are decisive now. I can't write you a love letter about them because the way we love each other is a simple and stupid and selfish way which doesn't lend itself to phrases and about which we have never pretended.

The trouble is that Esmond is an adolescent. There is no excuse to hurt him. He is not an Eric [Lord Dudley]. There is no evil in him and neither of us wishes him harm. His only sin is his wealth and that is not his fault and he has had little profit from it. He needs protection and if he *gave* a little more he would deserve it. Anyway, he needs it, and you contracted, in exchange for a lot of flim-flam, to give it to him.

You have extracted the maximum out of the flim-flam which he gave you and which you once wanted. You give happiness to countless people and luxury to a few whose lives would be grey without it. You would do still more if I didn't take up so much of your mind and vitality. You would do still more and could be a very

Guy Charteris, Ann's father

Ann with Raymond and Fionn

Ann, Nin Ryan and
Esmond Rothermere

A party at the American Embassy in 1947. *Back row:* Cecil Beaton, Laura Dudley, Michael Berry, Alastair Forbes; *front row:* John and Nancy Hare, Ghislane Alexander, Eric Dudley, Peggy Dunne, 'Chips' Channon as Mr Chips, Pamela Berry and Ann

At the Headdress Ball, with Lucien Freud and Frederick Ashton

Peter Quennell

Patrick Leigh Fermor at Kardamyli, Greece

Hugo Charteris

Ian Fleming

great person in England (as opposed to the shiny world) if you
wished and if someone beat you with a hairbrush once a day. But at
any rate you play with the little finger of your left hand a greater
part in Esmond's business than any other woman I know in any
other husband's business.

The children are another problem. They love you in a taken-for-
granted way. They shouldn't be shaken up again. They oughtn't to
be driven in on themselves anymore. Esmond is an excellent
stepfather for them. They are not easy children. They need peace
and stability and no more turmoil. The same thing applies to your
family who are under your wing, and particularly to Hugo and also
to Nanny who I am sure doesn't want to start wandering again and
whom I suspect you will always need, and your various relations
who I expect like to bask in the brassy glare and I dare say think it
their due in exchange for an escutcheon or two (dirty crack!).

The point is that a lot of people depend on you.

No one depends on me. I give nothing except my cherished
freedom. My love for you is entirely selfish and if I married you I
shouldn't give a hoot for what you had left behind. None of it means
a thing to me and, for your own *happiness*, I think you would be
well quit of nine-tenths of the weight on your shoulders.

So what is left? A warm but very prickly nest with shame for the
present and uncertainty for the future and a lot of squalling
obligations on your conscience. I would be worrying at what I had
taken you from (I suppose) and with no new stability to offer in
exchange for the old.

I can't go on, my darling darling. I want this to be a sensible
balance sheet, but it keeps on trying to be prose, and it keeps on
painting the picture too black.

I know all the other side. Our two lovely years, our basic love
and faith in each other and in our stars. They would be enough to
sail our ship if it weren't for the harm we would do.

You know it just as well as I do and it doesn't need anyone's
advice. We know enough to be good about it and don't let's cheat.
Something may make it easier. The world's in a funny state. Perhaps
one day we may get married. I hope so with all my heart. I know we
would be happy so long as it comes about the right way. Otherwise
we wouldn't. We both know it and that's the final argument.

I haven't said all the nice things because you know they are in
my heart. I love you so much more than any other woman and we

have had so much happiness that I am brimming over with you so that often when I think of you I almost cry.

But you don't like men who cry do you!

Darling Ann, I love you.

Ian

This is a week later and I don't know the date. It is late at night and a Thursday.

My beloved,

We have now had a week more or less together and I love you as much as ever and I have kept my other letter in my pocket and kissed you instead of giving it to you. But I feel the cream-puff fog ‚ncroaching more and more and the odds lengthening and I know it's no good unless the atom bomb falls. We shouldn't be happy unless it did.

We behave together in an uncivilised way and we love in the same way. We would be happy beside the blue lagoon but not in Kensington Gore. I would not have the patience or the tolerance and you would hate me for my harshness and lack of sympathy and I would hate you for putting the simple things second.

You are surprised that I wish to spend all my evenings alone, and I am surprised that you prefer 'company' – not the people you would choose, but just any people rather than none. You hate silence and I prefer it. You are natural and I am unnatural. I don't see how we can marry in these days and be happy when the way we mostly love each other is like furry animals. If once you had had dinner in bed with a book, rather than downstairs with Hugo and Esmond and spotty footmen, I would have thought that you had secret places stronger than the bars of the cage. But your life bears down on me with such an insistent weight that I can't push it away and isolate you and see you clear without your chosen carapace. (I mustn't write like Hugo might!)

My darling last night I looked round my room and saw all the bits of you. I have often looked at them before and almost counted the strings that bind my heart to yours. All the warmth in me comes from you. All the love I have for you has grown out of me because you made it grow. Without you I would still be hard and dead and cold and quite unable to write this childish letter, full of love and jealousies and adolescence. But meantime, with every day, you were being taken further away. More people, more success, more *Daily*

Mail, more responsibilities and more happiness were building walls around you. Your life was choosing you for one road rather than another. Now I believe the road is set and, all other things aside, I believe it is your happiest one.

Hell, this is a stupid letter and I am stupid to write it. I believe in my heart that we shall still live our lives together because we shall both come back to a love which is the true love, which not many people have known. But now, or tonight, I feel that I must say what I have said and make us both unhappy. I feel the weight of your public life upon me and I know I shan't shake it off and so I had better tell you about it and help you out of this dear blind life we have been living together.

When I have given you this letter let's try and grow up and if we fail please my darling let's come together again and live like furry animals and make each other happy. I believe we would, but I'm not certain enough now to want to go on tearing each other to tatters – and that's what the undertones in our voices say we are going to start doing soon.

My darling, darling, there are so many years left to us both. Please let's have some of them together.

I love you.

I.

To Ian Fleming

[Paris]   Tuesday [March? 1950]

My darling
        Everyone was very gay last night; they danced the farandole up and down the staircase. Hugo[1] was told he looked like Lord Byron and Alastair [Forbes] was also there looking like Lord Byron, they stood arrogantly at different corners of the room surveying the antics of the smart but rapidly ageing women; Hugo was particularly distressed at their age and saw no beauty in them. I behaved very well and sat on a sofa wrapped in black lace and talked to Duff [Cooper] about law and morality and to Palewski[2] about nothing at all.

Darling, I thought about you so much, because there was no one to make my eyes shine. I feel awfully sleepwalking and I can't think of a religion for us, I just look forward to Easter. I don't even know if I am happy or sad, and I wish a fairy would arrive with a wand and make everything all right: give Esmond a perfect wife and put me in your bed with a raw cowhide whip in my hand so as I can keep you well behaved for forty years.

Laura's eyes were shining last night, she was in white satin and I imagine was the belle of the 'jumping ball', and I expect the French champion had a wonderful time, tho' she tells me she still thinks of marrying Gerry [Koch de Gooreynd]. Gerry was at the jumping every night, and I wanted her to pick him [out] of his seat and fling him across her saddle and gallop into the ring with him; it would have been good for Eric [Lord Dudley] who looked beastly smug between the President [Vincent Auriol] and old Wallie Windsor.[3]

Darling, I wonder about your headaches and I wish we were at Southend, and I am finding it difficult to write to you, which worries me – but maybe it's because I went to bed at 2 a.m. or maybe it's because the future is so strange that my light touch is less light than usual.

An old Austrian who had drunk too much followed me around last night lamenting Salzburg and the past, he wouldn't believe that I had never dined in Salzburg with him or anyone else, it only resulted in tooth grinding when I thought of your carryings on in that city.

Be good, my love, and take care of yourself.

My love, love

Ann

1 Hugo Charteris had joined the Rothermere group in 1948 and, after a depressing spell on the Hull *Evening News*, had come to London as a sub-editor on the *Daily Mail*. He then became the group's correspondent in Paris.
2 Gaston Palewski (1901–84). Loyal supporter of de Gaulle, President of the Constitutional Council 1965–74. Nancy Mitford's lover and the model for Fabrice in *The Pursuit of Love*.
3 The Duchess of Windsor was then fifty-four.

To Hugo Charteris from Ann

Warwick House   Saturday [?March 1950]

Darling Hugo,

I shall have to challenge Duff to a duel; but Duff's opinions are at least less variable than yours. Once one recognises that Esmond does not mind very deeply about anything or anybody one ceases to expend violent emotion upon him and only regrets that fate has given him so much power – is it more evil to be negative with power than to use it like Max [Beaverbrook]? I think possibly it is for it becomes a breeding ground for thousands of ugly little powers with only the Charteris influence to combat them!

Every new idea in the office comes from MacLean.[1] I do not quite understand your dislike of him, we lunched together on Tuesday and he said saturation circulation point for the *DM* was $2\frac{1}{2}$ million and it would not pay to have more; this seems reasonable and I do not understand why E wishes for more, some vague undigested aspiration for competition with Beaverbrook. The *Daily Mail* can never be anything but a muddle, for even in the unlikely event of Esmond finding perfect lieutenants, the perfect lieutenants will be in the impossible position of quicksand power and no final responsibility; how can you completely trust or indeed help any person who will within cautious limits invariably listen to the advice of the last acquaintance he meets? Frank [Owen] and MacLean must hate each other and me. Esmond has a wonderful memory but, I have come to believe, no capacity for thought and very bad judgement of human beings.

The *Daily Mail* prior to my return bought most of the hoardings in and outside London to advertise a new London edition, but despite Esmond's morning conferences two days before it was due to appear no one had thought of anything new to put in it. Esmond returns from the office at 7.30 and says to me, 'I want a title for a gossip column that is to start on Monday.' I comment on the tardy approach, he blames Frank [Owen] and says, 'MacLean suggested asking you and is waiting at the office for you to telephone.' Six months ago I had discovered some editions of a magazine now dead called the *London Mail* and in it was a column called 'Things We Want to Know' done under headings of Who Why Where, so I telephoned MacLean who is delighted. Esmond has by this time returned from his bath and asks what I have arranged, when I tell him he turns white and says 'That column bankrupted the *London Mail* because of the libel suits.' However having put the hand to the plough I become interfering and insist that on Saturday Hallowes[2] should come to W[arwick] House so I can explain to him how it should be done. Hallowes (narrow but nice) produces a blurb, in which three dull paragraphs are signed by Ian Coster,[3] Peter Wildeblood[4] and another. I then become vehement and the present column was born with the initial wonderful start that when Coster heard his name was to be dropped, he gave notice and has finally and for ever left the *Mail*. The column is now being run by Kathleen Lyon,[5] Wildeblood and Wiltshire,[6] and most of the news comes from me. It is really a whole time job and I should love to edit it, because one could air injustices and run campaigns, but at the moment it invariably has the bite taken out of it by the subs. I lunched with Kathleen etc. and they all complained at the alterations and general cowardice. I am aspiring to get this fixed because although it might be *much* better it is attracting attention. Will you send some Paris items or rather send them to Kathleen and pay no attention to the teleprinter. I have anyway tried to improve that so you might let me know if there is a change.

Kisses

A.

1 Stuart MacLean, able Managing Director of the *Daily Mail*. Had been an officer in the Irish Guards. 'A dynamo of energy and ideas', he died in his forties.

2 John Hallowes, Deputy News Editor. Bought an orchard in Kent and worked part time for the *Kentish Express*.

3 Ian Coster had been a major in the Marines and was brought into the *Mail* by Frank Owen. He later had a column called Costermongering.

4 Peter Wildeblood, journalist and author. Found guilty of homosexual offences at the same time as Lord Montagu, went to prison and wrote about it courageously in *Against the Law*.

5 Kathleen Lyon, reporter, had married in 1948 Michael Christiansen, who became Editor of the *Daily Mirror*.

6 Maurice Wiltshire, a news reporter who moved into the world of entertainment.

To Ian Fleming

Tuesday 10.30 p.m.

Just Another Thought

Your philosophy is splendid in a selfish kind of way,
when your hair was black and curly but not now it is grey,
for you're well over forty and I fear you're getting fat,
you're apt to be forgotten and just an old bad hat.

This dear familiar face is not accustomed to neglect,
and still has the capacity to make other men erect.
So if by chance you meet a pretty Biarritz slut,
just pause for thought and hesitate before you stuff her up.

And if you need adventure it'll be [as]much as you can do,
to cope with the variety of your ever loving Shrew.

Boiled samphire to you.

My darling,

You have been so sweet on the telephone this week. I loved it that you missed me, and I loved it that you were fussing about us last night. I fussed so much last week that I am fussed out and determined to go busting along with you wherever you go; you can recognise the change of mood in the *beautiful love poem* on the front page. Oh Oh Oh I was angry with 'Just a Thought' how dare you, it was the crowning injury and I shall make you eat it Sunday night with the kedgeree or is it to be sausages?

Darling, keep safe for me. I love you.

A.

P.S. I wish you could write as well as you use paste and scizzors [*sic*], it's like having Don Iddon for a lover.

To Hugo Charteris

Shane's Castle

Tuesday
[?April 1950]

Darling Hugo,

Esmond must be stopped holding editorial conferences because the stories circulated about them do him little good: Miller[1] walks in and says 'What, no ash trays in here', Es apologises and dashes out to collect one from Queenie Davies [his secretary], or else Esmond says 'Why were the last editions bad last night?' Miller then turns to Pickering[2] and says 'Shall I tell him or you?' Pickering blushes and Miller says 'The last editions were bad because I went home early last night', Esmond says 'Oh' but does not ask for reasons and Miller is triumphant. I know Frank [Owen] is deeply resentful but he has only told me that they are a mistake because Esmond listens attentively to a great deal of showing off and never pulls anyone up or contradicts – alas, I am sure it is true. Frank is doing a quiet efficient job of sabotage, reading between lines I feel his spleen is entirely directed at Esmond and not MacLean. Esmond has never had a showdown with him and the present set up is ideal for him, for many things have been done without telling him, which gives an excuse and I suspect there is a section of the office who are on his side. For instance the W. Column,[3] which I regret ever having started, was resented by Frank and I think till last week he did what he could to destroy it, but last week he brought its present editor, Laurie Wilkinson, to lunch and Laurie naïvely said it had been easier since he had Frank's support. I am told by good friends that it is very undignified for me to tout gossip for the office and when Es returns I am going to resign, it is sad because it need not have been cheap boring trash, but having lunched with Mr Wilkinson I realise that nice though he is, he is dull, average, and full of fear; he has improved it a little but I fear his horizon includes little beyond Princess Margaret and the Hon Peter Ward.[4] I am going to implore that we cease to publicise the Princess's night life and occasionally write up her serious activities. Like you, I am now seriously worried about the *Mail*, because faithful old readers are complaining of its cheapness – last batch was Sniff [her father], Tommy and Joan[5] and many others of that type.

Esmond is more to blame than MacLean and it will be hard to change his mind because the circulation has risen a great deal, is still rising and the highest readership on gallup polls is still (oh boomerang) the W. Column.

Julian Fane[6] has joined the staff and his first suggestion is that we serialise T. S. Eliot's *Cocktail Party*,[7] Boofy [Gore] is encouraging it and MacLean has taken it home to read, my faith in him will be shaken if he does not realise that it is popular popular highbrow. I read it a week ago, enjoyed it enormously and will certainly go to the play when it arrives from New York.

Oh well, why worry, I expect if you were Editor I should fight with you, and you would certainly fight with Esmond, and all the shares belong to the Harmsworths so why should the Charterises get stomach ulcers on the outer perimeter of power? Your reactions are much like mine – vainglorious, arrogant moths to a tawdry callow candle.

I must to bed and Raymond is drinking hot skimmed milk under my nose, which makes me vomit. . .

Love to you both and to Richard.[8]

Ann

1 Jack Miller, Deputy Night Editor.

2 Sir Edward Pickering (1912–). Managing Editor of the *Daily Mail* 1947–9, Editor of the *Daily Express* 1957–62, Executive Vice Chairman of Times Newspapers since 1982.

3 'Who? Why? Where?', later changed to 'Tanfield's' and edited by David Edgar.

4 Peter Ward (1926–). Son of the Earl of Dudley and so Laura Dudley's stepson. He had had to deny rumours of an engagement to Princess Margaret. Married Claire Baring in 1956.

5 Joan Thesiger (1895–1971). Married in 1920 Alan Lascelles (1887–1981) who was Private Secretary to George VI and was to be so to Elizabeth II.

6 Julian Fane (1931–). Brother of the Earl of Westmorland and writer, best known for *Morning*, 1956.

7 *The Cocktail Party* ran for 325 performances from 3 May 1950, but was not serialised.

8 Virginia Forbes Adam (1922–) was married 1948–70 to Hugo Charteris, and their son, Richard, was born in 1949.

To Hugo Charteris

Sussex   11 June [1950]

Darling Hugo,

Your poor sister has once more been crucified by *Time* magazine[1] and there has been quite a frenzy in the office; when the warning wire came from Iddon it implied no mention of me and I tried to soothe Esmond's panic by saying how little publicity mattered, how soon it would be forgotten and how sad I was that on this occasion it would be no acquisition for my scrapbook but only oblivion! MacLean has taken the blow hardest and wishes to bring an action for libel, it is sad that E. is unable to persuade that it is all of singularly little consequence.

I have seen Schofield[2] but once since the new reign, he dined with E., me and Martin [Charteris], we discussed that well worn topic, *The Cocktail Party*, which Schofield had found most disappointing. Personally it is a relief to have an editor who treats one as a human being. Martin and E. decided he must have Jewish blood, and I suppose he could be described as a bourgeois intellectual, but most important he is sane, sober and convinced and as good a mould as one could get to pour our liquid chairman into and hope that he will set.

This is written from Sussex, Peter [Quennell] is the only guest and he and E. are swimming at Seaford, the weather is delectable and the 'temple haunting martlet' has started a mud nest under the eaves which should bring luck to the house; it has been a quiet weekend except for summer lightning at dinner last night, we were discussing a possible supper dance to greet the American ballet and I unluckily suggested caviar, which innocent if extravagant thought put Esmond into a frenzy. 'Who' he said 'is going to pay for it? People of wealth like me have to be responsible and careful and cannot afford to be talked about, it would' he said 'be a social outrage to give the guests caviar'. At this point Peter showed unwonted courage and suggested that perhaps caviar was less outrageous and irresponsible than *Caroline*.[3] '*Caroline*' said Es 'what harm has *Caroline* done, jolly good entertainment.' Peter, brave brave Peter stuck to his guns (or his caviar!) and said he suspected that *Caroline* had increased masturbation statistics by 15%, at which Esmond gave a mirthless laugh and said 'Caviar loses money, Caroline makes it', this put me into a white passion and poor Peter regretted his temerity and spent a sorry evening trying to extinguish the flames!

Best love

Ann

1 See following cutting from *Time*, 5 June 1950.
2 Guy Schofield had been Editor of the *Evening News*, which with great success he had turned into a sunny, optimistic paper. He was the new Editor of the *Daily Mail*, where he earned the nickname of 'The Silent Killer' as members of the staff resigned or were fired; one however found him 'very staid and honest and parochial. Nice man.'
3 Popular novel being serialized in the *Daily Mail*.

Time, 5 June 1950

The Eleventh Man

Esmond Cecil Harmsworth, 52, second Viscount Rothermere, owns London's stoutly Tory *Daily Mail* (circ.
2,280,000) and for three years fiery, loquacious Frank
Owen, 44, has been the editor. But it has long been
common knowledge in Fleet Street that the real boss
wears a petticoat.

For several years, pretty, vivacious Lady Ann Rothermere, 36, has tried to run the *Mail* from Warwick House.
Without consulting Editor Owen, she often summoned
staffers to her home to assign stories or suggest new
features. Six months ago, Stuart MacLean, advertising
manager of the *Mail* and a friend of 'Annie's', was
appointed managing director of the paper. Overbearing,
tight-pursed Director MacLean moved in on editorial
authority, in some cases firing, shuffling and promoting
editorial staffers, without consulting Editor Owen.
(Complained one *Mail*man: 'He wants to run the paper,
but he thinks he can run it like a cash register.') Owen
fought back, but fought a losing battle. In recent months,
eight top editorial executives and writers and two directors have been fired or quit. Last week, as fed up with
Warwick House as Warwick House was with him, Frank
Owen quit.

To Hugo Charteris

Warwick House   [July 1950]

Darling Hugo,
    I can't express myself or spell tonight as I am still in the grips of
exhaustion from the Warwick Ho' dance; the result of Esmond
refusing to entertain more than 200 people and my hatred of half
the Mayfair inhabitants was very nearly disastrous, it was a perfect
summer night and the terrace was so popular that the drawing-
room was almost empty; my basic disregard of the herd instinct
made me overlook the vital factor that a successful party means a

mob of hot bodies and I was so nervously exhausted myself that my impressions of the evening are very hazy, in fact I hated every moment of it having badly overestimated my physical resilience and spent the previous two days on a step ladder with a mouthful of drawing pins instead of being ironed by Elizabeth Arden; strength of purpose has never been my forte and I tried to give two parties at the same time, firstly a good supper for ballerinas, intellectuals and aged economists and secondly a riotous dance, the first succeeded and the second failed, or very nearly. Esmond thinks it was a tremendous success and I am not disillusioning him because I should like to try again. The evening started at Covent Garden at 7 p.m. when Freddy Ashton nervously pushed me and the Duchess of Kent into appropriate places to watch his new ballet[1] and ended at 6 a.m. with Caroline Duff making me tea in Paulton's Square. Freddy's new ballet had a pornographic dance in it which shocked the Duchess and as she was unable to compliment him on it or Cecil [Beaton] on the clothes, they were both a little depressed and not in very good form, however we all trouped back to supper and champagne and the warm night and floodlit garden made that part of the evening great fun, but when the other guests arrived I discovered too late that many of them were actors or old and wished supper conversation and then bed which is what I too should have preferred but I felt it incumbent to try and make the party go upstairs and immediately became haunted by there being so few people that Letty and Jeremy Benson[2] were always in view! Despite all this gloom the party continued till 5 a.m. with occasional people appearing from the river party in Edwardian boating costume including the Paget girls[3] looking lovely and Evelyn Waugh grotesque as an able-bodied seaman; I was having a last glass of beer with the Pagets when Esmond appeared and said he must immediately talk to me alone, which filled us all with curiosity, but he was insistent and pompous so I meekly went into the hall where I found Martin [Charteris] and with exaggerated solemnity they told me a man and woman were asleep in Martin's bed and what should be done; of course I told everyone and we rushed upstairs, but Esmond so seriously insisted on discretion that I finally went alone to identify the bodies, and found passionately entwined not a man and a woman, but two men; they looked so happy that I left them and put Martin in Nanny's bed for what remained of the night.[4]
[remainder lost]

1 *Les Illuminations*, choreography by Frederick Ashton, music by Benjamin Britten, decor and costumes by Cecil Beaton, based on poems by Arthur Rimbaud and danced by the New York City Ballet. The main parts are the Poet, the Dandy, Sacred Love and Profane Love.

2 After the death of her husband Lord Elcho in 1916, Lady Violet Manners [Aunt Letty] had married in 1921 Guy Benson. The architect, Jeremy Benson (1925–), is their son.

3 Daughters of the Marquess of Anglesey. Lady Elizabeth Paget (1916–82), who had married in 1939 Raimund von Hofmannsthal, Lady Mary Paget (1918–), Lady Rose Paget (1919–) and Lady Katharine Paget (1922–).

4 The butler, Mr Wright, was less amused, threw up his hands and cried, 'Oh, I must go and check his Lordship's bedroom.'

To Hugo Charteris

Shane's Castle   18 August [1950]

Darling Hugo,

There is no point in writing of my emotional state for it is static owing to lack of courage to leap from the merry-go-round. I should not miss the fleshpots but I must confess that I enjoy the excitement. Noël Coward wrote a lyric 'so obsessed with second best that no rest she'll ever find'.[1] It applies to both your sisters or at least to one side of them. If E. would push and I. would pull it would be easier, but one cannot blame Ian for only saying 'Barkis is willing' because it would frighten any man to be more insistent when as he rightly says he cannot offer the public life and in fact hates social gatherings, and so I hesitate to take the step until I am certain that I can discipline myself to be led instead of leading, on the other hand I love Ian and if I continue this way I shall probably lose him and find Esmond is as remote as the north pole – anyway I am fairly certain that I am doing myself more harm than them. I have spasmodic guilt about Esmond's lack of occupation – he is alone in Sussex with tennis pro. – but even if we were happy together I should have still to be in Ireland at this time of year, and he is doing much the same things as when we met – tennis tournaments and dances in Eastbourne, and I think he genuinely prefers that CLASS of society to our CLASS of society. He has deserted – for an American blonde – but I don't think it is serious.

Interruption for a trunk call from I. in Vermont USA which has made me feel lonely and destroyed my peace of Irish mind. He has been bitten by a snake and is surrounded with golden orioles and sunshine; he had to go to America on business, on Kemsley business, and is spending weekend with the Bryces who are rich enough to afford transatlantic calls; I would rather he was in London but he hates it in August when I am away so this was an excuse for a holiday, but it sounds gayer than mine. I love being with the children but the climate makes me melancholy, I hope you will not find that Scotland has too much effect on you,[2] the eternal soft rain and dripping trees make me sad and introspective and indeed mad.

With much love and affection

Ann

1 *Dance Little Lady* from *This Year of Grace*, 1928.
2 Charteris wished to write novels in the country and was about to move to Little Ferry in Scotland, where for a time he continued to get £500 a year as a stringer for the *Daily Mail*.

To Hugo Charteris

Warwick House   2 November 1950

Darling Hugo,
    I enjoy your letters so much that I must immediately reply to the one which has just vastly enhanced the pleasures of my breakfast. Many channels have been swum since Sammy the Seal's escapade, it was a poignant meeting for brother and sister, if we had been lovers it would have had something of Tristan and Isolde, especially when you waved your lily white hand so sadly in the direction of France.[1]
    The delay in writing was partly caused by health, partly by work for textiles and Ideal Homes and also the change of gear necessary for Esmond's return.
    Esmond arrived with winter; and falling leaves and bonfires remind me of the last two years when I was able to anticipate sunshine and an Eden shared with an Adam, who though he may not be the solution to all things at least [watched] coloured fish and lizards with a sympathetic enthusiasm; and apart from my love for him, it was also six weeks away from Roswell,[2] Wright [the butler], O'Neill trustees, telephones, newspapers and the paraphernalia of people who gnaw away one's vitality and whom one has not sufficient character to resist. Christmas without Ian seems a bleak

affair, he was always there at Christmas, long before Esmond, and he gave the children presents about which he had taken trouble. I cannot face Wraxall so we are going to Gstaad; the children will love it and Esmond and I will play canasta with Tanis[3] and her current beau; and after Christmas the children go to Ireland, Esmond to Monte Carlo and me to where? Esmond is being very very nice, he is well and happy; I don't think he likes close personal relationships, but according to his fashion he loves me; and who would organise his fun and his work if I went?

My love to Virginia and Richard and yourself, I will write again very soon and will send the poetry book. I preserve your letters with the children's and look forward to them. Ann

1 Swimming the channel was much in the news and it had been arranged that Sammy the Seal should do it. This he duly did preceded by a boat from which fish were scattered to urge him on and followed by a boat full of sea-sick journalists. Ann was on the beach near Dover, Hugo among the journalists, who were not permitted to land.

2 Miss Roswell was employed as secretary by Lord Rothermere but continued to come once a week and do secretarial work for Ann after her divorce.

3 Tanis Guinness (1908–). Married to Drogo Montagu 1931–5, to Howard Dietz 1937–56 and then to Teddy Phillips.

To Hugo Charteris

Shane's Castle   Wed. eve [?December 1950]

Darling Hugo

I found some old letters from Es here; written at the peak of our romance from Monte Carlo, they are almost identical to the ones I received this summer! Oh dear, when I think of the passionate love I lavished on him; neither of us, alas, understood affection which is so important to marriage. None of us had affection in our tempestuous childhood and I have only seen its necessity very late.

Esmond was well and cheerful while in London, we were friendly but nothing intimate was discussed – he didn't want to; he supported my expensive venture in Ideal Home decor to the discomfiture of the office, and he asked and took advice on many minor matters, and it was all friendly but not personal.

I went to a card party of Noël Coward's with Loelia and Ian, and suggested it was funny to see Ian and Loelia play together, which lighthearted words produced a conflagration between Ian and myself which lasted a week; he says I regard the men in my life as part of the social furniture and would sooner die than admit love in public, I pointed out that the sad situation we were now in came from excessive public affection, but he maintains that at social functions my ears and eyes close and all humanity is sacrificed to being a public entertainer – ah me.

This is not an answer to your letter or perhaps in some ways it is. I agree with so much of what you say, but you are not simple. . . you will fling a very worthwhile success in the faces of your (pop!) contemporaries because you believe in something and Virginia who is loved by all and a most remarkable person will be there to help you. You know I have never met anyone who disliked or criticised V; ask her from me how she got her values so right, values is a horrible word but she is the most remarkable mixture of goodness and charm, serious and light and great understanding.

With best love to Père, Mère et Bébé

A.

To Lady Diana Cooper

Blue Harbour, Port Maria   10 February [1951]

Darling Diana

This is a letter to say thank you for the lovely weekend at Chantilly last October – we both enjoyed it so much but immediately after[wards] you came to London, so I thought it sensible to save genuine happy gratitude for a moment when there was also some entertaining news.

This remote tropical island has become a playground for that fraternity of gentlemen in whom I find most pleasure – the joy of putting Cecil [Beaton] and Oliver Messel[1] in underwater masks and introducing them to a new world of fish and coral design; Cecil was tremendously brave and seeing a sneering dangerous barracuda chased it 'because it looked like a disagreeable dowager'. Oliver appeared unable to swim a stroke and constantly sank in bubbling ecstasies while his friend the 'great dane' was like all faithful dogs too scared to enter the water and barked anxiously in the shallows.

Alas, the friendship of a lifetime has ended – Noël C. and

Edward Molyneux[2] are non-speaks after a series of painful meetings all ending in schoolgirl brawls; I am sorry for Edward, he has had a nervous breakdown and until last week could only drink, weep and scream, I have no idea what he said to annoy Noël, but on the last occasion Noël accused him of being jealous of Dior and refused to go to his farewell party; poor E., the party was last night and at vast expense he managed to transform a charming tropic hotel and an exciting native band into an Old English bourgeois beano, 'Roses of Picardy', roast beef and hot champagne; instead of hot music, planter's punch and spiced curried goat.

Our greatest excitement has been a real genuine coral reef 18th century-print wreck, and only a hair's breadth that no lives were lost; the Ivar Bryces and Tommy Lighters[3] [sic] put into the local harbour in a luxury yacht with several million dollars of jewellery and several hundred dollars of drink; the American crew paid no heed to gale warnings, the captain went shopping leaving no watch, the crew got drunk and the storm broke at dusk an hour before they were due for dinner with Ian. Noël, Ian and myself imagined no such incompetence and thought they had put to sea to ride out the gale, but as we were swigging martinis the door broke open and four of the USA's richest citizens fell into the room snow white and dripping water, they had the black marks of lifejackets round their necks and purple bruises from diamonds crushed between skin and jacket – they had had to jump from yacht to launch and Mrs B.[4] was in great pain for she had the world's 4th largest diamond forced mercilessly into her bosom while they were tossed from coral crags through huge breakers onto the shore; from then on it was a blissful blissful night – Noël was able to play 'In Which We Serve', Ian was Masterman Ready and I was 'Admirable Crichton'. Noël and Ian rescued the crew while I poured disinfectant into the diamond wounds and handed out rum to dull the pain, and then Noël took the prettiest sailors to the nearest hotel and rubbed them down with brandy – it was a small Mafeking night for the British. The following day we formed a wrecker's company, Noël got a small expensive piano, Ian salvaged the gin, and I collected two lush bamboo chairs and a canasta tray that came in with the tide – but none of us have found any jewels.

Back to work on March 3rd, Bestest love to you and Duff, and I hope hope you are very very well.

Ann

1 Oliver Messel (1904–78). Theatrical designer, who then had *Ring Round the Moon* by Jean Anouilh running in London and Copenhagen, *The Little Hut* by André Roussin, translated by Nancy Mitford, running in London and New York.
2 Edward Molyneux (1891–1974). Fashion designer. Noël Coward had written on 23 December: 'Edward rather pissed. I warned him gently about not being too impulsive about White River [a property] whereupon he flew at me and really was quite insufferable. I kept my temper with a great effort . . . He has so many wonderful qualities but he is curiously petulant and spoilt and he always was.' They made it up.
3 Tommy Leiter, described by Ivar Bryce as 'a gentle, friendly millionaire', was one of the Chicago family who made a vast fortune at the end of the nineteenth century. Boats had gone astray under his charge before and were to do so again. James Bond's ally in the CIA is called Felix Leiter.
4 Marie-Josephine ('Jo') Hartford married Ivar Bryce in 1950. His account has them safely on shore when the storm broke.

Lord Rothermere had delivered an ultimatum that included Ann not seeing Fleming for six months.

To Ian Fleming

[Paris]   Friday

My love,
    I am sending all these scraps of letters, and now I have to dress and argue about the bill. I look forward to talking to you this evening.
    It was bad of me not to allow Gerry [Koch de Gooreynd] to come over, but I gathered he wanted to tell me that Esmond wanted me much more than he could express when with me – and I didn't want to be upset.
    Oh, my darling, I know I should try and make an effort; the most serious side of me has always felt that we should be without each other for six months, because if it is real love it should easily survive that length of time and perhaps we should be happier if we used that much self-discipline. I am very bewildered and unhappy and I want you so much; you have been so wonderful in the last month, so calm, so deeply loving and affectionate that I don't see how I can really leave you; but do you think we ought to try for a bit my sweetest? My darling, I long for Easter and dread afterwards.

A.

To Hugo Charteris

Seaside   29 September 1951

Darling Hugo,

Warwick Hut has been in turmoil because I have bought a talking parrot; I found an exquisite brass regency cage and while at the *Mail* autumnal flower show I told MacLean I wanted a parrot, he advertised for one without warning me and I was deluged with letters and shocked by the prices (£50 to £60) but at last a letter arrived offering 'Jackie, he don't swear, he say "Old Buzzard, Hello darling" and he like Scotch music and sopranos', £25 and I could return him after two months if we didn't make friends. His home was Shepperton so I asked Catton when free to collect him as he sounded the perfect bird; that evening Esmond appeared in a rage that none of my other failings had ever produced and said he would not have a parrot in the house and that if I persisted the parrot and I must leave together! This was awkward as the money had been sent, La Roswell was very indignant and said she was lonely and the parrot could live in the office when not with me, so the bird-loving Charles was sent to collect him and he was smuggled upstairs; Wright in the meantime disclosed to Roswell that some twenty years ago Esmond read an article on parrot disease which frightened him so much that the nursery parrot was immediately strangled and there had been a ban on parrots ever since, can hypochondria go further! At least he might have explained, and I do not yet know whether he realises it is in the house because it is moping for its home and will only say 'Hello darling' to Charles, but it is only a question of days before the cage is moved to the drawing-room and he says 'Old Buzzard' to Esmond. Miss Roswell and the housemaids worship it and Miss R. asked to be allowed to take it home for the weekend; perhaps Es will cite the parrot instead of Ian, or perhaps I shall be thrown out with a parrot in my arms, either would make a Northcliffe news story if not a Schofield one.[1]

Dined with Laura Thursday who was entertaining D. of Windsor, D. of Westminster,[2] young Max Aitken[3] and Fred Cripps,[4] pleasure- and beauty-loving brother of Sir Stafford; the gaffe of that evening was the D. of Windsor saying to Esmond 'You know Jamaica well, is the native problem worse than Nassau?' Laura's nudge unseated me from the sofa but I managed to squeak into the painful silence 'It's me what's been there, Sir.' My biro pen's leaking and Peter and Ian talking, they send their love but make concentration difficult and I must away to make a spaghetti mess for their dinner. I will write again soon.

With love and all wishes for the embryo book.[5]

Ann

1 The parrot and the brass cage eventually left with Ann and lived in the library at Victoria Square. The parrot bit Princess Alexandra's finger.

2 Hugh (Bendor) Grosvenor (1879–1953). Succeeded as second Duke of Westminster in 1899. He had been married to Violet Nelson 1920–6, Loelia Ponsonby 1930–47 and was now married to Anne Sullivan. He was very rich indeed.

3 Max Aitken (1910–85) was married to Violet de Trafford that year, he for the third time. A fighter pilot in the Battle of Britain, he had been a Conservative MP 1945–50 and joined Beaverbrook Newspapers of which he became Director and Chairman. Succeeded Lord Beaverbrook in 1964, disclaimed the barony, accepted the baronetcy.

4 Frederick Cripps (1885–1977). Succeeded as Lord Parmoor in the last year of his life. He too was married to Violet Nelson, in his case 1927–51. His austere brother had become the Labour Chancellor of the Exchequer in 1947.

5 Charteris's first novel, *A Share of the World*, was to be published in 1953.

Patrick Leigh Fermor on an election party at Warwick House on 26 October 1951:

Greta Garbo was there, absolutely amazed at the din . . . Ed Stanley, just out of hospital, arrived in a wheelchair in black spectacles, a black wideawake hat, and a heavy black beard – a mystery still unexplained . . . when Conservative victories began to predominate, there were outbursts of cheering largely led by Ann waving a glass and shouting 'Hooray!' as though at a boat-race, occasionally changing her note when some Labour member who was a friend lost his seat: 'Oh dear – poor old –' whoever it was; elsewhere cries of triumph went up. Harold Nicolson,[1] toying with the thread of a monocle I never saw him wear, murmured, 'I do *deplore* this partisan *booing*.'

1 Sir Harold Nicolson (1883–1968). Author, diplomat and diarist. Married Vita Sackville-West in 1913. National Labour MP 1935–45.

In November of that year Richard Charteris, Hugo and Virginia's 2½-year-old son, was drowned.

To Virginia Charteris

Shane's Castle   6 December [1951]

My Darling Virginia,

I should have written sooner but there was a rush of plans for holidays, a promotion party for Noël Coward, a television party to get funds for children's hospital and all the other dementia of Warwick Hut.

Darling, I have never suffered such grief as you; I held my baby's hand for one minute and was amazed how long the torture lasted, my deep love for Ian is based on his understanding of [my] mental condition at that time, so when I think of you it is by a large multiplication sum and I know a little how utterly drab and remote all else must seem and I continue to mind for you quite dreadfully. I don't know about faith as I prefer to believe or rather try to believe in some vague colossal plan, and that is partly because I have an optimistic character and though casually religious I think prayer is strengthening; but I'm sure Colin[1] is the person to talk to, I have a passionate hero worship for him and he has many of the qualities that I shall hope to find in the vague deity I believe in.

Papa, the eternal child, is here; it is many years since I have been quietly in a country house with him, and I must say he is a delightful person to have around, he has something unique to add to every occupation of the day, whether it is a duck shoot, a wireless programme or merely sitting in the bath in Fionn's riding hat! The more I see of Vi the fonder of her I become, it was wise of Hugo to help tie the final knots.[2]

We had a wonderful supper party for Noël Coward, after the first night of his play;[3] we did him proud by taking Princess Margaret and the Duchess of Kent; receiving them at the theatre became Marx brotherish as Esmond's shyness made him unable to proceed or recede, but after I had curtsied he suddenly shot like a lobster from its hole across Noël and in the general confusion he and Noël bowed to each other leaving their royal Highnesses' white hands waving feebly in the air.

I become increasingly interested in Princess Margaret and dished up Freddy Ashton, Alec Guinness[4] and Trevor-Roper[5] in the hope of broadening the Ward Wallace[6] circle, however she collected Orson Welles[7] by herself and seemed quite happy alternating him with [Lucian] Freud and [Mark] Bonham Carter.[8]

Vi and Papa have returned from duck shooting, so I will end this and write to Hugo tomorrow.

Very very much love darling

Ann

1 Colin Forbes Adam (1889–1982). Virginia Charteris's father.

2 Violet Porter had married Guy Charteris in 1945.

3 *Relative Values* with Gladys Cooper and Angela Baddeley, a success.

4 Alec Guinness (1914–). Actor. He had directed himself as Hamlet that year in London. Knighted in 1959.

5 Patrick Trevor-Roper (1916–). Consultant ophthalmic surgeon at the Westminster Hospital since 1947, and author of many books including *The World Through Blunted Sight*. A lasting friend, and travelling companion of Ann's in her last years.

6 William (Billy) Wallace (1927–77). Escort of Princess Margaret; married Elizabeth Hoyar Miller in 1965.

7 Orson Welles (1915–). Director and actor in both theatre and cinema. Ten years after Citizen Kane and two after his performance as Harry Lime in *The Third Man*, he was then at the peak of his career.

8 Mark Bonham Carter (1922–). Director of William Collins and soon to become Liberal MP. *See* Appendix of Names.

To Hugo and Virginia Charteris

Hotel Schweizerhof, Grindelwald   January 1952

Darling Hugo and Virginia,

Last October it was agreed by mutual desire that I should depart from Esmond, and I decided that the easiest way was that it should take place while I was in Jamaica;[1] I might have told you sooner but it was supposed to be a secret, and mysteriously it has been easier for me to discuss it with no one until it is a *fait accompli*.

There are no hearts to break and my only anxiety is the children; there is no excuse for me except I like interest and affection – but there, you both know all about it; I knew that this year was a turning point and at one moment did not know which way to turn, but the thought that I should have to embrace the Kingsleys and Keeper-Coos[2] and Monte Carlo and watch MacLean and fight MacLean and wade through the tundra and desert of Esmond's heart and soul was too much, particularly since losing Ian would be like losing a leg. Please write to me at length in Jamaica, and please continue to take the *Mail* money, I am not an unjust woman and I know that Esmond owes me a very great deal, besides there is no bitterness and he says that whenever he wants an honest opinion on anything he will come to me. As a matter of fact I know he won't because divorce is divorce and by any other name smells just as foul.

I cannot make this a long introspective letter because there could be no termination for several thousand words, and it's all so trivial and sordid compared to the valley of shadows in which you have been plunged.

Bless you both, and send me some encouragement, or rather both of us, it is quite a step for Ian after 43 years of chosen solitude.

With much love

Ann

1 The decision was therefore taken before Ann became pregnant with the child she had in August 1952.

2 Nickname for Lorna Harmsworth, daughter of Lord Rothermere, and her husband since 1941, Sir Neill Cooper-Key, who was a Conservative MP 1945–70.

To Hugo and Virginia Charteris

Goldeneye, Jamaica   1 February 1952

Darling Hugo and Virginia,

Thank you both very much for loving and encouraging letters. Ian sends his love and says to tell you he is marrying me so as to have dinner with Lucian Freud every night! But to be more serious all goes well and Ian has coped with kindness and understanding with all unexpected complications at reaching our jungle home; alas, in Nassau and indeed mildy before leaving Warwick Hut I was stricken with that almost universal complaint haemorrhoids or piles, to me they had always been a joke to be read about on the Bromo container, and to be tortured with pain, misery and embarrassment was wholly unexpected; I survived New York by willpower and collapsed in Nassau. We were staying in a smart [hotel] and while I was reduced to the doubtful consolation of a brilliant Levantine doctor Ian was exposed to cocktails and dinners with millionaires, all tax-dodging, of varied nationalities. It is a hideous island, 50 miles of golden sand polluted by rich villas, pasteboard invitation cards, conversation on money and entertainment high poker; he was only fairly rude – on the 'Duff-Hugo'[1] side – but says his social manners are exhausted for the year. Two days ago I was well enough to fly and we had a tailwind, such a strong tailwind that we reached Jamaica in one hour instead of two but were unable to land our side of island, and after two descents from stratosphere in gale and storm we were blown up up up again and had to bump our way over the mountains to Kingston, and when we finally landed I was near unconscious.

The first part of this letter will be difficult to read because Ian threw a beetle at me and unbalanced a glass of water which spilled over everything; a further interruption has been caused by the intrusion of two crickets, they make a noise like a buzz saw and when I finally found them they were entwined in a sexual embrace – splendid vitality to make such a din at the same moment.

The expression 'the marriage has been dissolved' applies to me and Esmond with an aptitude which is alarming, the strong ugly 'divorce' has no bearing on it – but I will not embark upon the subject for it would take too long, let it suffice to say that I am surprised that I have not once looked over my shoulder at the fleshpots and that no one has been hurt – it seems, as it always did, quite natural to be living with Ian, and I hope we can marry here to brush the smell of registry office from the nostrils.

My anxieties have been you and Boofy; Peter Q is a fixture and A. Forbes an enemy;[2] I wrote to Boofy and hope he will answer but he has the Cecil and correct attitude towards broken vows, and I admire it though curiously it was [at] the thought 'aged 50 at the Villa Roche Fleuri'[3] that my stomach turned and I knew I must desert not a marriage but a job and seek humanity.

I hope that you will continue to take the DM arrangement and if E. prolongs it ACCEPT. If not Beaverbrook is easy to fix and possibly Kemsley. Talking of Kemsleys, they have been nice to us, we spent our last night in England with them and it was only spoilt by the Dudleys coming to dinner, it is horrible to accept the narrow kindly vulgarity of the Ks and then to be ashamed before them of one's brother-in-law. Eric [Dudley] lost his temper with me and said 'I always knew you were a – a – a' but fortunately did not say 'bitch!'

Darlings I must stop now, if this letter is incoherent it is because there is too much to say. I hope my dear god-daughter [Frances] has cut her teeth and ceased to cry.[4] Some day, somehow you must come here, it is healing, beneficial and inspiring.

Your letters made me happy and I think of you often.

With much love

Ann

1 Duff Cooper and Hugo Charteris both had explosive tempers.

2 'This was one of Ann's many aberrations of judgement. She and Ian were much touched on arriving back in London for the first time after their Jamaican wedding to find flowers and an affectionate welcome home message from Alastair Forbes, the only Rothermere employee to make such a friendly gesture,' says Alastair Forbes.

3 The love-nest, comfortable rather than beautiful, kept by Lord Rothermere, Ann's father-in-law, in Monte Carlo.

4 Frances Charteris (1950–). Now a photographer who in 1983 married another photographer, Valentine Chong.

From Somerset Maugham[1]

Villa Mauresque, St Jean, Cap Ferrat.   8 February [1952]

Annie dear,

I had not heard from you for so long that I thought you had dropped me and suddenly it occurred to me – to be confirmed by your sweet telegram, for which my grateful thanks – that you had run away with your husband. In my young days such a procedure would have shut all the doors of Mayfair against you, but I daresay in these degenerate times you may get away with it. But tolerant as people are now I don't think you ought to make a habit of it. After all, it is rather frisky.

All the same I send you my fond love.

Willie

1 Somerset Maugham (1874–1965). Writer and close friend of Ann. *See* Appendix of Names.

To Hugo and Virginia Charteris from Ian Fleming

Goldeneye, Jamaica   23 [February 1952]

Dearest Virginia and Hugo

Your sweet letters made us both very happy. It was kind to dispense some of the encouragement and affection from your bulging cornucopia and I only hope that the death of the golden goose, while making our lives, won't harm yours. I don't expect so.

A. is fat and freckled and *détendue* and we are having a marvellous honeymoon among the hummingbirds and barracudas. The absolute won't be through until 24 March so we can't write until about 1 April! Then home about the 5th.

One of our first tasks will be to outfit the spare room at Cheyne Walk for you both and Guy and Vi [Charteris]. Hard lying, I fear, after Warwick Cage but anyway it will be there for your black and golden heads when you want it.

We are of course totally unsuited – both Gemini. I'm a non-communicator, a symmetrist, of a bilious and melancholic temperament, only interested in tomorrow. Ann is a sanguine anarchist/traditionalist.

So china will fly and there will be rage and tears.

But I think we will survive as there is no bitterness in either of us and we are both optimists – and I shall never hurt her except with a slipper.

These are disjointed thoughts which I must now take into the grey valleys of the sea.

                                                  Ian

To Cecil Beaton

Goldeneye, Jamaica   29 February [1952]

Darling Cecil,

. . . We dined with Noël, Wilsons[1] and Lunts[2] last night, the conversation was not sparkling. Noël was making eminent playwright conversation to leading lady, I chatted to Mr Lunt which I liked and Ian was left with the Wilsons and would have been happier if it had only been la Wilson – he detests le Wilson. The answer to Noël is that he should be used as a cabaret and not as a guest, he does not understand the give and take of talk and the deserts of pomposity between the oases of wit are too vast, he has written us a poem 'Don'ts for my Darlings' of which I enclose three verses. Ian wishes to replace Cecil with Quennell but Noël won't spoil the rhythm!

> Don't Ian, if Annie should cook you
> A dish that you haven't enjoyed
> use that as excuse
> for a storm of abuse
> at Cecil and Lucian Freud.
>
> Don't Ian, when friends are arriving
> By aeroplane motor and plane
> Retire to bed with a cold in the head
> And that famous redundant 'migraine'.
>
> Don't either of you, I implore you
> Forget that one truth must be faced
> However you measure
> Repentance at leisure
> You haven't been married in haste![3]

After this effusion it is ungrateful of me to be catty, but while he continues to pose as intimate friend of the royal family it is irresistible. When we arrived last night he said with great drama 'My dears, I have dispatched my letters to the Queen, such a relief as the formalities one must observe obscure the feelings, but between the conventional beginnings and ends I was able to put in my whole heart'![4]

Best love and blessings from us both

Ann

1 Princess Natalia (Natasha) Paley (1905–81), daughter of the Grand Duke Paul of Russia, married in 1937 Jack Wilson, who was the close friend and business manager of Noël Coward, though their relationship was at this time deteriorating.
2 Lynn Fontanne (1892–1983) married Alfred Lunt (1892–1977) in 1924 and they became the most brilliant acting partnership in the American theatre.
3 Ann wrote to Clarissa Churchill of this verse, 'I have suffered considerably from his reading it aloud in front of strangers.'
4 George VI had died on 6 February. In April Noël Coward 'woke after dreaming vividly of the Queen Mother and there was a registered airmail letter from the Queen herself thanking me for my letter of condolence. A very charming gesture to write it herself when she must have so many thousands to deal with.'

To Clarissa Churchill[1]

Goldeneye, Jamaica   3 March [1952]

Dearest Clarissa

The Hultons[2] have left a tremendous sense of chaos, they twittered and chattered and thoroughly awoke the authoritarian in Ian, who finally took charge of what they should wear and eat and when they should sleep; Teddy bathed in thick beige woollen pants stretched in the most unfortunate places, we forced his mongoloid head into an underwater mask but he persistently submerged the periscope and being too witless to drag the mask from his face came near to drowning – an anxious moment as it would have meant another source of lush entertaining closed down; on the other hand in these rural surroundings he relaxed and revealed his north of England blood by becoming a cross between Stanley Holloway and Gracie Fields; he gave a curious rendering of Jamaican calypso and proved himself word perfect in 'Itchycoo' and 'Tarara Boom Deay' – a real gift of clown comedy.

We shall be home at the end of March. I hope London is recovering from funerals[2] and winter.

                              With love

                                Ann

1 Clarissa Churchill (1920–   ), neice of Sir Winston and cousin of Randolph, was one of Ann's closest friends in the 1950s. *See* Countess of Avon, Appendix of Names.

2 Princess Nika Yourievitch married Edward Hulton in 1941. Both wrote books; he owned magazines, including *Picture Post*, and was knighted in 1957. The couple had been staying at Goldeneye.

Ann's Diary, Jamaica

This morning Ian started to type a book [*Casino Royale*]. Very good thing. He says he cannot be idle while I screw up my face trying to draw fish. Noël came to dinner and made all our favourite jokes about the dinner-table benches, and the dreadful discomfort of them. My favourite jokes because I hope they will be heeded. Played canasta.

Telegram arrived saying 'Milk River Hotel staff on strike' and cancelling our bookings. We were all packed, masks and spears, in the boot of the car and a cutlass for me to cut flowers. Ian decided to ignore telegram. He brooks no interference with his plans. So we started for the mountains that lie between north and south of the island. I watched the banks for new flowers. Ian stopped whenever I shrieked, for it was marvellous new territory. Two day lilies with stems inches thick, cutlass useful. Dug both out to plant at Golden-eye. Ian found scent of mixed flora made him sick. I refused to part with them, and suggested lunch the minute we could see from the mountains to the south. Despite the height, it was already much hotter than the north of the island. Found a piece of shade and a view. Nothing missing in the picnic basket. Huge thermos of iced limeade, bottle of gin, hard boiled eggs, b. and b., marmalade, sandwiches and fruit. Very good feast. Very brief siesta owing to mileage and me wondering where we would sleep if the closed hotel refused sanctuary.

Now the road was bordered with amaryllis lilies, smaller and far more appealing than the hothouse variety. They are very delicate pale salmon colour, or else salmon and white stripes. Presently green valleys of lemon orchards in flower, then baked fields with vast watermelons ripening upon them.

As we became tired, the landscape changed for worse, all vegetation ceased except an occasional cactus. We remembered the area was radioactive hence the fame of the baths supposedly more curative than any continental resort. It was in the desert that we found the spa hotel. Planter-built in the 18th century it was not unpleasing visually, though unexpectedly small and not recently painted, it stood dusty on the dusty banks of the Milk River, no sign of life only a sign of death – a dead alligator below the door step. We were both very happy. Ian rang bells and dashed about until he discovered the proprietress. He exerted every bit of vitality and charm and finally overcame her objections and [she] allowed us to move in, and share her dinner of lobsters straight out of the sea. The small dormitory bedrooms were empty, each furnished with a truckle bed, and no valance to hide the large chamber pot beneath.

In the night we were overcome with thirst and all taps we could find contained spa water – it was nauseating.

The baths are hacked out of rock below the hotel, so one sits in a large rocky excavation being tickled by shrimps and innumerable indescribable river fauna.

Ian easily persuaded the proprietress to let us stay on and produce a kind of picnic lunch. The heat was overwhelming, we had to wear shoes on the burning sand and the sea was not refreshing. Retreating from the beach we found a large blue pool of ice-cold radioactive water, containing a shoal of sizeable and interesting fish and edged by scrub giving three feet of shade. The pool was extremely deep with submarine cliffs and I was worried when Ian descended with the spear gun. He shot three fish which we took home for dinner. They tasted of mackerel and looked like unspotted trout.

We had arranged to go alligator shooting by moonlight, but alas, it is raining. One goes by boat, and their red eyes shine in the moonbeams, and one shoots when one sees 'the red of their eyes'.

To Hugo and Virginia Charteris

Goldeneye, Jamaica   15 March 1952

Darling Virginia and Hugo,

This will be the last letter from the Lotus Islands, we marry on the 25th, New York 26th and home on the 30th – I hope. Lord K. [Kemsley] sent us a charming cable full of good wishes and giving us an extra fortnight's holiday; though an idiot he is a goodhearted old tycoon. I had forgotten that spring comes to the tropics, it is now light from 5 in the morning till 7 in the evening, so we are asleep by 10.30 and bathing at sunrise, writing, painting, shooting, eating and snoozing for the rest of the day – it is frighteningly agreeable. We have just returned from a trip to the crocodile rivers on the south east. Alas, no crocodile, we embarked on the river at night armed with a rifle and anxiously watching for a beautiful pair of red eyes in the torchlight but the weather, already threatening, broke into smashing rain, and everyone was discouraged except the giant mosquitoes. It was a sad climax to bargain with Chinese traders for a skin the next morning, incredibly expensive and badly cured it will probably make one pair of shoes for Frances.[1]

I wish I could hear the first reading of the book, and I hope Irene[2] is pleased and excited, would it be possible for me to have it in April? I shall be at St Margaret's with Fionn and it would be a good moment to read it and possibly invite Rosamond [Lehmann] to stay. I cannot say the half there is to be said because I have had many letters to answer, too many kind things said by friends, which add to my guilt because it cannot be integrity to leave anyone whether he is a millionaire or a dustman, nor is it a martyrdom to live with someone you love in a scented garden eating steaks cooked on charcoal and bananas and cream! I fear Ian's martyrdom *is* imminent with intrusion of talking parrot, saxophone, R. [Raymond], F. [Fionn], and self to his perfectly run bachelor establishment and as the beautiful Austrian maid is in love with him the immediate future looks rather chaotic.

I cannot remember when Hugo's contract with the *DM* expires. If E.'s reply is unsatisfactory I think it would be better to try an arrangement with Hulton magazines; I think I could arrange as they are friends in spite of Ian refusing him hot milk at bedtime!

Let me know if finance is too difficult, I don't quite know about me till I return but I can certainly help.[3]

I hope Hugo has taken my suggestion and interfered in the Countess's grisly romance,[4] I have not had a letter from her and she will have been enraged by mine, but I do think Sara's season should come first.

Best love to you both,

Ann

PS You must read *Mutiny of the Caine*[5] and *Venture to the Interior*.[6] Unlimited novel expenditure will have to cease, shall I join the Times Library for both of us and send you one or two per month?

1 Frances Charteris was not yet two.

2 Irene Lawley married Colin Forbes Adam in 1920 and was therefore Hugo's mother-in-law.

3 Ann received a settlement of £100,000.

4 'Bobby [Casa Maury] was physically attractive and we had a short love affair. . . it never even crossed my mind to go off with him.' Laura, Duchess of Marlborough in *Laughter from a Cloud*, 1980. Her daughter Sara, born in 1934, was then eighteen.

5 *Caine Mutiny* by Herman Wouk, 1951.

6 *Venture to the Interior* by Laurens Van Der Post, 1952.

The marriage took place a day early, on 24 March, and Coward recorded, 'Cole [Lesley] and I were witnesses at Annie and Ian's marriage in Port Maria – a very simple affair, rather nicely done. Later dinner at Goldeneye, which was hilarious.'

From Evelyn Waugh

[April 1952]

Dearest Ann

I too disapprove of divorce.[1] That is one of the many reasons for rejoicing in your escape from the arms of Esmond.[2]

I am afraid it is no good trying to put Randolph [Churchill][3] off anything by telling him it's vulgar. Since the matter is up, I too am curious. How much *did* you get?

Will you please tell Ian that I am home now & will go into the Queen Anne Press project[4] as soon as I get my letters answered.

Can't you get him made a Viscount? There isn't long for the Conservatives to flow as the fount of honour. It would be a shame to unpick all the coronets on the underclothes. Coronation honours is the time.

Love from

Evelyn

1 Ann had replied to Waugh's letter of congratulation 'I disapprove so deeply of divorce that I had anticipated total social ruin and was amazed that New York society treated us as Tristan and Isolde.'

2 Lord Rothermere had been divorced from Margaret Redhead in 1938.

3 Randolph Churchill (1911–68). Journalist, Conservative MP, lasting friend of Ann's. *See* Appendix of Names.

4 The Queen Anne Press belonged to Lord Kemsley and Fleming was a director. It published the *Book Collector* which Fleming was to buy for £50 in 1955. It also published Evelyn Waugh's *The Holy Places* that year but Waugh wrote to Nancy Mitford, 'Don't have anything to do with Ian Fleming's Queen Anne Press. They are dreadful people to deal with', and subsequent projects came to nothing.

MRS iAN FLEMING

THE FIRST YEARS 1952-9

The framework of the Flemings' lives was to rest on events already in train or soon instigated. At the end of 1951 Fleming had taken over the lease of Noël Coward's house on the Kent coast, White Cliffs, and early in 1952 they found a house in Victoria Square. Goldeneye remained. The first James Bond novel, *Casino Royale*, had been started in January 1952 and a preliminary draft was finished six days before the wedding. Caspar Robert Fleming was born on 12 August.

With these ingredients a routine emerged. At the beginning of each year Fleming would fly to Jamaica and start a new novel. Ann feared aeroplanes and they had differing views as to whether Caspar should come but she almost always joined him there. Friends would come to stay. In March they returned to London, Ann leaving first (giving them the opportunity to write to one another). During the rest of the year the general tendency was for Ann to go on European jaunts to see Lady Diana Cooper at Chantilly, Somerset Maugham at the Villa Mauresque in the South of France or Patrick Leigh Fermor in Greece, while Fleming went farther afield to Las Vegas, Istanbul or the Seychelles. Each of Ann's husbands complained about the friends with whom she liked to surround herself and the complaints were not entirely unreasonable. Fleming, who had had more than forty years to form his habits and was a natural solitary, came to see Victoria Square as permanently festooned with effeminate intellectuals. To the writers, painters and politicians who flocked there it became a centre of gaiety and interest. It is true that some of them mocked Fleming's novels and that as his success grew, so did the mockery, and it is also true that those who got on with Fleming say 'I used to like Ian' in a mildly defiant tone, as if it were a point sufficiently surprising to be worth making.

Ann's two main correspondents were in broad agreement with Fleming's view of Victoria Square. Hugo Charteris had exiled himself to Scotland to write novels. These were often so clearly based on friends and family that rows and even censorship ensued.

Ann for her part would not allow a version of her life with Lord Rothermere as husband and Fleming as lover to appear. She also pointed out what she saw as the faults in his books. Charteris felt that both Ann and Laura were leading worthless and corrupting lives and should offer support to their struggling brother who was not. It did not help that he disliked Fleming intensely. Though Ann never quarrelled with him irrevocably, their relationship became stormy and their letters infrequent.

Evelyn Waugh dismissed most of Ann's male friends as 'fuddy-duddies', a term used to describe Lucian Freud, Peter Quennell, Alastair Forbes, Malcolm Muggeridge, Stephen Spender and Frederick Ashton among others. He did, however, share her affection and admiration for Lady Diana Cooper, the Duchess of Devonshire and Clarissa Eden. As he became her principal correspondent he influenced both the tone and the subject matter of her letters. Her style is heightened and she catches something of his technique of exaggeration; naturally she dwells on the people he knows and takes an interest in his family and his activities. She refers to Fleming almost entirely in flippant terms, even when things are going less smoothly between them.

By 1956 each was having an affair, Fleming in Jamaica and Ann in London. She no longer enjoyed Goldeneye and went less often. White Cliffs became unbearable but when they moved to a house near Canterbury, she detested that too. Fleming's novels were steadily becoming better known and more remunerative so that he felt able to resign from *The Sunday Times*, but Ann's settlement from Lord Rothermere was dwindling. These developments however are presented to Waugh in a light tone, quite different from that of the less frequent letters between husband and wife.

To Hugo and Virginia Charteris

24 Carlyle Mansions   16 July [1952]

Darling Hugo and Virginia

The second instalment [of *A Share of the World*] is with me and Rosamond Lehmann does not answer her telephone, but maybe she is away for a few days.[1]

My reactions on reading the manuscript are manifold: the poor Forbes Adam family, no wonder they spent some time in thought before sending an opinion, it must have been a shock to see the family so thinly disguised and immortalised in tragedy – that happy Yorkshire home! I think they are heroic not to complain, poor Irene typing away with grim courage and with feelings which must – surely – must have been slightly hurt?[2]

I cannot possibly give a serious opinion of this piece of the book, but can it be, dear brother, that you are seeing too much of people's failings and not an all round picture? You have a devastating eye and the studies of Papa, Irene and Colin are clever but do not convey their charm, and they are all people who have that quality in high degree, to say nothing of the virtues of Virginia's parents which you manage to denigrate throughout the book; it left me with a bitter after-taste such as I experienced with Theodore Dreiser's *American Tragedy* and some of the early Huxleys. This is not a criticism of the book but merely the ponderings of a sister and should be accepted as such and again, I repeat, we need an outside mind as soon as possible and I will do my uttermost to convey it to Rosamond this week.

My energy decreases and the heat wave was most trying. I have reached the stage of permanent discomfort[3] but I may be released by Caesarian around the opening of the grouse shooting season, I do not know which to hope for, early release or three weeks more and a natural event – I hear the verdict next Wednesday.

This weekend we entertain Fiona,[4] Boofy, Mark Bonham Carter, Eliz Cavendish,[5] Lucian Freud and Gerry [Koch de Gooreynd], so the house is fully extended, and if there is no sunshine the living room will be congested and very noisy; Gerry is invited to play golf with Ian who is temperamental if denied golf and exposed to non-stop conversation; we can only offer prawning as alternative to a tennis court, but they are most lush and magnificent prawns and should excite all but the least imaginative.

Cyril Connolly has spent his all on tropical shrubs and is amazed that they do not thrive, but he enjoys *angst* and it will no doubt please him to see the winter kill them one by one.

I went with Quennell to the Hamish Hamilton[6] party to celebrate the successful 21st birthday of the firm, I was amused and he was appalled by the appearance of the middle-aged lady authoresses, who all have horse faces and girlish hearts and were dressed to a woman in pink lace and organdy with blue bows.

I must to rest now, I hope V. is not tired and I long to see Frances,
With much love

Ann

1 Rosamond Lehmann had promised to read the novel as a friend, and as professional reader for her brother John's publishing firm.

2 Irene Forbes Adam typed the manuscript with tears pouring down her cheeks but no attempt was made to stop or alter the book.

3 Ann was eight months pregnant.

4 Fiona Colquhoun (1918–   ). A joint cousin of Ann's, she married in 1937 Arthur 'Boofy' Gore, who succeeded his brother as Earl of Arran in 1958. She set a world record by doing 102 miles per hour in a powerboat on Lake Windermere in 1980.

5 Lady Elizabeth Cavendish (1926–   ). Sister of the Duke of Devonshire, Lady-in-Waiting to Princess Margaret, close friend of John Betjeman.

6 Hamish Hamilton (1900–   ). Founder of the publishing firm and Chairman 1931–81.

From Ian Fleming

24 Carlyle Mansions, Cheyne Walk.   Saturday evening.
[August 1952]

My love

This is only a tiny letter to try out my new typewriter and to see if it will write golden words since it is made of gold.[1]

As you see, it will write at any rate in two colours which is a start, but it has a thing called a MAGIC MARGIN which I have not yet mastered so the margin is a bit crooked. My touch just isn't light enough I fear.

You have been wonderfully brave[2] and I am very proud of you. The doctor and nurses all say so and are astonished you were so good about all the dreadful things they did to you. They have simply been shuffling you and dealing you out and then shuffling again. I do hope darling Kaspar[2] has made it up to you a little. He is the most heavenly child and I know he will grow up to be something wonderful because you have paid for him with so much pain.

Goodnight my brave sweetheart.

* * * * * * * * * * * *

Ian.

1 Literally gold-plated. Fleming had ordered it in May in New York in order to continue work on *Casino Royale*.

2 Caspar Robert Fleming (variously called Kaspar, Kasper, Kasbah) had been born by Caesarean on 12 August. Ann wrote to her old friend Clarissa Eden (*née* Churchill), 'We would both like it very much if you would be the female godparent to Kasper, this is not entirely because you are the FO's wife, because we decided in July that you would strike a happy balance between Noël and Cecil (my choice) and Peter Fleming and some stout golf player (Ian's choice), so if it is suitable company for you we should be very pleased.' The golf player was Sir George Duff-Dunbar, a barrister and collector of Wedgwood, one of the four people to whom Fleming left £500 in his will.

To Cecil Beaton

[St Margaret's Bay]   2 September [1952]

Dearest Cecil,

It was very nice to chitter-chatter this morning, and it will be lovely to see you Saturday, but don't do it if it is too exhausting a journey because I imagine you have a lot of work next week.

We would love it if you would be godfather to Kasper and take a picture of him as a christening present – he is prettier than Princess Anne!

I dare hardly admit it but Noël is a godfather, an act of treachery on my part as we thought he would be offended if not asked as he considers himself responsible for the whole thing; when he appeared last Sunday he was quite delightful for the first hour including a demonstration of his best stage technique for the baby which instantly stopped crying and almost started clapping, and then he suddenly became so vulgar and dull that I longed to cancel the G-parent arrangement and be frightfully rude to him; my only false relationships are with him and Rosamond Lehmann and I cannot extricate myself from either.

Bless you and look forward vastly to seeing you.

Ann

To Hugo Charteris

[St Margaret's Bay]   3 September 1952

Darling Hugo,
I am on the low road to recovery, I thought once I got Kaspar to the sea that recovery would be immediate but instead I am pursued by demons, and have nightmares about long red rubber tubes and can't stop crying, for five days all normal functions and some abnormal ones were performed by tubes, one I had to swallow which was strapped to my upper lip, one inserted in a right arm vein dripping blood, one in a left arm vein dripping glucose, and a hole drilled in my stomach for a larger one to drain me, it vanished into an infernal machine which occasionally made hiccuping noises under the bed and which doctors and nurses did things to and then carried noisome stuff away in a bowl – however they were reasonably generous with morphia; and all this because I was going to burst with wind! They decided to do another Ceasarian [*sic*] because the baby's head was very large and my last operation in some mysterious way meant that a normal birth might rupture and split me open like an old pea pod.

However Kaspar is perfectly well and starting at 9 lbs 4oz at 8 months and one week, he is still rapidly gaining. It is very nice to have Nanny [Joan Sillick] back. Raymond spends all free time from Aldershot in the nursery and I think would like to climb into the cradle and put Kaspar on the barrack square. The doctors have advised no more babies – rather strongly, which is depressing but did not surprise me, as I had known better than them that Edinburgh had left me permanently less healthy.

I have thirty people to thank for flowers and I am sitting here indulging in such letters as I feel like writing, so far Willie Maugham, Evelyn Waugh, C. Beaton and yourself. There awaits a difficult list headed by Esmond who sent many roses and a note –

'Dearest Ann, best wishes to you and your son', the hospital was awash with tears of what might have been. Oh what a strange character, in sixteen years that one line showed more feeling than when he took my body and vitality utterly for granted. The next letter to the Editor of the *Sunday Dispatch*, dear Mr Eade whom I always slanged. And then Lord Beaverbrook whose flowers made me feel like Evita Peron's corpse and were sufficient to give the doctor's wife and decorate most of the general wards for many days – there's always an irresistible side to the old devil and it's exciting to see £20 of flowers edged sideways through a sickroom door, then dear retired Doc Lane Roberts who brought me magnolia buds and advised me to watch them open instead of dwelling on the miseries . . .

I fear Emlyn Williams'[1] shoulders are padded to an unbelievable degree, Lucian Freud pinched them in the crush bar at Covent Garden to find out, he turned swiftly round and thought it was me as Kaspar and I were a trifle unwieldy by then, however Welsh charm is alright in very small doses. . . .

Raymond is progressing towards officer rank with no trouble and Fionn has passed school cert. at high level, which is all cheering.

Well, it is 9 p.m. and my bedtime, do you know a poem called 'Dover Beach' by M. Arnold? That's how it is here.[2]

I long to see you both and F.

With much love to all,

Ann

1 Emlyn Williams (1905–). Actor and playwright, at that time enjoying his greatest success impersonating Charles Dickens reading *Bleak House*.

2 Dover Beach begins:
> The sea is calm tonight.
> The tide is full, the moon lies fair
> Upon the straits. . . the cliffs of England
> Stand glimmering and vast, out in the tranquil bay.

Evelyn Waugh wrote on 22 October in answer to an invitation to White Cliffs: 'Laura [his wife] alas cannot get away from the milking-shed but if you wish to have me without her, I shall love to come. . . I have turned over a faded leaf and am all honey and flowers now, so rest assured I won't squabble with any of your guests. I can't say that the three you name are my favourite people. Why not David Cecil or Frank Pakenham or Connolly [without his wife]? But why ask others? It is you and Ian I come to see.'

Patrick Leigh Fermor remembers a weekend at White Cliffs, perhaps this one, when 'Duff and Diana were there, and Evelyn Waugh who was wearing a violent tweed cape and a cap of the same material which was a sort of polygon of tweed segments meeting at the middle at a cloth-covered button which he said was called a Sefton. Ann enjoyed the fact that Duff and Evelyn didn't get on; nor for that matter Ian and Evelyn. She revelled in being close friends with people at loggerheads.' Waugh's suggestion of Connolly might have been no happier, as Ann had written the month before, 'On Sunday we went to tea with Cyril Connolly. We found him in a great rage, he had just received a presentation copy of Evelyn's war novel *Men at Arms* and the dedication was "To Cyril, who kept the home fires burning". Cyril said, "If he's referring to my firewatching, it's libel."'

To Cecil Beaton

Goldeneye, Jamaica   6 February 1953

Darling Cecil,

I decided I mustn't write a letter of *groans* about Noël! But we had an epic evening with him, Cole,[1] Michael Redgrave[2] and Bob Michel;[3] Noël insisted that Clemence Dane[4] would have more posterity fame than Cyril Connolly, and said Cyril's only claim to fame was the good fortune he had had in being sent to Eton; it is difficult to protect Cyril but that was going too far. However seconds later he laid down 'that Shakespeare, thank God, was not an intellectual'. I managed to kick Redgrave into the argument and was amazed how intelligently and tactfully he routed Noël without giving profound offence: Ian complained afterwards that I shouldn't gaze with hatred and contempt at Caspar's godfather!

Lucian has had a curious holiday with Raymond in Ulster, he was in pursuit of Lady Caroline[5] and was socially a disaster in that parish pump border state and of course I am blamed for encouraging bizarre tartan-trousered eccentric artists to pursue virginal Marchionesses' daughters. Raymond was entertaining the Prime

Minister[6] and new governor Uncle Wakehurst[7] to a pheasant shoot, and Lucian retrieved the birds faster than any retriever which shocked them deeply; later Maureen [Dufferin][8] left for Switzerland and Caroline went to stay and was discovered with Lucian on the hearthrug beneath dimmed lamps by the agent; the agent is a pompous ass and he told R. that that kind of thing would do him no good. Oh dear.

Noël has a splendid part as King Magnus, he gave me *The Apple Cart* to read and it is a good idea of Binkelstein's[9] but I was sad to hear that it had been promised to my beloved Alec Guinness, and when Alec was told Noël was to have it for the first three months he refused to take over – this I was supposed not to repeat but it tried my self-control sorely.

Tomorrow we go to Max B. [Beaverbrook][10] for two nights and then a flora and fauna trip to the mountains.

Bless you darling,

love

Ann

1 Cole Lesley (1911–80). Born Leonard Cole, he started as Coward's valet in 1936 and became secretary, manager, legatee and biographer.

2 Michael Redgrave (1908–). Actor. He showed Coward his new film of Terence Rattigan's *The Browning Version*, in which he had scored a great success. Knighted in 1959.

3 'A dear friend to me, and to my whole family, he stayed for twelve years', *In My Mind's Eye*, an autobiography, by Michael Redgrave, 1983. Eventually Michel returned to America, where he died in 1975.

4 Winifred Ashton (1885–1965). Novelist, dramatist, painter and sculptor. She took the name because she was told that she should be called 'something inescapable like Westminster Abbey' and while pondering this found herself opposite Saint Clement Danes.

5 Lady Caroline Blackwood (1931–). Writer, daughter of the Marquess of Dufferin and Ava. She was married to Lucian Freud 1953–7; he asked Ann to be best man at their wedding.

6 Viscount Brookeborough (1888–1973). Prime Minister of Northern Ireland 1943–63.

7 Lord Wakehurst (1895–1970). Married Ann's aunt Margaret Tennant in 1920, and became Governor of Northern Ireland in 1952.

8 Maureen Guinness was married to the Marquess of Dufferin and Ava 1930–45, Major 'Kelpie' Buchanan 1948–54 and in 1955 to Judge Maude.

9 Hugh (Binkie) Beaumont presented Coward in Shaw's *The Apple Cart* to general applause in May. Hugh Beaumont (1908–73) was Managing Director of the production company H. M. Tennant, and so the most powerful man in British theatre.

10 Lord Beaverbrook had a house in Montego Bay.

To Hugo Charteris

Goldeneye, Jamaica   2 March [1953]

Darling Hugo,
    I shall make no attempt to answer your letter for it is late, and the guests are chattering.
    We went to Kingston to greet the SS *Cavina*,[1] combining it with a dinner at Government House and a night spent with rich influential Portuguese Jews; they got us special passes to be first on the pier and have promised influence to return our parent to England; we were guilty of accepting their hospitality but excited when three black slaves prepared an early breakfast in our bedroom, they appeared ebony black in starched shocking pink and no nonsense of breakfast trays, a vast mahogany table was dragged from the wall and spread with linen and silver, the first course was exquisitely prepared grapefruit, pawpaw, pineapple slices and peeled banana; Ian grew very excited and said 'a nabob's breakfast' but alas, the silver coffee pot was half full and the scrambled eggs a grey mush.
    We reached the pier at 9.30 a.m. and ten minutes later a gale sprang up and when the *Cavina* appeared on the horizon my hair was blowing perpendicular and we could not hear each other speak. 'She can't berth till nightfall' the authorities told us. You have never seen Kingston so you cannot realise what a terrible blow this was, it is torpid sweating shadeless heat, it was Saturday the shops and institute shut and the American navy was in, two destroyers and an aircraft carrier, so the hotel and restaurant was a sweating mass of gum-chewing Yanks, by three o'clock I was near death and oblivious of every shade of public opinion I went to sleep on a sofa in the Grand Hotel with my shoes off and hair over face, Ian read a book beside me and was asked if he was responsible for 'poor sick vagrant lady'. At sundown the wind dropped and with joy in our hearts we observed the *Cavina* moving in, we dashed to the car, and stood, two pulverised blancmanges on the pier waving frantically, the deck was a-swarm with people but never a well-known face and the flag was at half-mast. I panicked but briefly, for suddenly an old Gloucestershire apple fell between us and there was Pop in your tropical outfit and his most Puckish humour; we were immediately arrested because it is against the law to import foreign fruit that bring disease, and while Ian was explaining away his father-in-law

the boat tied up and the immigration authorities went on board; the Portuguese Jew had arranged for our friends to be disembarked first, so while Ian argued and I threw pieces of Didbrook apple into the sea, another frantic message to say 'would Commander Fleming step on board as Mr Freud needed help'. It appeared Mr F. had only ten shillings, and they thought he would add to the unemployment problems so Ian had to swear to be financially responsible for him during his sojourn! We were exhausted by the time we motored over the mountains, and Ian's temper quite remarkable considering the heat and provocations. Now everything goes well I think, Papa is very happy and Vi a faithful sweating follower, he has found 50 birds and tomorrow we camp in the wilderness.

Bless you both and love from us all.

Ann

1 The ship in which Lucian Freud and Guy Charteris travelled to Jamaica.

Peter Quennell imagined the scene in a letter from London: 'Palms wave – waves ripple – tarantulas crawl – barracudas undulate – Lucky snares the Birdwoman – The Commander groans quietly under the horror of his unwanted guests.' Lucian Freud had to stay on for a while before he could return via Miami, New York and Holland. He wrote, 'I am still sitting in the banana wood in almost the same place and am now such a fixture there that birds sit on me and spiders use my head to hold up their new webs. There was a moment of slight tension when Violet was handing round the vegetables in a glass dish, and, mistaking her fingers for sausages, I tried to help myself to them, but luckily for Violet they were the other side of the glass . . . the clouds appear only when I need them. . . .'

To Evelyn Waugh

White Cliffs, St Margaret's Bay, Dover   Good Friday
                                                        [3 April 1953]

Dearest Evelyn

We are returned from the tropics and I should like to see you. We enjoyed two months of freedom from care, there was constant sunshine, black slaves, and solitude save for occasional intrusions from celebrities, for instance a shocking encounter with Katharine Hepburn;[1] she was wearing brief shorts from which protruded an immense length of bone and old skin knitted together by vast purple varicose veins, she must be the oldest gamine in the world. The *ménage* that interested me most, however, were your friends Graham Greene[2] and Mrs Ralston[3] (I can never remember her name correctly). I immediately continued the pursuit I started at the D'Arcy dinner,[4] his address was Number One Bungalow, Tower Isle Hotel, I bombarded them with invitations but was unable to smoke them out though I finally extracted an invitation to cocktails, so I put on my best frock and accompanied by Ian and Freud went in search of Number One Bungalow; it took us some time to find it as it was several unchaperoned miles from the hotel, a perfect place for lovers, two bed, two bath, one patio private beach and swimming pool. Mrs R. was dressed as a French porter but it did little to disguise her charms, Mr Greene was very over anxious about the making of dry martinis, and offering peanuts and quite impossible to engage in seductive conversation. Finally the *petits soins* were accomplished and I turned my beady eyes on him when, oh horrors, a smart stationwagon drew up and out stepped Lord and Lady Wimborne,[5] Lord Brownlow and Mr and Mrs R. Benson and the evening was totally ruined. It was all very strange and improbable, and I am now more interested in Mr Greene's character. Can he like such people? Is he living in sin? Is he tortured? He remained remote from all, totally polite and holding the cocktail shaker as a kind of defensive weapon – please explain it all to me.

We are in 16 Victoria Square though it is not yet finished, our telephone number is Tate Gallery 2300, so please telephone anytime after 20 April, we are going on a secret mission to France for the next two weeks.

There is a new saga at Connolly cottage, the animal[6] is a female animal and she is now grown up and from obvious dog-like symptoms Cyril knew she must have a mate or satisfaction, he was unable to provide either and now the animal hates him, has bitten him to the bone twice and chases him snarling round the house; Barbara's[7] comment is that the house is full of unsatisfied women.

Do *NOT* repeat this story, as I don't care to fall out with the neighbours, and I am also devoted to them.

Love to Laura and yourself

Ann.

1 Katharine Hepburn (1909–). Actress and film star, who had appeared in *The African Queen* the year before.

2 Graham Greene (1904–). The novelist, who had married in 1927 Vivien Dayrell-Browning.

3 Catherine Crompton (1916–78) married Henry Walston in 1935. He was a Labour MP and agricultural expert, created Lord Walston in 1961.

4 A dinner party for the Jesuit priest Father Martin D'Arcy to which Waugh had taken Ann. As well as Graham Greene, Waugh's mother-in-law Mary Herbert, Randolph and June Churchill, Eddie Sackville-West and T. S. Eliot were present. Waugh 'thought it all pretty beastly but then I was already in general despair'. He had to pay for the wine.

5 Lady Mabel Fox-Strangways married in 1938 Ivor Guest who succeeded as Viscount Wimborne the following year.

6 A coati.

7 Barbara Skelton had married Cyril Connolly in 1950.

To Lady Diana Cooper

White Cliffs, Dover   2 May 1953

Darling Diana

Chantilly was its usual high standard of beauty and entertainment, thank you so much, and particularly for taking so much trouble to ship us to Newhaven. Your Dieppe friend is a delightful character and loves you deeply, he gave us a dramatic imitation of your dockside driving, the speed at which you leave the harbour keeps him awake at night. *The Apple Cart* was enjoyable and particularly foregathering in Noël's dressing room with Graham Greene and Mrs Wolfstein [Walston], she has an enviable gift for flattery and praised the length and straightness of Noël's legs – apparently only comparable in beauty to Greene's shanks – there was nothing for me to do but relapse into morose silence.

Anthony [Eden] was over three hours on the operating table,[1] I went to the clinic to be with Clarissa, a grim day for her – sixteen doctors and Winston tampering with the bulletins. Poor girl, to have to give her Apsley House dinner to Aunt Clemmie [Churchill] and possibly no coronation.

Let me know when you are [among us] as we have Lady Sysonsby's old cook.[2] Hope the grandbaby[3] flourishes. Much love and thank you for the Chantilly treat.

Ann

1 Anthony Eden had an operation for inflammation of the gall bladder on 12 April and another on 29 April after which his condition was described as 'satisfactory'.
2 Lady Sysonby was the mother of Loelia, Duchess of Westminster, who arranged the transference of the cook, Mary Crickmere, and comments, 'I never did Ann a better turn.'
3 Alice (Artemis) Cooper (1953–). Edited A Durable Fire, 1983, the letters between her Cooper grandparents.

Mary Crickmere (1910–83) was Welsh, dark and had a strong presence. Ann left the menus to her, stipulating only that she should avoid having chicken all the time. When Ann complained of the cost she told Ann how many people had eaten in Victoria Square that month; when Ann did not believe her, she drew up a list of names. There would usually be either two lunches and a dinner, or two dinners and a lunch each week. As Ann would leave for the country on Thursday evening or Friday morning and return on Monday, that was almost half her London meals. If alone Fleming would have six scrambled eggs in front of the fire, whereas Ann would retire to bed. Edgar Crickmere (1911–) was valet to Fleming, drove a bit and waited in the evening, but not at lunch. As Mrs Crickmere would not come into the dining-room, footmen had to be hired; Ann protested several times, but Mrs Crickmere would not give in. Crickmere produced the wine as his wife did the food, with a minimum of overseeing. Ann would say nothing more specific than, 'I liked that, get some more.'

There was only room for eight at the round dining-room table, though Ann would sometimes slip in one or two more, but Crickmere remembers the guests as vociferous: 'The noise in there! They all talked, nobody listened . . . but she was a good listener.' Guests would come after dinner and fill the drawing-room on the first floor and the landing outside, which was a sort of open library or study. It was thus impossible for Fleming to come back from his club and get to bed without being seen. The Crickmeres stayed until 1964 and then used to return to do dinners.

To Evelyn Waugh

16 Victoria Square   2 June [1953]

Dearest Evelyn

I have lost my voice, I suspect it is psychosomatic, not desiring to discuss young people's dinner parties with other mothers.

Before I lost my voice I motored Freud and Sylvester[1] to Oxford to address the art society. Sylvester is my new friend, he is well mannered and vastly intelligent, he is the Art Editor of *Encounter* and bullies Stephen Spender.[2]

Poor Mrs Ed[en] was ill and did not enjoy Geneva or get to know any of the Chin-chin-chinamen,[3] very soon you will be sorry for her.

I was at Oxford for the anniversary of Bill Deakin's[4] arrival in Yugoslavia – the man who did all the dirty work before you and Fitzroy[5] arrived; poor Bill gave a dinner for the occasion and invited several Yugoslavs including the Ambassador, they were all looking forward to booze and boasting of heroic deeds but they made a terrible error in inviting Sir Maurice Bowra,[6] he arrived booming 'Yes, yes, epic occasion, epic occasion, important celebration, important celebration' and then proceeded to expound loudly on topics more interesting to himself and indeed to me and made it clear that Bill's exploits and Yugoslavia were to be given little prominence – I have felt guilty ever since.

When are you coming to London? Is this prolonged absence because you are working or have you resumed your horrid chloral drinking habits?

Why not come to luncheon the week after next, 15th, 16th or 17th?

Love

Ann

1 David Sylvester (1924–   ). Writer, mainly on painting.

2 Stephen Spender (1909–   ). Critic, poet and friend of poets. Co-editor of *Encounter* 1953–67. Knighted 1983.

3 Clarissa Eden accompanied her husband to the Indo-China conference at Geneva attended by Chou En-lai.

4 William Deakin (1913–   ). Led First Military Mission to Yugoslavia (which included Randolph Churchill, the Earl of Birkenhead and Evelyn Waugh) in 1943. Warden of St Antony's College, Oxford 1950–68. Knighted 1975.

5 Fitzroy Maclean (1911–   ). Foreign Office 1940–3, Conservative MP 1941–59, Brigadier commanding British Military Mission to Yugoslavia 1943–45. Baronet 1957. Has written several books, including *Eastern Approaches*, 1949.

6 Sir Maurice Bowra (1898–1971). Warden of Wadham, Oxford 1938–70. Knighted 1951. Among his books are *The Greek Experience* and *Memories*, but his writing was not as stimulating as his conversation. A stream of notes from him and John Sparrow to Ann in which they frequently comment on each other are too slight to be reproduced.

To Evelyn Waugh

16 Victoria Square   1 September [1953]
                                        arrived from France yesterday

Dearest Evelyn

No date on your letter, it has probably been here some time and by now you have regained your mild obesity and the affections of little Margaret, you should be pleased that her preferences are so normal and healthy.[1]

I was refused admittance to a Benedictine monastery for being trousered and bareheaded, finally they allowed me to attend Mass in Ian's macintosh, the discomfort was horrible but the Benedictines made a beautiful noise and an exquisite colour scheme, white acolytes, black monks and a shocking pink prior.

The same evening I was refused admittance to a casino for wearing espadrilles, and was forced to attend a people's casino where I placed 400 francs on zero and won – an exhilarating experience.

The Pyrenees are inferior to Scotland and fearfully depressing, we stayed in an inn with no modern conveniences and my stomach was upset from over-indulgence so I was unable to climb to the cave and spent the time fighting with [an] old French gentleman for access to the only thunderbox; Ian was guided to the cave by the priest who was to say Mass over the mouth of the cavern for the soul of the speleologist they dropped last year,[2] it was a four-hour climb and martinis and champagne trickled from his pores and he returned less enthusiastic about the centre of the earth, and for a week was unable to walk downstairs without falling flat on his face. We then went to Biarritz where there were plenty of thunderboxes but one had to be nippy to escape boredom and drowning, the sea was rough and the beach populated with Spanish Marquesas and international flotsam and jetsam such as Mrs Randolph the first,[3] Rose Bingham Warwick Fiske[4] and the new hostess Mrs Charlie Clore.[5]

I hope you are at peace with Lady Norwich[6] and I sympathise with delaying a truce with Churchill, I am told he has purchased the country house but no one will go and stay with him, he telephoned last night to invite us but I pretended the room was full of people. I am so fond of him when he is not physically present but only retain warm memories of his gusto.

Alert me of your next visit,

Love

from

Ann

1 Waugh had written that, after his cure for obesity he was 'light as a feather and feeble as tissue paper. My clothes hang round me like classical draperies.' Also that his daughter Margaret showed a marked preference for the company of her brothers, sisters and cousins.

2 Marcel Loubens had been killed when his safety harness broke a thousand feet underground. His companion Norbert Casteret was leading the expedition which Ian, aged forty-five, had joined in order to descend through the second deepest cave in the world to a vast subterranean river. In fact he was only allowed to stand at the entrance and watch.

3 Pamela Digby (1920–   ). Married 1939–46 to Randolph Churchill, not yet remarried.

4 Rose Bingham (1913–   ). Married 1933–8 to the Earl of Warwick, 1938–40 to William Fiske, 1945–50 to Lieutenant Colonel John Lawson and in 1951 to Theodore Basset.

5 Frances Halphen married the financier Charles Clore in 1943.

6 Duff Cooper had been created Viscount Norwich in 1952 so Lady Diana was Viscountess Norwich. She disliked the name and though he protested 'A little

Norwich is a dangerous thing', she announced in *The Times* that she wished to retain her former name and title, as she still does. A row was in progress because Waugh had refused to stay with Randolph Churchill when he heard that the new Viscount was to be present. It lasted another two weeks.

To Virginia Charteris

Victoria Square   12 September [1953]

Darling Virginia

I was *very very* excited when Boofy showed me the *D. Sketch* cutting, I have not seen Mark[1] and did not know *the Book* was a Book Society recommendation, it should mean a wonderful Christmas sale, I am so happy that it will have such an auspicious start, I felt so inadequate to judge it.

Ros Lehmann comes to dinner next Tuesday, she wrote Ian the most remarkable fan mail letter about his cave articles, I thought they revealed only too clearly that there was no story to write but Ros said they churned her inside and that no doubt he had thought of 'caverns measureless to man – down to a sunless sea' and she was now certain that Coleridge must have been transported to that particular cave in his opium dream. Ian was very angry when he read it to me and Fionn and was received with shrieks of laughter.

Best love to you both and tell Hugo I will write to him very soon,

Ann

1 Mark Bonham Carter had just published *A Share of the World* at Collins.

To Patrick Leigh Fermor

16 Victoria Square   7 October [1953]

Darling Paddy,

There is suddenly a tremendous craving, an obsession for you, it is running like wildfire through warm autumnal London – it began some days ago with the advent of Diana [Cooper] who is agitating for your return and subsequently told a massive luncheon party you wrote better letters than anyone, it continued with Martha Gellhorn[1] who is complaining she was not allowed access to you in

Rome, it continued with Joan[2] telephoning Ian to know your whereabouts and it spoilt Cyril's 50th birthday party for me because I had caught the infection and missed your gaiety and vitality, you would have prevented my nervous constriction at the million possibilities that something would spoil Cyril's evening. I think Cyril enjoyed it but I lost control of dinner and allowed Bowra to bellow across me and Cyril to Clarissa, whereas they were both intended to concentrate on Connolly; I was also worrying at Ian sitting beside Mary Campbell[3] who bores him, with the result that I became intoxicated and had a pain in the stomach and did not enjoy it.[4] Can we have a party to celebrate your return? That prospect would cheer me enormously.

I am pleased *The Violins of St Jacques* are to appear as a book,[5] it is a *wonderful wonderful* story, every ingredient I enjoy including tears at the end.

Come back soon,

Love Ann

1 Martha Gellhorn (1908–). War correspondent and writer. Married to Ernest Hemingway 1940–5.

2 Joan Eyres Monsell (1912–). Married 1934–47 to William Rayner and in 1968 to Patrick Leigh Fermor.

3 Lady Mary Erskine (1912–). Married 1933–44 to Philip Dunn, 1946–59 to Robin Campbell, 1962–9 to Charles McCabe and 1969 until his death once more to Philip Dunn, who had meanwhile succeeded to the baronetcy.

4 Cecil Beaton recorded his impression of the evening in his diary:

> This week [Ann] gave a dinner to celebrate the fiftieth birthday of Cyril Connolly, and the small group she collected had unity and character. A lot of talent, brilliance and erudition was gathered here between 'Empire patterned' walls. They were people, born in all sorts of different strata of life, enjoying the fruits of success in the company of others they respected or had most in common with. The talk was on target: no one wasting time in banalities.

5 *The Violins of St Jacques*, 1953, had already appeared in the *Cornhill Magazine*.

From Sir Maurice Bowra

Wadham College, Oxford   October [1953]

My dear Ann,

What a delicious dinner, and what an enjoyable evening. I was much depressed at having to do a Cinderella departure, and sorry not to see the Second Mrs Connolly[1] – but others seemed more resigned at the deprivation. Mary Campbell surprised me by saying how much she liked her and how easy she is to get on with. Odd. I hope Cyril was not sick, as you were afraid he might be. He does it quite neatly but is full of guilt afterwards, which spoils his evening. It was clear that Clarissa has no intention of making Roy[2] a peer. Very disloyal of her.

Yours ever

Maurice Bowra

1 Bowra missed Barbara Connolly on another occasion and commented, 'I am beginning to think that I shall never meet the Second Mrs Connolly. She is becoming a dream figure with green eyes and copper hair, very jolly.'
2 Roy Harrod (1900–78). Economist and biographer. Knighted in 1959.

To Hugo Charteris

Goldeneye, Jamaica   January 1954

Darling Hugo,
    What nonsense did I write in my last letter?[1] I cannot remember, I only know that for many moons there have been many things I wished to say but it always sounds wrong, perhaps I slightly resent your vaguely superior attitude to most other people – perhaps it isn't superior, perhaps your nerve tentacles are over sensitive – I know every letter of mine has been critical, more so than I intended, but I thought you were becoming dangerously subjective for a novelist – not subjectively analytical – but perhaps pigheaded! Anyway I thought if the book was a success it would be the moment to talk – but it wasn't really because I was sad for you about its successor – my last conversation with Mark [Bonham Carter] we agreed that it was worth the altering but that must be your decision.[2]
    This year is a bad writing year for having avoided the guests all day we play a canasta game in the evening – we stipulate it shall be one and play a quarter their usual stakes, even that is expensive as I always fall asleep and give the pack. Yesterday was disaster – owing to an exhausting struggle with an octopus I was barely able to see the cards and we lost £5.

The villain in Ian's new book is called Hugo Drax,[3] not Connolly Drax as I suggested, I enjoy a Connolly tease and he hates the Waugh character named after him,[4] but possibly a blood and thunder villain might please him; the heroine is a policewoman called Gala, she has perfect measurements. I was hopelessly ignorant of such important facts and apparently the inches I suggested had the hips and breasts of Mrs Blow and a waist like Laura, fortunately Noël brought a Mainbocher saleswoman for a cocktail and all is well.

Diana's behaviour during our last week in London was in keeping with her character and all youthful episodes;[5] she was tragic – genuinely tragic because the face slipped sideways and the blue eyes became more fixed and glassy but it was a very public grief, a terror that people might avoid her, a wish to be surrounded by friends to describe every detail to everybody and to be hopelessly intoxicated every night; it was strangely obvious that Duff had been the easy human being and that those whose company Diana craved were a [rum] crew. She wished to join David Herbert[6] in Tangier and then Jenny Nicholson [Clifford] in Rome; Paul Louis[7] was immediately at her side offering to give her a house in Paris and also in London; when I left Ali was in charge giving full rein to his own isolation and craving for love, and Auberon[8] was splendid – but he has a real goodness and is different to the others.

Much love to Virginia, Frances and Jane and yourself,

Ann

---

1 Three letters from Ann mainly devoted to criticising Hugo Charteris's novel have been omitted. Her next letter to him begins 'Perhaps we had better cease arguing by post and have days of conversation when you come South. . .'

2 Charteris's second novel libelled his Colquhoun relations and has never been published.

3 'One cannot forget *Moonraker*, 1955, for the vivid, rounded depiction of its villain, Hugo Drax, and what is probably the most gripping game of cards in the whole of literature.' Kingsley Amis in the *Dictionary of National Biography* 1961–70.

4 General Connolly in *Black Mischief*. The evacuee children of *Put Out More Flags* were also named after Connolly.

5 Duff Cooper had died in the first hours of 1954.

6 David Herbert (1908–   ). Brother of 17th Earl of Pembroke. He went to live outside Tangier in 1950 and became the leader of society, louche, expatriate and otherwise. Lady Diana arrived 'in a scarlet cloak and floppy black felt hat with her "emblem" – a gold unicorn – pinned on one side. . . Diana wished to meet people,

to go to parties and be distracted; so the days passed successfully enough – the nights were very painful.' *Second Son* by David Herbert, 1972.

7 Paul Louis Weiller was a rich and loyal French admirer of Lady Diana. He gave her a mink coat from Dior costing £4500 in 1951 which she christened 'the coat of shame'.

8 Auberon Herbert (1922–74). Waugh's brother-in-law, whom he detested.

To Evelyn Waugh

Goldeneye, Jamaica   7 February [1954]

Dearest Evelyn

The weather reports are alarming, why are you not with us? Today we ate saffron rice with octopus conch and lobster, caught by me; I was sad about the octopus, the entrance to his lair was scattered with exquisite seashells, he had eaten the contents and was holding them with his tentacles as a protective front door. I prized them from him one by one, put them inside my bathing dress, put both hands in the hole and with tremendous courage pulled and pulled, he poured forth black ink which strengthened my resolve, I was the stronger and collected him at the cost of a few scarlet railway lines round the wrist; you will have gathered he was a small octopus and not a giant squid.

We have just said goodbye to Tanis and Teddy Phillips, they were with us twelve days, twelve interminable days. I had always liked Tanis in France and England, and Teddy seemed harmless, but here their perpetual marital endearments in high drawly voices were nerve-grinding; she is 'Lion' and he is 'Bear' or 'Bearingtons', Ian said I was to tell them they must not call 'Lion' and 'Bear' to each other while he was writing but I could think of no tactful approach; finally Ian whose tact is notorious said at luncheon 'We should love you to continue using the house but we are going away for three or four days.' An appalling silence fell. I had not been warned of this violent move and where could we be going? The meal was ended amid awkward silences and I had to do some incoherent explaining to Tanis, she was mollified but Ian said I was a traitor, however they did not hurry their departure but treated us like natives, they went shopping and bought Ian two bottles of whisky and me a pair of moccasins which we received with Indian grunts.

The purpose of this letter was to say I was sorry to miss you in

London, I telephoned White's twice to try and persuade you to dinner and help with poor Diana, but missed you; you missed nothing for the cook was in Rhondda valley burying her miner father and it was cold ham, vodka and hysteria.

Send me a postcard, for there are no jolly jokes in Jamaica.

With love

Ann

Note by Ann Fleming on travels in Europe.

I think Ian was happiest when he, me and the Thunderbird flew from Lydd to Le Touquet. After the customs officer released the machine he would park it outside the airport restaurant, and we would eat omelette *'très baveuse'* (he always insisted on *très baveuse*) and plan our journey south.

In early days when he was still working for *The Sunday Times* we were usually in a hurry, but even later when it was no longer necessary I found the mileage per day exhausting.

On re-reading diaries [lost], the drive through Provence in the spring of 1954 was specially beautiful. Our destination was Marseilles. Ian was to write of Commandant Cousteau who was exploring the wreck of a Greek trading vessel off the coast. Cousteau's ship was in harbour listing to one side with its weight of amphorae and other terracotta objects strewn on the deck. Ian was determined to deep dive to the wreck. When he sailed with Cousteau I went down the coast to Willie Maugham anxiously to await his return. Ian proved too old for the depths, the pressure was great, but he adored the adventure despite severe headache for several days. It was the beginning of affection and admiration for both Cousteaus.

Ian joined me at the Villa Mauresque, and was delighted by Willie's company and well-planned day. There was a strange resemblance between them, luxurious symmetry, the perfect martini served in a sunny garden, a high standard of cooking, a variety of menu, a choice of wonderful smells in the bathroom, soap, essences and shaving lotions.

A curious feeling that they both regarded 'women' with mistrust. Years later Willie said to me 'Ian's public will not let him rest.' This was sadly true. I told Willie that Ian (by then ill) would constantly repeat 'How can you expect me to make you happy, when I am not happy myself?' They both had a basic sadness and a desperation about life. In the spring of 1954 we were all happy, the fourth being Willie's friend and companion Alan Searle.[1]

1 Alan Searle (1904–   ). Maugham's lover, then secretary and companion from 1946. Son of a Bermondsey tailor, Lytton Strachey had called him 'My Bronzino boy'.

Ann and Maurice Bowra had been to stay with Joan Rayner and Patrick Leigh Fermor on the island of Hydra.

To Hugo Charteris

[St Margaret's Bay?]   [August 1954]

Darling Hugo,
From Athens to the island of Hydra – four hours by slow boat on a glassy sea of palest blue with a sky to match was indeed miraculous beauty; we slunk along the mainland with islands and strange rocks on our left and hills on our right. The Grecian hills have a remarkable simplicity of line, neither dramatic nor menacing; those nearest to us were ochre with valleys of lemon and olive trees and dark cyprus spikes. The further peaks pale honey to cream till they become part of the sky, it explains mythology, temples and oracles.

Joan and Paddy have been lent a painter's house at Hydra,[1] it is the most barren and burnt of the islands and after a week I wished I had someone to take me to other islands or to Delphi but the heat is so tremendous in August and they had all seen everything at more clement times of year; in spite of this I enjoyed it all – only the four of us except short visits from Freya Stark[2] and Isobel Lambert.[3] We dined frequently at the harbour cafés and after drinking the resinous wine Maurice [Bowra] and Paddy would recite in a variety of languages tho' I tried to steer them to English and French; the conversations were largely on events before the birth of Christ so I have become a good listener! Although Maurice and P. are supposed to detest each other they appeared to have totally similar tastes including Joan Rayner – they both love Greeks, Greece, talking, reciting, war, medals and royalty; I had not realised how much Maurice had enjoyed 1914–18, and staggering up the hill from the harbour to home we invariably sang 'Keep the home fires burning'. Our return journey was nightmare.

The sun shone yesterday and today, an excitement in England, I bathed and have a pain, it was too cold.

This letter is not an answer to two of yours but I may do better from Ireland, the east coast air makes one sleepy, Ireland is relaxing.

Love to Virginia and the children and yourself,

A.

1 Belonging to Nico Ghika, the Greek painter, sculptor, engraver, architectural planner and writer. Member of the Athens Academy. Married to Barbara Warner since 1961.
2 Freya Stark (1893–   ). Traveller and writer. Made Dame of the British Empire 1972.
3 Isobel Nicholas married Constant Lambert, the composer and conductor, in 1947. He died in 1951. A painter and stage designer, she executed the sets for his last ballet, *Tiresias*.

Patrick Leigh Fermor wrote of Ann's visit to Hydra:

Later, when we settled for a couple of years in Nico Ghika's house in Hydra, she came once, or perhaps twice, overlapping with Freya Stark for two or three days, but for the whole time with Maurice Bowra. Cyril and he, old friends, overlapped as well; but this may have been – and I think it was – another year. Ann didn't know Maurice well, but they got on at once and were great pals ever after, which made us feel pleased. Burnt down now, this lovely house was white and grey-shuttered at the top of a steep escalade of terraces with crags above it and gorges shooting down to the sea. In summer it was so hot we had luncheon in a sort of cellar dining-room and dinner under the stars or the moon on one of the terraces or in the port. The scenery was exactly that of one of Ghika's pictures. When Ann and Maurice were catching the 'plane back I went to Athens with them, and after Maurice had gone to bed, we climbed into the ruins of the temple of Olympian Zeus – huge columns, some tumbled but many still standing – and wandered among the giant Corinthian capitals scattered there.

To Joan Rayner and Patrick Leigh Fermor

16 Victoria Square   23 August [1954]

Dearest Joan and Paddy

I am ashamed of the lapse of time between regretfully leaving Hydra and thanking you for its manifold joys: it was a wonderful mixture of rest, stimulation and beauty, I miss the gay talkie-talk silencing the cicadas, the taste of retzina and even the loo – I became fond of the lavender on the window sill and I now constantly forget to pull plugs; I enjoyed the 'oozo' and the 'Gazoozo', Isobel, Freya and above all Maurice, without whom I should never have made the journey; it was lovely to be with you both, I had often longed for a glimpse of your adventurous lives and I hope you will constantly have houses in romantic places and I may become an annual visitor.

The journey home was uneventful until Rome when the skies became dark and we were delayed two hours because the aircraft had developed a 'snag', it was humid hot and no sign of Fionn, I became restless and nervous and when the dread signal came was relieved to see her wandering blindly towards an aeroplane bound for Hong Kong weighed down by cedarwood boxes, one containing an Etruscan drinking cup, the other the head of a Florentine stone lion, she seemed surprised I had no Grecian urns and said 'Surely Sir Maurice gave you something.' I was still confessing that I had seen nothing of temples or sculpture when we flew into an electric storm over the Alps and everything became a grim nightmare, two vomiting screaming children, Fionn throwing up over London Library volumes and a clutch of beastly businessmen whose horrid jokes were silenced by fear, I shut my eyes and said 'Cows in a field, Cows in a field' over and over again, it had a miraculously calming effect but we were thrown higher than pressure level and arrived at London airport gasping for breath. When we reached at last Victoria Square, we were confronted by Raymond who said his appendix had to be removed immediately, so there was a flurry of surgeons, nursing homes to say nothing of muddles at St Margaret's and having to let Nanny have a rest and to say nothing of Ian's arrival from the USA covered with running sores – 'syphilis' I shrieked over the barrier at the airport but apparently it was allergy to some Borgia American pill taken supposedly to kill a cold in the head. These are my honest excuses for a monstrously late letter; less valid reasons were being sucked in[to] a short August silly season, a handful of close friends, luncheons at the Etoile and cinemas at night. They are all mutual friends so I will briefly tell of their news.

James Pope-Hennessy[1]

PLUNGED IN GLOOM. A fortnight's solitary confinement with Lady Crewe[2] who is economising by no longer producing an Edwardian grog tray, no longer does a discreet footman enter at ten o'clock with muted footsteps and a pleasant clang of glasses and decanters on a silver tray; but alas, she did produce four more cabin trunks of letters and papers of no political or romantic interest to be ploughed into the last quarter of James's life of her most uninteresting husband: so like the fairytale princess he has been trying to turn straw into gold, but not so fortunate his hair has changed from ebony to ash.

Cyril and 'BABY' [Barbara Connolly]

Lunched with them at the Grand Hotel, Folkestone – they remember Hydra with pleasure but as something pleasant that happened a long time ago. No offers for the cottage, no money in the bank and Baby unable to return to the cooking routine so they are on a raw vegetable diet and ate three helpings of roast beef, Yorkshire and horseradish to make up.

Colin Tennant[3]

All headlines of yellow press devoted to his visit to Balmoral for Princess Margaret's birthday and inferring an immediate engagement, he had to be smuggled onto the London Express and travelling under the name of Archie Gordon appeared amongst us thriving on the situation and pretending he did not wish anyone to know his whereabouts or the date of his departure for Venice with Judy Montagu;[4] Judy thinks nothing will come of the situation but I believe Colin is serious and would enjoy being a Prince Consort.

Lucian [Freud]

Lucian returned from holidaying in Menton with Lady O. and B.[5] to finish the portrait of Colin. He was arrayed in discreet cotton-striped suits acquired in San Remo and unsuitable for English weather, he was in tremendous spirits and as Colin likes to sit to him from dawn till dark I suspect Lucian of being a strong influence in the royal drama.

Alan Pryce-Jones[6]

The season has never stopped for Alan, the quietude of August has not descended upon him and he is gaily juggling with committees and coronets while waiting for his holiday which is to be spent yachting in the Mediterranean with the American Ambassador[7] and other unknown American guests – he was amazed at my gasp of horror at the prospect of such a holiday.

Peter Quennell

Peter is feeding his birds on cuttlefish, cherishing Paddy's stuffed beauty and goes to Rory Cameron[8] plus Spider Monkey.[9] He is a little nervous about her impact on the sophisticated South of France.

I met Robert Heber-Percy[10] in the street, he had recently received a postcard from Daphne Fielding[11] saying how splendid for publicity that her book was to be published the same day as Lord Vivian's case comes before the judges.

Ian had a horrible time with Nin Ryan at Newport, the beach crowded with umbrellas and elderly ladies in picture hats and beyond that mountains of flyblown seaweed with noisy traction engines driving paths through it so that the rich could get a glimpse of the ocean and the more adventurous of them could bathe. Children were being kept indoors because someone had seen a crab.

Give much love to Diana and I hope you have not been inundated with strange Greeks and visiting British.

Thankyou again and again for so much fun and sunshine.

With love

Ann

1 James Pope-Hennessy (1916–74). Writer, Literary Editor of the *Spectator* 1947–49. In addition to his biography of Lord Crewe, he published *Queen Mary* in 1959, and *Verandah* in 1964. Ann liked his exotic tales of the homosexual underworld.

2 Lady Margaret Primrose, daughter of Lord Roseberry, married in 1899 the Marquess of Crewe (1858–1945). He had been Lord Privy Seal twice and Secretary of State for India 1910–15. *Lord Crewe: the Likeness of a Liberal* by James Pope-Hennessy appeared in 1955.

3 Colin Tennant (1920–). A cousin of Ann's, he married Lady Anne Coke in 1956 and succeeded as Lord Glenconner in 1983.

4 Judith Montagu (1923–72). Daughter of Venetia Montagu *née* Stanley, Asquith's friend. Ugly, witty lifelong friend of Ann. In 1962 married Milton Gendel. *See* Appendix of Names.

5 Oonagh Guinness (1910–). Married 1929–36 to Philip (Gay) Kindersley, 1936–50 to Lord Oranmore and Browne and in 1957 to Miguel Ferreras.

6 Alan Pryce-Jones (1908–). Critic, author and journalist. Editor of the *Times Literary Supplement* 1948–59.

7 Winthrop Aldrich was American Ambassador in London 1953–7.

8 Rory Cameron lived at La Fiorentina near Cap Ferrat in the South of France, where he wrote travel books and his mother, Lady Kenmare, painted wallpaper and made toffee.

9 Sonia Leon, who was married to Peter Quennell.

10 Robert Heber-Percy (1911–). Known as 'The Mad Boy'. Inherited Faringdon House from Lord Berners. Married Jennifer Fry 1942-7 and Lady Dorothy Lygon in 1985.

11 Daphne Vivian (1904–). Writer. Married 1926–53 to the Marquess of Bath and 1953–78 to Major Alexander ('Xan') Fielding. Her brother Lord Vivian had been shot three times by Mavis Wheeler, a former mistress of Augustus John, and in October he gave evidence on her behalf. She was found guilty of malicious wounding, not attempted murder, and they were reunited when she came out of prison in February.

To Evelyn Waugh

16 Victoria Square   20 October [1954]

Dearest Evelyn

Before embarking on any ship with you I shall require a certificate guaranteeing your *mental health* and would prefer a *strong* male nurse to accompany us, otherwise the journey may terminate like your *Handful of Dust* with me reading aloud day and night to keep your warlocks and witches at bay.[1]

My first publication by the Queen Anne Press under Weidenfeld's wing is to be *Beds of Crime* illustrated with captions from the *News of the World*: I don't like being a publisher, it is the same sordid middlemanship as stockbroker or greengrocer.[2]

Ian is in America visiting Alcatraz, Nevada, Las Vegas and Los Angeles to collect material for a new plot,[3] so I had his least favourite people to stay – Pope-Hennessy, Quennell and the Freuds; we went to tea at Saltwood Castle with Sir K. and Lady Clark[4] and unluckily Lucian rang the mediaeval bell too roughly and it jammed, Edgar Allen Poe noises resounded through the building and Sir K. and his lady swept to the door and became quite hysterical in their efforts to unjam it; they payed no attention to us – not so much as 'good afternoon' – and displayed little manners or *savoir-faire*; when quiet was restored we were conducted icily round the icy ramparts and had a very solomn reception, it is a long time since I was made to feel so foolish and guilty.[5]

Come to London on the 25th and after a good dinner I will take you to a party Weidenfeld[6] is giving for Peter Q.

Love

Ann

1 The voyage to Ceylon fictionalized in *The Ordeal of Gilbert Pinfold* had taken place in February but the novel did not appear until 1956.

2 The plans for Weidenfeld and Nicolson to distribute for the Queen Anne Press fell through.

3 '. . . for three carefree weeks Fleming lived out the world he was soon to describe in *Diamonds Are Forever*. . . As Fleming drove Woodward's car and bet on the tote and took the mud baths at Saratoga he and Bond were one. They remained so in Los Angeles and Las Vegas and for the rest of the stay in America.' *Ian Fleming* by John Pearson, 1965.

4 Elizabeth Martin married in 1927 Kenneth Clark (1903–83).

5 Ann wrote later to Hugo Charteris, 'I was reduced to childish giggles with James while Peter took a ponderous interest in the operation and Lucian did his vanishing trick which is mental and not physical; I cannot say that the visit was a success but it made us all very happy for the rest of the evening.'

6 George Weidenfeld (1919–   ). Chairman of Weidenfeld and Nicolson since 1948. Created a life peer 1976.

To Patrick Leigh Fermor

16 Victoria Square   Sunday 28 [October 1954]

Darling Paddy

Last weekend a great buzz amongst the neighbours for Maurice went to stay with Sir K. and Lady Clark and managed to wind up the rusty portcullis tower, the drawbridge, and let in the *canaille*. Cyril arrived last with his scowling 'Baby' but finally it proved a merry party for Maurice had subdued his host and hostess by telling them that no matter how many castles they owned they would always remain bourgeois so with due humility they perched on a narrow seat below a mullioned window while Maurice filled glasses and held court in front of the fire. So at last Maurice met Baby but the results are unhappy for Cyril for Baby has declared that Maurice is frivolous and trivial and cannot be compared to Berenson and E. [Edmund] Wilson and to add to the disaster she had never met K. Clark before and finds him a mixture of Berenson, Wilson and Rudolph Valentino so Cyril is full of woe and says she already sees herself as Lady Clark and is planning the move from Oak Tree Cottage to Saltwood Castle – a matter of five miles.[1]

London is gay and pleasant, last Monday to *Figaro* and the Vienna State Opera, Tuesday to Freddy [Ashton] and *Firebird*: Freddy as the magician clanking gold nails a yard long – irresistibly comic to me and James [Pope-Hennessy] – we had to stifle giggles[2]: Margot[3] exciting and beautiful beyond belief. Wednesday Lennox Berkeley[4] and Alan Pryce-Jones's *Nelson* at Sadler's Wells. I went to a splendid film with Ian but attended Jimmy Smith's[5] party afterwards – the verdict was reasonably favourable but I did not hear much as I arrived last and hurled myself upon Freddy who was at an eightsome table which included Alan and the inevitable Duchess of Buccleuch,[6] Jamie [Hamish] Hamilton and divers pansies; Freddy not a wit nonplussed by the proximity of Jamie gave me a dazzling imitation of Jamie fracturing Freddy's ribs so as to install himself next to the Duchess.

My life is more social than was intended, for Evelyn Waugh ruined my chances of becoming part-time ancient student at the Kensington College of Art. He came to dinner the same night as Robin Darwin[7] and attacked Robin for several hours, referring to him as Gilbert Harding and being generally insulting. I barely know Robin and he appeared quite defenceless and rather humourless – finally he fled into the street sobbing 'why does he hate me so?'

Ian goes to Las Vegas beginning of November to plot the third novel [*Moonraker*] amongst twenty-four-hour divorce and gambling; I remain in London.

It is very easy to write to you compared to my brother, with whom a painful correspondence is in progress: the second novel was rejected, the third hangs in the balance because he refuses to alter his heroes, who are all overwhelmed with self-pity and megalomania; my plain speaking by post may well mean that I have to take the night train to Inverness and then a multitude of local trains to heal the breach at John o' Groats.

I have done little else except enjoy the Irish rain and celebrate Raymond's coming-of-age with exquisite linen and silver, dry rot hanging from the walls and a strange mixture of ancient relations.

Love to you both and Hydra,

Annie

1 Sir Maurice Bowra wrote to Ann, 'Mrs C. is plainly a cup of tea at a high level, but I can see she is not always very friendly . . . The old boy was on his best manners

– a great joy to see him. I have asked them to stay ... what a prospect.' The Connollys' marriage ended in 1954.

2 Sir Frederick Ashton comments on this performance, 'I exaggerated it. I enjoyed it.'

3 Margot Fonteyn (1919–   ). Prima ballerina. Married Roberto Arias in 1955. Dame of the British Empire, 1956. She was rehearsed by Karsavina, the original Firebird, who passed on from Fokine: 'Here is no human emotion'.

4 Lennox Berkeley (1903–   ). Composer, whose opera *Nelson* had a libretto by Alan Pryce-Jones. *The Times* found it 'the only heroic opera in English ...'. Knighted, 1974.

5 James Smith (b.1906). Director of W. H. Smith. Amateur singer and brother of 3rd Viscount Hambleden.

6 Mary Lascelles married in 1921 the Earl of Dalkeith who succeeded as Duke of Buccleuch in 1935.

7 Sir Robin Darwin (1910–74). Principal of the Royal College of Art 1948–67, Rector and Vice-Provost 1967–71. Evelyn Waugh recorded 'dinner at Ann Fleming's where she had asked a great booby called Darwin whom we mocked'. He and Ann thereafter called him 'Velvet'.

To Evelyn Waugh

16 Victoria Square   15 November [1954]

Dearest Evelyn

The long delay in answering your letter was because the annual journey to Jamaica is always a horrible problem to me though it appears to present few difficulties to rational human beings. I want to bring the baby and I thought we could all travel together, but Ian is appalled at the prospect and will not risk him in the tropics though I fear this is tinged with the terror of Nanny preventing him (Ian) bathing naked; so alas we shall have to take different routes – while you are enjoying *delirium tremens* on the ship I shall be mad with fear in the air.

I have consulted Elizabeth Cavendish on Princess Margaret's programme, at the moment it does not include 'Roaring River'[1] so perhaps you will come to us when you need a change of company and when next you come to London we will discuss it; I am pleased you are coming and am arranging a spear and goggles so you may share my passion for octopi, nasty food and an ice-cold swimming pool; it is frowned upon to bathe in the sea, which on a clear day may be seen in the distance.

A week has passed since I started this letter, is there any chance of your coming to London? There are a great many things I want to talk about, I have purchased the Queen Anne Press from Lord Kemsley, what shall I publish? Please write me ten thousand words on some saint with interesting habits, St Francis of Goa or Saint Cunégonde, there is a remarkable Rococo statue of the latter in the V. and A. exhibition, I have never heard of her but judging from the wealth of her costume she must have combined virtue with wealth. You may design the binding and choose the lettering.

Peter Quennell is coming to Jamaica, I have warned him that his holiday may become a Roman holiday for me, to escape you he may hurl himself into the sea and be eaten by sharks: it has depressed him extremely that you may be on the island let alone in the same house.[2]

Come to London soon for I would seriously like your help with the Press, and your last book was sold in a flash: I thought you might have some small unpublished work of a morbid character that could be illustrated by Francis Bacon.

With love

Ann

1 Lord Brownlow's house where Waugh was to stay.
2 Ann wrote to Hugo Charteris later, 'P.Q. showed real feeling and anger when I told him his holiday was to be a Roman one for Waugh was arriving. He called me a middle-browed Messalina with a taste for circuses.'

From Evelyn Waugh

Piers Court, Stinchcombe, Glos.   17 November 1954

Dearest Ann
    It is kind of you to offer me a good dinner on 25th. It is very long since I had one. But I don't know Wildenstein and I fear never shall.
    Nothing in your letter pleased me.
    The plural of octopus is octopodes or (*anglice*) octopuses. *Never* octopi.
    I can't understand why it is more comfortable for Kaspar to travel by air.
    You see I am falling into winter melancholy but I have finished my book [*Officers and Gentlemen*]. It is OK.
    I greatly enjoyed the first ½ of Daphne. Then contrary to all

expectation good taste & discretion intervened.[1] Your great friend 'Xan' [Fielding] can't read proofs.

I propose to tour Jamaica extensively, not only the fashionable resorts but the mountains & villages. I will buy a horse & recapture the lost pleasures of my youthful journeyings. I will visit you too, please.

Are you sure poor Quennell is not dead? His recent articles suggest that he is. Do Jamaicans raise zombies?

Love,

E

1 Waugh wrote of *Mercury Presides* by Daphne Fielding, 'The adult part is rather as though Lord Montgomery were to write his life and omit to mention that he ever served in the army.'

To Evelyn Waugh

[St Margaret's Bay?]   [29 December 1954]

Dearest Evelyn

One should always leave with one's guests, I have made the mistake of lingering in the country for a post-Christmas lull; our grand London cook and her John Dory mate who came to make us comfortable over the festival have left Nanny and our old-maid-of-all-work in savage moods, apparently they had not been given a decent helping of turkey, and on the day of departure the grand cook before catching her train had sat drinking tea at the kitchen table and passing remarks at the old-maid-of-all-work's efforts to produce a simple luncheon for two. I had not realised how serious the situation was and this morning ventured to pass a remark myself on the subject of baby's meat being grilled to rags and this finally shattered her nervous system, her sobs drowned the throbbing of the frigidaire, she threatened to leave by the next train, she ran to her room and from below we could hear suitcases slammed on the floor and the violent emptying of the chest-of-drawers, Nanny immediately forgot the scarcity of turkey and volunteered help so I was not outnumbered, in fact retreated to my own apartment to await a report: twenty minutes later Nanny appeared white and grave but with treacherously sparkling eyes to tell that Mrs Davies had nowhere to go on the train and had decided to drown herself and would it be wise to fetch a doctor. I was very relieved to hear she had nowhere to go and decided to risk suicidal tendencies and suggested a policy of inertia until teatime; my instincts proved correct for in the evening when Nanny appeared with the offspring she was obviously disappointed and said there had been no drowning, Mrs Davies had only had a hot bath!

One way and another it has been a tiring Christmas, we hired the next cottage to house the grand cook and mate but alas it caught fire on Christmas Eve. Its owner had left it in a horrid mess, twenty-five filthy old school ties on the dressing table, a soiled dressing gown and nether garments on the chair and unspeakable bath towels; I live in constant fear of losing the grand cook and had spent the morning hiding his horrid relicts in the linen cupboard and it was the linen cupboard that burst into flames: my father maintains that I threw a lighted cigarette into the cupboard with the dirty clothes but luckily it has been attributed to a 'short' in the electric system. The fire gave great pleasure to the neighbours and to Peter Quennell, who became a fire brigade bore and regaled us with anecdotes of his war fire service, presumably forgetting that I knew he had never seen active service for he was sacked on the first burning chimney incident for lighting a cigarette.[1]

I telephoned to you and Laura at the Hyde Park Hotel but there was no answer from your rooms, shall I see you before you sail? The Boxing Day air tragedy[2] has made me no happier and it is probable that I shall sail on the 19th with Lady B. Parsons[3] and fly from New York; Ian is very cross but if we both fly together neither has a sane relative to adopt the baby.

Fionn received a letter from Miss Laycock[4] yesterday telling [her] she was engaged to the ADC, she says he has very long arms and an enormous mouth but omits his name – a triumphantly conventional end for a *very fast* debutante.

I hope there was enough turkey for all the little Waughs, best wishes to you and Laura for the New Year,

Love

Ann

1 Peter Quennell was in the Fire Service for almost a year but it is true that on his first real fire (others had been false alarms), having hosed the wrong floor and drenched his companion, he had a cigarette stuck in his mouth by an acquaintance who observed, 'Have a fag, Quenn', and this led to his dismissal.

2 An aeroplane crashed at Prestwick and twenty-eight people were killed.
3 Lady Bridget Parsons (1907–72). Sister of the Earl of Rosse. James Lees-Milne wrote in his diary in 1943, 'She is ravishingly beautiful with her long, arrogant neck, golden hair, fair complexion and sulky mouth.' *Ancestral Voices*, 1975.
4 Tilly Laycock (1938–), daughter of General Robert Laycock, married in April 1955 Lieutenant Mark Agnew in Malta.

> Ann sailed from a frozen England at the end of January suffering from laryngitis. At first Peter Quennell was the only guest at Goldeneye, then Evelyn Waugh arrived.

To Hugo Charteris

Goldeneye, Jamaica   14 February 1955

Darling Hugo,
   I left England with great reluctance and complete loss of voice – laryngitis for three days is a pest if you incline to leave all arrangements till the last minute. I was tearful at leaving Caspar which broke the last vocal chord. Now I am here sleep sea and sun have lulled and restored the nerves.
   Peter is a peaceful and appreciative guest, he pursues the humming birds or corrects his *Hogarth*[1] proofs. Evelyn Waugh has arrived and left behaving with near-warm civility to Peter and removing Peter's fear-phobia; it was an occasion when Evelyn wished to please for he had been two weeks with the Brownlows and said it was a great intellectual strain to find words simple enough to converse with them – they are indeed a grisly household, gin from ten-thirty on, the women concentrate on a smooth sunburn and hairless bronzed shanks, the men lounge and yawn or play cards. Evelyn took gallantly to the underwater mask, but his rowing in a rubber boat over coral pinnacles became commando-courage. When his panama blew overboard, his little arms jerked up, sweeping the rocks, towards the edge of the reef and the giant breakers. I cried for mercy and said if he returned to calm water I would scramble and swim for the panama, but no sooner was swimming possible than I belly-flopped from the boat and dashed for the shore; he thought it very treacherous and was only half placated when I found him a sea-slug to squeeze – they shoot out a

mile of purple ink if touched. Poor Evelyn, he is deeply unhappy – bored from morning till night and has developed a personality which he hates but cannot escape from; he has gone to Kingston to bully the RC bishop and returns here for two nights before sailing.[2]

We are the only heterosexual household for 50 square miles, Sir J. Gielgud is on our left, Noël on our right and beyond two newcomers who have called their house 'Moot point'!

Write to me soon, I hope to be back in early March. I hope everything progresses; I asked John Perry[3] if he would read your play, he is Binkie Beaumont's paramour but of Irish county family and was sympathetic to the plot. He is also Binkie's partner and has had two successful plays put on both about old family homes – did you see the one where Sybil Thorndike (the old aunt in the play) sat in a sedan chair for two acts occasionally lowering the window to shriek abuse at her stepnephews and nieces?[4] Dinner approaches – we all send love. I will write to Virginia soon – I hope Frances is beautiful and intransigent – Jane[5] cuddly. Best love,

A

1 *Hogarth's Progress*, 1955.
2 Waugh wrote to his daughters on 23 February, 'I am staying with your cousin Ann Charteris-O'Neill-Rothermere-Fleming. She is a very different character here from her London self – up at seven, in bed at ten, hours spent in the sea, hours spent at the easel painting fish and shells.'
3 John Perry (1906–   ). Theatrical impresario and partner for thirty years of Hugh Beaumont.
4 *Treasure Hunt* by M. J. Farrell (Molly Keane) and John Perry, with Sybil Thorndike as Aunt Emma Rose in 1949.
5 Jane Charteris (1953–   ), then almost two. Now journalist and publisher. Married in 1984 Peter Clark.

After Ann's departure in March, Ian wrote:

Goldeneye, Jamaica   Monday

My darling precious,

When I saw that the big bird had got you up in its claws I went back to sunset and sat on the far groyne and swam and loved you for an hour and hated the idea of Edward [Molyneux] and Montego and Goldeneye and Jamaica without you. Then I sat with Carmen

[Pringle] for an hour and told her how wonderful you are and then I went to Edward's. At the bottom of his drive it was very exciting and all made for you, which made things worse. The night before a shoal of thousands of goggle-eyes (must look them up) had been seen and about fifty of the fishermen sewed their nets together and for the whole previous twenty-four hours they had been making a great sweep of the bay. And now the twenty canoes were in a circle and it was getting smaller all the time. So I found Edward and T. P. [Tony Pawson] and we stayed there until it was quite dark and the fishermen left men in two canoes with acetylene torches to keep the fish down and they all went home and I expect they all dreamed all night of the great circle of boiling fish. And the churchbells were ringing in Montego and it was madly romantic and like some great traditional fish festival in Italy. And they were due to come back to their boats at six in the morning and I told Edward that he had got to get up at five and be there and paint the whole thing. Then we had to leave it and go up to his airless and pretentious house[1] and talk about you and Edward's servants and how much he was 'tiefed' [robbed] and how Noël thought he was God. Then frozen New Zealand mutton for dinner and tomato soup and ice cream and after dinner Edward said What will you drink and I said Brandy and there was no brandy and T.P. played the *House of Flowers* record[2] and I wanted to scoop you by hearing it first but Edward talked about Billy Rose wanting to buy his house at any price. Then bed, with the empty twin beside me and no air and no darling sniffs. As a result I woke up earlier than usual and cursed you for not being there and went down to the sea and they were all there and the ring of net was getting smaller, but still as big as a house, and the fish were boiling and jumping and they were all about a foot long and very silver with big black eyes and the fishermen didn't want to hurry it, because the market knew about the catch and all the hotels were waiting and the longer they had to wait the more they would have to pay because of lunch and not having bought any other fish. So I went back and it was cold and I bathed in the dull pool and thought of you being woken up in NY by the hot air crackling in the central heating, and had breakfast with bad scrambled eggs but lots of matching china and the toast wrapped up in a napkin. Then I went down again to the sea and Edward was there painting away and finally the circle was as big as a stage and they started hauling up parts of the nets and the fish waterfalled into the canoes and as

soon as one canoe was full they started to fill another. I left after a
bit and they had filled four canoes solid with fish. Nothing else but
goggle-eyes. Then I finished correcting my book[3] which seems
terribly silly today and Edward's picture isn't bad, in fact I think the
best he has done this year, and he was pleased I had made him
(which shows there's something in the way I go on!) and agreed to
call it 'The Killer Net', which is what the blackamores call it when
the circle gets small. And now I'm getting tired and will shortcut the
rest.

I love you

Ian

1 Edward Molyneux's house was decorated in yellow, had yellow flowers and was
referred to by Coward and Fleming as Jaundice House.
2 Harold Arlen's Broadway musical with book and lyrics by Truman Capote had
opened on the last day of 1954. However 'an intangible gossamer grace rendered
the show somehow untheatrical' and it did not run.
3 *Diamonds are Forever*, 1956.

To Joan Rayner and Patrick Leigh Fermor

16 Victoria Square   27 March [1955]

Darling Joan and Paddy

There are terrible rumours abroad that neither of you will
return to us and you are to nest in Hydra forever. I think you should
return like Peter Pan and Wendy for a few months of the year.

I am a fortnight back from Jamaica and still bubbling with
health and delighted by old friends, icy winds and frost-nipped
primroses. Our guests this year were P. Quennell and Evelyn W.
The three of us went rafting on the Rio Grande while Ian was
polishing up horror comic number four. It was a strange party,
Evelyn wore blue silk pyjamas and a panama hat with pink ribbon,
he ordered a stupendous lunch from the Titchfield Hotel – wine
packed in ice in biscuit tins, cold roast fowls and legions of hard
boiled eggs – he treated Peter as a native bearer and we rode ahead
on the first raft, Peter and the biscuit tins behind us; whenever we
shot a tiny rapid he roared over his shoulder 'stop looking so
poetical and mind the lunch' but alas it was Peter's victory for the
river was in spate, our punter inexperienced for he lost balance and

fell overboard, we cannoned into the rocks and subsided slowly into the river – Peter said it was like watching an old-fashioned carriage accident.[1]

Poor Evelyn – killing time is his trouble and not a night without sleeping pills for twenty years – birds, flowers, fishes mean nothing to him but he learnt a great deal of the island by motoring with Jesuits. We became very fond of him, he became courageous underwater and even bathed once before breakfast.

Maurice Bowra comes to lunch on Wednesday before his cruise with Ladies Birkenhead,[2] Berry and Pakenham[3] and all their children – he will appear as a Turkish pasha. My only financial hope of Greece is to go on the *Achilles* with Elsa Maxwell in August,[4] she has been presented with a publicity trip by Niarchos – but alas the vulgarity is extreme and the guests abominable. I said 'Yes' in New York but have since discovered it may mean sharing a bathroom with Lady Fairbanks[5] and Mrs Gilbert Miller;[6] but I have a plot to wait in Venice with impoverished friends and when such VIPs as Claire Luce and Marilyn Monroe do not appear to dash aboard waving the Union Jack, burn the stars and stripes, make Elsa walk the plank and sail to Hydra.

Freddy, Isobel and Alan's Japanese first night[7] is Friday, they were to have supper with me but there is a plan afoot to move to the spacious Panamanian Embassy and enjoy the hospitality of Roberto Arias[8] – I wish you were here.

We lunched last Sunday in Folkestone with Cyril and Baby, it was arranged by Ian for Sunday and not Saturday so Baby was routed for she will only go to Folkestone on Saturdays; Ian's victory was expensive for Cyril for as she would not contemplate an early drive they had to spend the night at the Grand Hotel and wait for us. I gathered there had been some painful episode in Rome and Cyril had returned down and so depressed he was forced to spend ten days at the Ritz, but they are now in honeymoon mood.

Much love to you both and send a p.c.

Ann

---

1 'We were passing a flock of wading egrets. "Owls," cried Evelyn loudly, frightening them all away... We swam for the shore, Evelyn doing a slow breaststroke, blue eyes blazing and mood much improved, for he liked things to go wrong.' Ann Fleming in *Evelyn Waugh and his World*, 1973.
2 Sheila Berry (1913–   ). Writer. Married in 1935 the Earl of Birkenhead. Her

brother Michael, now Lord Hartwell, married her husband's sister, Lady Pamela Smith, the following year.

3 Elizabeth Harman (1906–) married in 1931 Francis Pakenham who became a peer in 1945 and succeeded as Earl of Longford in 1961. Biographer.

4 Elsa Maxwell with characteristic energy had arranged for 126 people to sail from Venice to the Greek Islands.

5 Mary Epling married in 1939 Douglas Fairbanks Junior who was made an honorary KBE in 1949.

6 Kathryn (Kitty) Bache married in 1927 Gilbert Miller, the theatrical producer.

7 *Madame Chrysanthème* with choreography by Frederick Ashton, music by Alan Rawsthorne and decor by Isobel Lambert came on at Sadlers Wells on 1 April.

8 Roberto Arias (1918–). Arrived as Panamanian Ambassador in London that year, and married Margot Fonteyn.

To Evelyn Waugh

[Telegram]   [July 1955]

Going direct boating party Dover unable lunch may I choose suite Granville for you discuss dates Thursday.
Presume Ivor Claire based Laycock dedication ironical Ann[1]

1 *Officers and Gentlemen* was dedicated 'To Major-General Sir Robert Laycock KCMG CB DSO. That every man in arms should wish to be'.

> In *Evelyn Waugh and his World* Ann wrote, 'When the war trilogy appeared I pretended to identify the caddish Ivor Claire with Bob and his [Waugh's] response was violent indeed but not wholly simulated.'
> Waugh's response was:

Your telegram horrifies me. Of course there is no possible connexion between Bob and Claire. If you suggest such a thing anywhere it will be the end of our beautiful friendship. . . For Christ's sake lay off the idea of Bob = Claire. . . Just shut up about Laycock, Fuck You, E Waugh.

> In his diary he writes that he has forbidden her to breathe a suspicion of 'this cruel fact'.

To Evelyn Waugh

16 Victoria Square   12 July [1955]

Dearest Evelyn

Panic is foreign to your nature and you rarely use rough words. Why do you become hysterical if one attempts to identify your Officers and Gentlemen? The book is a great delight, I am sad I have finished it, the evacuation of Crete was over too soon; I should have liked several hundred more pages and the microscope placed over more officers and gentlemen in trying circumstances; if I had had to choose a commando raiding party I should have taken you Bill Deakin and Anthony Winn and avoided all the Philip Dunns[1] with or without Es, but then after my behaviour on the coral reef you would not have taken me.

May I have permission when rereading the book to imagine that Trimmer McTavish is Lord Lovat?[2] – I won't tell anyone else. I am still sad about the beautiful young soldier's identity disc, Crouch-back was a very trusting fellow.

Thankyou so much for sending me *Os and Gs* – no complaints except Ritchie-Hook's disappearance, he was my favourite character last time and it was a frightful [?] to lose him so soon and promise a return three pages before the end.

Will you postcard me to St Margaret's on two points. A. Would the presence of P.Q. and Spider Monkey upset your bank holiday? I would sooner have you. B. Would the Grand Hotel Folkestone be too far?[3] Only twenty minutes and very comfortable and on the way to churches I wish to visit, Romney, Dymchurch etc:

Wish you had been at the water party, everyone so young and beautiful.

Love and thankyou and Fuck you

Ann

1 Sir Philip Dunn, Canadian millionaire and Philip Dunne (1904–65), Unionist MP, were both in Number 8 Commando with Waugh in 1941.

2 Lord Lovat (1911–). Waugh's enemy from the time in 1943 when he prevented Waugh joining General Laycock abroad.

3 Waugh stayed at the Grand Hotel where he found the staff 'obliging, but I must warn you that the cooking is very poor.' He went to St Margaret's Bay 'during the proletarian festival. It was a revelation and inspiration to see the indefatigable mother and housewife at full stretch.'

From Evelyn Waugh

White's, St James's, SW1   10 August 1955

My Dear Ann

It is splendid to have escaped from the two grinding stares of Lord Mersey[1] and Kaspar. Nothing can be more hideous than my memories of the Kentish coast except perhaps the horrors threatened by Miss [Elsa] Maxwell, whose despairing invitation to her cruise was awaiting me, which of course I have refused. But I must thank you for your kind hospitality on several occasions and for some miles of exhilarating transport.

A bugger (name unknown)[2] has just said 'I met you at luncheon with Annie.' It appears he conducts Assheton's [*sic*] band. He is much more obliging than Assheton and says he will arrange for spastic Hatty[3] to go to the ballet school.

And now I am off to true blue Cordelia Margaret[4] and to Goneril & Regan Teresa[5] and Hatty.

I do hope that old Kaspar has nightmares about his visit to Folkestone.[6] I shall, for many years.

Do please come to Stinkers soon. You will be most welcome, also Fionn. NOT OLD KASPAR. I will get mattresses laid out for you everywhere.

Read the life of Elinor Glyn for advice on bringing up chicks.

Love from

Evelyn

---

1 Viscount Mersey (1872–1956). Chief Liberal Whip in the House of Lords 1944–9. Waugh had recorded on 5 August, 'The man at the next table has introduced himself as Lord Mersey, Mathew Ponsonby's father-in-law. He tells me funny stories.' By 8 August, 'The persecution by Lord Mersey has made my meal times unendurable.'

2 Robert Irving (1913–). Conductor of the Royal Ballet at Covent Garden 1948–58, when he became Musical Director of the New York City Ballet.

3 Harriet Waugh (1944–). Youngest daughter, now a novelist. Married Richard Dorment in 1985.

4 Margaret Waugh (1942–). Biogragher. Married Giles FitzHerbert in 1962.

5 Teresa Waugh (1938–). Lawyer. Married Professor John D'Arms in 1961.

6 Ann wrote to Cecil Beaton of the week before: 'Evelyn was here for dinner last night and lunch today and we returned him to Folkestone and enjoyed an afternoon on the dodgems; he was furious that I would not put Caspar to sleep in his room with a spoonful of paraldehyde, send Fionn to the cinema and have dinner

with him. Waugh commented: 'Unbearable luncheon... Caspar is a very obstreperous child, grossly pampered.' Ann reported more fully in *Evelyn Waugh and his World*: 'The next bout of fisticuffs was in the sepulchrally silent tea room of the Grand Hotel, Folkestone. Evelyn was annoyed that I had brought my three-year-old son, who was perched on my knee; so he put his face close to the child's, dragging down the corners of eyes and mouth with forefingers and thumb, producing an effect of such unbelievable malignity that the child shrieked with terror and fell to the floor. I gave Evelyn's face a hard slap, overturning a plate of éclairs, and presently had my revenge by driving over a cart-track so bumpy that he swallowed half his cigar.'

From Evelyn Waugh

Piers Court, Stinchcombe, Glos.   26 August [1955]

Dearest Ann

Old Kaspar will not recognise me if (God forbid) we meet in the near future. I have given up wine (before 6) & bread and am as thin as R. Ironside.[1] Also I am growing a moustache to rival [Robin] Darwin & Lady Pamela [Berry].

If you see Mr Ironside please chide him about his *wrong* opinion of Holman Hunt's 'Shadow of Death' (which he misnames 'Shadow of the Cross'). I went to visit it in Birmingham last week – of course it is in the cellars – and found it a superb painting. The shadows on the legs are stunning. Had he examined it when he wrote so foolishly? He seemed to me a respectable young person and I am deeply shocked.

I had an exhilarating time among the Pre-Raphaelites in Birmingham. A civil, pretty young lady named Miss Bodkin showed me all the arcana.

On the way home I stopped to see *Titus Andronicus* at Stratford. So enjoyable that I have written an article in praise of it and of homage to Lady Olivier[2] whom I thought deliciously funny. Now someone says she was not meaning to be.[3]

I should not dream of making a joke about Quennell – I regard him as a subject for shame & sorrow.[4]

Next time you organise a 'charity' entertainment, why not produce the play in Nigel Dennis's *Cards of Identity*? It would be awfully funny.

My poor mother-in-law is entertaining 13 Soho bandsmen at Pixton.

Perhaps you will meet Miss Maxwell's party at Constantinople?
Laura's cows are dying of drought. She sends her love.
I hope poor O'Neill is a little happier now.

Love from

Evelyn

1 Robin Ironside (1902–1965). Painter, stage designer and writer.
2 Vivien Leigh (1913–67). She was married to Laurence Olivier 1940–60.
3 Waugh wrote a laudatory review in the *Spectator* of 2 September, ending:
'When she was dragged off to her horrible fate she ventured a tiny, impudent,
barely perceptible roll of the eyes, as who would say, "My word! What next?" She
established complete confidence between the audience and the production. "We
aren't trying to take you in," she seemed to say. "You're too clever and we are too
clever. Just enjoy yourselves." It was the grain of salt which gave savour to the
whole rich stew.' That Waugh had misjudged her intentions is clear from Lord
Olivier's autobiography in which he says that for once he agreed with Tynan in
condemning her performance.
4 Ann had written that Peter Quennell attributed to Waugh a rumour that he,
Quennell, had joined the Salvation Army. He considered it slanderous.

From Evelyn Waugh

Piers Court, Stinchcombe, Glos.   12 September 1955

Darling Ann

I don't think I can help with *Punch* and your underprivileged
children.[1] They have far too many treats & should all be sent to dig
coal for our coming winter. *Punch* is just a parish magazine for
television these days. I've never troubled with children so can't say
much about it – except the horrors of Old Kaspar. I have made
enquiries. At his age Septimus [Waugh] could walk five miles
without fatigue.

Laura's cook's husband has gone off his rocker and instead of
working in the garden hides under her bed all day (his wife's, not
Laura's) in the hope of taking her in adultery. He keeps her awake
all night torturing her to confess infidelities of which it appears she
is innocent. As a result her cooking – never good – has become
unbearable. I live on Rye-Vita and gin.

I thought Nancy's article,[2] of which she is as proud as a pea hen,
great nonsense. Nancy never lived in a stately home. Swinbrook

was a little house her father built & there were only women servants in it. They knew no other lords – that is why she thinks them unique.

How generous of you to buy a Darwin.[3] You could give it as a wedding present to Christopher Glenconner's boy who I see is engaged to a negress.[4]

Christopher Sykes[5] has written a very clever book – so clever I can't follow the plot at all. You have read it? If so please tell me who killed Lord Grinstead – old or young Portin? And what is the subject which James can never mention after marriage to Rose-mary? But it is full of funny scenes and good talk. It is named *Dates & Parties*.

My article on Titus Andronicus was really a fan letter to Lady Olivier.

I have a niece[6] being married in London next week & must go there that day. Could go earlier & stay later if you are free. Wedding is Tuesday. You must explain to me why Cyril wants Barbara. It is not as though she were rich or a good housekeeper or the mother of his children.

Ian shouldn't say 'fabulous' should he? About an hotel I mean.

I hope you have scolded Ironsides about Holman Hunt.

Miss Gasgoyne smiles furtively at Teresa on Miss Freeston's doorstep but no words have been exchanged.[7]

What hell Miss Maxwell's cruise sounds.

Mary Dunn and her monopode[8] were here yesterday. Both *very* nice.

Love

Evelyn

1 Ann had asked him to write for *Punch* on the horrors of travelling with children, which article would end with the address of the charity which collected for holidays for East End children.

2 Nancy Mitford had written on social behaviour, popularising the terms U and non-U, in *Encounter*. With Waugh's reply and some other pieces this eventually appeared as the book, *Noblesse Oblige*.

3 Ann had written, 'Darwin only sold one picture at his exhibition – the smallest and cheapest.' She had not bought it.

4 Emily Licos, not a negress, was married to James Tennant 1955–62.

5 Christopher Sykes (1907–   ). Writer and biographer of, among others, Orde Wingate and Evelyn Waugh.

6 Veronica Waugh, daughter of his brother Alec.

7 Veronica Gascoigne and Teresa Waugh were both attending Westminster Tutors before going to Oxford.

8 Robin Campbell (1912–   ). Painter who had lost a leg in the war. Married 1946–59 to Lady Mary Erskine.

To Evelyn Waugh

16 Victoria Square   29 September [1955]

Dearest Evelyn

Graham Greene has placed his daughter in a Chicago slaughter-house, would that appeal to Harriet? She kills bullocks and packs them in tins.

I wish I could have come to Brighton but we were searching for a modest house in which to spend our old age. When we found it, it was full of happy people but we propose to sit like foxes outside a rabbit hole and in time we must win.

Last night we accompanied Mr and Mrs Malcolm Muggeridge[1] to the first night of the *Punch* revue. Mr M. was very nervous, he dislocated two of my fingers during a feeble skit on 'collapse of stout party'; the programme was ablaze with illustrious names – Auden, Eliot, MacNeice – but alas at the end the gallery booed and the cheers from the stalls were half-hearted; your friend Mr Anthony Powell[2] was outraged because a young man dressed in full mess kit sang Miss Joan Hunter-Dunn wearing a white tie – apparently an unspeakable offence when wearing military fancy dress. The evening ended with a party on the stage where I was flattered by being acknowledged by Mr Graham Greene but I fear it was because I was advantageously placed at the buffet and able to supply him with food and drink; he scuttled away like a crab when his glass and plate were full.

Our survey of Ox, Bucks and Berks took us to Chequers for tea and Oving[3] for dinner; when we arrived at Chequers Clarissa flew out of the garden door and muttered in a stage whisper 'don't mention Burgess or Maclean';[4] we followed her into the garden and there was Sir [Anthony] on a *chaise longue* recovering from the flu' and gloomily reading bulletins from 'Ike's' oxygen tent.[5] Lady B. [Bridget] Parsons was reading the newspapers on another *chaise longue*, everyone was covered in Jaeger rugs and the atmosphere lacking gusto; luckily a servile private secretary poked his head nervously round a yew hedge and hissed 'I've got the Chancellor on the telephone, sir' – it was the voice I would use if I had cornered an octopus, hooked a salmon or shot a 'rhino', it had an electric effect on [Anthony], he shook off the rug and was clearly relieved to leave us; much to our joy the servile secretary reappeared twenty minutes later to advise us that he would not rejoin us.

I *shall never never* write any more about the [Edens] at home if you tell Randolph for he would immediately telephone Lady [E.] and I should lose a girlfriend, a snobbish entourage and a source of *great* entertainment.

When are you coming to London? Next week is Fionn week then pleasure week then Hugo week – could you lunch on the 11th or 13th? 13th you will find Aunt Cynthia, 11th Maugham, Sparrow[6] and Hartley.[7]

No one talks of anything except Jack Spot, Rev. Andrews,[8] Burgess, Maclean – have you a copy of Cyril's pamphlet?[9] I have bought the remainder from the Queen Anne Press and business is flourishing.

We watched the first commercial television from Mrs Crawley's[10] home, Lady Pamela's whiskers did not show and she was extremely good but alack, the machine broke when Mr Crawley appeared, his head became quite flat, his chin enormous and then he vanished like the Cheshire Cat – Mrs Crawley was very distressed.

With love

Ann

PS. S. Spender says will you write a letter to *Encounter* criticising N. Mitford!

---

1 Katherine Dobbs, a niece of Beatrice Webb, married in 1927 the writer Malcolm Muggeridge (1903–   ). He was Editor of *Punch* 1953–7.

2 Anthony Powell (1905–   ). Novelist, Literary Editor of *Punch* 1953–9.

3 The country house of Michael and Lady Pamela Berry.

4 The White Paper on the disappearance of Burgess and Maclean had been published and there was much speculation as to the identity of the Third Man (Philby).

5 President Eisenhower had had a heart attack on 24 September and had been put in an oxygen tent.

6 John Sparrow (1906–   ). Barrister, Warden of All Souls College, Oxford, 1952–77.

7 Leslie (L.P.) Hartley (1895–1972). Novelist and critic. Among his books were *Eustace and Hilda*, 1946, and *The Go-Between*, 1953.

8 Jack Comer, known as 'Jack Spot', was a notorious king of the underworld; the Reverend Andrews was a vicar of eighty-eight who had given evidence in his defence against a charge of malicious wounding and was being interviewed by the police once more.

9 Connolly had written a pamphlet on Burgess and Maclean in 1952, the year after they fled to Moscow.

10 Virginia Cowles (1912–84). American journalist who married Aidan Crawley in 1945. Aidan Crawley (1908–) stood as Labour MP 1945–51 and Conservative MP 1962–7.

From Evelyn Waugh

Piers Court, Stinchcombe, Glos.   1 October 1955

Darling Ann

Was [Anthony's] Chancellor Adenauer or Butler?[1] The photograph of Butler, stuffed with royal jelly, reeling up the steps of his house, was one of the keenest pleasures of last week.

Would you not like to spend your old age here? Last holidays decided me that I must move to somewhere larger and I am trying to sell. So far the only customer has been Sir Anthony Lindsay-Hogg[2] who came with Dudley Delavigne[3] as his advisor and seemed to like everything. Suddenly he turned green, called for aspirin, and left in a rush saying he could not possibly live here. Did he see a ghost?

Have you any memory of a house called Portlip near your old desecrated nursery? It has seen a lot of suicides and was going cheap and I wanted to buy it but it was snapped up. Ugly house, but delightful surroundings with a popish chapel.

I was invited to write for *Punch*'s Revue in one of those letters beginning 'Dear Evelyn Waugh' which, without Nancy's guidance, I long ago decided to leave unanswered. I am going to meet her at Momo's at luncheon on Thursday.[4] You too? I should like to write a detailed refutation of her notorious article, but can poor Spender afford me?

Bucks is an awful county to die in.

Love from
Evelyn

1 Dr Konrad Adenauer was Chancellor of Germany; R. A. Butler, the Chancellor of the Exchequer, was the one with whom Sir Anthony Eden had spoken on the telephone.

2 Sir Anthony Lindsay-Hogg (1908–68) did not buy the house.

3 Dudley Delavigne, a brother of Doris, Viscountess Castlerosse, was an estate agent.

4 Maude ('Momo') Kahn. Sister of Nin Ryan. Married in 1920 Major General Sir John Marriott. Their house was the gayest spot in Cairo 1940–42. 'Small, dark and vivacious, she prided herself on her long red fingernails, her girlish figure, her dress sense – her clothes might change in colour but never in style – and her reluctance to rise before mid-day.' *Randolph: A Study of Churchill's Son* by Brian Roberts, 1984.

Ann organized a dance to raise money for a charity supported by the Earl of Arran ('Boofy's beastly East End children'). She reported to Waugh how Robin Darwin arranged the use of the Royal College of Art, 'allowed me to complete my plans and then announced that he must have two thirds of the money. . . Tomorrow starts Hugo week, he will appear with my breakfast tray each morning and discuss Kant, Hegel and other frivolous topics. It will seriously interrupt my campaign against Shylock Darwin, I shall not have time to take my little soap box to the Junior Common Room and incite the long-haired ones to rebellion.' However she later told Hugo Charteris that, if exhausting, it had been a success: 'the very rich have so little to do . . . the final horror was to return from the Royal College after organising the Humphrey Lyttelton supper and the decor to find that they had all sent me flowers – a forest of white, lilacs, chrysanthemums, roses, lilies of the valley – no vases, no room, no time. Few people can have been so enraged by such lavish expenditure.' Patrick Leigh Fermor enjoyed the party and wrote on 7 January 1956: '. . . I wish you hadn't left so early. I stayed for ages and ages, enjoying it at a steadily increasing ratio, and swallowing immeasurable amounts of all kinds of delicious drinks. In fact, I'm not quite clear about the end of the evening. The mists of the dark ages set in, mimicking in a lesser degree the fall of Rome when the hoofs of Alaric splintered the Capitoline marbles . . . When the mists of oblivion parted, I found myself, at high noon next day, light-headed and unshaven in the middle of Knightsbridge, a lady's overcoat over my tarnished armour, still trailing that bloody trident and waving for a taxi in vain. . .'

To Hugo Charteris

16 Victoria Square   21 October [1955]

Darling Hugo,

Perhaps my flare-up was timely; it is a long while since I became exasperated by your attitude towards Laura, me and money[1] – may I ask what woman from here to Brora brickworks does not object to brass being thrown upon their sofa cushions? Your behaviour is like the last line of the old song 'They drink the wine she sends them, yet they never can forgive', you have for long condemned our morals but deeply feel that you should share in our marginal prosperity – for believe me it is very marginal, at my present rate of expenditure I shall be bankrupt in two years and once more dependent on the generosity of my mate who believes that entertaining is a waste of time, energy and money. I had meant to give you champagne on Wednesday night but your dictatorial letter, 'make it a binge, Penny and Timmy[2] live below subsistence level', happily set up strong feelings of resistance and the damage done to the cellar is reduced. You must realise that every year my wish to give you anything is reduced by your obvious contempt for any way of life except your own and your ill-concealed envy.

If the Skipwith estate[3] is worth the umpteen pounds you mentioned then Timmy should have curtains in his flat and it is more money than your father and all your sisters could ever accumulate.

This is a straightforward letter from an elder sister but the Forbes Adams are so nice to husbands and wives and you so seldom take to older people that I feel it will not come amiss.

You should be able to assess the vast difference there is in becoming grown-up in 1930–40. When I met Esmond in 1935, the word 'press-lord' meant nothing to me, nor newspapers, nor millionaires; I regarded newspapers as I did the arrival of groceries and milk and paid but little attention to them for I was more interested in 18th-century memoirs. I met Esmond in the summer by an Austrian lake, he put sun oil on my back and for the next six years I lived but for physical contact with him – of the final result I am not very proud; and all this is only to illustrate and convey to you that if you believe anything else our relationship must be a false one.

It saddened me that our week should end as it did for I am very fond of you, but I was very tired and had been maddened by your inability to be gracious and civil about telephoning to Virginia – Ian had seen you put the money in the ashtray and I think or we think that it was an ugly approach to a simple situation; no one grudges you a telephone call but it was you who made a financial issue of it.

I think you should read the second Amis book[4] for it is a study of the lives of the same type of persons and behaviour as you saw on Wednesday night.

Please, darling, don't be too adamant and complacent that your views on everything are the ultimate answer for it will make you so unhappy and exhausted. I have always had enormous faith in your writing, if you will impose some form on the content and keep open windows in your mind.

I loved seeing you but felt we were skirting issues and now I have said all I have to say, except I wish we had been longer together.

I hope you will find Perdita[5] and Virginia very well, Frances and Jane very gay.

Much love,

Ann

1 Hugo Charteris had come to think that his elder sisters should help if not support him. He had written to Mary Rose Charteris in 1953: 'I've written and asked Ann to give me a garden tractor (£100) – first time I've ever asked any of them for anything – but I thought she'd look silly if I collapsed one light midnight with a spade gripped in my rigor mortis. So I'm giving her the chance.'

2 Penelope Munday, an actress, married in 1954 Timothy Forbes Adam, Virginia's eldest brother. He too was an actor and they met in a repertory company in Dundee.

3 Yorkshire home of the Forbes Adam family.

4 *That Uncertain Feeling*, 1955, describes the social and amatory mishaps of a librarian in a small Welsh town.

5 Perdita Charteris had been born on 12 September.

To Evelyn Waugh

16 Victoria Square   23 October [1955]

Dearest Evelyn

Did Septimus ever read *Bumble the Pekinese* by Magdalen Eldon?[1] Poor old Hugo had luncheon with me and Magdalen and when the meal was ended he was prostrate with nervous exhaustion and foaming at the mouth; it will remain a mystery how this came about for we opposed him mildly and politely as one might humour someone who should be in a straitjacket, but before coffee appeared his hair was on end and he said that conversing with us was like trying to kick two concrete footballs. While I was apologetically bidding Magdalen goodbye he telephoned to his wife in Sutherland (costing me £1) and ordered her to destroy *Bumble the Pekinese* as it was insidious propaganda for a way of life that was best forgotten and might contaminate his daughters. He was not lucid in his explanations to me of this strange behaviour and could only say that Bumble's home was furnished with Adam mantelpieces and Chippendale chairs; his behaviour bewildered me still further when his friends came to dinner, he regaled them with long stories of how many high pheasants he had shot while staying with Lord Dudley, and they were clearly puzzled, and it seemed contradictory to his attitude towards *Bumble the Pekinese*.[2]

27 October

I was too exhausted to continue the letter last weekend, for *Bumble* preceded several family parties all packed with drama and very wearing to the nerves. Hugo's dinner party was costly, his friends drank 8 bottles of chianti, 2 bottles of brandy, ½ a bottle of whisky and ½ of crème de menthe – also martinis before dinner. We were only [six] souls, Nicholas Mosley,[3] Lady Betty Montagu (author of *Waiting for Camilla*)[4] and his brother and sister-in-law Mr and Mrs [Penny and Timothy] Forbes Adam. Mrs Forbes Adam is a contemporary Cinderella, for from midnight onwards her angry baby-sitter telephoned every five minutes demanding release or overtime. It was a dilemma for me, for the young mother was incapable of speech and the Crickmeres get very angry if the telephone rings after midnight. At one moment I thought I should have to collect the two infants and baby-sit without pay but towards one o'clock they all departed taking poor old Hugo with them and poor old Hugo had such a night in Chelsea that he will not forget for a long time. The young mother was sick and Master Mosley and Hugo had an orgy of squalor, which I maintain is typical of the Kingsley Amis world and the new generation of writers; Hugo is extremely annoyed by my theories and distressed by his friends' behaviour but somehow it was all my fault in the end.

It was sad you were not at Pam's dinner, there was too much dead wood and too many people who see each other every day, you would have been a welcome astringent wit. I was placed between Osbert Lancaster[5] and Nigel Birch. Osbert is becoming more repetitive than Ed Stanley and Nigel could only moan about the poor fare at Buckingham Palace the previous night – hot-water soup, cold white fish, tough steak, warm ice.

I think I had better post this letter for it will not improve. Could you come to the Chinese Theatre on Monday the 7th or to dinner on Monday the 14th? Ian has to be in Montreal those ten days – or else I could come to you on the 14th?

With love

Ann

1 Magdalen Fraser (1913–69) married the Earl of Eldon in 1934. Believed to have been the original of Lady Foxglove in *The Foxglove Saga* by Auberon Waugh.

2 Waugh replied, 'Thinking it over it seemed to me that pheasant shooting was a highly suitable subject for conversation with "unsophisticated" people.'

3 Nicholas Mosley (1923–). Novelist and biographer. Son of Sir Oswald Mosley, grandson of Lord Curzon, he succeeded to his aunt's barony in 1966, becoming Lord Ravensdale.

4 Lady Elizabeth Montagu (1917–). Novelist.

5 Osbert Lancaster (1908–). Cartoonist, writer and stage designer. Knighted in 1975.

From Evelyn Waugh

Piers Court, Stinchcombe, Glos.   Eve of All Saints
[31 October 1955]

Dearest Ann

I sympathise with Hugo's detestation of the Art of Lady Eldon. I do not know her Pekinese but her revolting mouse, which appears regularly in *The Universe*, has obliged me to discontinue reading that otherwise edifying journal. This mouse lives in quite humble circumstances. The motive cannot therefore be envy. Nor do I believe that is Hugo's real motive. He discerns, as I do, something profoundly nauseating, and rationalises falsely.

What an interesting life you lead. Far other than mine. I have been composing an essay in praise of Alfred Duggan[1] & spending my 52nd birthday reading the life of Hugh Benson. The cow man broke his legs so poor Laura has to milk night & morning. For a birthday treat I went yesterday to see Margaret [Waugh]. She is very robust with new common tastes, popular & successful at school. Well, that takes all the gilt off her gingerbread. I like girls to be wistful & difficult. I am a genuine Pre-Raphaelite, unlike Betjeman who really likes them strapping.

It is very kind of you to ask me to the Chinks on Nov 7th. No good I am afraid. But 14th is a date – here or at the Ritz Hotel.

Nancy does not want the French to know she is a communist agent so I am having to spoil my *Encounter* exposure.[2]

Dame Edith Sitwell was confirmed the other day in the presence of the cream of English Popish society.[3] I hear that the Archbishop, an ex-missionary, forgot where he was and conducted a catechism class making them repeat simple prayers after him word by word, again & again.

Let me know please soon about 14th.

Fond love,

E

1 Waugh's review of Duggan's novel *God and My Right* appeared in the *Spectator* of 18 November. Duggan had been a friend of Waugh in his wild youth.

2 Nancy Mitford wrote, 'You know I'm not a communist Evelyn, now don't you? ... Think of me as a Christian, *early* if you like.' Waugh replied that he had attributed her class-war battle cry to her admiration for Lloyd George and she accepted this: 'I know you can't tell the difference between Lloyd George and Stalin but other people can.'

3 Edith Sitwell became a Catholic that year at the age of sixty-eight. Waugh was her godfather.

To Evelyn Waugh

16 Victoria Square   13 January [1956]

Dearest Evelyn

I am despondent and melancholy for I feel I cannot leave old Caspar alone with old Nanny between falling cliff and raging sea so it is to be an octopodless year: I love scratching away with my paintbrush while Ian hammers out pornography next door and we are both very sad, but there seems no alternative. Ian leaves next

Wednesday and I go to Enton Hall with Miss Montagu for a week of fibrositis treatment: it is less fashionable than Tring but I was encouraged by the brochure for although the dining room looked melancholy the plates were heaped with food.

I had a feudal ten days in Ulster – devoted peasantry, icy ruins and youthful company; I intend to spend much time with the under-25 age group and batten on them like a vampire; I chaperoned Fionn and Miss[1] and Master Gage[2] to Dublin where a very un-eligible beau[3] of Fionn's was learning production at the Gate Theatre. We then spent a night at the luxury *beautiful* home of Sir Alfred Beit.[4] Perhaps we brought too much sunshine into their lives too quickly, for they seemed dazed and apprehensive at the gusto that was displayed at Scrabble, bridge and ping-pong.

Our Christmas was quiet, no excitements except a budgerigar flying out of Ian's new American car – the mystery remains unexplained, could it have religious significance?[5]

Oh dear, I am sorry that the Luce arrangement has fallen through, how is this man in a position to open the tycoon's letters?[6] Why don't you come to Enton Hall? It would cure your rheumatism and bring on fresh experience of insanity – so much time has passed since the last attack. I was hoping to come to Assisi for ten days with you and Diana [Cooper].

Diana and Judy [Montagu] tried to reach France the day of the great gale, they set forth for New Haven in Paul Louis [Weiller's] Rolls, laden with french commodes, *boiserie* and *marqueterie* that he had recently purchased but the Captain said it was too rough and refused to take so much weight on board, so they returned to London and I had the pleasure of hearing all about Mells.[7]

Lady Pamela far from boasting of her efforts to oust the [Edens] is whining and frightened and saying it was just a little tease. [Clarissa] is abed with a cold and maintains that Mrs Botts' washing line was hung across a lime avenue where the [Edens] walk on Sundays, far beyond the precincts of Mrs Botts' garden. Apparently [Clarissa's] request was humbly put but altered by the minion who delivered the message; if you did not see the unfortunate publicity that followed the incident I will lend you my copy.[8]

Randolph [Churchill] threw a coffee pot over me, swiftly followed by a jug of water which he said would prevent the coffee stains, but it was far too much water and very cold; he was in a difficult mood for when Ian Gilmour[9] was speaking passionately of ending capital punishment he started singing 'Lloyd George knew my father, My father knew Lloyd George' and as he would not stop we had to get a taxi and send him to White's.

Let me know your plans.

Love to you all,

Ann

P.S. Delighted T [Teresa] is to have a ball, who are the other two thirds?[10]

1 Camilla Gage (1937–   ). Art dealer. Married in 1965 Edward Cazalet.

2 Nicholas Gage (1934–   ). Farmer. They are the children of Viscount Gage.

3 Anthony Page (1935–   ). Director of films and plays. Artistic Director of the Royal Court 1964–5.

4 Clementine Mitford married in 1939 Sir Alfred Beit. They have a remarkable collection of pictures at Roussborough in County Wicklow.

5 Fleming had bought a Thunderbird for £3000. It had a four-barrel down-draught carburettor, Fordomatic transmission and a power output of 180 h.p. Ann said it was 'above our price bracket and below our age range', and once put sugar in the tank.

6 Henry Luce (1898–1967). Founder and Editor-in-Chief of *Time*, *Life* and *Fortune*. Waugh had written: 'A "Dear Harry" letter I sent to Luce was intercepted and answered by the man about whom I was complaining. So I must settle down to exploit my insanity.' *The Ordeal of Gilbert Pinfold* was published in 1957.

7 The Somerset home of Katharine Asquith, where Waugh had been playing Scrabble with Monsignor Ronald Knox. Waugh won.

8 Mrs Botts took her version to the *Daily Mirror*.

9 Ian Gilmour (1926–   ). Editor of the *Spectator* 1954–9. Conservative MP since 1962, Lord Privy Seal 1979–81. Succeeded as a baronet 1977.

10 The dance was also for Lady Christina MacDonnell, daughter of the Earl of Antrim, and Susan Baring, daughter of Lady Rose Baring.

After her visit to Enton Hall health farm, which she was often to visit again, Ann wrote to Lady Diana Cooper:

16 Victoria Square   24 January [1956]

Darling Diana

I am 4½ lbs lighter and free from pain, I have just eaten a Crickmere omelette and feel very guilty. I left Judy at the Godalming cinema this afternoon, she is 9 lbs lighter and determined to see it through, it is a pity she has to continue the sleeping pills. Poor dear Mr Riddell has no idea the amount of aspirins and sedatives that are concealed in the toes of his patients' shoes and wrapped in their handkerchieves; confidences were exchanged in the smoking cubby hole after 7 o'clock soup and before television; and Lady Veronica Hussey[1] shocked me by proclaiming to the crowded room that she had enough phenobarbitone in her douche bag to kill a regiment. I was more shocked by the hiding place than the drug.

Would it be possible for me to come for a weekend and possibly the fancy dress ball? Judy says you may take anyone, and we have forgotten starvation in planning a Chantilly weekend which terminates with us all dressed as Lady Hester Stanhope and Paddy as Lord Byron. It would be a treat and would stop me pining for Ian and the octopodes.

I have absolutely no news, no one broke through the sound barrier except – guess who? Randolph, who kicked the Crickmeres until they disclosed Wormley 333;[2] he wanted to tell me that when Andrew Devonshire[3] heard R. was travelling with [Eden] he said 'You'll be the camel who broke the straw's back.'

I am now overcome with delicious starvation lassitude. It would be lovely to come to Chantilly.

Much love,

Ann

1 Lady Veronica Blackwood (1910–   ). Married to Roger Hornby 1931–40, Squadron Leader Maddick in 1941 and Captain Thomas Hussey in 1947.
2 The telephone number of Enton Hall.
3 Lord Andrew Cavendish (1920–   ) succeeded his brother as Duke of Devonshire in 1950. In 1941 he married Deborah Mitford.

From Ian Fleming

Goldeneye, Jamaica   Sunday
                                                   [January 1956]

My love,
How different my writing looks from the others you get – from Peter [Quennell] and Evelyn and Hugo. That is the sort of thing one thinks about after 3 gins and tonics and 3 thousand miles of thinking about you. It was horrible leaving the square. I said

goodbye 3 times to your room and stole the photograph of you and Caspar. It's now behind a bottle of Aqua Velva in *our* bedroom so as not to be blown down by the wind. Things blown down by the wind worry me. For what it's worth, which, at this writing – as they say in America – is not very much to me, Jakie Astor[1] flew with me to America. Vacuum in New York. It's a dead dreadful place and I loathe it more and more. The Bryces were very suspicious about your absence. What had happened? Jo [Bryce] said you were the only woman I had ever loved and ever would. Good? Bad? I said, as I say to everyone, that you are coming later. NANA has changed. It doesn't belong to them any more. I took some money out.[2] Do you want a fur coat? What shape? What fur? I might get thin to smuggle it. Draw a picture. Give your measurements. Spent the night with the Bs. I *love* Ivar. I can't help it. He *needs* me (4 gins and tonics!) Second night alone in Grand Central Station Oyster Bar. What do you think I do when I'm abroad? Well I don't. I sit alone. In fact, I believe you'd rather I didn't. Any person rather than no person. (I'm beginning to write like Hugo. It's an obssession.) T. Capote[3] was on the *Avianca*. Just arrived from Moscow. Suitcase full of caviar for the Paleys who have built a house beyond Round Hill. V. sweet and nice, loves you. Fascinating about Russia. Met the real jet set there who loved him. Found beautiful powder blue Austin on arrival. Drove through dark. Beach miraculous after 4 weeks. Norther $\frac{1}{2}$ moon. Very sad without you. Today started book. Got two conches but no fun as you weren't there and sea *crawling* with lobsters. Also no fun. V. nice new gardener called Felix. It's a wonderful place and I can't sell it but you *must* be here. It belongs to you and you're stupid not to come here. You *must* get rid of your fears of things. Your fears of things are as bad as my fears of people.

(5th gin and tonic and goodnight my darling love and come if you possibly can) I love you only in the world.

I

1 John Jacob Astor (1918–) Conservative MP 1951–9. He remembers that on the aeroplane Fleming 'sat on the forward right-hand side of the first class and was wearing a light Burberry (and looked like a Graham Greene character who was clearly a secret agent).' Knighted in 1978.

2 The North American Newspaper Alliance, which represented a consortium of newspapers working together to acquire serial rights they could not have afforded singly. Ivor Bryce bought it and Fleming became European Vice-President in 1952.

3 Truman Capote (1924–84). Writer, maturing boy wonder. *Other Voices,*

Other Rooms had come out in 1948, *Breakfast at Tiffany's* was to come out in 1958. He had accompanied *Porgy and Bess* to Moscow and wrote a celebrated account of the trip.

To Ian Fleming

16 Victoria Square   25 January [1956]

My darling,

I am home in the empty house, in my bed and weighing only 9 stone.

I have had anguished moments at not being with you, the detail of our wonderful lives at Goldeneye suddenly became painfully vivid, I could see the bottom of the reef clearly and longed for the sense of well-being that I only have in Jamaica. I have thought of the bean soup and the clucking bird and of your typewriter, and the drunken Scrabble, and I don't believe you realised how much I wanted to come and how much I mind you being alone there. I hope you won't learn to be happy there without me. If I could summon the courage I would join you but somehow one month is very short. I don't feel at all interested in London life, but perhaps Caspar will cheer me up when he arrives on Friday for his party. I bought two brass horse pictures in Mayfair Mart for you for £8. I thought I would get both, for the 2nd one is an Arab pony saddled and bridled and very attractive.[1]

I have no news of the great big world, luckily some very funny letters awaiting from Evelyn about the ball he is to give and a p.c. from Willie [Maugham] of a camel and a pyramid. Give Noël my love and Coley [Cole Lesley] and tell them to let me know if you behave badly.

I miss you *very very* much and you must promise to take me for a holiday in the summer.

Goodnight and God bless you my darling,

Ann

1 Fleming particularly liked brass in all forms and had a set of brass silhouettes set on velvet with cherrywood frames. Ann sold them after his death.

From Ian Fleming

Goldeneye, Jamaica   Saturday
[11 February 1956]

My darling Treasure,
      Truman Capote has come to stay. Can you imagine a more
incongruous playmate for me? On the heels of a telegram he came
hustling and twittering along with his tiny face crushed under a
Russian Commissar's uniform hat. I told you he had just arrived
from Moscow. Anyway it appears he couldn't stand the Round Hill
life with the Paleys and Minnie[1] and Co and just came to me to be
saved and write his articles for the *New Yorker*. Anyway here he is
till Tuesday and of course he's a fascinating character and we really
get on very well though when I gave him a lobster without a head to
carry this morning I thought we were going to have another
Rosamond [Lehmann] act. But he was brave and went off with it at
arm's length. It has poured with rain since he arrived on Thursday
and is still crashing down. Just taking him off to Noël for drinks and
dinner. Ah me. Anyway the book is half done and buzzing along
merrily in the rain.

It is now Sunday and I'm in the garden between showers and spells
of hot sun. The Noël evening was typical. His firefly house is a near-
disaster and anyway the rain pours into it from every angle and even
through the stone walls so that the rooms are running with damp.
He is by way of living alone up there and Coley has to spend half the
day running up and down in the car with ice and hot dishes of
quiche Lorraine! A crazy set-up. N. is going to sell Goldenhurst and
Gerald Street and become a Bermuda citizen! So as to save up
money for his old age. I can see the point but I expect the papers will
say some harsh things.[2]
      Write again quickly. Your letters are wonderful and long.
                        I love you,
                              Ian

Truman and everyone send their love.

1 Mary ('Minnie') Astor married James Fosburgh, the painter. Barbara Mortimer
married in 1947 William (Bill) Paley, President of CBS.
2 Coward wrote in his diary for 29 January, 'The die is cast and from now on no
repining.' Goldenhurst, his farmhouse in Kent since 1926, and the studio in Gerald

Road that had been his London home since the early 1930s, were both sold. Though he became a resident of Bermuda he remained a British citizen. The papers said a great number of harsh things. Later, when he bought a house in Switzerland, he described it as 'overlooking a perfectly *ravishing* tax advantage'.

To *Ian Fleming*

White Cliffs, Dover   Thursday 16 February [1956]

Oh my darling,

I do love the thought of you and Truman resting together. Goldeneye was the last heterosexual household. What will its reputation be now! Anyway I am happy you have such good company, and I am not jealous.

We are living in glorious sunshine, exhilarating air and magical snow. Paris was very beautiful and the frozen lakes of Chantilly most romantic. I stayed four nights. Diana got me an invitation to Madame de Noailles' fancy dress ball; I had always wished to see one of these occasions, and alas, having seen one I should like to return again and again!

The theme of the ball was writers or painters of one's own country. It was all very serious and could never have happened in England. I was Harriet Wilson[1] and put myself and tiara in the hands of the grandest French hairdresser, who also insisted on painting my face. The result was dazzling but more *directoire* than Regency. Each guest mounted the splendid staircase separately, there was a fanfare of trumpets and the pseudonym was bellowed through microphones. Judy [Montagu] and Bindie Lambton[2] were nervous but I enjoyed every minute of it.

Madame de Noailles has a great cross-section of friends, literary, art and smart, the floors were strewn with playing cards and drink and food abounded, but the dancing was a bit solemn for me. We had dined in Pam Churchill's flat, a curious occasion for the hairdresser was in attendance and it was like a rehearsal with snacks in the dressing-room; women and pansies were lined up to have wigs, make-up, cod-pieces and ruffs adjusted – goodness how angry you would have been. Paddy Leigh Fermor was half ashamed and half fascinated by the expert tying of his Bulwer-Lytton cravat. Paul Louis Weiller was dressed as François Premier, very impertinent, but a vast improvement to have a beard and mediaeval hat. Judy was George Eliot and Diana, Lady Blessington.[3] Tony Pawson and Johnny Schlumberger as Calvin and Martin Luther – rather inappropriate.

When we finally arrived the British contingent clung together to watch the entrées, but I wandered into the ballroom and realised that it meant nothing to be a stranger because everyone was acting their part; leaning against the wall and gazing arrogantly at the crowd I saw a man of god-like beauty – tall, slender hips, melancholy eyes and black curls. I elbowed my way towards him and said 'Vous representez Lord Byron.' Alas, it was dear old Peter Glenville,[4] nice to find a friend but not romantic. Towards the end of the evening one became aware that the male French element were dressed as priests, an easy role for seduction, they advanced on any pretty woman and holding a crucifix said 'Je vois que vous avez quelque chose à confesser, mademoiselle!'

This is not a well-written letter but there is always so much to say that I cannot stop to consider grammar like I do when I write to Hugo and Evelyn – in fact I nearly put in another exclamation mark, sign of a lazy, ignorant writer.

Darling, darling, I wish you were coming home sooner. Two months is a long long time. You write nice love letters but do you really miss me? I suspect you enjoy your Jamaican nights. Paris was a short interval and there are no more treats. My only pleasure is that I am in better health than for ten years – no pains and high vitality. I should have had my neck unlocked years ago, it is very rejuvenating to have a flat stomach and a straight back.

Much and all love darling – I must go and have a long sleep – the snow is soporific,

A

1 Harriet Wilson (1789–1846). Courtesan, whose Memoirs begin, 'I shall not say why and how I became, at the age of fifteen, the mistress of the Earl of Craven.' Patrick Leigh Fermor commented: 'Ann went as someone in a high-waisted outfit – I can't remember who but she looked marvellous.'

2 Belinda Blew-Jones married in 1942 Viscount Lambton.

3 Lady Blessington was an Irish beauty who became a leading London hostess in the early nineteenth century and wrote several books, including Conversations with Lord Byron.

4 Peter Glenville (1913–). Director of plays and films. That year he directed his own translation of Feydeau's Hotel Paradiso with Alec Guinness in London, and Terence Rattigan's Separate Tables in New York.

From Hugo Charteris

Little Ferry, Golspie   [March 1956]

Darling Ann,

Fortunately there is no real danger of our quarrelling seriously
for the same reason that Zulu trade unionists and Chinese beetle
fanciers can never really get *at* each other, even when they meet. We
will each, for example, probably bask to our dying days in the
certainty that the other is enormously immature and without a clue
as to what is really going on in the world. So let us leave the matter
there, and never try to understand each other except about matters
that do not concern either of us personally, and about events that
happened more than fifty years ago. No – that's balls too – I should
not get on well with you there either. About paint perhaps – we
could talk about paint – not painting but paint – and communica-
tions, speed of. And about horse-sense.

My latest novel[1] ah me ah me dare I believe it is strong meat, and
some of it reads like an oyster going down. You simply don't know
it's gone except for the sensation. An extraordinary thing happened: I was lying in the bath after I had finished it, in a general float
mental and physical, staring at the picture of a Balinese beauty on
the wall, and thinking will Granny [Tennant] live to read this and if
she does, dear God if she does. . . . The mere thought mesmerised
me because there are some people whose defence mechanisms are so
virulently powerful that even to touch them is like tickling a
crocodile with no bars between: their *'righteous'* indignation is so
formidable that one is hypnotised half into accepting it. It is their
truth – so passionately that it feels like the truth – CRASH the
picture came down, paused erect on the toothmug rack and then
pitched forward to destruction on the floor. GRANNY WAS IN
THE ROOM.

Help! I shouted – help! And would scarcely be comforted.
Supposing I had heard that she had died that night. At about that
time. When would I have next slept soundly? Perhaps never.

Love from us all

Hugo

1 *The Tide is Right.*

To Evelyn Waugh

16 Victoria Square   23 March [1956]

Dearest Evelyn

The day you came to lunch I was almost as mad as you on your journey to Ceylon. My father had been most seriously ill in Birmingham and despite the flu' I had to relay the distressing bulletins to Hugo at John O'Groats, Laura in Paris and Mary Rose [their sister] at Braintree; it was most foolish of the doctor to give me dexedrine instead of advising another day in bed; I have vague memories of a coal-black sky, desirable paintings and the cowardice of your behaviour when we met Lady Eden and Lady Bridget, Peter Quennell could not have behaved worse than you did. Poor Lady Eden needs friends and she loves you, she says she is sad she was so unprepared for the brief encounter.

Lord Beaverbrook telephoned this morning, so I thanked him for your brother's book[1] and said you were with me when it arrived; to my surprise he broke into guffaws of laughter and said 'It's a pity that story is not true, it's a most magnificent story, it's a pity it's not true.' I said I was bewildered by his reaction – he chuckled some more and said 'Ah no, Ann you know as well as I do that Alec has made more money with his books than Evelyn and Evelyn is most horribly jealous.' I told him I was grateful for his gift but I had been unable to read more than one chapter, and thought there could be no jealousy as there was no comparison. He chuckled more horribly, Canadian gargling noises, and I gathered he was going to immediately telephone Nancy Spain to tell this glorious joke; twenty minutes later he telephoned again to say Nancy Spain knew how jealous you were of your famous brother and they both regretted that I had invented such an epic occasion – I am still bewildered.[2] Max's purpose in ringing me up at 8.30 a.m. had been to tell me that he had had a most glorious dinner the previous evening – Claud Cockburn,[3] Judy [Montagu] and Mr and Mrs Randolph Churchill, every time Claud called Randolph 'Randolph', there were screams, 'You shit, you have never met me before, how dare you use my Christian name.' By the time coffee appeared Randolph and Claud were unconscious beneath the table and June had buried her face in her napkin and was uncontrollably weeping – a most civilised and gracious occasion.

Ian returned on Wednesday, and was immediately asked to broadcast on Colonel Ivan Serov and to be televised in the Chamber of Horrors with other thriller writers. I was most disappointed that he refused both, particularly the latter for I longed to know how they would dispose of the thriller authors amongst the tortured and the dead and I thought it would be so nice for old Kasbah to watch his papa in such circumstances, it might give him an interesting trauma.

Cyril took China tea with me yesterday and [Barbara Skelton] telephoned every ten minutes reporting on winter damage to their tiny home. C. was looking very bonny and brown as a berry, he found it impossible to maintain the tragedy, and despite great efforts his crumpled face kept expanding into winning smiles and an unusual standard of wit and jolly jokes.

Goodness, how I look forward to hearing your self-portrait – how long do I have to wait?

With love

Ann

1 Alec Waugh's *Island in the Sun* was enjoying great success.

2 Nancy Spain (1917–64) wrote an article in Beaverbrook's *Daily Express* on 17 March which said that Waugh's sales were dwarfed by those of his brother. She had got her figures wrong; Waugh sued for libel and was awarded two thousand pounds in March 1957 and accepted a further £3000 as an out-of-court settlement for a second case. He wrote to Ann in May, 'I am chivalrously refraining from issuing a subpoena to you to sneak on Lord Beaverbrook's telephone confession of malice.'

3 Claud Cockburn (1904–81). Journalist and a cousin of Evelyn Waugh. Editor of *The Week* 1933–46.

From Evelyn Waugh

Piers Court, Glos.   Monday in Holy Week
[26 March] 1956

Dear Ann

I am very sorry indeed to hear of your father's illness. I hope you have better news of him by now. I had no idea you were suffering anxiety when I lunched with you. Had I known, I should have been much softer.

I am sorry & surprised that you can't enjoy *Island in the Sun*. I thought it very good. My brother has lived out of England most of his life and many of his expressions are unfamiliar and uncongenial, but the story is intricate & managed with rare competence – as well as Dr Maugham can do. Try it again when the dexedrine is out of the system.

Your censure of the manners at Lord Beaverbrook's table encourages me to think you have some respect for such things. May I therefore remind you of a point of etiquette you must once have known, but have now plainly forgotten? A is in a public place with B when they meet C, whom, A knows, B does not wish to meet. The only correct behaviour for A is to acknowledge C with a bow, smile & polite word and immediately help B in making his escape. For A to attach herself to C and shout at B to join them is ill-bred. To boast to others of B's embarrassment aggravates the offence.

Yours ever affec.
Evelyn

To Evelyn Waugh

16 Victoria Square   4 April [1956]

Dearest Evelyn

C. [Lady Eden] thinks B. [Waugh] behaved with good breeding and tact, C. is sad she was unprepared for the meeting. C. does not disclose what her behaviour-pattern would have been had she been forewarned. Clearly A's [Ann's] behaviour was very non-U but then she was the least inhibited person present and considers false pride should not come between friends, she considers Christianity more important than etiquette.

We had a very disturbed Easter, Boofy Gore has identified himself with a gangster called 'Boofy Kidd' in Ian's new horror comic, the passage runs thus: 'Kidd's a pretty boy. His friends call him "Boofy". Probably shacks up with Wint. Some of these homos make the worst killers. Kidd's got white hair though he's only thirty. That's why he works in a hood.' Lord Lambton telephoned Boofy, read the paragraph to him and advised him to see his lawyers; Boofy became demented, pompous, hysterical, telephoned to me, said his life was ruined, said Ian was Eton's most popular author and his son would read it, said his oldest friend had done him a grave injury; I pointed out that though married, Ian and I were separate entities, that I had neither written nor read the book – but that increased his misery and rage and he invoked the help of sister Laura. She telephoned when I was at church on Easter morning and hurled abuse at poor Fionn: 'Your mother may like pansies but other people don't, don't forget Boofy has a million friends and Ian has none.' I became very angry and when Randolph [Churchill] telephoned to ask if I knew anyone near Ashridge College where he would be welcome for the night, instead of slamming down the receiver I advised him to propose himself to the Gores and explained the situation – it was grist to the barren mill, he laughed horribly and twenty minutes later Boofy was on the wires shrieking and gibbering and shouting that Randolph was coming to stay to help and advise and that all Fleet Street would hear of it and he would be sacked from the *Daily Mail*. Since then silence has fallen, I wonder what mischief is brewing?[1]

I believe you should give up paraldehyde for mescalin. Since you bought the Richard Eurich painting and you admit you have no reaction to flowers, fish and natural beauty I have become convinced that mescalin would awaken your visual sense, you would then walk and breathe and sleep instead of talk, drink and write and you would become healthy and benign – but I would much rather you did not change.

We had a very jolly dinner, the Gaitskells,[2] Bonham Carters,[3] Boothby[4] and Randolph; Violet wrote to me and said that 'of the brass in your orchestra Boothby was more muted than Randolph'.

Cyril has divorced Barbara; Cyril had nowhere to spend Easter so I asked E. Rice[5] to entertain him; E. Rice is lonely for Marcella has to be with the dying Lady Curzon, so he was glad to have Cyril, but surprised when Cyril arrived with the divorced Barbara and an extremely savage animal called a ginette [*sic*];[6] but alas on Easter Day Barbara left with Weidenfeld and the ginette bit Cyril, Cyril became very sullen and I had to stop talking to Boofy and go and explain Cyril to his host, who was bewildered.

I hope you had a calm Easter.

Affec.

A.

---

1 The passage in *Diamonds Are Forever* remained and there was no lawsuit.
2 Hugh Gaitskell, (1906–63). Married Dora Creditor in 1937. A Labour MP from

1945 and Chancellor of the Exchequer 1950–1, his most important if frustrating role was as Leader of the Opposition from 1955 until his death, when on the verge of becoming Prime Minister. Bevan's unkind phrase 'desiccated calculating machine' stuck, but he could be a warm and emotional man. Ann showed him the pleasures of upper-class frivolity, and some of his colleagues disapproved.

3 Lady Violet Asquith (1887–1969), daughter of the Prime Minister, married in 1915 Sir Maurice ('Bongie') Bonham Carter. She was made Baroness Asquith in 1964.

4 Robert Boothby (1900–). Unionist MP 1924–58, when he was created a life peer.

5 Edward Rice was a charming and right-wing barrister and romantic adventurer with white hair and brilliant blue eyes. He opposed the war and was moved from his farm in Kent. His wife was Marcella Duggan, whose mother had married the Marquess Curzon and who died in 1958; later he married Nolwen de Janzé.

6 A genet is a small Spanish horse, or donkey. Goodness knows what this animal was.

From Patrick Leigh Fermor

Auribeau sur Siagne, Alpes Maritimes   Monday [August 1956]
Telephone Auribeau 6

Annie Darling,

I escaped two days ago from the top of the French Alps where the film of the capture of General Kneipe[1] is in full swing – the crossing of Mt Ida. I must say, it is terrifically exciting. Dirk Bogarde, who is doing me, is charming, a brilliant actor, and the whole thing is bewilderingly strange. It's very odd seeing truckloads of Germans in steel helmets bawling 'Lili Marlene' blocking those peaceful Alpine passes.

All the same, I was glad to get away. Fleets of cars, technicians, cameramen, props and make-up men, 'continuity girls', megaphones, cohorts of dawdling extras – agoraphobia strikes like a mallet.

Do appear in this part of the world soon. Telephone will get me any morning, and probably afternoon. This is a minute village on top of a green cone in the hinterland between Grasse and Cannes – 10 km. from both, and I spend my day scribbling in M. le Curé's leafy garden overlooking the meanderings of the ice-cold Siagne, most bracing of rivers. What is M. Maugham's telephone number? I might ring and ask when you are expected, and pave the way.[2]

Anyway, Annie darling, do please write at once. It will be heaven seeing you.

Love

Paddy

X X X

1 *Ill Met By Moonlight*, 1957, directed by Michael Powell, about Leigh Fermor's exploits in Crete during the war.

2 Ann had suggested that Leigh Fermor come over to the Villa Mauresque while she was staying there and perhaps invite himself to stay too.

To Evelyn Waugh

16 Victoria Square   27 August [1956]

Dearest Evelyn

I did have a jolly time at the Villa Mauresque, a beautiful slice of human comedy, Alan Searle persuading me that Willie's stutter always became worse before his daughter came to stay, tremendous under currents about 'The Will', and all three parties taking me for walks along those carefully raked gravel terraces and swearing me to secrecy. Alan incites Willie against Liza,[1] Willie loathes Lord John Hope, and poor Liza ill at ease but a cautious, discreet, ambitious girl. I had not realised Willie was so rich but your letter arrived too late for me to participate in the spoils, for I had wrecked my chances by introducing Paddy Leigh Fermor into the household. Paddy had been working on the Crete film with Daphne and Xan [Fielding], but when they departed he grew melancholy alone in an Alpes Maritimes inn, and when I arrived at the Mauresque there were letters, postcards, telegrams awaiting me, so Willie suspected a plot to use his house as a hotel and angle an invitation for a lover. Paddy was invited for lunch and arrived with five cabin trunks, parcels of books and the manuscript of his unfinished work on Greece strapped in a bursting attaché case: despite this inauspicious start luncheon went like a marriage bell, reminiscences of the old school were exchanged[2] and Willie told us that on his arrival at Canterbury he had been placed in the fifth form but stuttered when doing a Latin *construe* and the master and boys laughed and he was demoted to the third form, and many other surprising confidences. So when coffee was finished I was not entirely surprised to hear

Willie invite Paddy to stay and the minions carried in the trunks to a magnificent suite and Willie pointed to a splendid desk and said 'You c-can w-w-work there.' But, alas, that evening Mr and Mrs Frere of Heinemann[3] came to dinner and Paddy who never travels without a bottle of Calvados appeared more exuberant than one small martini could explain. The conversation turned to occupational diseases and Paddy shouted at length on the stuttering that typified the College of Heralds, I intervened with a swift change of topic and thought the situation saved, but Frere (nasty man) made us all angry by saying no author wrote for anything but profit, this put my voice up several octaves as well as Paddy's; worse was to follow [for] while I was endeavouring to include our octogenarian host in the conversation by praising his garden, our octogenarian host remembered that it was the Feast of the Assumption – no newspapers, no gardeners – he cannot bear to see the flowers unwatered and the gravel unraked nor can he believe in assumptions – while he haltingly complained of religious holidays Paddy broke in – 'Darling Annie, when I was with Robin Fedden[4] in the Louvre we saw the vast Mantegna painting of the Assumption and Robin said with that delightful stutter "that is a m-most un-un-w-warrantable assumption"': Alan and I exchanged glances of despair and the evening was wrecked, the Freres left at ten o'clock, Willie saw them to the door, returned to the unlivable living room, walked up to Paddy and said 'G-Goodbye you will have left before I am up in the morning.' He then vanished like a primaeval crab leaving a slime of silence; it was broken by Paddy who cried 'Oh what have I done?' and slammed his whisky glass on the table, it broke to pieces cutting his hand and showering the valuable carpet with blood and splinters. Alan and I were reduced to mad laughter; but in the morning Alan reported that imitations of stuttering drove Willie to frenzy and the car was ordered to deport Paddy and the cabin trunks to St Jean. When I went to tell Paddy the car was at the door, he was sweating with hangover and trying to strap the manuscript into the attaché case, unluckily he had placed it on the unmade bed and the last tug tore the sheet, a noise like Smee in Peter Pan and a huge three-cornered rent. It was a sad end after so promising a beginning.[5]

There is more to tell, the arrival of Mrs Stitch [Lady Diana Cooper][6] and much excitement, but it must wait for your family will be arriving.

I must see 'Stinkers' before it closes – middle of September Wed. to Friday any good?

With love

Ann

1 Liza Maugham (1915–). Daughter of the writer, married to Vincent Paravacini 1936–47 and in 1948 to Lord John Hope, who was later made Lord Glendevon. Alan Searle wrote with gloom a little later that Maugham had taken a great fancy to will-making and made a new one each week. In the event Searle received £50,000, all royalties for his lifetime and the contents of the Villa Mauresque; Liza Maugham the villa itself (from *Maugham* by Ted Morgan).

2 They were both at King's School, Canterbury.

3 Alexander and Pat Frere. She was Edgar Wallace's daughter, he was Maugham's publisher.

4 Robin Fedden (1908–77). Author of books on potry, suicide, Egypt, crusader castles, skiing and the National Trust. He worked for the National Trust 1951–74.

5 Leigh Fermor's account differs only in detail. There was no private supply of Calvados, the cocktails were sufficient to make him exuberant. Stuttering was first introduced by his saying that he had a passion for rash generalisations and that Diana Cooper had told him of three: that all Quakers were colour blind, that progressive members of the Liberal Party in Edwardian times always travelled with aneroid barometers and that all heralds stuttered. Mrs Frere said, 'How do you mean?' and he said, 'Stammered, you know, have an impediment in their speech.' Also there was a happy ending. Lady Diana arrived, championed Leigh Fermor ('I've never heard such nonsense') and, 'I was solemnly asked back to luncheon, a sort of feast of forgiveness. Mr Maugham and I were a bit embarrassed and very polite. I was pleased as I could not bear his thinking I had been so wounding on purpose.'

6 Mrs Stitch, who appears in *Scoop* and the war trilogy, is the most direct portrait to appear in Waugh's novels.

From Evelyn Waugh

Piers Court, Stinchcombe, Glos.   13 September [1956]

Dearest Ann

Alas Wednesday next is a very bad time to visit us. . . .

The mediaeval palace near Exeter was snapped up by a school so I have bought a dull, very private house of sandstone, hidden in a valley behind a demesne wall [three words erased].[1] Had I Lady Pam's money and energy I could make something of it. As it stands it will be a suitable place to end my days and there is a lunatic asylum bang next door which is valuable (a) for me if I get another go of barminess (b) in providing indefatigable gardeners at slave wages (c) husband for Harriet [Waugh]. Odd that you should like her.[2] Mr no I mean Major Muggeridge does too. She must be a modern taste like Henry Moore and Rock and Roll and Science Fiction.

You are lucky to be able to be interested in Suez. I find that anything the newspapers write about immediately drops dead for me. But you don't have to read newspapers I suppose living in the centre of the political web. Miss Macaulay has written a penetrating character study of Lady Eden in a book ostensibly about Trebizond – adultery and agnosticism and sad humour.[3]

Both my legs are all right and I use them a lot because I can't drive a motor car so that with Laura away I have to walk to church.

Trevor-Roper[4] is indeed growing infantile. His howlers in history would earn him the birch at a properly conducted school.

On second thoughts I have scratched out the name of my new house. I don't want Lord Noel-Buxton hanging round. I shall keep it secret and have all letters sent to a bank. Have you found a house yet? *Do* save Ston Easton from demolition.

Your affec. cousin

Evelyn

1 Combe Florey House, erased by Waugh. His son Auberon now lives there with his family.

2 Ann had described her as 'a great beauty with alarmingly intelligent eyes'.

3 *The Towers of Trebizond*, 1956. As a Roman Catholic, Waugh considered Clarissa Eden's marriage to a divorced man constituted adultery. Ann replied, 'I see no resemblance.'

4 Hugh Trevor-Roper (1914–). Brother of Patrick and Regius Professor of Modern History at Oxford 1957–80. Created a peer, 1979. He and Waugh had battled in the correspondence column of the *New Statesman* through December 1953 and January 1954 over Sir Thomas More and the word 'recusant'.

From Evelyn Waugh

[Postcard]   [27 September 1956]

Another point about Miss Macaulay's *Clarissa*. It is written in a very cleverly contrived language of its own – part *Young Visiters*[1] part *Gentlemen Prefer Blondes*[2] – to convey the thoughts of an ill-educated girl. No reviewer has noticed this. Because Miss M.

usually writes a stylish & correct English they assume she has done so this time & say so. Assess.

E

1 By Daisy Ashford, 1919.
2 By Anita Loos, 1925.

To Evelyn Waugh

[?Victoria Square]   Saturday 24 November [1956]

Dearest Evelyn

I have had three different kinds of flu' and far too much excitement, I started a letter ages ago but Ian says I am not to write all the weekend unless it is a diary. I despair of ever seeing you again and I wish I could join you and Paddy at Chagford.[1] I am to be the *Evening Standard* guest television critic next week, and I thought of having a set moved into the Easton Hotel, then you and Paddy could write it alternate nights and I could walk, talk and sleep away from the abominable telephone.

The departure of the Edens for Goldeneye was wrapped in mystery. Some nine days before, Alan Lennox-Boyd[2] telephoned and asked if he might borrow the house and how long would it take to prepare it, he said his visit was a secret so naturally I did not tell anyone, or rather naturally I did not tell anyone because it was such a dull secret; but on Monday last Alan went to see Ian and disclosed that dear old Goldeneye was considered an appropriate place for the Prime Minister to lick his wounds but I was not to be told; I was told but could do nothing to warn Clarissa of its disadvantages until she chose to confide in me which was not until forty-eight hours before departure. She seemed disconcerted to hear that if one wished a bath one had to give two days' notice, and that I did not know if there was a dentist on the island and that all the doctors were black. I warned her that shoes must be worn while bathing, and that the reef abounded with scorpion fish, barracuda and urchins, I forgot to tell her that if [Anthony] is impregnated with spines he should pee on them. [He] is to have the front bedroom, [she] the back bedroom and your old room is to house the two detectives. The plumbing is not good at the moment, after plugs are pulled noises of hunting horns are heard for at least twenty minutes – so they will have little privacy; I think Torquay and a sun-ray lamp would have been more peaceful and patriotic.[3]

Ian went to see Clarissa the night before they left, he found her practising with an underwater mask in her drawing room, no doubt part of the delusion that the Suez canal is flowing through it.[4] I love the dear girl but she does do things in an odd way. Ian was cross that I said anything detrimental about his beloved house and also says it will put up the value of the property, and would I keep my trap shut: alas, I did not take his advice and yesterday's *Daily Express* will mean a permanent breach with Noël Coward.[5]

We all missed you at Chantilly. Mr Gaitskell came to lunch and fell in love with Diana, he held her hand – apparently when he was at Winchester he fell in love with Felicity Tree,[6] so they had much to talk about. He had never seen cocktails with mint in them or seen a magnum of pink champagne, he was very happy. I lied and told him that all the upper class were beautiful and intelligent and he must not allow his vermin to destroy them.

This letter is to invite you and Teresa [Waugh] to dinner on Dec. 17th, 8.15 at the Ritz, for the annual fancy beano, the theme is Nursery Rhymes. *Please* come, it should be about the date of your annual vomit at the Hyde Park Hotel.

With love

Ann

1 The Easton Court Hotel at Chagford in Devon, discovered by Alec Waugh, was used by several writers as a retreat, among them Leigh Fermor and Waugh.

2 Alan Lennox-Boyd (1904–83). Conservative MP 1931–60, Secretary of State for the Colonies 1954–9. Created Viscount Boyd in 1960.

3 Lady Eden wrote from Goldeneye on 1 December to say that all was beautiful, problems about food had been overcome and white telephones installed in the drawing room, but admitted, 'I have slight trouble at night with all those squeaks and whizzings and then that liver-attack of fireflies in the room whenever one opens one's eyes.' Gardeners and policemen swarmed through the grounds.

4 Lady Eden's remark about the course of the Suez Canal had been much quoted.

5 Under the heading 'Fleming's private hideaway where Eden flies tonight' and photographs of Ann and Goldeneye the story quoted Ann as saying, 'We lent the house to Noël Coward seven years ago after he had a colossal flop in New York. He went there for a few months to lick his wounds. It was very successful.'

6 Felicity Tree (b.1895). Married Sir Geoffrey Cory-Wright in 1939 while he was still at Cambridge. 'A red-haired local belle' in Norfolk where Gaitskell was brought up, she regarded him 'as a dreamer, not a do-er'.

To Cecil Beaton

Goldeneye, Jamaica   15 January 1957

Darling Cecil,

Considering how much I love you I am ashamed at being the last to congratulate you on your decoration:[1] the general reaction amongst your friends was that you should have received a knighthood – they were just as excited as the soccer fans are about 'Matthews the dribbler'.[2] The honours list appeared when I was steering an exhausted course between operations, Christmas and an horrific interminable journey here on the *Caronia*, I did not even have time to enquire from Eileen[3] which country you were headed for.

In the meantime so many things have happened, had I been Clarissa and known it was my last honours list[4] I should have been tempted to scatter them like confetti – make Greta [Garbo] a dame and a small Victorian chain for Raimund,[5] as it is I know no details and have this minute written a vague letter to her not knowing how ill Anthony is or what their plans are. Every tree in the garden is engraved with 'God bless Sir Anthony' – the black police employing their leisure hours. Ian is dining with Noël, Binkie B. [Beaumont] and Clemence Dane tonight but I caught too many lobsters this morning and have a chill.

This is a very dull letter and I do not know where to send it, but let us try and catch up with each other as soon as possible.

Congratulations and very best wishes and love for the New Year.

Ann

1 CBE. He was knighted in 1972.
2 Stanley Mathews (1915–). The footballer. He received the CBE in 1957 and was knighted in 1965.
3 Eileen Hose, Beaton's secretary and friend.
4 Sir Anthony Eden had resigned as Prime Minister on 9 January.
5 Raimund von Hofmannsthal (1907–). Son of Hugo von Hofmannsthal the poet and librettist, he accompanied Lady Diana Cooper on a tour with *The Miracle* in 1925, and later worked for *Time*. He married Lady Elizabeth Paget in 1939.

To Evelyn Waugh

Goldeneye, Jamaica   19 January [1957]

Dearest Evelyn

Do not blame those friends of man – crème de menthe and paraldehyde – for 'boat barminess', it is happier to freeze in Somerset than to journey to sunshine – look what happened to poor Freud on the banana boat – you were both fortunate to recover. I fear I never shall, my experiences on the *Caronia* qualify me for sanctuary in your local loony bin – could I weed the garden with Hattie? I wonder how you survived the *Britannic*? We were eleven days at sea, eight in full gale and two in sticky heat. Nanny suffered seasickness, rheumatism and neuralgia, I remained mobile on dramamine and gin, O'Neill and old Caspar were very well and in need of constant entertainment, O'Neill ate *pâté de foie gras* and smoked salmon, old Caspar thrived on greasy cutlets and tuttifrutti ice cream. Old Caspar woke at six every morning and O'Neill wanted to be escorted to the night club every evening. Old Fleming took cabins for us on the sun deck so the day of the worst gale when the engines were at a standstill, we were tilted at the most acute angle and my curtains remained horizontal with the ceiling, I was in a stupor of fear and dope and old Caspar was also horizontal with the ceiling shredding scarves and handkerchiefs in the electric fan. It made a horrible noise and I wanted to cry but decided it was necessary to control myself, so I took old C. downstairs to be nearer the lifeboats and found the promenade deck awash with waves and broken glass and blood; we were told the Marquesa Casa Maury's portholes had been stove in, so walking like flies we went to comfort her and from there to the smoking room for gin; in the smoking room Reggie Winn[1] and Humphrey de Trafford[2] were discussing 'form' for Ascot next summer, they seemed oblivious of danger, and I was delighted when old C. blew fizzy lemonade at the insensitive beasts.

When we arrived at Bermuda the weather improved and Lady Astor[3] adopted the children, she had boxing matches with one and danced with the other, so I was able to indulge melancholia and madness, the madness increased because being on sun deck there is a constant stamping of feet on the ceiling, all sorts of horrible games played above one's head and jokes and laughter. I wonder why you did not go barmy on the *Britannic*? Did they have paper hats and balloons in the worst weather and was everyone old and ugly?

This morning a letter arrived from Clarissa, it was sad and short and contained very very small photographs of Anthony on the Goldeneye beach, Anthony reading in the garden, Anthony sunbathing; owing to my unhinged mind I was immediately in floods of tears.[4]

Noël Coward appeared last night with a party of persons called 'Perry', 'Terry', 'Binkie' and 'Coalie'[5]: he seems most annoyed he was not received by the Edens, he sent them a basket of caviar, cutlets, Earl Grey tea and Romary biscuits, and apparently gossiped with the detectives. I tried to appear disinterested but drank in everything he said – very low to gossip with detectives, and I should have told him so. Nothing he said is repeatable, it was distressingly intimate and conceivably true.

I enjoyed New Year's Eve, but the following luncheon was not so happy, you would not talk – very tiresome of you as you are much funnier than John or James [Pope-Hennessy?]. John was pulverized by Diana and not at his best, but recovered when you and Diana left and he could relax and pull James's hair.

I hope you have more hot water and the comforts and beauty of Combe Florey improve.

Love

Ann.

1 Reginald Winn (1899–   ). Brother of Anthony.

2 Humphrey de Trafford (1891–1971). Brother of Raymond, landowner in the West Indies.

3 Nancy Langhorne (1879–1964). An American, she married in 1906 Viscount Astor. Unionist MP 1919–45, and the first woman to sit in the House of Commons.

4 Ann wrote to Lady Eden commiserating on her husband's continued ill health, thanking her for the fresh crop of detective stories they had left behind.

5 John Perry, Terence Rattigan, 'Binkie' Beaumont, and Cole Lesley. Terence Rattigan's *Separate Tables* had been a success in London in 1954 and in New York in 1956. Knighted 1971.

From Evelyn Waugh

Combe Florey House   23 February 1957

Dearest Ann

Welcome home. I was on the point of writing to you in Jamaica when your letter arrived. When we last met I was very sad at the prospect of being kept in England all February by the opening of my season of litigation, but the weather has been warm so my old joints have not suffered, and the campaign in the Law Court has opened with highly successful skirmish.[1] I don't suppose you saw the newspaper reports. Anyway they omitted some jolly features. First, I told the Dursley parish priest that he would get part of the damages and that good man's prayers were dramatically answered. From the moment Shawcross[2] took the case against me he was afflicted by a series of disasters in his private affairs which culminated in a well-nigh fatal accident to his mother-in-law at the very moment when he had me under cross-examination & was making me feel rather an ass. Poor Miss Spain lied sturdily on oath. The judge was a buffoon who thought he was a character out of Gilbert & Sullivan. He summed up inviting the jury to dismiss both cases – mine & Miss Spain's counter-claim. That would have left me with costs to pay. At any moment in the last six months I would have settled for £500. At the end of the second day I would gladly have taken a fiver. During the jury's long deliberation my lawyer apologised for having let me into the business & it was hinted that costs would be about £5000. I contemplated changing my name to Quennell or Forbes and flying to Australia. But they were a splendid jury – middle-aged, prosperous-looking, deeply prejudiced against Lord Beaverbrook and not the least amused by the judge's facetiousness. They dismissed from their noble minds any consideration of Miss Spain's libel of me, or mine of her, and decided to fine Lord Beaverbrook for his impertinence to the Royal Family. So they gave me £2000. Now I have a second and much graver case against the *Express* which should ensure that the evening of my life is not spent in utter penury. Miss Spain behaved in a gentlemanly way & congratulated me and I sent her a bottle of pop.

I have had a mass of 'fan' letters. The simple fact is that all four million readers of the *Express* detest the paper, are ashamed of reading it, & feel that any damages they can impose on it slightly exonerates themselves.

I shall be in London soon & will call on you.

Love

Evelyn

1 The libel case against Nancy Spain and the *Daily Express*. Waugh was claiming that he was represented as 'an unsuccessful writer who had made a false and malicious attack on Miss Spain for reasons of personal spite against her; that he was a writer whose name carried insignificant weight with the general public, the film rights and options of whose books were not worthy of purchase, and who was not worthy of consideration for the writing of articles.'

2 Hartley Shawcross (1902–   ). KC since 1939, Labour MP 1945–58, Attorney General 1945–51. Created life peer in 1959.

To Evelyn Waugh

16 Victoria Square   15 March [1957]

Dearest Evelyn

Two weekends at Oxford have reduced letter-writing time to a minimum, but now Ian has returned [from Goldeneye] and domesticity and peaceful weekends [resume].

You will be rewarded in the next world for your virtue[1] and next time we meet your face will be shining with goodness and perhaps your hearing will have returned – a miracle brought about by sacrifice.

This morning the Ritz and marble halls were filled with interior decorators and painters and the only customers were Diana and Randolph; Randolph was surrounded by marble tables piled high with innumerable copies of *What I said about the Press*.[2] Some were being packed into parcels for Diana to sell at Chantilly and others put in baskets for me to sell at Victoria Square: Diana thought the only hope was to say it was a banned book, so inspired by this I covered my quota with brown paper jackets and wrote 'Castle Flagellant' for a title, with crossed birches drawn beneath. At this moment we were interrupted by a drunken American woman called 'Jo' Forrestal, widow of the American politician who defenestrated himself because of unkind columnists – she reeled up to our marble tables and said to me 'You are Patsy Ward[3] aren't you? Tell me about the horse racing world.' I was extremely cross and know nothing about the horse racing world but took advantage of her unfortunate condition to sell her a copy of *What I said about the Press* for a pound and did not give her any change. Then Lord Stanley and Joan Aly Khan[4] appeared and Mrs Forrestal congratulated Lord Stanley on having married such a beautiful woman, while this situation was being untangled Violet Trefusis[5] materialised and gave Diana grizzly bear hugs, in the confusion I managed to sell them all copies of *What I said about the Press* and while Randolph was autographing them Diana and I escaped to the 'Etoile' and enjoyed a peaceful lunch with Lucian Freud and Tony Lambton.[6]

Fionn gave her party in a draughty cellar, six crazy paving stones for a dance floor and seating accommodation, wooden alcoves lit by green and orange lamps – a gramophone played 'Rock and Roll'. It was difficult to place old people and it was inevitable that I shared my loose box with Maurice Bowra, David Cecil and Mrs 'Pussy' Deakin, they all behaved very well, David did the Charleston with me and Maurice kept shouting that the music was on purpose to annoy him, oblivious of the happy young couples dancing. Miss Waugh, Miss O'Neill and Sweet Alice partnered by Sykeses, Lytteltons, Rothschilds, Pryce Joneses and other most beautiful and entertaining young men. I fear Sweet Alice[7] took the biscuit and was more alluring than our daughters though obviously not nearly so reliable.

The cost of these revelries was £83 – enormous, as the champagne was hot and sweet and I brought the smoked salmon from London; alas, Fionn had not discovered that the cellar was in liquidation, and so there is no one to argue with.

Now I must entertain Ian. The weather is lovely here – why not come to Folkestone?

Love,

A

P.S. I presume you watched Randolph on the television last Monday? He was interviewed by Woodrow Wyatt[8] on the *Panorama* programme and managed to 'plug' all his books. Miss Judy was in the studio and has a fine account of his mastery of Woodrow and white-faced officials trembling 'stop him, stop him, stop the plugging', but alas, Woodrow made matters worse by asking why he had brought a dispatch case to the studio, this was in a vain endeavour to arrest the flow of talk about *What I said about the Press*. It was a fatal slip, for like an accomplished conjuror Randolph snapped open the case and produced the manuscript of *Lord Derby*[9] and was able to once more proclaim 'these books will be published by Country Bumpkins, East Bergholt, Suffolk – now have you all got the address, once more – Country Bumpkins, East Bergholt, Suffolk'; he was *very very* drunk and at the end of his act was delighted to find that the next turn was a parade of men's fashions and when Miss Judy attempted to take him from the studio he embarrassed everyone by shouting that he must watch the Buggas march past.

1 Ronald Knox was dying and Waugh accompanied him mournfully along the south coast to a series of hotels.

2 His new book. It cost one shilling.

3 Patricia Ward, sister of the Earl of Dudley.

4 Joan Yard-Buller (1908–), married to Loel Guinness 1927–36 and to Aly Khan 1936–49. She is the mother of the present Aga Khan.

5 Violet Keppel (1894–1972). Vita Sackville-West's lover 1918–21. Writer in English and French, restless socialite based in Paris and Florence. In 1946 James Lees-Milne had found her 'like a basilisk. Upright in carriage and very ugly.' *Caves of Ice*, 1983.

6 Viscount Lambton (1922–). Conservative MP 1951–73. Disclaimed title of Earl of Durham, in 1970. Published a collection of stories, *Snow*, 1983.

7 Alice Jolliffe (1937–), married to John Chancellor 1959–69 and to Richard Windsor-Clive in 1969.

8 Woodrow Wyatt (1918–). Labour MP 1945–55, 1959–70; journalist, started *Panorama* in 1955. In *Confessions of an Optimist*, 1985, he records, 'He [Ian] was sardonic and often morose, with a smile like a swift flash of sun through a storm-cloud. He had the appearance of an underfed stray cat . . . [Annie] could be sharp but she was a splendid woman, funny to and about her friends and enemies, but a warm, true friend. She liked to be at the centre of events.'

9 *Lord Derby, King of Lancashire*, 1960.

From Ian Fleming, who had gone to Tangier to write.

Tangier   Saturday [Easter 1957]

My precious,

Your letters have been lovely and have sustained me here. I simply couldn't write before because my brains have been boiling over with writing about five thousand words a day – a terrific job.[1]

But it has been very exciting and the story is sensational – at least I think so. Please don't say a word about it or we may be stopped publishing.

This is a pretty dreadful place and the weather has been ghastly, freezing cold and constant wind. The paint is peeling off the town and the streets are running with spit and pee and worse. The Arabs are filthy people and hate all Europeans. My life has revolved round a place called Dean's Bar, a sort of mixture between Wiltons and the porter's lodge at Whites. There's nothing but pansies and I have been fresh meat for them. David [Herbert][2] is a sort of Queen Mum. He calls himself Lord Herbert and has that in the telephone book. Says he can't get them to change it as they don't understand 'honourable'. He's been very sweet to me but I'm fed up with buggers. They all do absolutely nothing all day long but complain about each other and arrange flowers, which I must say are quite wonderful here. I even went so far as to buy three dozen roses for myself! Jimmy Smith has arrived with Diana Campbell-Gray[3] and they are staying with David and getting thoroughly depressed by the weather and the stagnation. Francis Bacon is due next week to live with his pansy pianist friend who plays at a bogus Russian restaurant. Otherwise there is Ali [Forbes] who lives secretively with his girl and is rarely seen. He has been a solace to me and we have had meals and walks. He knows he can't write and asks me how to. Rather pathetic. He is very frank about his disabilities but desperately lazy and the only hope for him is to marry a rich woman. He knows he's unemployable. He's now been recalled to London for 'consultations' and fears the worst. There's a new editor and Eade has resigned. He's going next Tuesday. He's really got a sort of death wish about his job. The girl is very beautiful – a sort of softer Barbara [Skelton] and calls him 'Papa'. Ali likes this plus incest.[4] They have a very nice modern flat looking over the harbour and I was very privileged to be invited there for drinks. He's an endearing but hopeless character. I suggested he should put an advertisement in *The Times*: 'Experienced nest-fowler offers services. Can make jokes and drive car into walls.'

My Zulu [Gavin Young] is an exceedingly nice man and a great boon. The town is madly intrigued by us and we have laid a false trail about a coelacanth. We even thought of carrying around a mysterious tin canister into which he would drop worms from time to time. Even my secretary, a good girl with a drunken nose, is besieged with enquiries about us. We go for immense walks along the wet windy beaches and I collect shells while he stamps on the Portuguese men of war that litter the beaches. They make a loud bang. Some nice shells including small Venus Ears . . . [remainder lost]

1 'The Diamond Smugglers', which appeared in *The Sunday Times* in the autumn.
2 David Herbert (1908–). Younger son of the Earl of Pembroke, who has lived in Tangier for many years. Fleming had got him the job in the war, liaising with spies among the French fishing fleet.
3 Diana Cavendish (1909–). Married 1935–7 to Robert Boothby MP, 1942–6 to Ian Campbell-Gray, 1971–83 to Viscount Gage. Champion racing demon player.
4 Unincestuous Alastair Forbes explains that he was asking Fleming for clues about the golden formula for making money rather than for lessons in style and comments, 'As the possessor of no less than seven pretty sisters, for none of whom I felt the slightest carnal desire, my references to incest were merely the lighthearted pendant to my explanations of the Arabic word *Baba*, meaning Father. My dusky Barbary love had adopted this appellation to explain my prematurely white hair, a phenomenon unknown in North Africa.'

To Evelyn Waugh

16 Victoria Square   4 May [1957]

My dear Evelyn
    One of those brave soldiers so dear to your heart has been drinking with us, his name is Bernard Fergusson[1] and he wears a monocle: despite very distressing jokes he was interesting – is he a White's Bar friend of yours? He has invited me to hear military bands play at Dover Castle.
    I hope you will be sad to hear that Alastair Forbes has been sacked by the *Sunday Dispatch*; the new Editor of the *Sunday D.* thought him the only asset the paper possessed and he was invited home with a view to promotion and greater glory, but alas, poor Ali delayed his return giving Ramadan as excuse for no aeroplanes from Tangier, but the new Editor was sufficiently sophisticated to know that eastern religious festivals do not interfere with international air travel, and when this lapse was followed by impudent letters he was briefly dismissed without a cheque enclosed: Randolph was informed and amassed hired mercenary country bumpkins from White's Club to march with pitchforks upon

Warwick House and set it on fire, he also alerted Michael Foot[2] and Ian Gilmour[3] to attack poor Esmond, and everyone was very happy; but I was sorry for poor Esmond and telephoned to warn him, and he was very kind and sent Ali £7000 which will keep him in Sulka shirts for several weeks.[4] Then Ali, Randolph, Judy and Mark Bonham Carter came to lunch and we drank Ali's health and Randolph gave him an 18th-century silver snuff box, and Randolph was very noisy because he had been drinking at White's and then going to Fortnum and Mason's to buy charcuterie to nourish his ghosts,[5] his ghosts love liver sausage and are always hungry.

I had a lovely five days' holiday with Diana [Cooper], she read me some chapters of her book,[6] all traces of Jenny Clifford are removed, and it reads like a good novel, one wants more and more; the language is original, the taste is impeccable; but she lives in mortal fear of what you and Mrs Katharine Asquith[7] will think of it.

Hugo's book[8] was recommended by the Book Society a few hours before Mr Rubinstein recommended Collins not to publish it – very sad and expensive for everyone.

I lunched with Francis Bacon to meet Colin Wilson (author of *The Outsider*),[9] he is very pretty, quite unlike his photographs, and has clearly never been angry in his life, he is a cross between Hans Andersen's little match girl, Sir Galahad and Little Lord Fauntleroy: after lunch we went to millionairess Anne Dunn's painting exhibition, and I introduced Colin Wilson to Clive Bell who congratulated him on writing *Anglo-Saxon Attitudes*,[10] both parties were very civil about the misunderstanding.

When will you come to London again?

Love,

Ann

PS. K. Clark has telephoned to the Rices to say he would love to take Lady Curzon sightseeing on Saturday afternoons, is he a saint, a snob – or both?

---

1 Bernard Fergusson (1911–80). Distinguished soldier and writer. Colonel of the Black Watch, Governor General of New Zealand 1962–7. Created Lord Ballantrae 1972.

2 Then Editor of *Tribune*.

3 Then Editor of the *Spectator*.

4 Alastair Forbes characteristically comments: 'Like many of Ann's letters to Evelyn Waugh, whom she was often almost desperate to keep amused, this letter fits the facts hardly at all. Having just returned from 2½ months in the US, I was

always planning on a long stay in Europe and had therefore booked passage for myself and my car to Marseilles. There I purchased a copy of the *Sunday Dispatch* which, though headlining me next to an unprepossessing passport photograph as "Britain's most pungent political commentator", had, in order to accommodate these doubtful embellishments, not only removed my never normally censored column from the space where readers for some dozen years had been accustomed to look for it, but also cut out the most relevant part of its comments on the important Sandys Defence White Paper of that year. I immediately cabled my displeasure in forthright terms to the new Editor, a Mr Terry, who, after sacking me unseen by return, himself, on the demise shortly thereafter of the *Dispatch*, left Fleet Street for ever for more useful and more gainful employment with the Ford Motor Company.

'Ann had nothing whatsoever to do with the compensation, rather larger than the sum she mentions, earlier offered to me by the Directors of Associated Newspapers, though the ever-kind "Boofy" Arran, spurred on by her sister Laura, definitely did.'

5 Waugh often referred to 'Churchill's ghosts' and threw doubt on the extent to which he actually wrote his own books.

6 *The Rainbow Comes and Goes*, the first of three volumes of autobiography. Jenny Clifford had worked on an earlier version.

7 Katharine Asquith (1885–1977). Married in 1907 Raymond Asquith, who was killed in 1916. Waugh too was apprehensive as to what she would think of his books.

8 *The Tide is Right* was libellous and never appeared.

9 Colin Wilson (1931–). Prolific writer. Won enormous acclaim for his first book, *The Outsider*, 1956, and was at the centre of that nebulous group described as Angry Young Men.

10 Clive Bell (1881–1964). Art Critic. Married Vanessa Stephen in 1907. *Anglo-Saxon Attitudes* by Angus Wilson had been published the year before.

From Somerset Maugham

Grand Hotel de l'Europe, Badgastein   3 June [1957]

My precious Annie

Who is this extraordinary man whom you have married?

When I arrived at Soefburg on the way to Munich, to stay the night at the hotel, I found the whole place in an uproar. They had had a telephone message so they believed from the celebrated Mr Ian Fleming and flags had been put up all along the streets and the municipality had arranged to give him a public reception.

In my small way I decided to stand him a drink on arrival and a simple dinner to follow. The chef burst into tears when he learned that caviar could not be sent from Russia in time. The manager put on tails, a stiff shirt and a white tie. The press and the photographers crammed the entrance of the hotel and traffic in the street was such that the police had to [hurry?] along to deal with it.

WE WAITED

WE WAITED

WE WAITED.

At midnight the mayor of the city and the general in command of the troops with tears streaming down their faces broke the news to the multitude that Mr Ian Fleming could not be coming and they had better all go to bed. It was a sad sight. I can't tell you how many disconsolate virgins asked me where Mr Fleming was and you can imagine how humbling it was for me to have to say

I DONT KNOW.

Willie

To Evelyn Waugh

16 Victoria Square   14 June [1957]

Dearest Evelyn

I hope you found the peacocks less insubordinate when you returned from Monte Carlo – that was a very enjoyable letter and so was the account of Winston eating.[1] How kind of you to give Lord Sheffield publicity; the poem alleviated his terrible unhappiness for at least two weeks, he preferred my version to his and was very pleased when I allowed him to copy it.[2]

It was a disappointment that you did not lunch with Lady Pamela the day you were expected, it's always a treat to see you and I anticipated a clash with the guest of honour – Mr Mike Todd[3] – director of *Round the World in Eighty Days*;[4] at one moment he turned to his hostess and said 'I'd like to bite your tongue out.' I encouraged him and said we would all be grateful but alas, he lost his nerve. Lady Pamela and Mr Mike Todd are organising a film première of *Round the World in Eighty Days* in aid of the Press Benevolent Fund. The tickets are being sold at £100 each and every person will get a carpet bag containing a copy of the *Daily Telegraph*; afterwards Mr Todd has hired the Festival Gardens where he and Lady Pamela will give a party and the guests will be transferred from the Astoria cinema to the gardens in ships laden with caviar and champagne; it would be quicker by road as the Astoria is a long way from the river. My invitation was couched in particularly insulting terms – Lady P. telephoned and said that obviously £100 was beyond my means but she was allowed to invite one or two friends to the party, apparently it is only two for my orders were to take Malcolm Bullock[5] to the gardens at midnight and wait for the ships to arrive. When I asked how we should occupy our time she said there was a dance band and we would be given fish and chips wrapped in copies of the *Telegraph*. I pointed out that Malcolm on crutches was not my favourite partner and fish and chips at midnight gave me indigestion, she said I was very ungrateful and should not sneer at this unique invitation – will you come with me?

Mr 'Rab' Butler[6] came to lunch and told us that at the last cabinet meeting the Prime Minister put boxes of tranquillisers in front of each member of the cabinet, it was taken as a jolly joke and no one partook of them, but David Ormsby-Gore[7] slipped his into his pocket.

I should be writing to Hugo, he was in London staying with us for a week and then despite Ian's protests came to St Margaret's for the weekend. It was a most unhappy occasion for in London I had not had time to see his lantern slides of African ladies having their clitorises removed with red hot scissors, and I forgot to suggest this treat during the weekend, his sensitive swollen ego did not permit him to suggest it a second time and I have had pages of abuse from Scotland. He says that some of the slides are so pretty they would have been a kind of present to me, it's a difficult letter to answer because I have to gently explain that I hate lantern slides and if one is mated to someone who takes in *Life*, *Time*, *Tide*, *Fortune*, *Match* and *Holiday* one has had a surfeit of wonderful photographs of African tribes doing all kinds of things.

Aunt Cynthia is going about in a laurel wreath woven for her by Ernest Thesiger.[8]

Let me know when you will be in London.

I hope Laura's cows have arrived.

Love

A

1 'We sometimes see Sir Winston (at a respectful distance) gorging vast quantities of rich food. His face is elephant's grey and quite expressionless. His moll sits by him coaxing him and he sometimes turns a pink little eye towards her without moving his head.'

2 Waugh had sent an annotated copy of his poem to Ann:

'Trusty as steel,[1] more valuable than plate,[2]
Aspiring Sheffield knocked at heaven's gate.
Peter[3] (who reads *The Times*) pronounced his doom
Simply remarking: "Stanley, I presume."[4]
(1) Sheffield was famous for steel and for silver. (2) Plated copper. (3) The Peter referred to is the first pope who is popularly supposed to hold the keys of heaven. (4) An American journalist named Stanley pursued an English missionary into Central Africa and greeted him with the words "Livingstone, I presume."'
This was to mark Lord Stanley, whose family had an older Irish barony, taking the name Baron Sheffield and Stanley of Alderley.

3 Mike Todd (1907–58). Producer. Had been married to Elizabeth Taylor, the film star, since February 1957.

4 The biggest film of its time with fifty stars and 68,894 extras wearing 74,685 costumes on the largest screen yet invented.

5 Sir Malcolm Bullock (1890–1966). Sociable Conservative MP 1923–53. Created baronet 1954.

6 R. A. Butler (1902–82). Conservative MP 1929–65, he was then Home Secretary, Lord Privy Seal and Leader of the House of Commons. Master of Trinity College, Cambridge, from 1965. Created a life peer in 1965.

7 David Ormsby-Gore (1918–85). Conservative MP 1950–61, at this time Minister of State for Foreign Affairs. British Ambassador in Washington 1961–65. Succeeded as Lord Harlech in 1964.

8 Ernest Thesiger (1879–1961). Actor of 'outrageous' parts who also scored a success as Captain Hook. 'Ernest once complained that Somerset Maugham never sent him anything: "B-but, I am always writing p-parts for you, Ernest," said Maugham. "The trouble is that somebody called Gladys Cooper *will* insist on p-playing them." (*Secrets of a Woman's Heart* by Hilary Spurling, 1984.) Ann's aunt, Lady Cynthia Asquith, had appeared on a quiz show in America and successfully answered questions about Jane Austen.

To Evelyn Waugh

16 Victoria Square   5 July [1957]

Dearest Evelyn
    You made a mistake in missing Lady Pamela Berry and Mr Mike Todd's party at the Festival Gardens to aid the Newspaper Benevolent Fund and publicise the film of *Round the World in Eighty Days*. Those of us who wished the maximum pleasure embarked at midnight from Charing Cross pier in a flotilla of river steamers, rain was falling and the cabins and bars were filled with Jewish film producers, publishers and interior decorators. On each deck was a brass band playing 'Rule Britannia' and other appropriate tunes and the remaining available space was occupied by us foolish goys,

singing to keep up our spirits while our satins and muslins and dinner jackets became wet and sodden and our teeth began to chatter; it was half an hour before the procession started for Battersea, it was then raining mercilessly and from each bridge Todd's publicity men threw pamphlets at us, they stuck to our faces and clothes. When we arrived there was a queue from the bank to the entrance of the gardens, so, escorted by Paddy Leigh Fermor, Vivien Leigh and myself made a dash for the wall of the pleasure gardens where with the aid of George Dix[1] and other helping hands we climbed five feet up and scrambled twenty feet down: Vivien climbs like a small exquisite cat, my descent was less graceful, but at least we had achieved our object, and were issued with macs and umbrellas and could survey merry-go-rounds, hamburger stalls and dance floors. Apart from the discomfort of waterproof over wet satin it was a comical scene – Stephen Spender looked handsome in a black sou'wester, the Warden of All Souls [John Sparrow] was in transparent white plastic, John Betjeman and Elizabeth Cavendish wore identical pale transparent blue, and some ladies managed to remain trim beneath huge umbrellas. Ed. [Stanley] and Paddy wished to experience the centrifugal force of the rotor, but Ed. tried to climb the walls when the machine was at its fastest and left half his nose on the side, he fell bleeding to the floor and the centrifugal force whipped the blood in circles and spattered all the nice macintoshes; I had a good view of this from the side. Paddy was disappointed in the free issue of cigarettes for they were not in cartons but loose on trays and the weather had turned them to nicotine puddings. The food was disappointing, each counter represented a different country but at two in the morning few people want Indian curry or Chinese bamboo shoots, there was nothing so simple as eggs, bacon and beer.

As I did not attend the performance I missed transportation by bus from cinema to river but Patrick Kinross[2] reports that many of the guests had not been on buses before and descended the stairs backwards.

Malcolm Muggeridge is deeply moved by *Pinfold*, apparently he had never perceived the underlying tragedy of your previous books, he had intended to be very acid at the Foyle's lunch but [he] has softened and he has a fellow feeling for poor Pinfold.

On the 18th there is a *Spectator* cocktail party – will you attend it?

I look forward very much to seeing you and reading *Pinfold*.
With love

Ann

PS. Not a good letter – but the house is full of young people playing skiffle music.

1 George Dix, the New York art dealer. 'George a sweet and guileless American, full of enthusiasm for the social life, for which one does not dislike him.' James Lees-Milne in *Caves of Ice*, 1983.
2 Lord Kinross (1904–76). Writer and journalist, sometimes as Patrick Balfour. He had succeeded in 1939.

To Evelyn Waugh

16 Victoria Square   3 August [1957]

Dearest Evelyn

Alas, I stuck an old safety pin into a small spot and a seven-headed Hydra of a carbuncle grew upon my right cheek, it rose like a soufflé, I could not open my mouth – it was very frightening and painful, on the seventh day the doctor pulled it out with forceps and fear became panic, for it has left a large hole.[1] I do not know whether to put my tongue out of my mouth or through my face, and will have to spend the rest of my life with Bacon and Freud who consider that pox, boils, burns and blemishes add beauty and excitement to the human phiz.

It was under these circumstances that I read *Pinfold*; the laughter was torture, the tears came easily, it was over all too soon; the Little Margaret seduction scene and the advice from her blimpish papa brought the Hydra to a head, my face cracked with delight and I read it several times. Thankyou indeed for my elegant copy which is respectfully in my bookshelf for I thought it better to cover Ian's cheap one with penicillin ointment.

I was very disappointed in Muggeridge, he was unable to make an honest speech, I fear *Pinfold* was too near some of his knuckles, for he understood the book but did not have the courage or control to stop the toads jumping out of his mouth.[2] I hope it will sell very well but I doubt if the Americans will understand it – too subtle for them. My respect for Mrs Pinfold is increased and my only complaint is that, like caviar, there is not enough of it.

My only outing has been to the Crystal Palace for the picnic, it was the day before the doctor said the poison was located and before it became too painful to move; we had the misfortune to meet a *Daily Mirror* reporter who recognised Edward Boyle[3] by his black coat, pinstripe trousers and enormous bulk; they wrote a malicious paragraph accusing him and Tom Driberg[4] of lighting bonfires in marble vases. The paragraph put Driberg in a terrible flap, he thought it would spoil his career and he made Paddy Leigh Fermor write to the *Mirror* and confess that he was responsible. Surely burning picnic litter is the least of Driberg's crimes?

Fionn has got a second, she was very cross at not being viva'd for a first: she has a socialist German Jewess girl-friend[5] staying with us who talks constantly about the 'Marxist approach' and other things I cannot understand, all the socialist German Jewess's friends have got firsts, so it cannot be a good thing and you must pray that Teresa gets a third or fourth – more hope of sanity and success afterwards.

Your peppery postcard was undeserved for this is the first letter I have written, and I am still very toxic and tired. When I am better I will ask you to explain the conversation I enjoyed at the Foyle lunch with Father D'Arcy – it was about Original Sin. I enjoyed the Foyle lunch and I thought your speech very good – Andrew [Devonshire] full of charm and Malcolm a mistake.

With love and thankyou,

A

1 Waugh replied, 'I am distressed to hear of your carbuncle. Those who have never suffered from such a thing speak of it facetiously. I had one once during the war in Italy, on the back of the neck, and I know it to be excruciating. The most painful experience of my life and very weakening. You must recuperate slowly. . .'

2 Waugh replied, 'I did not attend to Muggeridge's speech at Miss Foyle's, being occupied with composing my thoughts for my own few words. His words were too many and what I heard indecent and irrelevant – all about Negresses practising contraception.' Malcolm Muggeridge comments, 'I found *The Ordeal of Gilbert Pinfold* a very moving and honest book and said as much in my speech. As E.W. took out his hearing aid – a trumpet – ostentatiously as soon as I began to speak, he cannot have heard anything I said . . . A total invention I assure you.'

3 Edward Boyle (1923–81). Conservative MP 1950–70, at that time Parliamentary Secretary in the Ministry of Education, later the Minister. Vice-Chancellor Leeds University, Pro-Chancellor of Sussex University 1965–70. Created a life peer in 1970.

4 Tom Driberg (1905–76). Journalist, politician and homosexual. A school friend of Waugh's at Lancing, a gossip columnist for the *Daily Express*, Labour MP and, it has been suggested, double agent. Created Lord Bradwell 1975.

5 Freda Strauss married Leslie Stone and is now a member of the SDP.

To Evelyn Waugh

16 Victoria Square   26 September [1957]

Dearest Evelyn

Today Randolph came to lunch, he was pale grey, quite silent, bright pink eyes streaming tears, it was a hangover not a tragedy; the only other person present was sister Laura, she also has weak eyes, and placed opposite to him her tears also began to flow and finally we were all three weeping, he asked her to marry him once or twice, it was a very dismal occasion.

It is many weeks since I intended to write and thank you for a most happy visit to Combe Florey. I was shy at being an only guest in the centre of a united clever family, and I deeply regret the long afternoon sleep and missing the clearance of Devil Island, but I enjoyed myself very much and should like to be invited again.

The delay in thanking you was because of long difficult letters to my daughter – like those that Doctor Summerskill[1] is publishing in the *Daily Mail* to her daughter – also, I have been in France.

How noble of you not to relate the Chatsworth chamber pot story,[2] haply Nancy told me in Paris.

The only social event of my week with Mr Maugham was a luncheon party for Sir Winston and Lady Churchill, the other guests were Lady Pamela Berry and her mate. Mr Maugham delights in being a year older than Sir Winston, and triumphantly exhibits his nimble movements, good eyesight and hearing in comparison to poor Sir Winston's old rogue elephant's swaying and total lack of hearing.

You wrote a wonderful description to me in the spring, when you watched 'Rhinestone Wendy'[3] attending to his feeding, he seemed to me like a remote benevolent baby existing in a happy limbo. I think he was longing for Lady Churchill's return to England and his removal to Wendy's villa, he regarded my scarred face and Lady Pamela's orange whiskers as a brief moment of purgatory, he showed signs of life when I told him that independent television had invited a prostitute to speak on the Wolfenden Report, but my back was turned and I could not see his expression when Lady Pamela shrieked 'I too Sir Winston live in the past and think only of my father.'

Lady Eden comes to dinner on Monday night, she came near to

buying a house a mile further up the Combe Florey valley, but decided the Somerset lanes were depressing and did not care for hillsides of stunted heather. Lady E. is staying with Lady B. Parsons and we both have to give dinners, it is a difficult social problem, Beaton and Ashton are in America so who can we invite? I have collected Maurice Bowra and we shall watch Ian being interviewed by Richard Dimbleby on television *Panorama* at 8.30, so conversation will be solved without reference to Suez, for I have hired a machine for the occasion and it is to be installed in the dining-room.

I went to the Second Empire exhibition in Paris and by force prevented James Pope-Hennessy sending Clarissa a postcard of 'La Parure de la Canal de Suez' – a collection of necklaces, brooches and bracelets presented to the Empress Eugènie.

Let me know when you will be coming to London.

The Tom Kitten has been to Ireland and returned in health and spirits, it's a very agreeable creature.

With love to you and Laura

Ann

PS. Alack, I missed your answer to horrible Priestley.[4]

1 Edith Summerskill (1901–). Labour MP 1938–61, published *Letters to My Daughter*, 1957. Created a peeress 1961.

2 Waugh had discovered an unemptied chamber pot in his room.

3 Wendy Reeves was married to the literary agent Emery Reeves who had worked for Sir Anthony Eden and Sir Winston Churchill. They had a house at Roquebrune which had belonged to Chanel, and an extensive collection of pictures and furniture.

4 J. B. Priestley had reviewed *The Ordeal of Gilbert Pinfold* in the *New Statesman* of 31 August and, under the heading 'What Was Wrong with Pinfold?', argued that Waugh had been driven insane by his attempt to pass himself off as a country gentleman. Waugh sent Ann a copy of his reply in the *Spectator* of 13 September: 'Anything wrong with Priestley?'

To Evelyn Waugh

16 Victoria Square   9 November [1958]

Dearest Evelyn

This afternoon Manchester television rang me up, and invited me to take part in a programme called *Youth wants to know*; it was suggested that I should fly to Manchester for the day and that young men and boys should ask me what qualities a woman hoped to find in a husband. I was told that Mrs Antonia Pakenham Fraser[1] and another young married [?] would complete the panel, but they wanted someone older and more experienced. I suggested I was not the right person and admitted I had been married three times, this they appeared to know and was the reason for the invitation, they said I knew my own mind. I did not involve myself in an argument, though I should have thought that my life proved that on this important topic it was clear I did not know my own mind. I suggested they should invite Lady Pamela Berry and Mrs Aidan Crawley, so I hope to watch the Manchester Teddy boys making Aunt Sallys of them.

The Jebbs[2] are very displeased because the doors of the British Embassy have been defiled by nocturnal prowlers who wrote 'Voltaire doesn't love Nancy' on one side and 'Nancy Go Home' on the other.[3] I think it must have been Lord Sheffield, it is suspected that it was a member of the Travellers' Club.

The Fleming brothers are having a tough time with their mother,[4] she inclines to dress like Lady Ottoline Morrell or the Casati, so every morning Peter, Ian and Richard[5] go to her hotel and force her into hospital matron clothes. On Friday the poor old thing wished to wear a yellow satin picture hat with grey pearl hatpins the size of tennis balls – they had her out of that in a trice. The flu' has prevented me attending the court but Miss Montagu who spends much time in the public gallery assures me that public opinion is against Marchioness Bapsy, I fear this will not help, for it appears that it is worse to 'harbour' than to co-habit. I had always assumed that once past the possibility of sex one was free to harbour whom one wished.

I wish you had stung Priestley into a further reply. I dislike him very much.

With love to you and Laura.

Ann

---

1 Antonia Pakenham (1932–   ). Writer. Daughter of Lord Pakenham, who succeeded as the Earl of Longford in 1961, she was married to Hugh Fraser, the Conservative MP, 1956–77 and in 1980 married Harold Pinter, the playwright.

2 Cynthia Noble married in 1929 Gladwyn Jebb (1900–   ) who made a great success as Permanent Representative of the UK to the UN 1950–4 and was Ambassador to France 1954–60. Created Lord Gladwyn 1960.

3 Nancy Mitford's *Voltaire in Love* came out that year.

4 In 1951 Evelyn Fleming, then in her sixties, had been engaged to the Marquess of Winchester, who was approaching ninety. He married Bapsy Pavry, daughter of a Parsee high priest, the following year. In 1954 Miss Pavry sued Mrs Fleming for enticement and with a second case and an appeal the struggle dragged on until 1958, when Mrs Fleming won. Her sons supported her in court throughout the embarrassing ordeal.

5 Richard Fleming (1911–77). Merchant banker, and Chairman of Robert Fleming Holdings 1966–74.

Ann had very much wanted to leave St Margaret's Bay and the Flemings had bought in haste a house called 'The Old Palace' at Beke outside Canterbury. It was haunted, doors banged, ghostly footsteps were heard. A disused tunnel was said to lead to the Cathedral. Worse, it was too close to the railway. Their marriage had not been going well and the move did not improve things. Ann left a note about Fleming again going to Goldeneye alone, saying 'I thought I should stay with Caspar', but this was not the whole truth. Fleming had a mistress there and when Ann discovered this she turned violently against Jamaica. It was the more bitter as Goldeneye had been the setting for their happiest days together. She was in fact having an affair with a married man in London, though it has been suggested that friendship rather than passion predominated.

To Evelyn Waugh

16 Victoria Square   15 December [1957]

Dearest Evelyn

Alas, unselfishness should be practised when young, it was too late for me to sacrifice myself and live in a 'golf box' in the suburbs of Canterbury to please Ian: my misery was confirmed by Fionn who dislikes it as much as I do. I am very unhappy.

The BBC in its wisdom has given Randolph a television programme to edit and organise. Its title is '*Conversation*', it will be televised at Bergholt, the first performance will be Jan 3rd. Poor Randolph is amazed that Gilmours, Shawcrosses, Lambtons, Rootes,[1] Amerys[2] have refused to take part. He telephoned Ian Gilmour and when Ian refused on behalf of himself and Lady

Caroline, he said wearily, 'Ah, well, I must try and get the Gaitskells.'

The result of this importuning is a team of persons generally regarded as clowns. Trevor-Roper, Lady Za-Za Roper,[3] Colonel Pryce-Jones and me. I did not have the heart to say no, it will be an epic occasion, and before 2 Jan I hope to persuade him to allow me to stage-manage, choose the people, and prevent him making a fool of himself, and us.

The *least* you can do is to *volunteer*, you have always been brave, and this is a test of loyalty, friendship and courage.

Happy Christmas and New Year,
and love to all Waughs,

A

1 Marian Hayter married in 1946 Geoffrey Rootes who succeeded to a peerage in 1964 and became Chairman of Chrysler United Kingdom 1967–73.

2 Catherine Macmillan married in 1950 Julian Amery, Conservative MP who was at this time Financial Secretary at the War Office.

3 Lady Alexandra Haig (1907–). Daughter of Field Marshal Earl Haig. Married in 1954 Hugh Trevor-Roper, now Lord Dacre of Glanton.

From Ian Fleming

[Goldeneye]   Sunday
                                          [?January 1958]

My darling
    It is all just the same except that everything is bigger and more. The flight was perfect, only five minutes late at Mo Bay. Mrs D'Erlanger[1] was on board with her daughter, which may have helped. She seemed quite pleasant and was very queenly with the ground staffs at all the stops. I arrived in a tempest and it has stormed more or less ever since – torrential winds and rains which are going on now and look as if they would go on for ever. Thank God for the book[2] at which I hammer away in between bathing in the rain and sweating round the garden in a macintosh. . . The sofas were covered with the stains of rat shit as it appears the servants have used the house as their own since I left. Paint peeling off the eaves, chips and cracks all over the floor and not one bottle of

marmalade or preserves. So I have had to set to and get in the painters etc. who are still banging away after a week. Noël and company aren't coming out till April. The *Nude*[3] is to have a season at San Francisco. Apparently Noël wears a crew cut in it which must look horrible.

Well, that's what Flemings call a Sitrep, just to show you I'm alive. I can't write about other things. My nerves are still jangling like church bells and I am completely demoralised by the past month. I think silence will do us both good and let things heal. Please put your health before anything else. Try and put a good face on the house and don't let your hate of it spread to the others or we shall indeed end up a miserable crew, which would be quite ridiculous to say the least of it.

Take endless care of yourself.

XXX

Ian

1 Edwina Pru married Leo d'Erlanger, the banker, in 1930.

2 *Goldfinger*, 'one of the easiest of his books to write'. (*Ian Fleming* by John Pearson, 1965)

3 Coward was to have a success in his own play, *Nude With a Violin*, in California after indifference in New York.

Ann was neither well nor happy. Hugo Charteris wrote to their sister Mary Rose, 'I thought Ann better – after a bout of Enton – but still pretty shaky and indirect. I've reached the point of no return with her and can talk of very little safely. I think she was frightened of Ian, perhaps with good reason. But by now she can do nothing but see it out. Besides, in a way I think it's true when she says defiantly, "I know he's a child. But I love him."'

From Ian Fleming

[Goldeneye]   20 January 1958

My love,

At last a letter from you after more than two weeks. They both arrived together – a left and right hook! Well, if life somewhere else will make you happy we must move, as anyway living with an unhappy you is impossible. But do remember that one cannot live by whim alone and that chaos is the most expensive as well as the most wearying luxury in the world. And for heaven's sake don't hurry. Do let's take real backbreaking trouble before we spend all this fresh money and have to spend more keeping up the sort of house I suppose you are looking for. And I beg you to have a stream or a river in the grounds, I shall simply pine away if we go to live in the middle of a lot of plough with deadly little walks down lanes and dons every weekend. But anything, anything to make you smile again and find you somewhere where you will rest and not tear yourself to pieces. I'm terribly worried about your health and I pray that Enton's prison walls have mended your darling heart and somehow got you off this tragic switchback of pills which I implore you to stop. They have nothing to do with the Palace but are a way of life which is killing you, and me with you because it horrifies me so much. You've no idea how they change you – first the febrile, almost hysterical gaiety and then those terrible snores that seem to come from the tomb! Darling, forgive me, but it is so and honestly all I get is the fag end of a person at the end of the day or at weekends. If a new house will help all that let us move as soon as we can and I will have to invent a new kind of life for myself instead of golf which I shall want to play neither with Michael Astor[1] nor Hughie.[2] I'm fed up with other people's neuroses. I have enough of my own. But don't pretend that I am always travelling or that I am always going to travel. One changes and gets older and anyway by next summer I shall have seen the world once and for all. Here is different because it is peace and there is that wonderful vacuum of days that makes one work. And do count the cost. Your pot is down to about 70,000 and two more years at 10,000 a year will reduce it to your iron ration of 50 after which we shall just have to live on income. Mama can easily live another ten or twenty years. Living on our combined incomes means that we shall not have more than

5000 a year which is as rich as one can be. One can live well on that in one house but not in two. These facts have got to be faced just as it had to be faced that we should leave St Margaret's quickly.

My darlingest darlingest love get well and write me a happy letter. I would give anything for one. Bless you and hugs and kisses.

I

1 Michael Astor (1916–80). Writer, painter, Conservative MP 1945–51 and later a close friend.
2 Hugh, Duke of Northumberland (1914–   ). Lord-Lieutenant of Northumberland since 1956.

Several distressed letters from Fleming written at this time have been omitted.

From Ian Fleming

[Goldeneye]   Tuesday
                                                               [undated]

My sweetheart,
    A vulture is sitting on top of the roof above my head. It is squatting on its stomach across the gable like a hen roosting and looks too ridiculous. When I walked out into the garden just now away from my bondage I thought this would be a bad omen and that there would still be no letter from you. I have spent a whole week getting up and peering towards the tray to see if something has arrived. But the funny vulture was a good omen and there was a nice fat packet from you which I have now devoured. I think you manage to write very sweet letters in answer to my vehement ones most of which I always regret when they have gone, and I promise I understand every bit of your point of view. If I FIGHT my case it is just for the same reasons as you FIGHT yours. We both feel the other is getting too much of the cake when in fact there's plenty for both if only we'd sit down peacefully and share it instead of grabbing. I envy you your life of parties and 'the mind' and you envy I suppose my life of action and the fun I get from my books. The answer is that compared to most people we are both enviable and lead enviable lives. I perfectly see your point about the house and I

only beg that where we finally settle will have something that appeases my savage breast – some outlet for activity, because I am hopeless and like a caged beast in drawing- and dining-rooms and there is nothing I can do about it. It's instinctive. You used to sympathise with it and in a way admire it in me, but I realise it must be hell to live with and I can only say that if it has an outlet I can keep it under some sort of control.

I must now go and bathe in the grey sea and then go for a long walk up a mountain to sweat the glooms away. I shall be home in a minute my love. Kisses and kisses and kisses.

Ian

Ian returned from Goldeneye in March. Evelyn Waugh meanwhile went to Rhodesia (Zimbabwe) to see Lady Acton as part of his research for the biography of Ronald Knox.

To Evelyn Waugh

16 Victoria Square   29 March [1958]

Dearest Evelyn

The 'African' letter was a great joy, it has been much appreciated by a variety of people to whom I read it, and it is now safely filed away, only slightly discoloured by lipstick in the handbag; Fionn insists that your letters are cared for, for she has asked me to bequeath them to her in my will – it is probably all she will get, poor child.

Speaking of reading aloud, did you see that Eisenhower had been forbidden to read to himself because it blistered his lips, what do you make of that?

Permanent exhaustion and life in the suburbs of Canterbury prevented my answering your letter sooner. Seaweed in the sitting-room and boulders of chalk on the head were the disadvantages of St Margaret's Bay, but here we have to entertain or be entertained by the neighbours, they fall into that category of person which is ever increasing and neither 'landed' nor 'peasantry'. The doctor's wife gave a cocktail party for us in a low raftered room, Ian could not stand upright and was unable to protect himself from the advances of a rapacious old virgin, she was wearing a handpainted skirt, crafty-arty sandals, and used an ebony cigarette holder as a weapon. I was delighted by Ian's misadventures, as it was upon his insistence that for Caspar's sake we were looking for other parents. [The lady] writes fourth leaders for *The Times of India*, she has also written to me to invite us 'to join just a handful of friends around noon on Easter Sunday'.

I gave a party for Lucian after his private view at the Marlborough Gallery. The Marlborough Gallery has a rich smart clientèle, and the Mrs Ryans, Momos and Kitty Millers were surprised and alarmed to find themselves rubbing shoulders with Teddy boys wearing day-glo socks and flat-chested flat-heeled young women in torn polo sweaters. There is a very splendid portrait of Lucian's favourite thief, which Ian has bought with his pornography money for Caspar; I suspect the Waughs will do better with Augustus Egg.

The Sotheby sale was a comic occasion. I went with a view to leaving a bid for the watercolour of Cézanne's gardener, but alas, it was sold for 19½ times my limit. The place was packed with people who wished to appear wealthy and knowledgeable; Ed. Stanley was there all day, also George Weidenfeld leaning against Genesis.

Randolph has had a rough time in Torrington,[1] he was thrown out of three hotels and finally a kindly *Express* reporter allowed him to sleep upon the floor in his room, but in the morning the landlord said he didn't hold with that kind of thing and ejected Randolph before he had breakfasted.

I stayed with Maurice to attend dinner at Magdalen College as guest of A. J. P. Taylor;[2] Maurice disapproved and made me late. I had only met Professor Taylor once and was flattered and curious; he is a clever man who makes a great donkey of himself. It was disagreeably cold in the Magdalen cloisters and disagreeably hot at the high table, the port, madeira and nuts room, and finally the common room. The worst ordeal was the port, madeira and nuts room; smoking was forbidden so to keep my nervous fingers busy I worked the railway which carries the decanters to and fro across the fireplace, apparently this is skilled labour and a male prerogative, so after a near disaster with the madeira I was forced to talk to a drunken history don known as 'Tom Brown',[3] he gesticulated with violence and finally stuck one of his fingers up my nose.

I long to see you, and surely it is time you had a rest from Anglo-Catholics.

With love to you and Laura

Ann

1 Mark Bonham Carter won Torrington for the Liberals in a celebrated bye-election. Churchill was there as a journalist.

2 Alan (A.J.P.) Taylor (1906–   ). Historian and journalist. Tutor in Modern History at Magdalen 1938–63.

3 C. E. Stevens (1905–76). The Ancient History tutor of Magdalen. Well known as teacher, polymath and eccentric, he was first called 'Tom Brown' as a schoolboy at Winchester.

To Evelyn Waugh

16 Victoria Square   6 April [1958]

Dearest Evelyn

I feel displaced by the Anglican clergy, but I have no pride and would await their decisions if I were not to be in Ireland that week – I am taking old Caspar to join the thieves' kitchen at Lismore[1] – come with me? We can enjoy the company of Debo and her court, we can call upon Elizabeth Bowen[2] and Eddy Sackville-West,[3] and while you are chasing Lucian and Robert Kee[4] I can enjoy the peaceful melancholy countryside and forget the misery of the suburbs.

Lord Lambton hired a 1920 saloon Rolls-Royce, far warmer, more dignified and comfortable than a Thunderbird; he conveyed me in its dusty beige luxury to luncheon with the Edens at Donnington Grove; we asked the chauffeur to take us to the smartest pub in Newbury to fortify ourselves against the meeting – Anthony has been very ill recently – and the chauffeur chose 'Chequers'. It made matters worse for I refused a drink on arrival because I had already had one, and when Clarissa asked me where we stopped I mumbled foolishly. Lord L. saved by saying 'The Dog and Duck'.

Anthony and Clarissa are very thin, and he grew excited at lunch about Suez. When I was alone with Clarissa I said I thought we should have avoided that topic, but apparently the memoirs start at Suez in looking-glass fashion – 'in case he falls down dead', said Clarissa.[5]

Mr Bonham Carter said that his victory at Torrington was due to Lady Pamela Berry's eldest son,[6] he headed the Conservative Office campaign and toured the villages in a loudspeaker van drearily intoning 'Sons of the soil, vote for Royle',[7] Laura Grimond[8] followed with brilliant mimicry.

Very low vitality accounts for brevity and scribble.

Love,

A

1 The Duke of Devonshire's house in Ireland.

2 Elizabeth Bowen (1899–1973). Anglo-Irish novelist. Married Alan Cameron in 1923. Had published *A Time in Rome*, 1955.

3 Edward Sackville-West (1901–65). Critic and author.

4 Robert Kee (1919–). Author and broadcaster. Lasting friend of Ann.

5 *The Times* published extracts from the memoirs of Anthony Eden in January 1960. *Full Circle* was published that year; *Facing the Dictators* late in 1962 and *The Reckoning* in 1965.

6 Adrian Berry (1937–). Scientific correspondent of the *Daily Telegraph* and author of *Apes to Astronauts* and *The Next 10,000 Years*.

7 Anthony Royle (1927–). The defeated Conservative candidate at the Torrington bye-election, he won Richmond the following year and became Parliamentary Under-Secretary of State for Foreign and Commonwealth Affairs. Knighted in 1974, created Lord Fanshawe 1983.

8 Laura Bonham Carter (1918–), Mark's sister, married in 1938 Jo Grimond, Leader of the Parliamentary Liberal Party 1956–67. He was made a life peer in 1983.

Fleming went to the Seychelles in the Indian Ocean after Easter. He wrote more calmly of the discomforts of the journey, entreated Ann to rest and become well and planned for them to meet in Venice on his way home. Unfortunately he got coral poisoning and a fever. Ann left a note:

In Rome [Ian] did not feel well and the wound was still festering. We went to Venice, me for the first time. Ian had taken the Princess Margaret Suite in the Gritti Palace Hotel. It comprised a marble bath and a sitting room with horrible gladioli in tall flower vases. The price was so astronomic that we swiftly moved to a back double room smelling of old canal.

Venice was a way of life we both enjoyed, hours of walking, and he would drink Campari and read the newspapers, while I sightsaw the churches.

I would willingly have lingered, but there was a plan afoot for Ian to write the history of the casino at Monte Carlo, so despite Ian not feeling well we flew to Nice.

To Evelyn Waugh

16 Victoria Square   30 June [1958]

Dearest Evelyn

Family and middle-age inertia prevented me writing sooner. Thank God, that Bron will recover.[1] It is a horrible story of misfortune and I am truly sorry for you all.

Freddy Ashton and Lucian Freud have suffered broken and lacerated noses. The Jaky Astors saw Lucian's little girls crying on a pavement while their bloodstained father was being shoved into an ambulance, Jaky took charge of the little girls and to his surprise became Lucian's next of kin to the hospital authorities – it is at least a Jewish kinsmanship.[2]

Ian is in America struggling with Columbia Broadcasting lawyers, he was offered a wacking sum to write thirty Bond episodes over two years: the prospect of thirty plots and how to save the money from the tax vultures has made him an unendurable life-companion and a nervous wreck, however we shall have expenses abroad and we go to Kitzbühel for August. I was praying for Italy but Ian does not feel inspired and thinks Caspar would prefer lake bathing to *quatrocento* paintings.

Had a jolly dinner with Debo, Lucian, Stephen Spender and Freddy Ashton. Stephen was at his silkiest – due I suppose to Duchess-awareness; Freddy was a great success with Debo – if she is going to frat. with Teddy boys she might as well meet the nicest of them.

I went to Oxford for the Encaenia luncheon and a jolly dinner at Wadham. I was late for the investiture and as the doors were closing in my face was hooked in amongst the dons by Trevor-Roper, I got my umbrella entangled in his gown. The Prime Minister [Harold Macmillan] looked beautiful, the leader of the Opposition [Hugh Gaitskell] looked like the Queen Mother.

The White's Club [*sic*] had their annual golf at Sandwich, the same figures as in 1935, but now sadly lacking in glamour and very neurotic at the thought of two thousand pounds. Michael Astor had spent a thousand pounds on golf lessons and £500 on golf clubs, he was defeated in the first round.[3] Owing to domestic troubles Ian had to take me, Fionn, Caspar and Quennells to lunch at the golf club. Quennell was the subject of rough jokes about his golf handicap. It was rumoured that Anne Tree[4] had found a lizard orchid on the course, so after lunch I organised my party as beaters are organised for a shoot, it chagrined the members of White's but I found three specimens of the orchid.

When will you be in town? I do hope to see you soon.
With love to you and Laura,

Ann

When little Margaret grows up do *not* behave like John Barrymore did with his daughter Diana. John Barrymore who was sitting with Errol Flynn said as Diana passed by 'Ever f——d her?' Errol Flynn had, but as the girl was sixteen, he thought it wise to show surprise and denial – 'Don't miss it,' said Barrymore, 'she's terrific.'

1 Auberon Waugh had been in Cyprus doing his national service. On 9 June he had been correcting the elevation of a Browning machine gun when it started firing. 'Six bullets later I was alarmed to observe that it was firing through my chest and got out of the way pretty sharpish.' ('The Ghastly Truth' in *In The Lion's Den*, 1978, by Auberon Waugh.) He received the last sacraments and startled a corporal by saying, 'Kiss me Chudleigh.'

2 There had been an accident involving a taxi. The Astors are not Jewish.

3 Ann was quite sharp about Michael Astor, who was to become a close friend. The year before she had written to Waugh: 'Michael Astor came to lunch today to escape from his mother Nancy Astor and I left him to sleep on the sofa while I took Caspar paddling and when I returned he had departed for London after painting a balloon and basket on Ian's favourite picture – it is a painting in the manner of Richard Wilson and much loved by Ian, don't you think the rich should respect the pathetic possessions of the poor? I have sent Michael a telegram saying "You have ruined our Richard Wilson, you ignorant beast." I think Michael's knowledge of pictures is limited and he may panic and send me a compensating Renoir.'

4 Lady Anne Cavendish, sister of the Duke of Devonshire, married Michael Tree in 1949.

To Evelyn Waugh

Villa Pengg, Kitzbühel   16 August [1958]

Dearest Evelyn
    A great joy to return from three days culture in Munich and see

your beautiful handwriting on the crudely carved hall table of the Villa Pengg.

Alan Pryce-Jones has been here for two days, he talks incessantly making agreeable conversation as if at an embassy dinner, he has a fathomless facility and chatters about his wife's death from cancer and the paintings of Kandinsky without a change of inflection; fond of him though I am, he is so unreal I am very pleased to be alone again.

I live on a cuckoo clock balcony gazing at the Walt Disney scenery or painting the flowers. Ian has a rip-roaring life with mediatised princes at the golf club, they are indistinguishable from Raimund Von H. [Hofmannsthal] and very tedious.

There are two paintings of great indecency in the Rococo exhibition, one unquestionably is 'Waiting for the Enema', the other of a nymphet with a lap-dog's tail between her legs shocked me more, painted by Fragonard – it says in the catalogue 'the subject was considered in doubtful taste and a note on the engraving by Bertony reads "*Ce sujet ne doit pas être mis a l'étalage*"'. I bought two photographs of it, one for darling Quennell and one for darling O'Neill.

Twice a week there are confetti battles in the town and a band plays, it usually rains and the confetti is thrown with great violence, the English nanny of some German Jewish acquaintances of the Munsters lost an eye last Saturday; these confetti orgies have great significance for Ian, he spent his nineteenth and twentieth years here being coached for the Foreign Office, they remind him of his youth and though he insists on my accompanying him I am invariably in disgrace. The first occasion he bought us each three bags of confetti but said it was no fun with a wife and I was to walk by myself and meet him at the hotel. I walked with one hand over my eyes and only encountered an old man on crutches and two small children, it seemed a shame to blind them and as the light drizzle had become thunder and torrential rain and no sign of Ian at the hotel I proceeded to march home. The tourists were sheltering under the buildings and so unluckily was Ian, he was very cross and said it was exhibitionist to walk in the centre of the street without an umbrella, that everyone was staring at me – alas, worse the next morning. I gave the surplus confetti to the children who failed to blind each other but succeeded in stamping it into the carpet from which no Hoover can remove it so I suppose we will have to buy Frau von

Pengg a new Wilton. Last night's celebration was again disastrous, the weather was glacial and my shoes were too small; when I removed them the town wags filled them with confetti and I did a jig to keep warm with Nicholas Lawford, Ian then reappeared having failed to find romance or enjoy his nostalgia but had been partially blinded by encountering our stalwart German maid who has a heavy hand with puddings and confetti. The sight of me dancing barefoot while Austrian youths poured confetti from my shoes over my head drove him mad with rage, so tonight he goes alone and I am writing to you.

Home in early September, let's meet soon.

Love,

Ann

To Evelyn Waugh

Old Palace, Canterbury   28 November [1958]

Dearest Evelyn

This morning I reluctantly left the clinic[1] and emerged into a black wet adhesive fog. I shall terribly miss those dedicated happy Catholic nurses and midnight feasts of cocoa and gingernuts; my room was next to the labour ward and there were several births in the dawn hours, I did not enjoy this so much but became accustomed to the pattern of noise, the hurried trundling of the hospital bed, the mutterings of doctors and nurses followed by a tremendous clatter and banging and rushing water, such as scullions would make washing up after a banquet of Lady Curzon's; accompanying this *fracas* was the protesting wail of the infant and silence till the male parent arrived sounding cross and apprehensive – never jubilant or loving.

I wish you had been in London, and we might have had a caviar orgy like last time.

Read Iris Murdoch's *Bell*, the critics did not notice that it is quite tremendously funny, the only person except you who makes one laugh aloud and tears pour down the cheeks.

My smart friends tell me that Randolph threw Rab Butler into his own fire and he was dragged from the flames by Mr and Mrs [Julian]Amery, this was the surprising sequel to a quiet Sunday supper, but poor singed Rab had provoked Randolph by suggesting that some passages in his *Life of Sir Anthony Eden* were in poor taste.[2]

I bought a book about you – but in the first chapter it said you retained your early Oxford friendships and Peter Quennell was still your best friend, are the other facts as inaccurate? R.s.v.p. so that I may know if I should continue to read it.[3]

Willie Maugham continues to clamour for Freddy Ayer[4] so that he may be constantly assured that there is no afterlife, very masochistic occupation for an octogenarian.

I have had one dinner-party enjoyed by no one except me. John Sparrow, — and Hugh Gaitskell read Yeats aloud, they all sat in a row holding hands because in early life they loved each other in the same set, this was depressing for Paddy Leigh Fermor who is just as exhibitionistic, and he was not allowed to read at all; Ian arrived in the middle, very intoxicated from high gambling and champagne, and recited in Russian the Cossack baby's cradle song; he temporarily silenced the eminent 'homos', they did not look at all pleased. The Duke and Duchess of Devonshire were very bored and went home.

I do hope you will be in London before Christmas. Could you dine on the 8th to present Diana with a unicorn? Could you come to 'fête champêtre' at the College of Art organised by Kisty[5] and Robin Darwin on the 16th? Could you come to dinner on the 18th to help F. Ayer tell H. Gaitskell how to organise education – not that the poor devil will have the opportunity.

With love and let me know if we may meet,

A

1 'A dull, tedious, tiny op. on womb', Ann wrote to Lady Diana Cooper.

2 *The Rise and Fall of Sir Anthony Eden*, by Randolph Churchill, 1959.

3 *Evelyn Waugh, Portrait of an Artist*, by Frederick J. Stopp, 1958. Waugh had made a few corrections and found it 'an interesting book – interesting at least to me.' Waugh's hostility to Quennell remained. He had written in August, 'It is getting very difficult now to buy ordinary writing ink – Stephens' I mean. There are awful liquids named Quink. Have you noticed how everything beastly begins with Q? Like Quennell and queers and the Queen, quibbles, quod, quagmire, quantum theory, queues, quiffs, most Quintins, questionnaires, quarrels – well, everything.'

4 In April 1961 Alfred Ayer was staying with Somerset Maugham who took him to dinner with Lord Beaverbrook. The conversation turned to life after death, 'to Freddie Ayer's dismay, for Beaverbrook was an ardent believer and Maugham was an equally ardent non-believer. Asked point blank for his opinion Ayer made the Solomon-like pronouncement that Calvinist doctrine stated that some were chosen at birth to be saved, which Beaverbrook was quite prepared to believe since he was

convinced that he was one of the chosen, while Maugham did not think it mattered whether one was saved or not, since there was no after-life.' (*Maugham* by Ted Morgan)

5 Christian ('Kisty') McEwen had married in 1949 Lord Hesketh, who died in 1955.

From Evelyn Waugh

Combe Florey House   3 December 1958

Dearest Ann

I had no idea you were in hospital. I would have called had I known. I am very glad to hear you are at liberty again.

Margaret [Waugh] and I shall be keeping Christmas at the Hyde Park Hotel but you will presumably be with Old Kaspar in his Old Palace then. Our ostensible reason is to protect Bron from the worst of the Welfare festivities – he fears a Saturnalia when all the nurses dress as surgeons and the surgeons as nurses and sing carols. My motive is to escape the Saturnalia at home, Margaret's to visit the theatre and the cathedral. It will be easier to keep her sober when I have my eye directly on her.

I cannot tell you the truth of Fionn's attempted enticement of Mr Chancellor[1] because I was tight at the time. I was tight all that weekend, driven to secret swigging in the dining-room by the plethora of guests. What I think happened was that the Papists went to Mass in Taunton & returned about 11.30 expecting to take Fionn and Mr C. on to cocktails at Tetton. There was no sign of them and some coarse chaff of Alice [Jolliffe]. The rest of the party went off & I got tighter. About 12.30 Fionn & Mr Chancellor returned with a fairly plausible story of having walked to a Protestant service three miles off. The weak point on which Diana [Cooper] fastened was that there is a perfectly good Protestant church within 100 yards of the house. I think I probably chaffed Mr C. By the time the Tetton party returned Kisty [Hesketh] had come and Diana was down and I was spifflicated. Diana had not seen Alice's departure but was convinced she had left in tears. Perhaps I observed or invented this detail which worked strongly on Diana's imagination during luncheon where she ate a great deal more heavy food – Yorkshire pudding and suet – than she is used to. It went to her head like wine and I think she upbraded? upbraided? upraided?

– can't spell that one – Fionn while I was urging Mr C. over the port to submit to the claims of the Roman Church. I am sorry I cannot give better evidence.[2] Fionn wore an evening dress made of I don't know what strange fibres but she was a very nice guest and she may come and gloat on me whenever the passions so move her.

I read Miss Murdoch's popular *Bell* in the wrong spirit perhaps. Didn't laugh once and thought it a great fraud. The only scene which was at all convincing was when the heroine had a bath in the journalist's flat. I will search it anew for jokes.

I went up for Campion Day at Campion House. An expected circle of dons, Bill Deakin, David [Cecil], [Isaiah] Berlin. They all left Common Room at 10.30 saying they had to 'work'. I thought that ineffably vulgar. David has not written a single word of his life of Max Beerbohm.[3] When I told him I was in the last chapter of my opus [*Knox*] he looked at me askance as though I was a reporter for *Life*. I looked at him benignly thinking him a talkative sloth. But when he said he had to 'work' at 10.30 I thought him a humbug trying to be contemporary.

Thunderbird has been lecturing the Oxford University Pornographical Association. They thought him a man to emulate. I tried to explain that all his [money?] was inherited and that he lives on your various jointures and makes nothing with his pen, but they were sceptical.

Bron is starving in the Westminster Hospital and entirely dependent on hampers from my friends. He has no pleasure except for visitors. The other day there was a letter in some paper like the *Spectator* from an atheist Cambridge don taking exception to a statement that charity and church-going are connected. In all his experience, this don said, he had never noticed that professing Christians are kinder than atheists. I thought of writing to say that in the last five months Bron has been able to keep a pretty accurate count of those who have troubled to visit him. *All*, except two brother-officers and one devout Protestant cousin, are Catholics. Dot Head[4] & Pam Berry and other near neighbours write the name of his ward in their engagement books and do nothing. No particular reason why they should, but they all say 'What can we do?', and I say 'Drop in and see him.' People like Mia Woodruff[5] & Frances Phipps[6] who barely know him go two and three times a week. Even Harold Acton[7] went twice during his brief visit.

Look out for *Memento Mori* by Muriel Spark. It deals with

geriatrics in the most gruesome way. I read it in proof. It should be out soon.

My house is too cold. I long for Africa. I see in this morning's paper that the Queen Mother is to be there at the same time [passage deleted by EW] which means that all government officials will be in a state of high over-excitement and the police painfully vigilant. I shall have to keep well clear of her route.

Sir J. Rothenstein[8] was at the Campion dinner. He told me he felled your Australian clown Cooper with a sock on the jaw. True?

Love

Evelyn

1 John Chancellor (1927–   ). Married 1959–69 to Alice Jolliffe, known as 'Sweet Alice'. His brother Alexander Chancellor was Editor of the *Spectator* 1975–83.
2 Fionn remembers that she went for a walk with John Chancellor, got lost and was late for lunch. She was indeed scolded by Lady Diana.
3 Lord David's *Max* did not appear until 1964.
4 Lady Dorothea Ashley-Cooper (1907–   ). Married in 1935 Viscount Head.
5 Marie Acton (1905–   ). Married Douglas Woodruff in 1933.
6 Frances Ward married in 1911 Eric Phipps (died 1945), Ambassador in Berlin and Paris.
7 Harold Acton (1904–   ). Writer, aesthete. Oxford friend of Waugh. Knighted 1974.
8 Sir John Rothenstein (1901–   ). He did strike the art critic Douglas Cooper (who was not in fact Australian) at a party in the Tate Gallery, of which he was director 1938–64.

To Evelyn Waugh

Shane's Castle   2 January [1959]

Dearest Evelyn

It has been a hard Christmas, I mean work not weather, just try walking through Belfast on the Eve carrying five pillows, four lampshades, a pound of Stilton, a crate of tangerines and smoked salmon for eight. I was too tired to go to church the following day and Thunderbird on his return said he, Raymond and Fionn had agreed I took too much on myself – no justice.

When I arrived [O'Neill] had ordered no food, blankets or pillows, and there were no lights in the bedrooms, only stereophonic sound relayed from his library; the library and his bedroom were oases of comfort apart from stereophonic sound, but without all was unfurnished, cold and black, the cellar and larder were empty save for a bottle of whisky for Quennell and a bottle of vodka for Ian; I summoned the keeper and told him to shoot pheasant and woodcock, I filled the cellar, decorated the Christmas tree, turned on the central heating, and with the aid of Nanny collected sufficient peasants to staff the house, then Fionn arrived with the bubonic, Caspar got a fever, and O'Neill turned off the central heating as an economy, my poor old father turned blue and had to be revived with brandy; but now, Thank God, the festive season is over and with the help of vitamin B injections I am beginning to see some point in life. I am very devoted to poor O'Neill, but he is in danger of becoming a most eccentric peer.

I was deeply impressed by Bron, he has amazing courage, he appeared serene and cheerful, far more than his pagan visitor. I imagine Christmas in London would be horrible, hence the telegram; I spent one Christmas in London when Hugo was born and I have not forgotten the misery though it is thirty-five years ago.

My unrewarded but ever devoted admirer Mr Gaitskell is coming to lunch tomorrow to look into unemployment on feudal estates; the agent is planning to shoot him and O'Neill says the visit will do him no good with the county.

With love to you all,

A

To Clarissa Eden

16 Victoria Square   15 January [1959]

Dearest Clarissa

The pirates gave great pleasure and occupied much of Christmas afternoon – 'She always chooses well' said Caspar, thankyou very much for sending him another lovely present.

I would have written sooner but it was a hard Christmas, when I arrived in Ireland Raymond said he was about to telephone and suggest that we all went to the nasty old palace, the reason was horribly clear – no bedside lamps, no blankets, a scarcity of chairs, central heating temperamental, the lavatories flushing scalding water, the taps ice cold, it was three days' slave labour to prepare for the family and on the happy festival morn I collapsed with a bubonic flu' imported by Fionn from Bethnal Green.

I enjoyed the postcard, but if that is the only available bathing your Christmas can have been little happier than mine – at the moment I feel anyone in the sun must be happy, London is a morgue of frozen dirt, Mickey has not allowed Bridget to return from Ireland because he cannot face her despondency when confronted with the shambles of Lennox Gardens – he still has only a candle and a camp bed.[1]

My only day in London I took Caspar to *Peter Pan* in the afternoon and went to *Madame Butterfly* in the evening with Joan and Garrett[2]; Garrett's guest of honour was Mr Heathcoat Amory[3] from whom he was hoping to extract some state aid for the opera; I had never met the shy Chancellor before but formed the opinion that he was not only tone deaf but positively antagonistic to music – during the tragic climax he was placed between me and Joan in the circle, he creaked and groaned like a sailing ship in a gale and seemed in grave discomfort, which was considerably increased when the lights went up and he saw our tear-stained faces, he could think of no suitable comment but asked me if all opera houses were the same shape – I could think of no suitable answer.

Garrett forced him to go home with Austrian Scharzenpuss,[4] it was clear from his reluctance that despite the weather he was indulging in his favourite occupation of bicycling and did not care to admit his machine was parked in Floral Street.

I do hope Anthony is well and there are some enjoyable aspects of S. America. With much love and thank you,

Ann

1 Michael Renshaw had bought a house in Cyprus but it had been ransacked by the Turks and he had to return to London. He bought a house in Lennox Gardens and made flats for friends – the Bryces, Diana Campbell-Gray (who became Viscountess Gage) and Lady Bridget Parsons.

2 Joan Carr married in 1935 Garrett Moore (1910–) who succeeded as the Earl of Drogheda in 1957. He was Managing Director of the *Financial Times* 1945–70 and Chairman of the Royal Opera House 1958–74.

3 Derick Heathcoat Amory (1899–). Conservative MP 1945–60, Chancellor of the Exchequer in 1958. Created a Viscount in 1960.

4 Prince Johannes Schwarzenberg was Ambassador 1955–66.

To Evelyn Waugh

16 Victoria Square   1 May [1959]

Dearest Evelyn

I am beset with cares so please answer this letter at once, for when I see your handwriting upon the breakfast tray my spirits rise and I become much happier: I did enjoy the Rhodesian traffic check and the Tatters and Rags.[1]

The Crickmeres gave notice last Tuesday and we are still negotiating, they have tumbled to it – that they are a unique and dying species. To crown [this] Fionn had an emotional crisis, and as we talk better when walking we did two or three Aldermaston marches, very inconclusive and worrying to me; needless to say Fionn's loved one[2] has no money and a background wrapped in mystery. Fionn reluctantly brought him for the weekend fearing I would find him non-Mitford, but he seems to have found me non-Mitford, and said it was impossible that I should ever meet his mother while refusing to disclose his mother's address and circumstances. Fionn tried a light-hearted approach and said she would not mind if like Ernest he had been found in a bag at Victoria station, but this made him very hostile and resentful. Oh dear, but this is <u>TOP SECRET</u> and I am trusting you, for alas, the importance of Ernest is very important to her, and when you can afford marble halls or risk V. Square I will tell you other comic details.

Poor Lucian [Freud] went to Aspinall's gambling hell and lost ten thousand pounds, mostly to the Earl of Derby;[3] when I asked him if it was true, he replied, 'not strictly, for I have not ten thousand to lose.' I then asked why Aspinall was so free with credit, and he said it was all run in a very gentlemanly way![4]

Loelia, Duchess of Westminster is eking out her pin money by being paid £100 a week by a low-born rich Italian girl who is to marry a high-born poor Italian man and wishes to learn how to be a lady. Loelia expects all invitations to be extended to the girl. Liz and Raimund [von Hofmannsthal] gave a banquet for important *Time* editors and Andrew Devonshire was placed between Loelia and the Roman protégé, he looked very unhappy.

The Turkish Ambassador[5] came to lunch and said he had not read *Lolita* because he preferred to see such things and not read about them; I disclosed this to other guests and he got in a flap and seemed to think he had made a diplomatic blunder.

Horrible treats this week include Lady John Hope's ball, I am engaged to dance all the supper extras with Dr Maugham. Dr Maugham malignantly telephones his daughter every morning and asks who is the host. He is paying for the ball and has not spoken to his son-in-law for five years, so anything may happen for Dr Maugham is very strong and lately injected with Niehan goat glands.[6]

Well, I was delighted to hear Auberon was recovered, I hope all your daughters are engaged to millionaires and you have as many domestics and cows and you and Laura desire.

Loving

Mrs Thunderbird

1 Waugh had written: 'The report in the newspapers about cars being stoned arose from the Public Works Department in Rhodesia making a traffic check. A black man was found with a basket full of stones at the side of the road and, asked what they were for, said, "For cars, sir." He couldn't count so he had been told to put a stone into the basket for every car that passed.' Waugh had also dined with a paramount chief who had said, 'Don't dress. Come in your tatters and rags.'

2 John Morgan (1929–). Married Fionn O'Neill in 1961, when he was a First Secretary at the Foreign Office. The marriage was dissolved in 1975. Ambassador to Poland since 1983.

3 Earl of Derby (1918–). Major in Grenadier Guards, which he left in 1946.

4 The great success of the gambling club in Berkeley Square named after John Aspinall (1927–) was widely attributed to the accuracy with which it was gauged whether a debt would be settled eventually or not.

5 Nuri Birgi (1908–). Turkish Ambassador in London 1957–60.

6 Dr Paul Niehans, who had cured Pope Pius XII of hiccups in 1954, had told Maugham that he had lovely soft testicles and that the best protection against cancer was rejuvenation of the sex glands. The treatment proved satisfactory so that spring he and his secretary 'once again had their buttocks filled with the thick pink fluid in the horse syringes'. (*Maugham* by Ted Morgan)

From Evelyn Waugh

Combe Florey House   [?May 1959]

My Dear Ann

Today is Margaret's 17th birthday. She has chosen a Knox Bible, a mantilla and a night's visit to Oxford sightseeing, as her presents. Yesterday was the anniversary of Bron's shooting himself in Cyprus. I gave him 3 suits of clothes. Very expensive.

I am sorry you have lost the Crickmeres. It was inevitable. Good servants are very sensitive to loss of tone in a house. You could not expect them to serve Freud & socialist MPs with the zeal they devoted to Clarissa and me in your better days.

I hope your anxieties about Fionn's proletarian suitor are over.

My elder peacock has developed an unnatural passion for a Muscovy drake. He approaches it *backwards* with tail spread. The drake is entirely normal and much disgusted.

Class consciousness is in the air again. Connolly was greatly titillated by Diana's *Common Day*[1] and described those adventurous and eccentric men Belloc & Baring as 'tame' and the candid Conrad Russell as 'pawky'. Now my friend Frankie Donaldson has written a book to prove how low-born she is and how different the upper classes are.[2]

I lunched with Maurice Bowra in Oxford. Get him to read you an excellent poem about Betjeman & Princess Margaret.[3]

Your story about *Lolita* and Turkish Ambassador is the best I have heard for years.

Do come & stay with us when you need a rest.

Yours affec.

E.W.

---

1 *The Light of Common Day*, the second volume of Lady Diana Cooper's autobiography, had been reviewed in *The Sunday Times* by Cyril Connolly.

2 *Children of the Twenties* by Frances Donaldson. She was born in 1907, the daughter of the playwright Frederick Lonsdale, and married in 1935 John Donaldson, who was created a life peer in 1967. *See* Appendix of Names.

3 Princess Margaret had presented John Betjeman with the Duff Cooper Prize in 1958 and Sir Maurice Bowra had written an ode to her in Betjeman's style. The first of seven verses goes:

> Green with lust and sick with shyness,
> Let me lick your lacquered toes.
> Gosh, O gosh, your Royal Highness,
> Put your finger up my nose,
> Pin my teeth upon your dress,
> Plant my head with watercress.

To Evelyn Waugh

16 Victoria Square   24 July [1959]

Dearest Evelyn

There is a new theory concerning you and the Chatsworth chamber pot, it is that you filled the pot yourself; the theory was advanced by William Plomer and all present agreed it was most probable and in keeping with your nature – it was earlier than Mr Pinfold thought and it distracted his distracted mind while waiting for dinner to be announced.

Thunderbird is resigning from *The Sunday Times*,[1] it has something to do with money; I am very cross for I wished daily accounts of the new régime, I told Max [Beaverbrook] to invite Roy Thomson[2] to dinner to meet me and Lady Diana, but Max said he would not understand our conversation, he cannot be very literate can he? He has already (Thomson) asked the Labour Party for a peerage in exchange for support and he intends to 'Poor boy' *The Sunday Times* – to 'Poor boy' means cut wages, sack staff and collect cash – however he has forgotten the unions, for apparently the *Scotsman* is a non-union house.

Pryce-Jones invited me to a television lunch to discuss how the public would like books reviewed, authors interviewed, literary discussions etc. At the moment ITV has one book programme a month, but no one looked at it and they wish to attract an audience. It was a lovely lunch, the guests were Osbert Lancaster, Angus Wilson, Siriol Hugh-Jones,[3] Jack Lambert,[4] G. Fraser,[5] Antonia Fraser, John Raymond[6] and strangers, the heat and lights were torture and the sweet white wine boiled over the brims of glasses; at pudding time Pryce-Jones initiated the debate and invited us to give ideas; thinking of you I said, 'See the author in his home, wife, children, housemaids' – housemaids was a slip of the tongue and the starving poet next to Thunderbird was awfully cross and started growling at him: after lunch they showed us the results, I looked like an over-animated witch, horrible nervous twitchings and nut-cracker grimaces, Antonia a static beauty, calm and clever, Siriol Hugh-Jones, an ugly dwarf in life, became a beauty on the screen, it was most discouraging; the only man who was good was a [–] called Tom Maschler,[7] the worst man was that inferior book reviewer Jack Lambert, but Jack Lambert has been offered a contract and was considered a great success.

It has been a long hot day, we motored to Broadstairs to see a smart private school called Wellesley House, notable because the Duke of Gloucester's sons were educated there and the Under-Master is Ian's golfing friend whose Xmas card I showed you. The golfing friend proudly showed us a trunk inscribed 'Pratt' and said 'Camden's son',[8] he also pointed to a small boy and said 'son of Cameron of Lochiel, chief of his clan', these splendid names seemed the only asset for the dormitories were overcrowded, thirty beds in one room and down the centre a repellent row of primary-coloured plastic washbowls with attendant grimy sponges and toothbrushes, and they took a pride in being a non-scholarship establishment and giving little time to the classics: so I am clinging despite Thunderbird to Summer Fields.

OH DEAR – last night two golfers, and now Ed [Stanley] has arrived – no painting, no writing, a grim struggle between pity and boredom – he has come from a Benedictine monastery, dismissed the Dover taxi, and nothing to be done except invite for the night and deposit at White's tomorrow morning, he has not had a bath for three weeks and I hoped for a respite while he cleaned himself, but he says not till bedtime and he is sitting downstairs waiting to tell untrue, unfunny stories. No one can carry his suitcase upstairs because it is laden with books that Auberon [Herbert] made him buy for retreat reading, they are religious works written by Poles and of such a length and dullness that the monastery would not accept them as a gift.

We had a romantic evening at the Tate Gallery, Sir Kenneth Clark told Leslie Hartley that he had hung the romantic pictures to create a rhythm of feeling, that in each room one should experience a sense of uplift and downcast. We all tried to experience this spiritual switchback but we did not succeed: nothing happened except Debo got intermingled with the Queen Mother and said 'Oh, Mam, you must see the picture of Charles the First being beheaded.'

Time you had your hair cut again, I shall be in London 10th to 20th.

And now to 'Ed.

Love

A

1 It was a friendly parting. Fleming continued to be paid £1000 a year and attended the conference on Tuesday mornings at *The Sunday Times* but he moved to Fleet Street with a new office and secretary for his own work.

2 Roy Thomson (1894–1977). Canadian millionaire press baron. Founder of the Thomson Organisation, he had just added *The Times* and *The Sunday Times* to a collection that already included the *Scotsman*. Created Lord Thomson of Fleet in 1964.

3 Siriol Hugh-Jones contributed to *The St Trinian's Story* that year and married Derek Hart.

4 J. W. Lambert (1917–   ). On *The Sunday Times* 1948–81. Literary and Arts Editor 1966–76, Associate Editor 1976–81. Member of numerous committees.

5 Perhaps G. S. Fraser, a Bohemian poet who had published *The Modern Writer and his World* in 1953.

6 John Raymond (1923–77). Critic and author.

7 Thomas Maschler (1933–   ). Fiction Editor at Penguin Books 1958–60, Chairman of Jonathan Cape since 1970.

8 Lord Michael Pratt (1946–   ) is the son of the Marquess of Camden.

To Ann Fleming

Combe Florey House, Nr Taunton   28 July [1959]

My Dear Ann

Thank you very much for your letter. It is very agreeable to have the duty of answering it instead of writing about my days in Africa – a work of ineffable tedium & triviality.[1]

I am sorry Thunderbird has left *The Sunday Times*. As long as his fastidious mind brooded over its pages I felt that the spirit of Edmund Gosse was still with it. Now there will only be the *Observer* and that has become purely a black man's paper. How painfully slangy the Devlin Report[2] was. Judicial summings up used to be models of English prose. De Quincey, by the way, says that the custodians of good prose are well-born spinsters who forgo marriage rather than pollute their blood with plebeian strains and console themselves for the loss of family life by writing letters to men of culture. Tell Fionn.

Did you observe that at Eckington (next village to Renishaw) natural, explosive gas was bursting through the stones of Pinfold Street? I speak literally. It was reported in yesterday's paper.

Even if I had (which I had not) filled the Devonshire pot before dinner Debo's housewifery is condemned. An old-fashioned, well-trained housemaid empties pots when she turns down the beds.

I hope this Canadian (why did you want to meet him?) will not sack poor Connolly, dreary as he has been lately. I am sure he is not a trades unionist.

What honourable motive can you have for lunching on television?

In choosing a school one consideration is paramount. It must be near either friends or a civilised town. I have had to stop seeing my son James since I sent him to Stoneyhurst. It is ghastly taking little boys (and girls) out from school. A neighbouring marble hall alleviates it a little.

Sheffield is much better company than most of your friends.

Mrs Ian Fraser gave birth to a daughter[3] yesterday in Taunton. Mr Fraser came to Mass on Sunday wearing an open orange blouse, blue linen trousers and sandals like something from Villefranche or San Tropez in the late '20s. Auberon Herbert has taken to welcoming his dinner guests bare to the waist. An American friend of Teresa's came to stay here without a dinner jacket.

What dull people have been dying recently (except Brendan)?[4]

I say what about Boothby giving champagne to 17-year-old tramps?

I can't express the horrible boredom of my African reminiscences.

I sent Margaret to hear Sir J. Gielgud. She was enraptured. Also much exhilarated to find he does not aspirate 'humour'. She has always thought this a discreditable peculiarity of my own. I have sent her to Bath today to buy tiny, very expensive discs of glass to adhere to her eyeballs.

Do you remember an Edwardian glass porch on this house? I have pulled it down revealing a splendid doorway, like something in Genoa. Now I am building double balustraded steps to it. Then I shall have to restore sash windows throughout. Then terrace the east lawn & then I shall be too poor to live here any longer.

Now I must describe the amenities of Mombasa. Hell.

Your affec. kinsman

E. Waugh

1 *Tourist in Africa*, 1960.

2 Patrick Devlin (1905–   ), Justice of the High Court 1948–60, life peer in 1961, had chaired a committee which recommended the formation of the Central African Federation.

3 Anne Grant (1939–84), Waugh's niece, had married Ian Fraser (1923–   ) who became Chairman of Rolls-Royce in 1971 and Chairman of Lazard Brothers in 1980. Each of her four children was born in July and this, the first, was named Consuelo.

4 Viscount Bracken had died in 1958.

To Patrick Leigh Fermor

Hotel de la Mer, Le Touquet   [August 1959]

Darling Paddy

I am in Hell, there is a cacophony of cars, screaming brats and a vast *piscine* from whence the results of swimming and diving contests are announced by very loud speaker: we transferred from Kent to Pas de Calais this morning and I doubt if I can stick it more than ten days. Send a postcard to this nightmare resort and save me.

Ian has the casino and the golf club and infernal friends, the children will no doubt enjoy the beach, and I think it will not be too wicked to desert them for more sympathetic surroundings.

Peter Q. spent the weekend with us; he caught a chill from bathing, I was not surprised for his bathing technique is eccentric, he walks slowly into the sea until shoulder-deep, fists clenched and arms aloft, he then circles slowly, gazing at the heat haze over Thanet or towards the Goodwin sands, he then remains stationary and stares at the horizon in a trance, but he makes no gesture to aid circulation.

Last London evening a grouse celebration with Beaton, Bacon and Ashton – Francis was restless for he had a date with a Ted at Piccadilly Circus, I persuaded him to collect the Ted, though warned by Cecil that he was known to be equipped with bicycle chains and razor blades and though worshipped by masochistic Francis was a danger to normal mortals; it was therefore an anti-climax when Francis returned with an undergrown youth with most amateur sideburns and drainpipes – he was named 'Ron', blushed when spoken to, a refined cockney accent and a lamblike disposition – I was most disappointed and refilled his glass assiduously hoping to promote rage, but it failed to perturb his most gentle disposition.

Not in a mood for letter writing and aware that I have provoked Ian's less gentle disposition by curling myself in an angry ball on the bed plus books, writing paper and ear plugs instead of hurling myself into organised fun.

My first telegram to Joan was because Ian intended going to Venice with the Bryces, but when he chopped this noxious plan, we decided a family holiday and plans became vaguer.

Much love

Annie

and PLEASE send a p.c.

To Evelyn Waugh

Hotel de la Mer, Le Touquet   31 August [1959]

Dearest Evelyn.

Thunderbird has devised a summer holiday for the family of a typically sadistic nature ... Thunderbird is very happy, he plays golf daily with an expatriate general who owns a rich American wife and a villa with slippery floors and elaborate cocktail arrangements, T-bird suspects he has gone too far and to placate said he had arranged lovely treats with the general's son, the general's son is a nob at the College of Heralds, he is called 'Rouge Poursuivant' and said he would be honoured to drive me around the Pas de Calais and explain heraldic motifs on ruined castles; at mealtimes I have to cope with old Caspar's passion for French food, especially snails, crayfish and mussels; he makes a horrible mess.

T-bird says this is all revenge because I took old Caspar and old Hugh Gaitskell to tea at the Sandwich Golf Club, neither of them had combed their hair or wore ties and they were very unpopular and an extra price was put on the bill, old Hugh Gaitskell hoped it was easier for Ian because Lord Cohen[1] shook hands with him, but he is only a summer visitor so it made no difference.

We have bought a home near Faringdon, it has a romantic garden and a better piece of water than yours, but, alas, there is a ballroom, billiard room and 40 bedrooms to be demolished[2] – the Carolean wings are lovely and we need a good architect and advice: if I was to meet you at Swindon would you come and advise? Have you views about architects?

I am now in a back bedroom and only subject to kitchen smells.

Raymond went to Majorca with a Marquess[3] and two daughters of earls,[4] he went by pale blue Chevrolet with a speedboat on a trailer, Fionn went to Greece 4th class tourist and writes that she will never marry a member of the upper classes and that the Parthenon is vulgar. Hugo went on a coach tour from Dundee to Paris, and from thence goes to distress poor old Jung in Switzerland; his activities will be in the *Daily Telegraph*: I should hate to be on a coach tour with Hugo or with a speedboat or with Fionn tourist –

when the house is habitable I shall remain permanently at home.

Let me know how your family are spending the summer, I shall be here till the 8th and would like to see you

Love

Ann

1 Lord Cohen (1888–1966). Judge of High Court of Justice 1943, Lord Justice of Appeal 1946, Lord of Appeal in Ordinary 1951. Created a life peer in 1951.

2 Sevenhampton Manor when finally done up by Ann was admired and loved by many and fulfilled Fleming's worst fears. The 'piece of water' was a lake that when dredged into existence was almost stagnant. It was not precisely 'in the middle of a lot of plough with deadly little walks down lanes' but 'dons every weekend' there certainly were. It was far nearer to 'some huge palace that we cannot afford to heat or staff and where we have to dress for dinner every weekend' than 'a small box'; and there was no golf course.

3 Marquess of Hamilton (1934–). MP for Fermanagh and Tyrone 1964–70. Succeeded as Duke of Abercorn 1979.

4 Camilla Roberts had married Earl Erne the year before and Sheelin Maxwell, daughter of Lord Farnham, married Viscount Knollys that year but the only earl's daughter in the party was Lady Diana Herbert, whose father was the Earl of Pembroke.

Patrick Leigh Fermor recalls:

When did Sevenhampton first come into being? I remember driving over there soon after Ann and Ian had got it – or when they were on the brink – and thinking what an extraordinary place it was: the old house, rather dilapidated on the side of the slope, the stretch of water that looked more like a lake than a flowing river, the tall, unkempt mass of trees with some of the heavy boughs split and fallen across the leaf-choked paths as in the picture of the cat-that-walks-by-itself. An islet was tangled with weeping willows and the trees and the water seemed to vanish into misty distances, giving an illusion of vast extent. There were stagnant patches of duckweed, frogs and rooks croaking, swarms of moorhens; and two herons rose and winged away down this dim vista. We wondered whereabouts the Warneford-Fettiplace duel had been fought. (One of them had been killed: was the place haunted?) There were overgrown hedges and currant bushes and vegetable beds run wild and to seed, espaliers untended in a walled orchard and faded brick stables tumbling to bits. The clock on the lantern had stopped and the weathercock was seized up with rust.

With what seemed like miraculous speed Ann had changed it into a place with a slightly different kind of enchantment; for, wisely, the atmosphere was not unlike that of the first wild vision. The enormous trees and the water retained their solemnity, nothing was too raked and trim, demolition was kept to a minimum and the additions were made out of the same rough, random, undressed Cotswold stone as the original fabric. Similar shingles covered the fresh area of roof and identical moss soon spread. The grass, sinking across the vista in a great curved swoop to the reeds and the water, was cut now in those lighter and darker stripes of a different grain that come with careful mowing so that they sailed away in a diminishing perspective to where a colossal, brilliantly placed Roman urn, leading the eye onwards to the trees, stood on its plinth like a Piranesi monument. The fallen boughs were only lopped where they hindered. The grass creaked with splitting conker shells and in season there was a heavy smell of elderflower. Pricked with pink and white candles, spatulate green chestnut shadows fringed the sky and among them soared tall elms which disease was later to ravage. Beside the grassy paths wandering along the water, the biggest wild hemlocks I've ever seen shot up. They might have been giant umbellifers in imaginary illustrations of the miocene age. Flowers, when they appeared, were scattered at random in the short and the long grass rather than dragooned into beds. The top of an uninspired Victorian belfry showed over the tree-tops; the only hint, in spite of a nearby side road, of the outside world.

The moorhens multiplied; did coot and tern haunt the place? There was always a great aquatic flurry of dark flotillas on the move. I think there were a couple of swans there at the beginning but not later; and perhaps there were Muscovy ducks. I'm sure there were some Australian geese, huge birds which were later banished for bullying. But there was a whole troop of mallards which crossed the grass at first light every morning to form up outside Annie's sash window, on which a bold spokesman banged its beak. The vast bird population always woke one when it was hardly light and if one looked out, there below was Ann's pale nightgowned figure barefoot in the dew scattering mallards' breakfasts. Herons were there occasionally. I think they nested one year, but on the whole they were gatecrashers from the heronry at Buscot. The great thing about these surroundings was the green unbroken expanse of sward, while up above the contrasting hues and shapes of leaves formed caverns of green gloom and sleep as well as unloosing green thoughts in a green shade etc. There was something Marvell-like about the whole place.

The steep slope it was built on made half the house drop – or rise – a floor; and this took away the look of a country house in a Hobbema or Ruysdael background – a comparison prompted by the semicircular gables – that it might otherwise have had; nothing could be less Dutch than that tilted and timbered setting. Indoors, leaving the long wing where the birds came meant crossing a flagged hall with an Angela Connor bust of Lord Goodman, then climbing a sweep of steps branching to a gallery and the bedrooms on the right, and on the left to a passage full of books and Lucian's Ann and Henry Lamb's Maurice Bowra. This led to a dining-room with books all over one wall – many of them works of reference ready to settle all mealtime disputes – and then through double doors into a great light drawing-room. Vast yellow sofas flanked a fireplace stacked high with logs, Aubusson flowers and foliage spread underfoot; there were hefty inlaid marble tables for drinks and books, masses of roses and other flowers were dotted about, and over the windows Martin Battersby had painted emblematic semi-circles: card-playing monkeys with chains or ribbons about their necks, trumping each other's leads with flourished kings and aces. A metal snake clasped a cylindrical clock on the chimneypiece, and its forked tongue marked the time on the revolving enamel digits. One wall had a splendid Victorian equestrienne in a feathered hat and a flowing crimson and tawny habit, another carried a dashing Augustus John of Ian's and Peter's mother; burning-eyed, plumed, and holding a violin. At the far end a bow window like a ship's poop looked out at grass-level, while double doors on the left opened on a balustraded platform from which, to deal with the steep drop in the lawn, two nearly semicircular flights of steps branched down again in Palladian curves to the lower level of the grass. Here, lolling round a white metal table on hot days, one looked over the water, the trees, a clump of enormous willows, two stone muses standing at random in the grass, the urn, and the striped sward with its croquet hoops over which a flat-footed deputation of mallards was sure to be advancing.

To Patrick Leigh Fermor

16 Victoria Square   3 October [1959]

Darling Paddy

The heat of summer and the beauty of autumn makes the weather historic, though somehow the unusual warmth makes it even more melancholy: we picnic every day and never question the possibility of rain, the earth is cracked and there are no mushrooms or indeed toadstools.

Joan [Rayner], Stephen [Spender] and Lucian came to dinner, I subjected them to a Tory television programme, otherwise it was a friendly quiet evening. The Tory television programmes are blimpishly vulgar, the Labour are slick, John Hare was shown in a supermarket with horrible housewives pushing shopping baskets over his feet, while he said 'We shall see the ladies have what they require', the Labour Party showed Lady Pakenham [later Countess of Longford] peering over *The Times* saying 'You, the workers, are the Top People, you are the ones who count.' It is all very horrible. Arthur Koestler is going to vote Conservative for the first time. Oh dear, this is a dull letter, but there is an election lull that is affecting the most unpolitical people and one feels nothing will be quite normal till next Friday.

Monday 12 October

On polling day my first task was to collect a dropsical centagenarian who lives immediately opposite Robin Ironside, her husband had been taken to the hospital the previous night with 'water stoppage', I said I hoped it did not mean an operation, and her reply was grisly – 'They took four pints off 'im in the surgery and 'is weight remained the same.' It took hours to remove her swollen limbs from the car and then she burst into tears because it was the first time she had voted without ''im' for twenty years and leant sobbing upon me, luckily a young policeman sprang to my rescue and we led her to the poll, where she inscribed a cross to ensure a slimy bastard called Hylton-Foster[1] should be elected by forty-five thousand votes; she was very maternal about Robin, for the poor waterlogged pair do not sleep well and wonder 'why the young painter's light is always burning at all hours of the night'. I immediately called on Robin who went whiter than his wont and said 'What else did she tell you?' – I fear I added to his permanent condition of anxiety.

14 October

Just returned from Oxford and a *vin d'honneur* to celebrate the publication of Evelyn's *Ronald Knox*, the *vin d'honneur* was in a poky Roman Catholic bookshop, and the combined smell of linoleum floor, cheap champagne, priests and religious tracts was very discouraging; the author was purple from wine and exhaustion, for the party had been preceded by a luncheon of many courses and vintages.[2] I spent the night with Maurice and the Waughs came to dinner, Maurice had sensibly skipped the cocktails and slept off the lunch so there was no voice or vitality to compare with his, or contradict his outrageous statement that for two years he had foretold that the Conservatives would be returned with an extra twenty seats.

Kisses and thankyou

A

1 Sir Harry Hylton-Foster (1905–65). Speaker of the House of Commons from 1959.

2 Waugh wrote to Lady Acton: 'An absolutely ghastly *vin d'honneur* was given for *Knox* under the Old Palace, in what used to be a wireless shop, now a bookshop. It was black with clergymen and I was deafened and asphyxiated.'

To Evelyn Waugh

16 Victoria Square   [November 1959]

Dearest Evelyn

I fear there has been no intercourse for ages, and very ill-mannered not to thank you for the exclusive luxury edition of your book, *Ronald Knox*. I read every word of every line on every page, and I wrote to you and then destroyed the letter; I would now like to know all the things you did *not* write. I did enjoy it, because I like to read about sad lives, and to me he seems a very sad person. I should like to ask you questions about him – especially the Greek cruise with Daphne Acton, they must have been very in love, one doesn't chuck lipsticks and thrillers into the sea for nothing, it is a much better story than 'Rain'.[1] Did you give sufficient proprietary rights to Lady Lovat[2] and Lady Eldon? Did he throw Lady Lovat's lipsticks into the sea? Someone did, for she has been pale mauve ever since I can remember.

The first letter I wrote was serious, now this has become too frivolous, couldn't you come to London and have an orgy? What about the annual vomit at the Hyde Park Hotel? Or would you come to 'Velvet' Darwin's dance on the 15th?

Ian has been round the world in eighty days; he met Dr Maugham in Tokyo and they spent hours in a jujitso emporium, Ian picking up a trick or two for Bond and Willie delighting in the little boys.[3] Poor Thunderbird couldn't get a girl in Japan because he dosen't know the language and recent visitors such as C. Beaton and T. Capote have convinced the Japanese that the British only like boys; he was more fortunate in Macao where he found a skyscraper brothel called 'Seventh Heaven', the 7th floor providing the best food and the youngest girls, but by that time he felt old and tired, the girls were very understanding and said 'All Englishmen too much gin.'

On the Japanese air line to Hawaii he was given a present every ten minutes – Happi-coats, Happi-socks, Happi-hankies, all the passengers were gently persuaded into Happi outfits by gentle doe-eyed air hostesses and twenty Happi minutes later a Happi smiling pilot announced 'Starboard engine on fire, we 1000 miles Tokyo, 1000 miles Hawaii, hope make Happi forced landing on Wake Island' which Happili they did.

I am recovering from three weeks of influenza, and very depressed. Lady Eden came to stay while I was suffering, her dinner plans were cancelled and I offered her various alternatives but she preferred to dine alone, she seems to have lost all desire for friends but is calm and funny – very rum girl; she bought assorted Penguin and Pelican books to entertain herself and Anthony during the winter months on St Vincent and Antigua, they do not propose to speak to anyone.

I did enjoy your review of the Avedon photographs, and the slaughter of poor little Truman,[4] I should like to know what Cecil thinks but he returned from America in a sadly exhausted state and has gone to Enton Hall for starving and silence.

Flu' prevented my enjoying the inaugural weekend at Chatsworth, Debo collected 'Mr Tom' and Mr Parker Bowles to shoot the pheasants and Chelsea girls in black stockings or trousers to pick them up. Lucian is painting the walls of the state bathroom.[5]

Now I must continue my convalescence, I can't write until I am accustomed to not smoking – it's torture.

I do hope Bron is alright, and Theresa's love affair progresses.

Fionn's life is chaos, and Raymond refuses to leave Ireland because — oh no, you are too indiscreet. Anyway the whole family are being very provoking.

Are you enjoying the winter? Have you made a plan with *The Sunday Times*?

Please write,

Love

A

1 Maugham's story of a clergyman destroyed by his love for a whore had been successful as a play with Jeanne Eagels and as a film with Gloria Swanson, 1928, Joan Crawford, 1932 and Rita Hayworth, 1953.

2 Laura Lister married Lord Lovat in 1910. She is described as 'an important figure in his [Knox's] middle years'. She had accompanied Knox on a cruise in 1930 but retained her lipstick. Lady Eldon was at his death-bed and asked if he would like her to read from his own New Testament. He said 'No' faintly, seemed to lapse into unconsciousness and then added, 'Awfully jolly of you to suggest it, though' – his last words.

3 Ian Fleming ran into Maugham at the Imperial Hotel and they lunched and went to the Kodokan gymnasium 'where fifty young men were practising breakfalls, while in another room a group of girls obligingly staged a mock fight. On the next floor, in one vast hall, two hundred bouts were in progress.' (*Maugham* by Ted Morgan)

4 Waugh reviewed *Observations* by Truman Capote and Richard Avedon in the *Spectator* of 20 November, under the heading 'The Book Unbeautiful'. He found fault with Capote's grammar and wrote of Avedon, already a well-known photographer: 'So far as he has any consistent style . . . it seems to spring from an aptitude to give all his sitters, irrespective of age or sex, a faint look of Mr Maugham.'

5 Tom Egerton and Derek Parker Bowles stayed and Lucian Freud painted flowers on the bathroom walls. Chatsworth had been a girls' school since 1939.

MRS IAN FLEMING

THE LAST YEARS 1960-4

The letters of the early 1960s are almost exclusively to Evelyn Waugh. Ann writes gaily of her travels – to Naples, where the gangster Lucky Luciano is a disappointment, to Capri for lunch with Gracie Fields and Graham Greene, to Portofino, where Waugh's mother-in-law has a house full of Poles, to Chantilly which Lady Diana Cooper is sadly leaving, to Goldeneye, no longer a sure source of pleasure but excellent comic material. In England they both make expeditions to Oxford and see Sir Maurice Bowra, they both go to Forrest Mere for their health, they both have children's marriages to cope with. Ann's social round is energetic, friends come to Victoria Square, she meets Harold Macmillan first at Chatsworth and then at Petworth, and her reports are sparkling. Waugh is more sedentary and it is clear that he is beginning to tire.

The publication of books by friends and relations is often mentioned. Lady Diana Cooper's autobiography is a great success, Auberon Waugh's first novel upsets some but not Ann, Hugo Charteris's career makes progress. Most spectacular of course is the rise of James Bond. In March 1961 President Kennedy reveals himself a fan and the American boom gets under way. Fleming struggles with projects for television and films until *Dr No* comes out in 1963. The money is welcome for they have moved into a flat in Sandwich from which Ian plays golf and Ann continues with her grandiose plans to transform Sevenhampton. Wings are torn down, a lake created, new rooms thrown out. As we have seen, this was not the country house Fleming had envisaged, indeed he regarded with dread the prospect of dons coming to lunch on Sundays, as Bowra and John Sparrow, among others, were soon to do.

This was however only one source of friction between them. Into the amusing correspondence with Waugh, which only hints at problems, there suddenly cut some fierce letters between husband and wife which make it entirely clear how tense things have become. A fragment which Ann herself must have preserved states her case. A letter to Peter Quennell gives a comic but ferocious account of a row in Jamaica. Fleming had a severe heart attack in 1961, became engulfed in a plagiarism case and sometimes sounds desperate. He became both courageous and difficult. Sometimes he stayed at a hotel near Brighton and refused to see Ann, sometimes he insisted on living the life he was used to, the life the doctors had forbidden. The doctors were right and on 12 August 1964 he died.

To Evelyn Waugh

Goldeneye, Jamaica   Tuesday
                                                      26 January [1960]

Dearest Evelyn

We went to *Our Man in Havana*[1] on New Year's Eve, Ian reviewed it on the Third Programme; it was a curious evening, for Ian did not tell me we were going and I did not tell him I was giving a party to welcome the new decade, so we had to take F. Ashton, W. Plomer, and little Cecil Beatnik. Ian as usual could not, would not, take Diana [Cooper], but I blabbed about our destination and she acquired a cheap ticket and was waiting in the foyer – Thunderbird gave me many a hostile reproachful glance while paying to bring her alongside us.

Cecil Beatnik was determined not to laugh at Noël Coward, very difficult because he was very funny, but I fear the film was ill co-ordinated and the audience bewildered. Alec Guinness gave a faithful interpretation of his part, and I thought much better than the critics allowed.

Did you know how angry Cecil was at being called 'Beatnik' at Lady B.'s [Berry's] party? I was fearfully loyal to you and said it was a most unmalicious joke, but he is very very cross, and said you were childish and insulting – it was foolish of him to repeat it, because Ashton and Plomer thought it very funny and did not conceal smirks.

I hear your agent asked *The Sunday Times* £5000 to send you to Monte Carlo; does this mean you are snowballing at Combe Florey or have you escaped by other means?[2] Anyway wherever you are your climatic conditions are better than ours. We have endured six days of rain and gales, and we are not equipped for such weather, the sofas and sheets are sopping, sticky damp and the ill-fitting shutters drip all day: the rivers belch yellow water and coconut husks into the sea in widening circles of bile and filth, the dainty beach is piled high with refuse, and landslides block all the roads; no one enjoys it except Caspar.

Mr Gaitskell was here, but because of the [Eden] legend his party said he could not come to Goldeneye because everyone would make jolly jokes; I went rafting with him and he is blind and deaf to natural beauty like poor you and poor Sparrow, but he is a much stronger swimmer, and the river being in spate he disappeared for several minutes, and we were about to form a human chain when he rolled onto the shore like an amiable hippo.

How I wish Teresa was governessing Caspar, I fear our poor Miss Mona Potterton is on Thunderbird's nerves; she travelled in a pleated white velvet bonnet and on arrival Thunderbird gave me one pound and said 'Take her to buy a straw hat, and forbid any raffia decorations.' Subsequently we were mystified by the hours she spends in the bathroom at night, till Thunderb. banged on the shutters and said in a thunderous voice 'Lights out Miss Potterton'; they were immediately extinguished and presumably she stumbled to bed in the dark; she describes the weather and the taste of tropical fruit as 'very pleasant', she has no other words – very monotonous.[3]

Please swap this dull letter for an exciting one, I dare not write my funniest story because you're so indiscreet. Home early March, and deeply regret being too far away to dine with you.

Much love to you and Laura

A

1 Carol Reed's film of Graham Greene's novel.
2 Waugh had been in Venice as well as Monte Carlo 'having a ripping time at the expense of the *Daily Mail*'.
3 Mona Potterton was described a month later to Lady Diana Cooper as, 'A gem of a governess. She seems to physically dematerialise, possibly levitate, she remains calm without companionship, reads aloud superbly and makes no demands.'

To Evelyn Waugh

16 Victoria Square

Mothering Sunday
26 March [1960]

Dearest Evelyn
    Caspar tells me it is 'Mothering Sunday'. Nanny forced him to put flowers on my breakfast tray and stick shells on a box, he is very

anxious to remove the box as he claims he was forced to stick shells on which he could have sold for a fortune. I don't mean the kind of box that figures in *The Ordeal of Gilbert Pinfold*.[1]

Miss Judy [Montagu] much enjoyed your visit to Rome, and I was interested to hear of the latest development in your romance with your daughter [Margaret]: I thought you would ruin her morally but I gather she is ruining you financially, that to enjoy her favour (not *favours*, a different implication) you have to buy her fur coats and jewellery. She seems to me to be developing splendidly, I am fed up with Fionn and Theresa's generation who wish to live in attics, save the Negroes and march to Aldermaston: if you promote 'Little Margaret' skilfully, she will marry a Greek ship owner in Westminster Abbey and you will end your days on a luxury yacht with plenty of grey pills and chloral.

I dined with Lord Beaverbrook and my fellow guests were Randolph and a shrewd woman called Christopher, Lady Dunn:[2] Randolph's condition prevented my exchanging many words with her but she conceived a passion for me and has sent a dozen bottles of whisky and a dozen of 1947 red Bordeaux; I was to end my evening at the Hyde Park Hotel where Lord Antrim[3] was entertaining [Patrick] Kinross, Devonshires, B. [Lady Bridget] Parsons, Cyril Connolly, Leigh Fermor and kindred spirits, but I could not rid myself of Randolph, he was abusive when I attempted to dislodge him from the taxi at the White's Club and claimed that Antrim was his best friend and they would all be pleased to see him. I doubted these words but it was less effort than calling a policeman. When we arrived in Lord A.'s private room he was in a different state of intoxication, a shambling, pitiful object, much like King Lear on the heath; so I was amazed at Devonshire's reaction for I did not know there had been a 'Suez' row – he shot to his feet said he was unable to remain if Randolph did, and so the party was ruined. Kinross said it was very agreeable before we arrived.

Mary Rose has had the pneumonia and the DTs; it is *grand guignol*, for her husband does not wish her to stop drinking, nor does she wish to stop drinking; and I do not know what to do. On my arrival home I found a letter from Laura saying the doctor advised her to keep out of it owing to their bad relationship in schoolroom days, also a letter from Hugo from John o' Groats, saying I should never leave M.R.'s bedside and pay the bills. Diana says that I should allow M.R. to drink herself to death, and that she is advising Cecil to let his mother drink herself to death; it sounds splendid, but I pointed out that one has to hire someone to pick them from the floor, mop up, and prevent them making rows in the street.

When shall I see you? I want to hear all about the travels.

Come to Chantilly next weekend.

Love to you and Laura,

Ann

PS. Your Jamaica letter was *very* welcome. Not at all nice there.

1 In Waugh's novel there is a black box which, some believe, effects miraculous cures.

2 Marcia Christoforides married Sir James Dunn 1942–56 and Lord Beaverbrook 1963–4. She was thus step-mother to Philip Dunn and his sisters.

3 Earl of Antrim ('Ran') (1911–77). Chairman of the National Trust 1948–64.

From Evelyn Waugh

Combe Florey House, Nr Taunton   31 March 1960

Dear Ann

Pray note that Taunton is in Somerset. Since it is the county town there is no need to say more. When you add 'Gloucestershire' your eagerly welcomed letters are delayed.

I am very sorry to learn that your sister has the DTs. It is no good people telling you to 'let her die of drink'. It is almost impossible to die in that way. When it occurs death is prolonged and painful. On the other hand those whom I know who have been cured emerge greatly reduced in character from the experience. Paraldehyde is the best palliative.

I am greatly puzzled by the statement in this morning's paper that poor Bridget has been locked up for drunkenness in the German Embassy.[1] I should have supposed an extradition order necessary for her arrest there. But I understand less & less of what I read in the papers. Why, for instance, does Esmond pay me £2000 for five articles & then cut out the few jokes and points of interest in them?

The American season has begun. I have had the first letter this year from a group of total strangers who write to invite themselves here. Perhaps you were wise to demolish your commodious house near Banbury. I had a very odd printed postcard from Thunderbird announcing that he had set up as a solicitor in one of the Inns of Court.[2]

Your cousin Margaret has failed for Oxford. Perhaps it is not a bad thing. The place was never intended for girls & has the most deplorable effect on them. I am sending her to work for the Jesuits in Mount Street arranging for the canonisation of Edmund Campion. She had an instructive tour of Athens & Rome & was an agreeable companion. She has the mentality of a child of twelve. Alas, she is in very bad looks at the moment.

Why on earth should General de Gaulle ask Laura & me to a party? Who makes out his list for him? Must be mad.

Your cousin Margaret must not marry a Greek in Westminster Abbey. An Englishman at the Oratory is what is needed.

Nancy says *Hons and Rebels* is false & cruel.[3] I have not read it.

Yours ever affec,

E.W.

How pleased the fuddy-duddies & welshers must be to have you back in London. Is Bill Patton's death a happy release or a sorrow to Susan Mary?[4] You might let me know as I should write to her & don't know quite what terms to apply.

1 Lady Bridget Parsons had been arrested for drunken driving in Belgrave Square and taken into the German Embassy until a police car arrived.

2 Fleming's new office off Fleet Street.

3 *Hons and Rebels*, 1960, by Jessica Mitford. An account of her childhood, which had appeared lightly fictionalised in her sister Nancy's novels.

4 William Patton (1909–60) married Susan Mary Jay in 1939. He worked at the American Embassy in Paris 1944–55 and then at the Paris branch of the World Bank until 1958. She married Joe Alsop, the journalist, in 1961.

To Evelyn Waugh

Chateau de St Firmin, Vineuil, Oise   Low Sunday
                                             [24 April 1960]

Dear Cousin E.

'Baby' is very patient with Viscountess Norwich. I find the Viscountess opinionated, exhibitionistic and obstinate; yesterday she criticised *G. Pinfold*.[1] 'Baby' was rushing in and out of the room carrying lilac trees and took no part in the argument but the Viscountess, determined to prove her point, fetched the book and we went through it page by page until she was forced to retract her foolish point of view; by that time 'Baby' was rushing in and out with apple trees but took a breather to give me support, and I was able to escape to feed the carp. Yesterday evening Viscountess Norwich swung the Norwich heir[2] round and round by his heels until he was sick on the carpet, I find her newly discovered maternal instinct very suspect.

Lord Haddington[3] is here; though sixty-five years of age he has seldom ventured from his Scottish home and is very bewildered and excited by it all, specially when Diana pulled up the maid's skirts to show the company the prettiness of her cambric petticoats – Lord H. did not dare look at anything but the ceiling.

You are missing many horrible treats: the pillaging of the royal box at the Opera House after the ballet gala; it had been decorated by Beatnik with carnations, and after Armstrong-Jones left Beatnik tore down his garlands and wound them round 'Baby', Mrs Osborn[4] and me, so we left be-bouqueted like Madame Callases and were gazed at with envy and disapproval.

Lady Bridget comes up for trial on Monday, all the rank and fashion attend and we think she will be acquitted because her inability to stand between two wardresses will prove ill health and not intemperance;[5] she is very cross because the Lord Chamberlain did not put 'The' before 'Lady' on her wedding invitation.

I wish I had answered your letter sooner, but Hugo is south with his family, Mary Rose needs constant attention and now Cynthia [Asquith] has died there is no one to help, and the Easter vacation was fraught with egg hunts and the Quennells, also the doctor's son got badly hurt at the egg hunt and the doctor came round roaring for vengeance on old Caspar; old Caspar was innocent for once, it was poor Mary Rose's sneaky child[6] who had hit the doctor's child with a spanner to gain possession of a chocolate rabbit.

Longer letter soon; please come to London. Why not Armstrong-Jones Day? I am giving the reception, seagulls' eggs and champagne on the floor, and all the hot news from the Abbey.[7]

Love,

Ann

1 Lady Diana Cooper and her daughter-in-law. Waugh addressed Lady Diana as

'Baby' when writing to her – 'embarrassing, but there it is'. Anne Clifford had married John Julius Cooper in 1952 and he succeeded as Viscount Norwich in 1954. She is happy to allow this description of herself to stand so long as it is understood that she felt much the same about Ann.

2 Jason Cooper, then aged one, was not sick on the carpet, according to his mother, but simply 'drooling with pleasure'.

3 Earl of Haddington (1894–   ). Lord Lieutenant of Berwickshire 1952–69.

4 June Capel (1920–   ). Married in 1948 the pianist Franz Osborn, and in 1966 Jeremy Hutchinson QC, who was made a life peer in 1978.

5 The Duke of Devonshire and Lord Kinross gave evidence as to how little she had drunk at dinner and she was indeed acquitted.

6 Francis Grey (1951–   ). Largely brought up with Caspar after the death of his mother. Member of the Royal Green Jackets 1971–9 from which he emerged a captain. Now a chartered surveyor.

7 On 6 May Princess Margaret married Antony Armstrong-Jones in Westminster Abbey. He was created Earl of Snowdon in 1961. Judy Montagu and Sir Harold Nicolson were among Ann's fifty guests and the latter found Ann's hat 'like a frigidaire from the Ideal Homes Exhibition complete with paw-paws, yams, passion fruit and bananas'. Noël Coward thought it 'a wild but beautifully organised lunch party . . . a glorious mix-up'.

To Evelyn Waugh

16 Victoria Square   2 May [1960]

Dearest E.

Very sneaky of you to come to London without telling me and take another girl [Lady Mary Lygon] to marble halls; and why do you send a postcard boasting of your asparagus? You must have acquired a very good cook recently for asparagus is easily spoiled, they are my only culinary defeat – burnt bottoms and hard heads – has Laura taken a course at the cordon bleu?

Leslie Hartley spoke loud and bold at Aunt Cynthia's memorial service, I had expected a shy nervous twitter; it was a strangely unmoving address, we had all been crying during the preceding hymn but he stopped all that – can't be right, can it?

We had a very jolly dinner here to mix Oliver Lyttleton Chandos[1] with the Gaitskells and Tony Crosland; you wouldn't have approved but Oliver was very happy and stayed till 2.30 a.m. to perfect his mimicry of my left-wing friends. [Unsigned.]

1 Viscount Chandos (1895–1972). Unionist MP 1940–54, Secretary of State for the Colonies 1951–4. Created a Viscount 1954. Chairman of National Theatre Board 1962–71.

To Evelyn Waugh

Hotel Excelsior, Napoli   25 May [1960]

Dearest Evelyn

I enclose a fragment of a letter uncompleted to show I was not disinterested in the excellence of your asparagus; the fragment was not finished because the Charterises invaded London, they are always ravenously hungry and cannot afford restaurants, they made Mrs Crickmere's feet swell, she was indignant and said 'In plain English, Madam, tell them to bugga off.'

I persuaded Thunderbird that Naples was a thrilling city as I wished to visit it. I over-egged it – stories of the rich façade of hotels and murder and dope-peddling in the back streets, and 'Lucky Luciano' organising vice gangs. The afternoon we arrived I said I was off to the National Museum, Thunderbird was very perturbed – 'Surely you can't go alone, you must not leave the hotel without me.' I returned unmolested and found a very excited Thunderbird because his journalist friends had persuaded 'Lucky Luciano' to meet him, the meeting was for 4 o'clock the following day and it was clear that my presence would be unwelcome, and indeed at 4 o'clock I was sleeping off fish soup and pasta, but at five I cautiously approached the hotel lounge and peering round the door I saw Ian with a little old Italian gentleman, benign, sedate, distinguished; to my surprise they were sipping China tea and lemon, a beverage loathed by Thunderbird. I thought there was some mistake but I was introduced to Mr Salvatore Luciano, and settled to listen respectfully; T-B was growing impatient – 'Didn't you deserve a sentence at all, Mr Luciano?'

'I was framed.'

'What about the narcotics racket?'

'It was white slavery they framed me on, and I disapproved all my life of men living on top of women. Dewey was the son-of-a-bitch, if Madam will forgive the expression, he framed me.'

'Why don't you write your life story?'

'People want to hear bad things, they wouldn't believe the truth, Mr Fleming.'

'What about the dope going from Naples to America?'

'Nothing happens in Naples the law doesn't know about, Mr Fleming.'

I thought he said 'Lord' and hopefully enquired the name of the church that contains two corpses preserved by pouring gold in their veins, he was very startled – 'That sort of thing doesn't happen in Naples, Mrs Fleming!' 'It did in the middle ages' I said firmly, and being tired of it all rose to say goodbye and added 'I'm proud to have met you, Mr Luciano'; he bridled, took off his spectacles, revealed the eyes of a toad and replied 'They say people only come to Naples to meet me and the Pope, Mrs Fleming.'

Alas, I am so tired that it is a dull account of the comedy – wish you'd been there, you would have enjoyed it.

When T-B is making a city 'thrilling' he never stops to look at anything – how do you account for the success of his articles?

Siena was particularly disastrous because the width of the car and the narrow medieval streets forced T-B to stop, his face was redder than the walls; yesterday we did the Museo de Capodimonte in ten minutes – three cubic miles of paintings and ceramics.[1] This morning the curator of the National Museum is taking us around in person, do you suppose his august presence will slow down T-B's speed?

I am choked with dust and deafened by noise, and longing for streams of lava to submerge all these horrible Fiats, motor bikes and Neapolitan Bonds. I suppose it is old age making me as irascible as you, or possibly nervous exhaustion for our itinerary in the last week has included Noël Coward, Charlie Chaplin,[2] Père Bise restaurant at Annecy (Ian sick all night following five-star dinner and my left eye bitten by poisonous mosquito), Turin (injections of penicillin for poisoned eye), Florence (eye still poisoned so Cyclops approach to Uffizi – and only allowed two hours), Rome (day with Roman princes, organised by Miss Judy – they all had black hair and black mats on their chests, and took dope – a beach party, that's why I know about their chests), Tiberius's bathing pool, a freak circus with only living female spider who looked like Hattie (I wondered if you had decided upon that instead of the ballet) for it was the head of an English-speaking blonde child who was clearly limbless for the head emerged from a small, black leather bag with spider's legs attached – I was sick that time.

I return on June 8th, and would like to discuss my thrilling travels with you – surely you are due for London soon?

Love to you both,

A

1 Fleming said when the project was discussed that he 'had often advocated the provision of roller skates at the doors of museums and art galleries'. Leonard Russell, features editor of *The Sunday Times*, had reassured him, 'We don't want that kind of stuff from you.'

2 Coward recorded: 'Annie and Ian's visit [to Les Avants in Switzerland] was a great success and they were both gay as bedamned and very funny. I took them to dinner with Charlie and Oona [Chaplin] and a good time was had by all, except, secretly, me. George and Benita [Hume] were present and Benita and Annie took one of those heartfelt female dislikes to one another. Under cover, of course, but clear to me. Charlie went into his act a thought too thoroughly and was a trifle embarrassing, but maybe I am hypercritical.'

From Ann and Ian Fleming to Evelyn Waugh

[Postcard]   [3 June 1960]

Written in a Neapolitan harbour restaurant. Tweedle-ee-wee of many Neapolitan bands and Thunderbird beset by pimps – 'You want a very nice Rose?' – 'You want a very feelthy picture?' – It's very feelthy sphagetti [sic], and very feelthy wine – and now a hunchback has arrived selling very feelthy lottery tickets.
[*Ian Fleming adds:*]
This is a splendidly horrible town. It has a ghastly zest which I would prefer to London if the food were better. A. stands up well under its pressure & it's a change to see her out-shouted in decibels &, I suspect, in content. The place still smells & cheats as badly as one's first visit abroad which is exhilarating for the elderly.
                                        Saluti
                                        Ian

To Evelyn Waugh

16 Victoria Square   10 June [1960]

Dearest Evelyn
    Absence of gossip sheets is due to decay of body,[1] and the last months have been fraught with the problems of an alcoholic sister; but your letter was most welcome in Naples though I was sad to hear of your relapse: let us discuss it all next week.

In Capri we had lunch with Gracie Fields and the Russian electrician[2] that she married, Graham Greene and Mrs Walston joined us for coffee and green chartreuse, the Russian electrician said to me 'Your accent is most majestic, do you not come from the same district as Gracie?' It was very nice to have a good stare at Mrs Walston, she behaved much as you described her in the shop of a lame shoemaker; she seized my battered straw hat and declared it a most enviable possession, she tried it on at various angles and prinked and preened, then she displayed the same idiotic enthusiasm for Ian's old walking stick and pranced about with the uninteresting object expressing a violent desire for it. I suggested a swop for her frock at which she started violently undoing the bodice – she's a very maddening woman.

Later we accompanied them to Anacapri and Graham Greene talked of blue cinemas, displays in brothels and the printed tariff issued by the fishermen of Capri for pleasuring American tourist ladies, the price varied from five thousand lire to twenty-five thousand lire. I was quite relieved when we left them and took the chair-lift to the top of the mountain, it is a very nice chair-lift for your feet trail through the vines, then the umbrella pines, and at the top you are within jumping distance of astonishing wild flowers – no vertigo.

I returned home via Chantilly, meeting Caspar and Nanny at the Gare du Nord, a very foolish thing to do on Whit Friday, thick crowds and surly porters. Caspar kicked a trail while Nanny and I carried the luggage on our heads.

Diana was doing far too much and had the collywobbles, previous to our arrival she had suffered night starvation and gulped a plate of cold curry; there was a heatwave and Whit Saturday morning no plug would pull so Diana in bonnet and nightie was flying about the place filling cans and placing them strategically, she refused all assistance.

I hear the Heads are to govern the new Rodesia – has it an H?[3]

Lady Dudley [Ann's sister Laura] becomes Mrs Michael Canfield[4] on Monday, she is ten years his senior.

John Betjeman's daughter[5] has the chic and poise of a Paris model, the wit of her mother and the originality of her father – you might fall in love with her.

Lord and Lady Lambton spent twelve thousand pounds on their ball, but my friends tell me little about it – Diana said 'Beastly, like all balls' and Quennell said 'I had a very agreeable time, but I don't remember details' – a lesson to us all not to spend money on balls.

I had a very jolly [Armstrong-]Jones wedding day, I motored Fionn and Leigh Fermor to the occasion: Fuddy-duddy Fermor enjoys his grey top hat and was in despair when I poked him into the rear seat of my tiny car – nobody could see him; then I couldn't turn the heat off but happily half way down the Mall I remembered the roof opened, so we were the only open car in a procession of funereal Daimlers and the cheering for us was loud and much chat about the identity of Leigh Fermor and offers from ladies to change seats with Fionn. The sun shone and the bands played – in Whitehall the Irish Guards were playing 'Danny Boy', and it was all so beautiful tears came into my eyes and I got out of time with the Daimlers and nearly telescoped.

Let me know soonest when we can meet.

Love to you and Laura,

A

1 Waugh had written: 'What pray has become of you? It is time you wrote me a long detailed gossip sheet. You must think of me as living in Tasmania eager for news of fuddy-duddies etc.'

2 Gracie Fields (1898–1979). The popular singer and film star married in 1952 Boris Alperovici. Fleming described her as 'this handsome, kindly, humorous woman from Lancashire', and he found Boris 'charming and intelligent'.

3 Antony Head was made a Viscount and the first High Commissioner to Nigeria that year.

4 Michael Canfield (1925–69). Publisher. Since 1953 Laura had been living with Anthony Pelissier, but he often disappeared without warning: 'He could never decide which of the arts to settle for. He painted, composed music, wrote and acted in early life . . .' After Christmas 1958 he had walked out again, and Frankie More O'Ferrall was coaxing Laura to a party. When she said that she had not even heard of Michael Canfield, she was told, 'Well that just shows how out of touch you are. He's the most attractive man in London.' Laura went, met him and, 'It was love, my heart sang.'

5 Candida Betjeman (1942–   ). Only daughter of Sir John, and author of children's and gardening books. In 1963 she married Rupert Lycett-Green.

16 Victoria Square   [June 1960]

Dear Evelyn

Yes, D. Fairbanks Junior does have graffiti on the undersides of his lavatories[1] – who told you? Little Margaret or the foreigners in White's?

On Wednesday went to Oxford for Encaenia luncheon, invited by Berlins. It was very jolly because of high summer weather and a splendid view from Isaiah's room and much to drink. I was able to watch the throng assemble and listen to the malicious commentary of Maurice and Isaiah.

The Prime Minister displayed little taste in conferring honours on Evelyn Sharp[2] and Lady Albemarle,[3] the former strode about with cigarette between clenched teeth and hands in pocket with gown flung aggressively back, and the latter minced, squeaked and gambolled girlishly, allowing gown to slip from one shoulder revealing hideous cotton frock.

At lunch I sat beside Isaiah, Lady Pam-bery on other side. Lady Pam's fur showed up very well in the sunlight from clerestory windows, and she was fearfully false and invited me to lots of lunch parties; opposite was Donald McLachlan[4] and the Editor of *The Sunday Times*[5] – a man I have never been allowed to meet; I knew Thunderbird had taken pictures of men dressed as women to the *Sunday Times* conference, hoping they would illustrate his piece on Berlin, so I asked him boldly if he would print them. He was embarrassed and cross, and said Ian had not shown the transvestite snaps but was no doubt waiting for R. Thomson's return from Canada with whom they would find more favour; so I will collect one for you. They are of increased interest since Fuddy-duddy Freud told me that Fuddy-duddy Bacon told him that the Riviera and other pleasure spots are populated with German homosexual youths who have been hormone-injected to grow breasts.

After lunch at Oxford I watched Lady P. and Lady Waverley[6] trying to approach the Prime Minister – they circled him like satellites round the earth, Lady P. made it first and picked up the hem of his scarlet robe and was obviously a gush of flattery. Then I was kidnapped by Maurice and we had cucumber sandwiches in the shade of his ilex tree. As we progressed towards Wadham we ran into the Prime Minister who exchanged banal courtesies with Maurice, it was almost hostile, and I was unrecognised by the great man and M. did not introduce me, so I stood and stared at the spires and also the P.M. and remembered the 'C' letters.[7]

Last night Jack Donaldson[8] took me to the Albany hideout for a drink; Mrs Walston was across the way with Graham Greene, the pictures were horrible, but it was pleasantly untidy; Frankie [Donaldson] was in the country and Jack had dined with me and the fruits of my womb, but they had gone one to a ball and other to review Quennell's book[9] for *Time and Tide*. There is something very impositive about Jack though I like him awfully.

Cyril Connolly upset the composition of last week's *Sunday Times* by returning Anthony Powell's book[10] to them on Friday with the feeble explanation that he was unable to review it because the Powells were spending the weekend with him and it would prove embarrassing.

I see you have been more courageous, the last paragraph of your review is intensely sad, it made me cry.[11] It is Ian's view, but he has not your command of language and beats his breast and shrieks that 'All men are islands' misquoting Donne's 'No man is an island' but it is unwise to contradict him.

Some men are certainly more islands than others; I have married three Formosas, perhaps it is more often a male affliction. Poor Maurice is a great sufferer, so is Dr Maugham, T. S. Eliot, Graham Greene. I suspect Lady Eden is an island. Harold Nicolson is less of an island – let's talk about it in marble halls.

Thankyou for the lovely caviar; let me know when next you come to see Little M. [Margaret], and we can have lunch at V. Square – cheaper for you. I can't write unless I see you occasionally.

Love

A

1 Believed to have been 'Hurrah! Daddy's home'.

2 Dame Evelyn Sharp (1903–). Permanent Secretary in the Ministry of Housing and Local Government 1955–66 and as such was to work with Richard Crossman and figure prominently in his diaries. Created a life peer 1966.

3 Countess of Albemarle (1909–). Among her many public works was the chairmanship of the Executive Committee of the National Federation of Women's Institutes.

4 Donald McLachlan (1908–71). Naval Intelligence 1940–45, Deputy Editor of the *Daily Telegraph* 1954–60, Editor of the *Sunday Telegraph* 1961–66. Married in 1934 Katherine Harman, sister of the Countess of Longford.

5 H. V. Hodson (1906–). Editor of *The Sunday Times* 1950–61. Author of several books on economics and on the British Empire.

6 Ava Bodley had married in 1941 Viscount Waverley, who died in 1958.

7 Waugh had referred to Macmillan as 'C' in his life of Ronald Knox, who tutored him, but Malcolm Muggeridge had blown the gaff in the *New Statesman*.

8 John (Jack) Donaldson (1907–   ). Farmer and politician. Married to Frances Lonsdale (*q.v.*). Created a life peer in 1967, joined SDP in 1981. *See* Appendix of Names.

9 *The Sign of the Fish*, the first volume of autobiography by Peter Quennell.

10 *Casanova's Chinese Restaurant*, fifth volume of *A Dance to the Music of Time*.

11 In the lengthy last paragraph of his review in the *Spectator* of 24 June Waugh quotes as the key to the whole of *A Dance to the Music of Time* a remark by the narrator: 'In the end most things in life – perhaps all things – turn out to be appropriate', and contrasts Powell's novels with those of Graham Greene: 'Mr Greene's characters never know anyone. Their intense, lonely lives admit of professional acquaintances, lovers and sometimes a single child but they are never seen as having ramifications of friendship, cousinhood and pure social familiarity. Their actions are performed under the solitary eye of God. Mr Powell sees human society as the essential vehicle of the individual. Everyone knows everyone else perhaps at the remove of one. Everyone's path crosses and recrosses everyone else's. There are no barriers of age or class or calling that can divide the universal, rather cold intimacy which the human condition imposes.'

From Evelyn Waugh

Combe Florey House, Nr Taunton   26 June 1960

My dear Ann

The sentence in my review of Tony Powell's book which caught your attention was intended to summarise *his* view of society, not mine.

The visit to the television factory was very rum. Margaret counted more than thirty men & women engaged solely in record-ing the dialogue of two. They were very civil, indeed deferential. The questions most odd. I presume the object of the programme is to satisfy the natural curiosity most of us feel about the way other people earn their livings. My interviewer[1] showed no interest in the literary life, or my aesthetic preferences, or my opinions of other writers, the places where I had travelled, the technicalities of composition or style – nothing like that. All he seemed to care about was my childhood – had I suffered very much from having no sister, that sort of thing. I did not see the result. Bron said I looked corpulent. He has come down and I am trying to bribe him to go abroad. He shows a painful affection for home life, unlike his exiled sister Teresa. I think I have persuaded him to go to Malta & Rhodes with the Clives[2] & Martin Dunne.[3] But I have to endure a young people's house party here next Sunday.

Somerset is over run by Roosevelts at the moment. My brother Alec came here for the first time last week. He has fallen victim to the continental regime of aphrodisiac injections and is leading a life that is not seemly at his age.

Yours ever affec.

Evelyn

1 John Freeman (1915–). Chairman of Weekend Television and once interviewer on the BBC's *Face to Face*. Labour MP 1945–55. Deputy Editor of the *New Statesman*, he became Editor for four years before being High Commissioner in India and Ambassador in Washington. Waugh had asked on a postcard, 'Do you know anything of Major Freeman, late Rifle Brigade, late advertising agent, late Labour MP, now connected BBC? Dirt welcomed.'

2 George (1940–) and Alice Clive (1942–), children of Lady Mary Clive, a sister of Lord Longford. Alice Clive married in 1962 Simon Lennox-Boyd, who succeeded as Viscount Boyd in 1983.

3 Martin Dunne (1938–). Son of Waugh's friend Philip Dunne.

To Evelyn Waugh

16 Victoria Square   16 July [1960]

Dear Evelyn

Why are you so unkind to Peter Quennell? He has been moping since he read your review and is at a loss to understand your aversion to him, he says you resemble Lord Chesterfield's description of life – 'nasty, brutish and short'.[1]

Chatsworth was very jolly, Debo carried Lord Antrim about in her arms and Antrim and Devonshire carried Osbert Sitwell[2] into lunch; their first effort failed and poor O. fell back upon the sofa all of a tremble; during the meal his fork started knocking against his plate, the din was awful, and it was difficult to maintain unembarrassed conversation.

It's very big, Chatsworth, isn't it? [Anthony] Powell and [Robert] Kee carried an elephant folio of Audubon's *Birds of America* from the library to the drawing room for my pleasure; they both complained of slipped discs on the completion of their task, and no table large enough so it was put upon the floor; while I was enjoying it Debo's labradors approached with muddy paws, I gave a shriek but Debo only said 'They're game dogs and only interested in birds.'

I am in bed with aches and bruises. Two days ago Thunderbird thundered into an ice-cream van, my head broke the windscreen. Thunderbird said it looked as if a 50 millimetre shell had hit it, very rum, because I have only slight discomfort when combing my hair. We were collected by two schoolmistresses, clearly their only pleasure in life is the frequent crashes at their front door. 'We put the kettle on when we heard the horn screaming' they told us while forcing strong tea upon us and enjoying the yelps of pain as they poured Jeyes fluid on my broken knees; they were very disappointed at our minor abrasions and said we probably had internal injuries; they must be constantly prepared for these excitements for the first aid kit was on the table and there was a satisfied happy glint in their eyes.

The *Cornhill* and the *Spectator* are a great joy this week in spite of the beastly ungrateful reference to my dinner-party. Edward R. F. Sheehan[3] writes well, you should give pleasure to your friends by inviting him to stay again.

Mrs Stitch is here and would like to see you.

Love,

A

1 The description was given by Thomas Hobbes, not Lord Chesterfield. Waugh's review of Peter Quennell's *The Sign of the Fish* in the *Spectator* of 8 July ranged from insult to faint praise: 'Mr Quennell wrote some pleasant post-Georgian, pre-Eliot verses. He shows proper modesty about his subsequent career. . . Is he quite the man to explore for us the mysteries of the creative impulse? . . . He writes nicely. He has nothing very original to say but he observes the rules of grammar and draws on a large vocabulary with notable tact of choice.'

2 Sir Osbert Sitwell (1893–1969). Author and champion of the arts. He was suffering from Parkinson's disease.

3 Edward Sheehan, an American, had stayed with Waugh when there was a fête and written an account in the *Cornhill* magazine (Summer 1960) called 'A Weekend with Waugh'.

Ann went to stay with Waugh's mother-in-law, Mary Herbert, in Portofino while the unwanted portions of Sevenhampton were pulled down.

To Evelyn Waugh

Portofino   31 August [1960]

Dear Evelyn

We are homeless until Christmas 1961. The last days at the Old Palace were like the last act of *The Cherry Orchard*, we sat upon our suitcases awaiting release from finality gloom, then Thunderbird went to Le Touquet for golfing and gambling, Caspar to learn his multiplication tables in Northern Ireland and me to Italy and the Berlins. Hourly we expect Auberon and Mary [Herbert] by car, Bowra by train; Auberon and Maurice may upset present routine. At the moment we have gentle Stuart Hampshire,[1] Julian [Ayer], and a quiet beach life with Russian evenings, for Isaiah has Russianised the Herbert agent's house – his personality and the cumbrous dark furniture, napkin rings, governess children, Jewish bride – it's very patriarchal and conversation continues long into the night. At 7 p.m. the American sputnik appears over the piazza, the Italians are much excited by this, they dance up and down and yell '*Sputniki, sputniki, sputniki*' – they are very cross if one is disinterested.

Graham Greene took us to Wilton's for dinner; while walking down Duke Street he said were we members of the Keyhole club, and took us down a mews to a courtyard where brilliant lights proclaimed striptease; we returned after dinner but missed the show – G.G. very disappointed. I will take you next time you come to London, and also Little Margaret.

There are two traction engines and a wooden scoop endeavouring to dredge our lake [at Sevenhampton]; the traction engines hoot mournfully and lawn is covered with sludge and dead eels; in December the house will be demolished and the rubble spread upon the other lawns; but we are very optimistic if only we can pay the bills.

Can't write – too hot.

Please RSVP to Shane's Castle, Antrim. I go there on 9th.

Love to Laura and you,

A

Enjoyed *African Diary* v. much.

1 Stuart Hampshire (1914–   ). Grote Professor of Philosophy of Mind and Logic, University of London 1960–3, Warden of Wadham College, Oxford 1970–84. Knighted 1979.

To Evelyn Waugh

[Portofino]   [September 1960]

My dear Evelyn

I do not know why you say the [Herbert] villa is uncomfortable, I have seldom been so happy anywhere, and had I a million pounds I would purchase it. I found it exquisite pleasure to lie in bed and gaze at the sea through Corsican pines. The rooms are spacious and could be made beautiful, it is true my bathroom lacked lavatory paper, soap and toothglass, but I collected these from the neighbouring bathroom inhabited by a Pole called Sigismund;[1] the Pole had ten razors and innumerable bottles of face lotion and medicines so I thought he would not miss the normal requirements.

Auberon is better walking than talking, his physical condition does not allow both. While walking he has to shorten his sentences and is far better company – indeed ascending mountains the talk is replaced by unnoisesome noises, difficult to know from whence they come, he apologises at length and says his mother does not like it. Auberon, Pole and I walked to Fruttuoso for lunch, it was raining and Pole carried basket, but he was a cunning Pole and wrapped his garments inside ours, so during lunch he was more comfortable than us.

Sir Maurice Bowra has fallen in love with your mother-in-law, he refers to her as 'Mrs Waugh, Senior', will your mother-in-law like this? I am also in love with her and was very pleased to see her again. She seemed to spend her time driving to Genoa to buy mosquito nets for Poles.

So despite a disconcerting arrival I enjoyed life with the Herberts; my arrival was disconcerting because the villa appeared untenanted save for a fat foreign-spoken gentleman whose English was confined to muttering 'I am Shakespeare, you are not';[2] thinking I was alone with a 'Pinfold' I hurried upstairs, where the names above the door clarified the situation and obviously the inspiration for your writing paper.[3]

Sir Maurice Bowra was not very happy in Portofino, the Berlins lodge guests in the Nazionale which inclines to be stuffy and noisy; I was delighted to leave it for the beauty and peace of the villa, but Maurice was then lonely and unable to walk uphill, so felt left out of things. We usually bathed at Paraggio, crowded and noisy, but the professors did not observe this because they made so much more noise themselves. I refused the Herbert bathing for fear of being wounded and maimed by the rocks. Jimmy Smith told me that when he bathed there the sea was red with blood, and the screams could be heard for miles.

Thunderbird is at a liver cure resort in Brittany with an old gentleman whom he loves. Disloyally I do not understand the success of his thrilling cities, but we need the money.

With love to you and Laura,

A

1 Sigismund Michailowski worked for Radio Free Europe in Munich.
2 Thought to be a relation of the Dorothy Shakespear who married Ezra Pound.
3 The names of poets were written on the walls in Gothic script. Perhaps Ann thought the foreign-spoken gentleman was referring to a named bedroom; perhaps he was.

To Hugo Charteris

Shane's Castle   16 September [1960]

Darling Hugo,

. . . I was very happy there [in Portofino]. Auberon owns a vast property, it is known as 'Il Conte Herbert' and is slightly more real than at home. He hopes to re-establish his finances by selling for a quarter of a million, and is constantly intriguing with doubtful-looking Italians on the piazza – I hope he has a good lawyer! I had forgotten how dynamic a personality Mary [Herbert] is, she bears little resemblance to her pink and white progeny. I think it possible that she unwittingly destroyed Auberon. I very much enjoyed seeing her again. I was told it was unwise to mention Bron's novel,[1] but a letter arrived from Boofy to introduce a junior partner of Chapman Hall[2] who had arrived for a holiday plus proof copy of the book. I felt Boofy was a'mischief making again, for I gather it may libel Magdalen[3] and set the Catholic clans fighting. Do not repeat this to Ian Fraser [her cousin] whom I dislike as much as I like the Herberts.

I hope your new novel is assured of publication, and you enjoyed Butlin's.[4]

I would have written before, but August was busy leaving house, getting flat in Sandwich, doubts and fears of ability to pay for new venture, Ian's blood pressure rising at night, post 'thrilling cities' exhaustion, and long beach days with Caspar and Francis [Grey].

Mary Rose started drinking when she visited Michael Asquith [her cousin] in Spain. Nigel [Grey],[5] convincing for once, said she sat up all night with Michael drinking white wine and talking of the past. She then recovered but started [again] when F. returned from school – I guessed because she was to come with Francis, but said she did not feel up to it, and when I collected him at the station he said she had been lying on the floor all day. Francis tells she was 'ill' the first two nights of their holiday, then alright. There is little one can do except keep in touch and send her to Enton if things get bad.

Raymond is in London, and we picnic every day: we use his vast Humber Hawk van with a silver eagle on the bonnet! Unluckily the clutch came away in my hand in the heart of the Sperrin Mountains. We were rescued by a turf-cutting family who enjoyed the situation, the silver eagle, the endless walking for help, and our final disappearance towed by an antique Morris.

See you soon I hope. Was sorry you did not materialise my brief night in London.

With much love to you, Virginia and all,

A

---

1 *The Foxglove Saga*, 1960.

2 Gillon Aitken (1938–). Literary agent, editor with Chapman and Hall 1959–66.

3 Some detected a resemblance between the sanctimonious Lady Foxglove and Magdalen, Countess of Eldon.

4 Nicholas Mosley, Raymond Carr and Hugo Charteris went to Butlin's with some of their children. Charteris wrote of the experience in the *Daily Telegraph*.

5 Nigel Grey (1891–1974). Married Mary Rose Thesiger *née* Charteris in 1949. Guy Charteris used to say that he had gone up to Oxford just as Nigel Grey came down. The Charteris family became obsessed with his age and insisted that he was older than their father, who was in fact five years the senior.

To Evelyn Waugh

Sandwich Bay, Kent   [22 September 1960]

My dear Evelyn

When Fuddy-duddy Quennell and Fuddy-duddy William Plomer read about the treatment of dear little Tarquin they rushed to the nearest receptacles and vomited.[1] Fuddy-duddy Quennell 'had laughed out loud, as one does in Evelyn's books' until he arrived at Tarquin's torture, but that broke his nerve.

Many descriptions of Tarquin have come to my ears, people speak of little else – I shall not allow Lady Eldon to adopt beautiful clever Caspar.

Connolly is quite right about your tensions,[2] but prosperity has nothing to do with it; you would not stink of paraldehyde if you had no tensions, or frighten fuddy-duddies by rolling your eyes at them. It's very nice to have tensions, it means you're a higher form of life than a jellyfish or a cabbage.

Who can be going to employ you in London and in what capacity?[3] I do hope it's true. I'm longing to see you.

The Donaldsons were alarmed that they had lost favour with you because no copy of your African adventures had reached them. I put their minds at rest. Next week I shall purchase a copy; at this moment I am reading Cynthia's *Married to Tolstoy*.[4] I enjoy it, knowing nothing of the story, but though in life she was astringent her literary efforts are sometimes embarrassing.

Do you read *Encounter*? You should not miss a piece in the August number by Arthur Koestler on yoga; if you are sufficiently versed in that art, you never when mating leave the stuff in the woman, it is too valuable, you take it back into yourself and it strengthens your body and mind. Thunderbird is very excited about it.

I terribly want to consult you about the house; T-B does not want to leave Sandwich, he is on the golf committee and his only happiness is pink gin, golf clubs and men. So he wants to alter the plans and keep a flat here and build a rabbit hutch for me instead of a mansion: he will come home occasionally. It's awful because I don't like an empty house at sunset – d'you suppose Bowra or Sparrow would live with me? Also I'm very excited by the plans, and the lake draining has produced torrents of water for black

swans. Shall I force him to build the mansion? We don't know yet if
we can get a builder to build: they are so busy one has to importune
them, and they can charge any price they like; it is also difficult to
find good stonemasons – a dying art. Perhaps I ought to stay and
cook for him here. It's delightful having no servants, I can cook and
paint all day, but one has to go out in disguise for fear of meeting the
Peter Thursbys, the Reggie Winns, and other 1920 persons who
seem sad and dull.

The Tate Gallery have an exhibition of Munich painters, a very
horrible collection of canvases by Kandinsky – red, white and blue
squiggles. The preview was followed by a reception at the German
Embassy, it is totally unfurnished and very large – just a few
photographs of pre-1914 politicians. But I had a nice time with the
French Ambassador[5] who took me to the buffet to prove that
despite the pre-1914 politicians they had betrayed themselves by
feeding their guests with slices of raw wild animals – and indeed
bleeding venison was the only fare. The French Ambassador says he
has to employ many Negroes from the French Africas to prepare
them for freedom, at the moment his 2nd secretary is Prime
Minister of Togoland, and spends all day telephoning to that
country.

Willie Maugham and Cyril come to lunch on Thursday – my
reconciliation with Cyril.[6]

Love

A

1 Tarquin was a baby adopted by Lady Foxglove in *The Foxglove Saga* by
Auberon Waugh: 'At the age of a year he was still completely hairless except for his
legs which grew redder and furrier every day . . . Tarquin ruled alone in the nursery
corridor . . . [they] first came across the beast cowering in a corner of the night
nursery but he scuttled sideways like a tarantula.' He was killed by a fall from his
rocking-horse.

2 Waugh had quoted Connolly, who wrote that Waugh was enabled to continue
writing in spite of prosperity by 'internal tensions', adding, 'What can the booby
mean?'

3 There had been a suggestion that Waugh should write the English screenplay of
Fellini's film *La Dolce Vita*.

4 Cynthia Asquith's biography of Tolstoy's wife appeared posthumously that
year. '. . . into all her writing she put the faith and hope that burned in her and the
charity that informed all her judgements'. L. P. Hartley in the foreword to her
Diaries 1915–18, 1968.

5 Jean Chauvel was Ambassador in London 1955–62.

6 Ann's relationship with Connolly had always been changeable. Waugh replied: 'I am glad you are chums with Connolly. He has botulism but it is not contagious. A man of great worth. Give him some tensions so that he can write books.'

To Evelyn Waugh

16 Victoria Square   12 October [1960]

Dearest Evelyn

I am not enjoying Diana's book,[1] I looked up all the references to you and thought them dull but kind: when I write my memoirs I shall shed more light on your character and spill the beans about the paraldehyde. Poor Little Margaret was brought up in an atmosphere permeated with alcohol and paraldehyde, that's why she has taken refuge with the Jesuits and incense.

Botulic Cyril came to luncheon accompanied by a skinny blonde,[2] but she is not hostile; she had no chance to speak because Angus Wilson, Thunderbird, me, and Cyril were all shouting at Willie [Maugham] who is far deafer than you. It was not a totally successful occasion because Angus said you were far and away the best living writer and Willie looked frightfully cross, but I kicked Angus under the table and he bawled at Willie 'the best novelist under sixty, UNDER SIXTY' – to switch the conversation I said to Cyril that you suggested I should give him some tensions so that his prose might flower once more, Cyril then looked even crosser than Willie, and said that cancelled the charming letter from you he was carrying in his pocket, and seconds later he said it was a pity your war trilogy was so dull, this annoyed me and Angus who again yelled that you were the best living writer and could never be dull, but it didn't matter because Willie was asleep like the Alice dormouse; he woke up with the pudding (treacle, his favourite, the French can't make it) and refused to deny that Cyril had stolen the only avocado pear that had ripened on his avocado tree: apparently Harold Nicolson wrote the story in a book and Cyril wishes to sue him for libel, but Willie remained silent except for stutter contortions, so I said that it was true, and Willie had told me himself. I find it irresistible to bully Cyril, I don't love him like you do.

T-B says that after the P.G.W. [Wodehouse] broadcasts the RAF sent a special flight to bomb the Wodehouse villa at Le Touquet, but

Ann and Ian Fleming with Caspar

Lady Diana Cooper

Sevenhampton

Evelyn Waugh with his daughter, Margaret

Cyril Connolly

Clarissa Avon

Nicholas Henderson

Judy Montagu

Theresa Gatacre and Roy Jenkins,
a talented croquet player

Arnold Goodman

Caspar Fleming

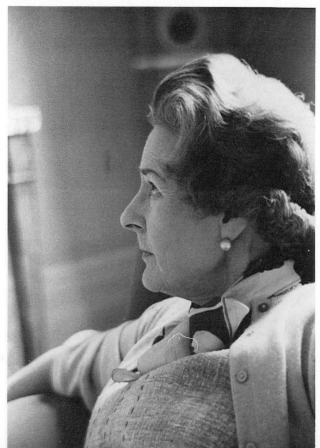

Ann in later years

they missed it and hit the villa of one of T-B's low golfing friends, the golfing friend is still complaining – this is true and T-B will give details if required.

Will you come to a lecture by John Sparrow on 'Great Poetry' – Nov. 2nd and dinner afterwards?

And now Thunderbird's dinner must be cooked; last night I gave him *'estouffade de boeuf'* – it prevented him from playing golf this morning, the meat had been marinated for two days in red wine.

affec. coz.

A

1 *My Grandmothers and I*, 1960, by Diana Holman-Hunt.
2 Deirdre Craig, who had married Connolly the year before. In 1977 she married Peter Levi.

To Evelyn Waugh

16 Victoria Square   7 November [1960]

Dearest Evelyn

Bron comes to lunch tomorrow to be 'lionised'. I promised him a monster – Douglas Cooper was certainly like Tarquin when a child – but alas, he is not coming and I fear Bron may think I meant Lady Bridget Parsons who is coming.

I enjoyed *The Foxglove Saga*, it's really funny, aloud laughter like your books, and I am surprised at the number of persons who are shocked by the Tarquin saga; it's the kind of story my father used to tell us when children at bedtime, perhaps it's Bron's Charteris blood; we were led to believe that any dark room contained creatures with eight legs, one or four eyes, superhuman strength and nasty natures.

I was with the Edens on Friday night, Bowra on Saturday and M. [Michael] Astor on Sunday. Lady Eden is a splendid housewife; the food is excellent and excessively rich, no human stomach can digest it, but Sir Anthony's American plastic model has no trouble with a menu based upon Guernsey butter and cream and washed down with three different wines; Lord Lambton and myself had to walk across Salisbury Plain and sleep like boa constrictors before we were well again. Sir Anthony talked with affection of his sow –

'the runt in every litter is called Anthony' said Clarissa, I thought this unkind but apparently it is customary to sacrifice a piglet from each family to the saint of that name – despite the legend she said it with some satisfaction. She is a devoted wife but ministers roughly, when she thinks his feet should be up she violently kicks footstools towards him – it must be a habit to which he is accustomed for he fields them neatly, if he did not the gesture might defeat the object and inflict a serious injury on him or the guests. Defence problems were discussed for six hours, poor Anthony Runt is only excited by politics and he sounded so sensible – tho' curiously his views are identical to Gaitskell's.

After talking to Lord Salisbury,[1] Lord Lambton and Anthony Runt, I conclude that some Conservatives hate Harold [Macmillan] as much as some Socialists hate Gaitskell.

Next time you go to Oxford look in at St Edmund's chapel, there is a modern painting of the Last Supper which is almost alright; I climbed over the red rope, but it is not signed and Maurice hurried me away because we had left muddy footprints on the green carpet around the altar.

Leslie Hartley came to collect me and Lady Waverley for John Sparrow's lecture on 'Great Poetry', his car was the kind of springless unwashed dung-smelling vehicle that is to be found at remote country stations, the driver resembled the art critic to whom you took such a fancy at Darwin's dump [David Sylvester] and was clearly very bad-tempered. Leslie sat beside him and gazed at him with love and fear while he rolled up the sleeves of his dirty red shirt and proceeded to drive us with horrid speed the wrong way down one way streets to the Royal Academy. Lady Waverley seemed oblivious of the angry hoots we provoked and continued to tell me her hat was made of a porcupine's pelt in memory of Lord Waverley, because he had once told her she was as defenceless as a porcupine in its prime. Later I asked Leslie about this man and conveyance, he had been found through an advertisement in *The Times* and his bad mood was explained because he had two daughters at Heathfield and had wished to take them out for the evening.

Our new home [Sevenhampton] was very jolly today, the roof is off, the windows gone, twisted lead pipes on the lawn, also two horses and a cow, and the welkin ringing with Irish songs, and the Irish demolitionists all wearing garish-coloured jockey caps and wonderfully good company, even the valley of brown mud and brown water did not depress me. Silly old Thunderbird was in such despair he went to see the television fortune teller who told him that the house would cost more than he thought and he would find a cheaper, smaller one nearer London – waste of £5/5 wasn't it?

When Nancy arrives tell her the dons are in a flap about 'Dior dons',[2] and poor Aline Berlin[3] was so distressed that tactful David [Cecil] over-egged by saying to comfort her that it was directed at Rachel.

Where is the *Daily Mail* sending you?

Love

Ann

1 Marquess of Salisbury (1893–1972). Elder statesman to the Conservative Party, resigned in 1957 when Archbishop Makarios was released.

2 Alfred in *Don't Tell Alfred* by Nancy Mitford, 1960, is an Oxford don who is made Ambassador in Paris. His wife recounts 'At this time, it is true, there were some rich, worldly dons whose wives dressed at Dior, and who knew about Paris and embassies, a tiny minority ... These Dior dons were not pleased by our appointment; they laughed long and loud, as kind friends informed us, at the idea of it and made witty jokes at our expense. No doubt they thought the honour would sit better upon them; how I agreed with them, really!'

3 Aline de Gunzbourg married Isaiah Berlin in 1956.

To Peter Quennell

Grand Hotel Kronenhof-Bellavista,
Engadine   30 December [1960]

Darling Peter

Today I have been marvelling at the pleasures of the rich. Me and Commander lunched with Daphne and Whitney[1] at the Corviglia Club, St Moritz. To reach the Corviglia Club you have to queue for the funicula, we stood on ice for forty-five minutes amidst an ill-mannered international ill-favoured jostling crowd, risking the points of skis in the eye and ski sticks through the feet, we then stood packed like sardines for a further claustrophobic horrific half hour while the overcrowded train jerked up the precipitous mountain – I had a strong desire to kill them all. The summit was indeed beautiful and only marred by winter sporters, and the Club was a very jolly joke, a smart chalet built apart from the tourists' restaurant, a helicopter landing ground, warmed lavatory seats, an Austrian prince in control, ready to repel all comers that did not exude wealth, confidence and vulgarity. I overheard Whitney explaining us to him 'She *was* Lady Rothermere'! It was lovely for the Commander, it really was, in a trice he was on the warmed lavatory seat and from thence to the sunny terrace, thighs wound in a delectable rug, sipping bouillon laced with vodka . . .

New Year's Day
I am deeply depressed by hotel celebrations, imagine Fionn, Duff [Dunbar], Caspar, Mona [Potterton], Ian and me at a table covered in crackers and paper hats! It was alright till Caspar took his high spirits and Mona to bed and Fionn vanished with her admirers, but there was an hour to go, a roaring band and stifling heat. I suggested bed, but Ian did not want, so we sat on, a grisly middle-aged trio, till at 11.30 I left them, went to bed in a fur coat, opened all the windows and listened to the bells – this was so melancholy the tears poured down, and when Ian appeared he was maddened by a freezing room and my face covered with icicles.

There have been some dangerous moments with poor darling Ian, Duff is in a very teasing mood and the height provokes easy laughter from me and Fionn – almost hysterical and nearly always at Ian's expense. Ian has not been very well, we are too high for high blood pressure – but I have taken him out alone once or twice so things have improved.

We return on the 12th, will you reserve Tuesday the 17th for dinner? Only chance to see you and Spider before Jamaica.

Hope you had a Happy Christmas.

Much love and best wishes to you both for New Year,

A

1 Lady Daphne Finch-Hatton (1913–) married in 1935 Air Commodore Whitney Straight.

To Evelyn Waugh

Grand Hotel Kronenhof-Bellavista,
Engadine   4 January 1961

My dear Evelyn
    I am in Switzerland, Ruskin may have found it soothing to his

sanity, it is having the reverse effect on mine; in the library (this hotel boasts a library) I have found essays by R. L. Stevenson corroborating my sufferings, I quote – 'A mountain valley has, at best, a certain prison-like effect on the imagination – the roads are indeed cleared, and at least one footpath dodging up the hill, but to these one is rigidly confined. There are no crosscuts over the fields, no following streams, no unguided rambles in the wood. The walks are cut and dry. Scents here are as rare as colours; unless you get a gust of kitchen in passing some hotel you shall smell nothing all day long but the faint and choking odour of frost.' I also share with R. L. S. loss of appetite and sleeplessness, would that you were here to puff paraldehyde over me.[1] The height has affected Thunderbird's blood pressure, and at night he has to be propped up with pillows because of panting, but he clings to youth and dreams of the days when he was the Kitzbühel Casanova; he is now better because a German girl aged fourteen called Lilo (hun for Lolita?) fastens his skis and collects him from snowdrifts.

Fionn has collected two hopeless suitors here, one a Cambridge post-scientific-graduate whose life work is the intestinal worms of the pig; her other admirer is sixteen, son of a stout gentleman I inadvertently collected on New Year's Eve. I became demented by hotel respectability and did the Charleston all by myself, an undignified display and rendered more so by being joined by a stout bald gentleman with a foreign accent; it has transpired that the accent was Lancashire, the gentleman a tycoon who has the monopoly of surgical bandages and Nivea creme, he told me he could not talk of the most paying side of his business, but after cross-examination revealed it was 'sanitary protection', he then chuckled and whispered that it was not a fluctuating market.

5 January

After lunch I buckled on horrid skis and tried to follow Old Caspar down the mountain, he went very fast and then he suddenly flew out of his boots and catapulted head first into a snowdrift, and when I extracted him he said it was all my fault and he would like to be in a taxi; so I'm taking the tickets to the *concierge* to try for sleepers on the 10th. If I fail, we shall be home at latest on the 12th – do come to London between then and the 20th when I have to go to Jamaica – I will pay for the caviar.

Your life does sound calm and happy, when the roof is on our home I shall refuse to be moss on a thunderball any more.

With love to you both

Ann

1 Ann wrote in similar vein to Lady Diana Cooper: 'White snow and white skies for a week – the Swiss suicide rate and Ibsen are now clear as a bell to me.'

To Evelyn Waugh

Goldeneye, Jamaica   4 February [1961]

My dear Evelyn

Thankyou for the caviar, it was a very jolly evening. I am becoming frightened of Little Margaret – what should I call her? I don't think she likes being called 'Little Margaret' – it took me 35 years to know what 'Sole Véronique' meant, let alone ask for it in a West End hotel. She has tremendous poise for a British virgin. You must ensure she makes a worldly marriage, or else leave her all your money so she may live in the way to which she is accustomed.

Thunderball has just completed his evening stint on the type-writer,[1] he boiled into the room because the chitter-chatter of me and Mrs Donaldson had disturbed his concentration, he is now disturbing mine by talking to Jack [Donaldson] about Buddhist monks, and now Jack is asking him about his writing technique.

When we passed through New York the temperature was below zero, and we both arrived here with bronchitis from the change of temperature. Ian had a high fever and was fearfully cross, happily Noël Coward came to call and proved himself a Florence Nightingale, changing Thunderbird's sopping pyjamas, turning the mattress, and fetching him iced drinks. Noël has always found T-B fearfully attractive and jumped at the opportunity to handle him. While Noël fetched ice cubes from the frigidaire T-B's language was something horrible, he blamed me for exposing him to homosexual approaches.[2]

The Donaldsons are peaceful delightful companions, Jack is very pleased with underwater life, he wishes to classify the fish, but somehow his reactions to visual joys are pedantic, I suppose he is all ears. Frankie also surprised me by thinking the faded butterfly prints in her room were real butterflies pinned in frames – I am always surprised when people do not notice closely the objects in a room. But I love them both and this is only comment, *not* for mischief making.

A malicious postcard arrived from V. Square *re* coconuts. I thought of sending you a case to mix with caviar but it is too expensive.

Yesterday [I found] a giant octopus, he was asleep against a rock, I fetched Thunderball expecting him to collect it for me but Thunderball was alarmed and would not prod it, he threw a stone and the creature unfurled a five-foot tentacle and explored, then I was much more alarmed than Thunderball and did my Victorian breaststroke for the shore. I dreamt about it last night.

Lord Brownlow imported a farm manageress, a maiden of fifty summers weighing fourteen stone, she gave a peremptory order to a sugar cane worker who promptly raped her, she took her riding breeches to the local doctor for analysis and also her person; a tremendous hue and cry is in progress but she has failed to identify the villain amongst a parade of Perry [Brownlow's] slaves; Perry is very ill as a result.

Love from

A

Donaldsons send love.

1 *The Spy Who Loved Me*, most ambitious of Bond novels, was published in 1962.

2 Coward wrote in his diary for 29 January: 'Annie and Ian arrived last Sunday, Ian with a temperature of 103. I went over with Annie, who had dinner with us looking exhausted and strained, and found him scarlet and sweating in a sopping bed and in a hellish temper . . . It was all *so* exactly like the scene in *Pomp and Circumstance* [Coward's novel in which the hero develops chicken-pox] that I expected him to burst out in a rash of spots. In fact I almost wished he would; it would have been so tidy and satisfactory. Their connubial situation is rocky. Annie hates Jamaica and wants him to sell Goldeneye. He loves Jamaica and doesn't want to. My personal opinion is that although he is still fond of Annie, the physical side of it, in him, has been worn away. It is extraordinary how many of my friends delight in torturing one another.'

To Evelyn Waugh

16 Victoria Square   25 March [1961]

Dearest Evelyn

Diana and I were much excited by the news of Bron's engagement, she dashed for Debrett and read aloud the family history. I
have heard well of Lady Onslow,[1] she is a friend of James Pope-
Hennessy, Peggy Crewe and Loelia Westminster; on one occasion
Loelia took me to Clandon Park, it was open to the public, the
coronets and robes were on view, and the Earl and Countess luring
the public to buy fruit and flowers. Will you and Laura be going to
visit there?

Will the two Teresas[2] share a double white wedding? It would
save a lot of expense and might prove sociologically interesting.

I went to lunch at Daylesford, the home of Warren Hastings and
at present inhabited by Lord Rothermere. Poor Lord R. is not well,
his heart has an uneven beat and he is allowed no tennis, no riding,
no work, but to my relief is finding solace in aquiring works of art
and Warren Hastingsiana. David Carritt[3] found a folio of Richard
Wilson watercolours of India, they are very beautiful and I suggested they should not be hung on too sunny a wall, but Lord R. said
they would see him out, which is a wrong approach.

When I arrived at Chantilly Susan Mary Alsop lost no time in
engaging me in earnest political conversation. 'What do you think
will happen in Angola?' It was difficult because I thought Angolas
were rabbits, but I was saved by Diana tripping through the door
overloaded with spring flowers and those strange wedge-heeled
shoes, and things took a happier turn conversationally.

There was no outward sign that Chantilly will soon be no
more.[4] I implored Diana to bring all the furniture to London and sell
it here, for she was talking a little wildly of giving away objects of
value, and indeed was very overtired: she had a graveyard cough
but maintained that she and the cough had separate identities; her
driving was more than usually precarious, for though she drives
more slowly she veers to left and right, and we had a nasty trip from
Paris in the twilight, the fragile van provoking much hostility and
angry flickerings of headlights from Citröens and huge lorries.

It was kind of you to mention Thunderbird in your excellent
Who's Who review, perhaps it will have to be revised after Friday's

law suit.[5] Thunderbird's secretary and Mrs Crickmere were very excited and said he was to be arrested at the airport, but happily it was only rumours of a writ that was in fact served on his publishers. It all comes of keeping bad company, we do not know what the next move will be.

I understand from Mrs Donaldson that all your children and you dote on Mr Gaitskell? Can this be true? I sometimes walk with him in remote parks, he wears dark spectacles and tells me his problems while my mind wanders and I watch the spring mating of the ducks – when I hear him say 'By the way, that's top secret' I ask him to tell me that bit again, but it's seldom very exciting – and by the way, *that's all TOP SECRET.*

Professor Derek Jackson[6] has given the Duchess of Devonshire a £500 dress from Paris, he had the impertinence to ask me to smuggle it to London for her. Is the Professor a friend of yours?

I hope bridal preparations will bring you constantly to London.

With love

A

1 Pamela Dillon (1915–   ). Married 1936–62 to the Earl of Onslow. The mother of Lady Teresa Onslow (1940–   ) the linguist, novelist and cook whom Auberon Waugh married that year. Waugh commented on the engagement, 'I regard it as a highly imprudent undertaking. . . the girl is pretty and seems sharp.'

2 Teresa Waugh was also engaged, in her case to John D'Arms (1934–   ), an American professor of Latin and Greek.

3 David Carritt (1927–82). Art dealer, for some years with Christies. He made several important discoveries, among them a Tiepolo ceiling in the clubhouse of Hendon Golf Course.

4 Lady Diana was being eased out of the Château de St Firmin at Chantilly, for which she had been paying £100 a year, by her landlord, Henri, eldest son of the Comte de Paris.

5 On 17 March Kevin McClory took out an injunction to prevent the publication of *Thunderball.* He had worked with Fleming on a film script and claimed that the novel infringed the copyright of that script. Publication was allowed but the ensuing case lasted two years.

6 Professor Derek Jackson (1906–82). A scientist married to, among others, Pamela Mitford 1936–51 and Janetta Wooley 1951–6.

On 12 April Ian Fleming drove to London for the Tuesday conference at *The Sunday Times*, eager to hear plans for the new colour magazine which was to start next year. During the conference he had a serious heart attack and was admitted that afternoon to the London Clinic where he stayed for a month.

To Evelyn Waugh

[29 May 1961]

Dudley Hotel, Hove, Sussex

Dearest Evelyn

We spent Whitsun with Edward Rice and his French wife[1] in her French castle, they had pressed us to stay till Wednesday but were forced to leave Tuesday themselves, they departed after much French shrieking and yelling and touching of forelocks by scullions, pastry cooks, gardeners and farm hands. Then silence fell and we discovered the cellar was locked, the larder was bare, the firewood sear and the only transport a jeep, poor T-B had to risk another coronary to start the engine so we could trundle to the nearest town for warmth and Calvados, for the serfs had all vanished with the master and mistress. Even before their departure it was a rum life, for Edward's too mean to give drinks before meals and the guests have to take him to a pub – a great effort in middle age to drive kilometres for a cocktail.

I dined at Petworth where John Wyndham[2] was entertaining the Prime Minister. Mrs Wyndham[3] was away, Lady Dorothy was absent, so the PM, John, Mr and Mrs Robin McEwen[4] and myself sat down to dinner at a table ornamented with golden candelabra, supped soup from golden plates while the Japanese deer stared through the windows. It was a splendid occasion to observe Mr Macmillan, he was suave with impersonal eyes, he ate and drank with extreme moderation and he talked from eight o'clock to one a.m., the only pause at midnight when he advanced to the door and we humbly followed expecting the great man's bedtime – but no, it was for a natural purpose – and in a trice he had returned to us and was at it again. Except for a weakness for anecdotes about the peerage everything he said was interesting, indeed very interesting. I doubt if he would enjoy a jolly jokes evening and all PMs are vain; no, not true, Eden was but Churchill wasn't – don't know any others. But I was very impressed by him and wouldn't care to play poker with him.

I am certainly coming to Quaglino feast. Would any of the family dine with me first?

Love

A

1 Nolwen de Janzé (1922–   ). She had a farm at Parfondeval in Normandy, and in 1948 had been married to a French protestant, Lionel Armand de Lille. She was now married to Edward Rice, a barrister and romantic adventurer with white hair and brilliant blue eyes. His political views were of the extreme right and when the German planes flew over, tears filled his eyes. He was not interned but told to leave his farm in Kent for Faringdon, a less sensitive area. She later married Lord Clark.

2 John Wyndham (1920–72). Private Secretary to Harold Macmillan 1957–63. Created Lord Egremont in 1963, succeeded as Lord Leconfield in 1967.

3 Pamela Wyndham Quin married John Wyndham in 1947.

4 Brigid Laver married in 1954 Sir Robert ('Robin') McEwen (1926–80), a barrister.

The marriages of Waugh's daughter Teresa to John D'Arms, and of his son Auberon to Lady Teresa Onslow took place in June. On the 10th Ann's daughter Fionn announced her engagement to John Morgan, whom Ann described to Waugh as 'Foreign Office Morgan. His parents are chapel-going folk and do not drink or smoke, his mother has only once been to London.' They were married six weeks later, on 26 July.

To Evelyn Waugh

Sandwich   5 August 1961

My dear Evelyn

We live in slum conditions, only sunshine could make them tolerable. The hired flat has dung-coloured wallpaper and curtains, the sea and sky match. The charwoman and Nanny chatter, the children fight, and Thunderbird waits morosely for midday when he joins the golf people and drinks.

Everything you say of weddings is true. You underestimated the price, the double event will cost £2000. I don't remember anything about the dance, it had been too long a day, including a sad scene in marble halls – poor Mrs Hugo Charteris wept throughout the pre-wedding rehearsal family lunch because I had failed to get bridesmaid frocks for her daughters and hired the Miss Lambtons at the last moment.[1] Hugo said viciously 'Everyone knows one can hire bridesmaid frocks' – well, I didn't know, and the Miss Lambtons are pretty little girls, while the Miss Charterises are very stout and have lost all their teeth.

John Morgan behaved very well at the party, he danced with his relations and our relations and Princess Alexandra,[2] and talked to the diplomats; Raymond did not dance with Princess Alexandra and we all forgot to say goodbye to her. Fionn was busy with old boy-friends and I did the Charleston with Freddy Ayer. I made a mistake in having Bowra and Sparrow to dinner, because at the hour I should have been in long white gloves receiving the guests we started reading aloud the new translation of the Bible. It's a family failing to pack too much into one day; I forced the bride to sell tickets she had taken for the Luther play[3] on the night of the wedding, it seemed a rum way to spend a wedding night to say nothing of the exhaustion. The Morgan side of the aisle was strewn with Lambtons, so they had a ready-made aristocratic family, for when asked I said they were cousins.

Cecil Beaton says he read every word in the *Spectator* except your review.[4] It was a very unkind review: I thought most of the reviews of his book hypocritical, all poor Cecil has done is to publish a true story of escape from environment – a very common practice. I have no doubt you did it too; I did my best to escape from Barry and William Morris wallpapers to the *Tatler* and Cap d'Antibes – only to beat a hasty retreat.

Loudspeaker vans patrol the coast warning the public to beware of jellyfish, they should threaten them with torture for leaving orange peel and old newspapers – I loathe the holiday public and hope they will be stung all over by jellyfish. The sea rescue helicopter and the Deal lifeboat have collected a dozen of children and some silly adults from floats, dinghies and lilos – there is no peace at all. I have been forced to cocktail parties to meet persons who have Caspar-age children, it's a strange world of very rich people who have houses here and at Sunningdale or Ascot, horrid furniture and pictures, ugly faces and dull minds. It's a waste of my ebbing vitality, because Caspar won't play tennis with the fruit of their nasty wombs because he has discovered a sand dune of human bones – he knows the Earl and Countess of Guilford were blown up in the vicinity during the war, and he loves bones and peers as much as he hates communal games.

T-B is not allowed to travel so I am about to telegraph Auberon, and – alas – not go to Portofino.

later

Perhaps you were not so unkind about Cecil's book, he has a horrid talent for conveying silliness, the visit to Hearst's ranch is really too horrible. Ungrateful of me because he took lovely free snaps of the bride, though he was very jealous that I allowed Lucy Lambton[5] (the one who was sick in the bathroom at Pixton, and you made Laura clean it up) to take snaps at the party. 'I bet nothing came out of that little black box' he said – he was wrong, for a bright voice on the telephone cried 'Mummy says you would like the intellectuals blown up' and sure enough a lovely picture of Connolly, Ayer and Kinross all in a row looking as sad as owls.

I find Hugo's new novel[6] unreadable, perhaps I am prejudiced, for he wrote to John Morgan saying that it was high time Fionn was removed from my influence because I was a Freudian penis envier. J. Morgan was very shocked.

John de Bendern[7] has a refined new lady-friend, he was overheard saying to her at dinner 'If you won't say pardon again I won't say fuck.'

Fionn and I still marvel at your generous, exciting wedding presents: I have not yet sent Bron his gift, my signature is not as valuable as yours, so it is trays not books.

Caspar was scared stiff when I told him you were going to be a page. I hope you are the right weight now and feeling well.

Let me know if you come up mid-week.

Love to you both

A

1 Ann had asked the Charteris daughters to be bridesmaids, done nothing about clothes and exchanged them for Lady Rose (1952–   ), Lady Anne (1954–   ) and Lady Isabella Lambton (1958–   ), who had suitably identical party dresses. Virginia Charteris had not been told until Caspar Fleming betrayed the situation at lunch.

2 Princess Alexandra (1936–   ). Daughter of the Duke of Kent and so a cousin of the Queen. Married Angus Ogilvy in 1963.

3 *Luther* by John Osborne with Albert Finney in the title role.

4 Waugh reviewed *The Wandering Years* by Cecil Beaton in the *Spectator* of 21

July: '. . . It tells the story of the early years of a young man unashamedly on the make. . . His camera carried him into the presence of the famous and the beautiful and, once there, he often established himself in warm friendship. . . he can't write for toffee. Neither in verbal expression nor in literary construction does he show any but the feeblest talent. . . I do not hear the authentic note of self-revelation even in his most shy-making confidences. . . I don't think people of the future will turn to him to elucidate the condition of his age.'

5 Lady Lucinda Lambton (1943–   ). Photographer. Married Henry Harrod in 1965.

6 *The Lifeline*, 1961.

7 John de Forest (1907–   ). Inherited Liechtenstein title of Count de Bendern.

To Aline Berlin

16 Victoria Square   14 August 1961

Dearest Aline

I fear summer holidays will not include you, Isaiah, Stuart [Hampshire], Auberon [Herbert] or Italy. I am very disappointed. Ian is no worse but should be better and has been dissuaded from travel. Please send me lots of postcards.

Hugh [Gaitskell] is a very inquisitive man – he has a long inquisitive nose like the ant-eating tapir, on the occasion of the party [Fionn's wedding reception] I was glad of this because I had taken dexedrine and remember nothing about it. The preceding dinner I do remember. John Sparrow arrived early in a torn shirt; while he was being outfitted from Ian's wardrobe the house began to throb portending Maurice's arrival – also early, I was longing to change from a new Victor Stiebel to an old French frock, the Stiebel was shocking pink and all wrong. Needing encouragement I consulted my father who said I looked like a *bon bon* – 'with a nasty soft centre' added Sparrow – thus encouraged I tried to be polite to the Hayters[1] and my stepmother when Ava [Waverley] telephoned to say she could not get a taxi – none of us stirred. Towards the pudding it was clear that Maurice intended to capture Ava from Sparrow, he roared at her across the table, not unreasonably for my stepmother and Lady H. are not very stimulating. By coffee time there was a general roar – topic: the seven deadly sins.[2] It was long past time for receiving guests, so I arrived late and distraught at the Savoy to find an unmixable assortment of persons, ancient aunts, strangers from the Foreign Office, Princess Alexandra and the

Gaitskells to say nothing of the senior Morgans and a gently disapproving son-in-law. The eldest Miss Lambton took photographs, Diana C. was very sharp with her and in revenge Miss L. has produced a remarkable picture of a ghost Diana, for through her one can see an energetic young couple doing the charleston; I am very pleased with it.

I have done nothing since the wedding except swim in the Channel and visit the Donaldsons. Jack is uneasy about his chicken battery, and so he should be. Three in a cage, they are mad and miserable, it is a horrible sight. It is an occupation unbecoming to high-minded Jack – he does not openly admit it but it is quite clear.

I hope Isaiah is very well and you are all enjoying yourselves, wish I was with you.

Much love to you both,

A

1 Iris Grey married in 1938 William Hayter (1906–), Ambassador to USSR 1953–7, Warden of New College 1958–76. Knighted in 1953.
2 *The Sunday Times* was running a series of articles on this subject. Waugh had written '*The Sunday Times* can't find anyone to write about Lust for their Seven Deadly Sins series. I have told them only women and buggers suffer from that temptation. Fucking bores men – at any rate they have nothing to say about it except to catalogue their partners. Driberg would write a stunner.'

To Evelyn Waugh

Shane's Castle   2 September [1961]

My dear Evelyn
    Paddy Leigh Fermor says Lust is too serious to write about, Quennell longs to express himself at great length upon this topic, so in my evening telephone talk to T-B I have made this suggestion: it will be interesting to know the increment offered Q. compared to the horrid difference of you and Connolly. I told Paddy (Gluttony) that Cyril's fee was £75 and yours £7500 – perhaps I'm wrong – Paddy was greatly worried at the gap between you and Connolly for his fee has not been divulged – he is planning his future on the hopes of £5000.[1]

    Would that I were in Somerset with you. I did not think you would care for Caspar, governess and lessons in your library,

Laura's room or on the Crystal Palace carpet. Here we are to have a summer school, Raymond Carr and his family – two boys to learn with old Caspar.

Love,

A

1 In the end the articles were published in a book, *The Seven Deadly Sins*, 1962, with an introduction by Raymond Mortimer. Edith Sitwell wrote on Pride, Cyril Connolly on Covetousness, Patrick Leigh Fermor on Gluttony, Evelyn Waugh on Sloth, Angus Wilson on Envy, W. H. Auden on Wrath and Christopher Sykes on Lust.

To Evelyn Waugh

Shane's Castle   11 September [1961]

Dear Evelyn

The last letter terminated abruptly because of my hurried departure for Eire to collect Sara, Raymond Carr and children from Pakenham Hall. Your name figures in the Pakenham Hall visitors' book, apparently you were present and took part in youthful pranks which resulted in the burning of furniture and defacing of paintings, your role must have been that of Paul Pennyfeather because you were the only guest not expelled for ever.[1] Perhaps in your day Pakenham was warm and comfortable, it is now sparsely furnished, damp, draughty and dirty. Thomas[2] was entertaining Mr and Lady Antonia Fraser & three children, Prof. and Mrs Richard Wollheim[3] & three children, Mr and Mrs Carr & three children, Mr and Mrs James Spooner,[4] Lady Judith[5] and Lady Rachel Pakenham.[6] It was baronial Bohemia, the guests were fed on sheep and bullocks slaughtered on the premises, cooked by a teenage girl and served by an ancient hunchback said to have been in the dungeon; no domestic attention in the sleeping apartments. I lit the fire in my bedroom but owing to a flaw in the chimney smoke billowed into the Frasers' apartment, they were asphyxiated and I gained no warmth.

I was awfully glad I only stayed one night and nothing happened except bats in the dining-room, Professor Wollheim fainted and the Ladies Pakenham put napkins on their heads and fled. I gave your love to Ran [the Earl of Antrim]; we went to tea at Glenarm, he and Angela[7] do not make for cheer: Ran and Raymond had a tactless conversation about the jollity of seeing 'To hell with the Pope' written upon walls, and Ran lamented the decrease of sectarian warfare in Ulster.

We return to London tomorrow, me to grave decisions between the values of the Cavendish or Westminster w.c.s and baths.

Do come up soon.

Love,

A

1 Paul Pennyfeather in *Decline and Fall* was an innocent by-stander but he *was* expelled.

2 Thomas Pakenham (1933–). Historian and farmer. Son of the Earl of Longford, he has never used his title Viscount Silchester.

3 Anne Powell was married 1950–67 to Richard Wollheim (1923–), Grote Professor of Philosophy of Mind and Logic at London University 1963–82.

4 Jane Glover married in 1958 James Spooner (1932–), director of several companies, Chairman of NAAFI since 1973. Knighted 1981.

5 Judith Pakenham (1940–). Poet. Married in 1963 Alexander Kazantzis. Does not use her courtesy title.

6 Lady Rachel Pakenham (1942–). Novelist. Married in 1967 Kevin Billington, director of plays and films.

7 Angela Sykes (1911–84) married in 1934 the Earl of Antrim.

To Frances Donaldson

[Postcard] Provence   [September 1961]

Ian has decreed a church a day, very mingy in this area. Have you ever thought of the terrible power of the driver on matrimonial motor trips?

Love to you both,

A

To Evelyn Waugh

16 Victoria Square   8 October [1961]

Dear Evelyn

Your letter found me with the 'Australian Booby' [Douglas Cooper] in his castle in Provence, I was crying when it arrived and it stopped me crying: there was a mistral blowing and Thunderbird in his Thunderbird had driven me too far and too fast, refusing to stop to gather autumn crocuses or to examine extraordinary churches on rocks in the Massif Central, and at meal times he disobeyed doctor's orders by stuffing himself with truffles, cream, burgundy followed by smoking hundreds of cigarettes.

The Graham Sutherlands[1] were staying with 'Booby', he seemed a Christian Catholic – good kind man; she a little flattering fluttering cooing woman to whom I took a great dislike; do you admire the paintings of Sutherland? I do, especially the portraits, and also toads and insects.

Did you read Mr Somerset Maugham's statement in today's *Sunday Times*? Do you suppose he will consider you and T-B 'needy authors'? It all stems from unpleasant family drama, apparently the insurance rates for paintings were raised because of Riviera thefts, Willie was too miserly to pay them and had sold his collection to some mysterious source. Lady John Hope was on to it like a flash and wrote claiming her share; it appeared some had been purchased in her name: her letter maddened Willie who has cut her out of his will.[2]

Angus Wilson sent me a postcard to tell me how delighted he was with your letter.[3] I have greatly enjoyed the first chapters, I missed most reviews while 'thunderbirding'.

I do not think Rose Macaulay's letters[4] should have been published. Who are the Cowley Fathers?[5]

When shall I see you?

Love

A

1 Kathleen Baring married in 1928 the painter Graham Sutherland (1903–80).

2 A not entirely accurate and certainly partisan account. Maugham had become worried about theft and decided to sell his pictures, some of which had been bought in his daughter's name because he intended to leave them to her and this would avoid death duties. She assumed they were hers and wrote a letter saying that she was sad he was selling them as she had thought she might keep one or two. Maugham flew into a series of rages, shouting, screaming, throwing things about. In May the following year he did sell some pictures at Sothebys and Lady John Hope sued for almost $650,000, just less than half, which she thought her rightful share. In January 1964 the case was settled out of court, three days before Maugham's ninetieth birthday, and Lady John Hope received $250,000. She had a strong case and could have got more had she been willing to drag her ancient father through the courts (from *Maugham* by Ted Morgan).

3 Waugh wrote a long letter to the *Spectator* in praise of Angus Wilson's novel *The Old Men at the Zoo*.

4 *Letters to A Friend* by Rose Macaulay, edited by Constance Babington Smith, told of Dame Rose's difficulties of reconciling a love affair with her religious beliefs.

5 Anglo-Catholics at Cowley near Oxford.

From Evelyn Waugh

Combe Florey House, Nr Taunton   9 October [1961]

Dear Ann

Please explain to Dr Maugham that what is required is not encouragement to young writers but consolation to the old. I don't belong to the Authors' Association. Dr Maugham had far better make a trust with you as sole trustee. A large annuity would be a great help to me – and to Cyril too I expect.

I was in London last week welcoming Harold Acton and signing copies of my last novel[1] – one for you though you won't understand it. It is for Christian consumption only.

Meg went to stay in Ireland with the Merseys.'[2] At luncheon, *à propos* of nothing, Lord Mersey suddenly announced: 'Ian Fleming is dying.' Meg piped up and said she believed he was in much better health. 'Nonsense. I know him well. He's got a very short time to live.' On another occasion he said: 'It is a curious fact that all the Tudor monarchs died violent deaths.' Meg questioned this statement. Lord M: 'It's a known fact.'

If you had read my treatise on Ronald Knox you would know all about the Cowley Fathers. He frequented them when he was a Protestant.

I have just read Loelia's book – quite competent and dignified and accurate.[3]

Harold Acton was very garrulous & malicious.

I went all the way to Bournemouth to see a picture reputedly by R. Dadd. It certainly wasn't by him but, having gone so far, I bought it. Now I regret it. Perhaps you would like to buy it from me.

I find I can't concentrate on my childhood while making plans for my death in Guiana, so the autobiography is in suspense.

Auberon Herbert has at last sold his home at Portofino but plans to build another in Sardinia.

I have found a series of novels called 'The American Blood Hound Series' which I greatly enjoy. Much cleaner than T-B.

Yours ever affec.

E

1 *Unconditional Surrender*.

2 Lady Katherine Fitzmaurice (1912–) married in 1933 Viscount Mersey (1906–79). She succeeded as Lady Nairne in her own right in 1944.

3 *Grace and Favour* by Loelia, Duchess of Westminster, 1961. Waugh is described as 'a formidable young man who looked like a furious cherub. His glaring eye was watching us, his sharp ear missed nothing. . . In 1930 *Vile Bodies* was published and with mixed feelings we saw how our *patois* looked in print.'

To Evelyn Waugh

16 Victoria Square   22 October [1961]

Dear Fat Coz.

Two copies of *Unconditional Surrender* caused rejoicing at V. Square. I was complacently expecting it but Mrs Whistler [Fionn] was near to tears with gratitude and excitement. I saved mine for this weekend; previous to the treat, on Thursday, Connolly was coming for a drink, but lost his nerve and telephoned; after apologies he asked if I had read your book, I told him my weekend plans and there was a pause, he then said 'May I see you on Monday to see if you have detected any resemblance between me and a character called Everard Spruce, Editor of a war-time magazine, *Survival*.'[1] Then followed an abusive tirade that you loved none but genteel well-born Catholics and officers. John Sparrow came to lunch and opened the book at random, it was a happy choice for it was the paragraph on expatriate writers and poets in the fire brigade. Peter Quennell and his wife dined that night; I told him of the felicitous page at which John had opened the book, Peter was so nervous and excited, suspecting insults and libel,[2] that he read the whole evening – very bad manners. I am now, alas, two thirds through the book and intend to tell Connolly that Ludovic and his *pensées* are based on *Palinurus*.[3]

I don't know why you disliked Lady Cunard so much,[4] but the 'Loot's' description of the Barrie evening[5] changed my mood from dismal Sandwich gloom to hilarity and joy. Ludovic, the parachute training, Mrs Troy, it's all *lovely* – thankyou *very* much.

Now, why, I wonder, do you admire Loelia's book? She is not a genteel poor Catholic lady, or is it because her 'ghost' is a genteel poor Catholic lady?[6] That is my assumption and I am spreading the rumour, and intend to tell the Catholic 'ghost lady'. The governess of the Duke of Westminster's daughters instructed me and Laura – I could write a more informative book about him. The party G. Weidenfeld gave to celebrate the publication of the book was a nightmare of drunken café society women displaying their withered shanks, scaly arms, sagging necks. Georgia Sitwell[7] was very drunk, and Liz [von Hofmannsthal] was the most intelligent as well as the most beautiful woman in the room.

Sad to miss last week's *Observer* and Rose Macaulay's letter on Graham Greene.[8] I wonder if he was asked if they might publish it? Leslie Hartley told me they had asked him if they might publish her reference to him being an irreligious man, he refused and was indignant at such a description.

Thunderbird made me cry last night and this morning, so I can't write any more now. T-B is unreasonable, he was making a muddle with his myriad of lawyers, so I did a little telephoning and straightened everything in a flash. I suppose if I had been wrong, he wouldn't have been cross.

I do hope Pamela Berry thinks your English as good as I do.

Love

A

1 Waugh wrote the next day to Connolly: 'A mischievous woman in London tells me that you identify a character named Spruce in a book I lately sent you, with yourself. I hope this is pure mischief. If not it is persecution mania. Just count the points of resemblance between yourself and that character and see what the score is.'

2 Peter Quennell was a poet in the fire brigade during the war.

3 Palinurus, pilot for Virgil's Aeneas, was the persona Connolly adopted for his collection of *pensées*, *The Unquiet Grave*.

4 Emerald, Lady Cunard who stayed, entertained and died at the Dorchester during the war, served as the inspiration for Ruby in *Unconditional Surrender*. 'In her hotel sitting-room, Ruby repined. Her brow and the skin round her old eyes were taut with "lifting". She looked at the four unimportant people who sat round her little dinner-table and thought of the glittering guests in Belgrave Square; thirty years of them, night after night, the powerful, the famous, the promising, the beautiful; thirty years' work to establish and impose herself ending now with – what were their names? what did they do? – these people sitting with electric fires behind their chairs talking of what?'

5 Lieutenant Padfield in *Unconditional Surrender*: 'I'm on my way to the Dorchester . . . Ruby had rather a misfortune last night. One of our generals over

here is a great admirer of *Peter Pan*. Ruby asked him to dinner to meet Sir James Barrie. She kindly asked me too. I was surprised to learn Barrie was still alive. Well, of course, he isn't. We waited an hour for him and when at last she rang for dinner they said room service was off and that there was a red warning anyway. "That's what it is," she said. "He's gone down to a shelter. Ridiculous at his age."'

6 Lady Mary Clive (1907–). Neither genteel nor poor, nor a Roman Catholic, she did help the Duchess of Westminster with her book. A sister of the Earl of Longford, she was married to Major Mersey Clive 1939–43, when he was killed in action.

7 Georgia Doble, a beautiful Canadian, married Sacheverell Sitwell in 1925. She died in 1980.

8 Extracts from Rose Macaulay's letters to Father Johnson of the Cowley Fathers in Boston, *Letters to a Friend*, were being published. Her first comments on Greene were 'What a mess his mind must be – nothing in it, scarcely, but religion and sex. . .'

To Evelyn Waugh

16 Victoria Square   25 October 1961

Dear Thin Coz.

Please take me to the Victorian exhibition at Agnew's, I should like a treat before Christmas, I should like to see if you are really thin,'[1] and Mrs Crickmere will cook us cokernuts in Portuguese chianti; your appetite was poorly on the last occasions that we met, but perhaps you are grown more healthy these days.

At this moment Thunderbird is roistering at the Dorchester with 700 members of the Eton institution called 'Pop'.

When Connolly called on Monday night Thunderbird was more unkind than me, he told Connolly that despite a ten-year stint on *The Sunday Times* forty guineas per week was sufficient, there was no occasion to raise it to fifty. Mrs Connolly has gained custody of children by previous marriages of assorted ages, so seven meals a day are served, but what grieves him most is Everard Spruce, and the review for *The Sunday Times*;[2] it is not Christianity but cowardliness than prevents his revenge, he went mournfully through the clownish and repellent rôles he has played in your books, and regretted that *Horizon* should have been mocked and reminded me of that whole issue of *Horizon* that was dedicated entirely to one of your more morbid works;[3] he asked if I did not think your wit had become bilious with the passing of the years, he has re-read *Men at Arms* and *Officers and Gentlemen*, and I look forward immensely to the result of such mental torture.

I dined on a tray in [Lady Diana Cooper's] bedroom last night, we had tongues to talk but no teeth; mine have been capped with gold to prevent nose meeting chin, and Diana had also suffered a change. I left her with Lord Kinross and Tony Guerilla.

Tomorrow luncheon with Willie Maugham and Alan Searle at the Dorchester, it is always an ordeal, excessive heat and champagne. I am to be told the saga of the picture sale and the flight from France. Yesterday Lord John Hope telephoned and said could he see me, that he and Liza depended on my *wisdom* and *kindness* to heal the breach with Willie. I was frightfully excited and enjoyed it all immensely, it was far from disappointing, after three whiskies and soda all the nonsense of 'that poor little love, Liza' sobbing on the bed because Father wouldn't speak to her was forgotten, and instead it was revealed that if Willie can move to Lausanne and rid himself of French law, he may prevent Liza inheriting the paintings. I pointed out that the sale of the villa would be quite something, and if the grandchildren were already subsidised things might be worse. I wonder why he trusts me as everything he says is a funny story for Willie? Alas, it isn't any more, for Willie is grown so old and has made himself so angry scribbling daily his autobiography and his hate of Mrs Maugham that I would not wish to aggravate the drama.[4]

Mrs Whistler [Fionn] has been advised by Mrs Crickmere that she must not buy a second-hand gas stove – 'All second-hand gas stoves is second-hand because someone stuck their head in the oven, and it ain't lucky' – ever heard that before?

I had forgotten that Lady Mary Clive is not a Catholic, and as you would not be so keen on a Protestant ghost I presume you sincerely admire Loelia's book, Kinross does not, and is going to say so in the *Telegraph* on Friday.

I would enjoy a whiff of paraldehyde before your voyage.

Love

A

1 Waugh had written: 'You are far behind the times in supposing that I am corpulent.'

2 Sir Maurice Bowra had written to Ann: 'I am not surprised that Cyril is wounded by Evelyn's presentation of him in *Unconditional Surrender*. It is not very like him, but sufficiently like him to be offensive. It is sad that Evelyn has such an urge to torture him. It must be a form of love. . . Cyril's review is remarkably kind and in its way very good. . .' Connolly wrote that the trilogy was 'unquestion-

ably the finest novel to have come out of the war'. However he was 'allergic to Apthorpe' and found 'the biliousness of Mr Waugh's gaze makes [the minor characters] too dreary to hold the attention'. Everard Spruce is unmentioned.

3 *The Loved One* was published complete in *Horizon*, February 1948.

4 Ann had written to Waugh the year before, 'It's quite tiring being Willie's pin-up girl, because of the deafness and the shouting. He is far deafer than you and has no idea of the loudness of his voice; at the American Embassy he did not observe the proximity of Mrs Whitney [wife of the Ambassador] and he yelled and stuttered 'I am not envious of these paintings because my own collection is much better' – a very barmy statement. I gave [him] a china piggy bank as a Christmas present, he did not observe the slit in its back nor, alas, the intended irony, so it is placed reverently on a stand beside a Henry Moore.'

Fleming was on his way to Goldeneye. Ann was to follow him. It was not a happy visit.

From Ian Fleming

BOAC [undated]

. . . you bring up how much you suffer over Caspar's day off. You have no idea of the torture those aimless querulous wanderings are for me and how much I am nauseated by his bad manners which you seem to tolerate so indulgently. I love him and I would take him anywhere alone, but watching his character deteriorate under your *laissez-faire* depresses me beyond words because I see him not being casually spoiled now but spoilt when it comes to facing the world. You say that I should impose my authority. I cannot when you abrogate the position of father as well as mother and when Nanny abets you. Those outing days slay me – apart from the long and aimless driving through those dreary TV villages and your complaints about the car. It's purgatory and we must make a new plan and above all decide who is father and who is mother and what their rôles are.

Well, that is to answer only one of your complaints this morning and yesterday.

There is so little to be said – or so much. The arguments we have had over the years, our different points of view, are stale – however valid they may be on one side or another.

The point lies in only one area. Do we want to go on living together or do we not?

In the present twilight we are hurting each other to an extent that makes life hardly bearable. That inhuman state of affairs has got to be ended. But it cannot be ended by my simply saying 'yes' to all you think you want, whether it is a real need or a whim. I get terribly exhausted and that's why I go to bed every night – even from the Portland! – at 10.30 and often sleep round the clock.

And that is one reason why I am going where I am, away from the sterile grind of Sandwich and London, to have a rest from it all – and regain some spirit, which, though you haven't noticed it, is slipping out of me through my boots.

If you were with me, happily, I would be totally contented.

As it is your distress and health and our futures will be things I shall try and help over when I have got back some confidence and strength and equilibrium.

In the meantime I hold you tight in my mind.

Ian

> In January Waugh had been to British Guiana with his daughter Margaret and visited Jamaica on his way back.

To Evelyn Waugh

Goldeneye, Jamaica   17 February [1962]

Oh, Uncozenly Coz. – to pass this way without notifying me . . . I was in Kingston.

Your friend Peter Quennell is here, writing about Shakespeare,[1] your other friend Stephen Spender was here lecturing for the British Council. We took both your friends to lunch on location with the film company producing *Dr No*:[2] they were shooting a beach scene, the hero and heroine[3] cowering behind a ridge of sand to escape death from a machine gun mounted on a deep-sea fishing craft borrowed from a neighbouring hotel and manned by communist negroes. The sand ridge was planted with French letters full of explosive – by magic mechanism they blew up the sand in little puffs. The machine gun gave mild pops but I was assured it will be improved on the sound track; all this endeavour was wasted because unluckily a detachment of the American Navy entered the bay in speed launches and buggered it all up. The American Navy was far funnier; despite the calmness of the sea the ablebodied ones were standing at attention in fully inflated scarlet life jackets, does the British Navy behave like that? There was a captain to each launch, they told us they were on French leave from Cuba and were in search of drink and women.

Peter Q. has made two women scream, the first occasion was when he disappeared in the moonlight with Ian's leading lady, the second was when we went swimming with Lord Wimborne and Lord and Lady Beatty;[4] despite the size of the Caribbean he managed to grab her leg under water, Lord Beatty was lazily swimming on his back but hearing the cry he went through the water like a swordfish.

Lord Wimborne, who has little to do in this world, has discovered the works of Scott Fitzgerald; he was bored by *Gatsby* but has become very fond of a short story about drunks in a lift, he reads it all the time.

In New York I dined with Alan Pryce-Jones, I did enjoy it. We met in his flat, I was only ten minutes late, but everyone was blind drunk. 'Everyone' was Auden, Isherwood and Tennessee Williams, each attended by a youthful curly-haired catamite.[5]

An American television company is sending a man all the way from New York to record Ian's views on the U2 pilot,[6] very rum.

God willing, I shall be home next week, and I would very much enjoy an account of your travels.

We are wondering why Lord Beaverbrook has 'killed' Ian's strip in the *Daily Express*, and also a profile on Ian and the film; it is wrapped in mystery and a slight economic blow to old Caspar. Possibly the old man has an advance copy of next year's book: it is more than usually erotic and nasty about Canada.[7]

With love

A

Love to Laura and please thank her for her 'incestuously jungled' telegram.

---

1 *Shakespeare: the poet and his background*, 1964.

2 The first James Bond film.

3 Sean Connery (1930–) and Ursula Andress (1936–). She was never to equal the effect she achieved by emerging from the ocean onto the Jamaican beach.

4 Diane Blundell married Earl Beatty in 1959 and, after his death in 1972, John Nutting.

5 These celebrated writers had produced respectively *The Dyer's Hand* in November, *Down There on a Visit* in March, *The Night of the Iguana* the year before.

6 Captain Gary Powers was shot down while working for the CIA over the USSR.

7 *The Spy Who Loved Me* is the most experimental James Bond story, the one that diverged furthest from formula. It is more realistic but told in the first person by a girl. Bond only appears in the last sixty-four pages. The heroine is Canadian and sympathetic but when she returns to Quebec she is disappointed: 'I found myself contemptuous of the screaming provincialism of the town, of the dowdy peasants who lived in it and of the all-pervading fog of snobbery and *petit bourgeoisie*.'

From Evelyn Waugh

Combe Florey House, Nr Taunton   27 February 1962

Dear Coz.

Welcome to winter. Meg & I have been back a fortnight. She has lost her suntan & her Guianese accent and one of her alligators died of cold on the drive from Southampton. Her bottle nose remains.

It would have been a treat if you had turned up at the da Costas.[1] Charles was a solicitious host, gave me more than I wanted to drink & read to me from a compilation of very recondite American jokes. When I was not looking, he kissed Meg.

The Editor of the *Daily Mail* has changed since I went away. The new one was polite but puzzled at my return. He can't think why I want to write about British Guiana. I have spent £2000 of his money there which I must enter as expenses in my income tax so he has jolly well got to print an article, tho' I have little to say that will interest his readers.

Meg proved a sturdy travelling companion, never repining at hardship but rejoicing in our rare encounters with luxury (the Hailes[2] live like fighting cocks), never queazy in the smallest boats in the highest seas. She grew very stout in the Antilles but looked skinny beside Ladies Lettice[3] and Magnus[4] with whom she played canasta every evening.

It is very shocking to come back to press cuttings. Worse than bills. Some wretch got hold of the story of Spender pawning my watch. By the way I have a letter of yours in which you say that Spender will pay for the damage. The bill was £14. I have put it in Lady Pamela's hands. She thinks he will bilk. You will be called in evidence.[5] Poor Beaton seems to have complained about me on the wireless. More press cuttings about that.

Civil war is imminent in British Guiana. All the blackamoors in the small islands will starve to death.

I hope you painted a lot in Jamaica. It must have been very trying having old Quennell hanging about. What does the poor booby think he can write about Shakespeare? I saw Cyril in London – very pretty but much embarrassed because, it appears, Beaton in the broadcast when he complained about me claimed Cyril as his best friend. I also saw Graham [Greene] who narrowly escaped being *plastiqué* in Paris.

Lord Wimbourne should read Fitzgerald's *Babylon Revisited.*

I was highly elated by John Sparrow's exposure of *Lady Chatterley.* I had not read the book since it first came out & innocently missed the implications. H. Nicolson said he had refused to give evidence for the defence because the implications were manifest to him. I hope all those ridiculous parsons read it – John's article I mean.[6]

Have you ever read the description of Coleridge in Carlyle's *Sterling*? Brilliant.[7]

Your affec. coz.

E.W.

1 Charles da Costa (1910–74). A Jewish Jamaican businessman, who claimed to have been beaten at Marlborough by John Betjeman. Waugh had stayed with him and Ann, without knowing this, had almost dropped in on her way back from taking Raymond and Sara Carr to the airport.

2 Lord Hailes (1901–74). Conservative MP, created Lord Hailes 1957. Governor General of the West Indies 1957–62.

3 Lady Lettice Lygon (1906–   ). Married Sir Richard Cotterell 1930–58.

4 Jewell Allcroft married in 1943 Sir Philip Magnus, the historian, who then called himself Magnus-Allcroft.

5 Stephen Spender had been taking Waugh's watch to be mended, when, much to his embarrassment, it was stolen from him. It was slightly damaged and Spender had it repaired.

6 John Sparrow wrote an article in *Encounter* to show from internal evidence that Mellors had sodomised Lady Chatterley. D. H. Lawrence's novel had recently been prosecuted unsuccessfully for obscenity, with many distinguished literary witnesses for the defence. Some now claimed that of course they had known all this before, others that it was not true.

7 *The Life of John Sterling* by Thomas Carlyle, 1851. Eleven pages are devoted to Coleridge who is seen as a sage 'who has escaped from the insanity of life's battles' to Highgate Hill where he is sought out by the young, among them Sterling. There, there was 'talk not flowing anywhither like a river but spreading everywhither in inextricable currents and regurgitations like a lake or sea.'

Having returned from Goldeneye without Fleming, Ann wrote him a letter from Victoria Square. Neither beginning nor end has survived though she seems to have preserved the middle intentionally. There was probably little before the first existing paragraph: 'Though I am really glad you are cheerful and well, and was pleased to receive so jaunty a letter, I am amazed that even you can so lightly dismiss my basic unhappiness and refuse to be in any way involved with it. I know that misery from far away will not put up your blood pressure, so I would be grateful if you could make an effort to see my point of view by reading this letter carefully.' She then says how much she has minded Fleming having a mistress in Jamaica, that while there had been any hope of sex between them she had not dared speak of his affair but that now such hope was dead. She adds, 'I beg you to cease saying I do not like sex, surely you remember our past?', though she concedes that since the birth of Caspar things have not been going well, and he has not been feeling well for some time. She continues, 'You will consider these things better left unsaid. I am saying them because if we are to continue to live together I want you to know that much of my despondency was due to this. . . I love you very much in many other ways, but I do think you must try and help me to be happy if you *mean* that you *only* want to live with me.' She continues:

To Ian Fleming

[March? 1962]

Firstly, I cannot ask you to give up Jamaica because of your great love for it, and because we are leaving Sandwich, but I can and do ask you to understand that a two months' holiday for you should be made bearable for *me* if we are not to break asunder. This means that you do not telephone [your mistress] the minute we arrive without talking to me about it, for however much you prefer to see [her] it is not possible, because of the past, to ignore my feelings and insult me in this way, unless you do not care how unhappy I am. It is a clear sign that you still want to see her a great deal. I fear that since the rise of James Bond you do not care for a personality that in any way can compete with yours, and no doubt there is more adulation to be had at —, and you refuse to see that it is an impossible situation for me. However, you have now two weeks for adulation and the chank shell on the desk and all the other visible signs of the tenancy of the once loved one and now friend [are removed?] No doubt that is why you wanted me to go. I would love to diminish the emotionalism of our lives but while she continues to be an adjunct of Jamaican life, and you take every opportunity of patronage and friendship to see [her] family I shall be neither calm nor happy. The fact that you saw her in the nursing home reveals your feelings for her, for you do not want to see many people. If you were well and we were both younger our marriage would be over; but I love you and want to look after you, and grind my teeth when you smoke, and am pleased when you refrain from the deadly gin after whisky, and because of these things I think it would be worth your while to put yourself out a little to do things with me and for me. Last year my happiness started when you were well enough to leave the nursing home and ended with those cruel words in the mistral, cruel because they were true and I did not have the self-sacrifice and the self-control to accept the truth. I fear I am not good enough for that. If I was it would probably not be virtue but indifference, and if I was indifferent to you, Caspar's home would be broken. It is an added complication that when I dared to talk to the Carrs until 10.45 you came roaring out, [it] was not entirely healthy for you to stay at the Portland until later hours. I do not know what it is except your personality has greatly changed with success, Bond and bad health – this is a *general* opinion. You need great love, calm and quiet, more than anyone. I can give you all if you give me little; but please devote a little of your vitality to keeping us close together, and share what you can of your life with me. I can in all ways be very useful. Though I have to write this letter I asked the Carghills[1] to keep you in view lest you get ill and I shall not be at rest until you pass the Scylla and Charybdis of Bryce and New York and get safely home.

It was very sweet of you to let me sleep in your room, I love your proximity and loathe the draughts in the other. I have wondered that you have never said that it is a pity there are not two decent bedrooms in the house. If there were I would less frequently trade upon your kindness and if you had expressed the thought I would have considered you considerate. I left an envelope of Dutch pipe seeds in the draughty room, I had not the heart to plant them.

I was to dine with Kitty Giles to see Mark Boxer,[2] but was unable. Kitty is not in the confidence of the hierarchy, but she said Boxer let fall a vague sentence inferring the possible decease of the coloured supplement, but she seemed unclear about it, though impressed by his sorrow and humility at the failure. The *'on dit'* through Lady Pamela is that you were discarded by Max because of the short story, but she clearly does not know and I have been too ill to tackle Max. [unfinished]

1 Morris Carghill (1914–   ). Solicitor, farmer and writer.
2 Mark Boxer (1931–   ). Cartoonist, editor, publisher. First Editor of *The Sunday Times* Colour Magazine 1962–5; now Editor of the *Tatler*. His cartoons, signed Marc, appeared in *The Times* 1969–83 and since then in the *Guardian* and elsewhere. Ann's literary executor.

A number of letters exchanged at this time between Ann and Ian have been omitted, and those that remain are difficult to date. This and the following letter from Ian give some indication of the anguish both were going through.

From Ian Fleming

Hotel Pierre, New York   [no date]

Wednesday
This is also *my* last effort.
I love you and I prove it by the efforts I make to make you happy. These efforts are not enough. All I get is a further string of complaints. When I want to do the things I enjoy, as this sudden trip to Jamaica, that is also a cause for complaint. You have had to get another man for a dinner-party!
    Your health? That too has been my fault for years. Now we find, as I have constantly said we would, that the trouble is organic. Why have I had to suffer so long before you could take the trouble to find this out? The East wind, the Thunderbird, the crash, the height of the mountains – it has all been laid at my door.
    And now these cruel letters and cables hurled at me.
    Can you wonder that I'm fed to the teeth?

But for my love for you and Caspar I would welcome the freedom which you threaten me with.

It has all been getting worse and worse and I knew this year would be decisive. Either we survive it or we don't. There is no one else in my life. There is a whole cohort in yours. I am lonely, jealous and ill. Leave me my pleasures as I leave you yours.

Above all, have compassion.

Ian

To Evelyn Waugh

16 Victoria Square   11 March 1962

Dearest Evelyn

I have suffered several varieties of influenza since my return to winter; depression from the disease and the antibiotic remedies induced a suicidal condition ill-suited to correspondence or any activity. My only outing was to dine with Lady Antonia Fraser; Hugh, it appeared, had lunched with you at White's, he seemed surprised by the incident.

I sat next to a terrible red-haired creature named Paul Johnson, he claimed to be in perpetual communication with you – is the link religion? I doubt if you would approve of him otherwise, his manners are abominable, though writing for the *New Statesman* he tells me he is a Conservative.[1] He also told me he had seen Bron passionately embracing Teresa (wife not sister) in an alleyway off Fleet Street.

I enjoyed your letter but would like to hear of the jungle episodes. Stephen Spender was told at one of the government houses where you narrowly missed each other that you had made much play with your ear trumpet and had invited Meg to tell you later of what the Governor spoke. The Governor was not hoodwinked.

Mrs Morgan [Fionn] is obsessed with happy childbirth, communal exercises, communal delivery and the presence of the husband throughout the grisly proceedings, I consider it a return to the middle ages and have forced her into privacy and the services of an expensive obstetrician. Are you and Laura to become grandparents?

Love

A

1 Paul Johnson (1928–) writes: 'In August 1958 I published in the *New Statesman* an attack on Ian Fleming's James Bond books. It was called "Sex, Snobbery and Sadism" and created a minor sensation at the time. It upset Fleming deeply and thereafter Mrs Fleming pursued an intermittent vendetta against me.' Johnson's break with the Labour Party was still more than ten years distant.

To Evelyn Waugh

Good Friday
[20 April 1962]

16 Victoria Square

Dearest Evelyn

I did *not* totally misunderstand the cause of your consternation at the Hailes revelation,[1] I am convinced you overestimated the capacity of your audience to appreciate your particular brand of wit and charm . . . While women of wit, beauty, and discrimination like Nancy and Diana seek your company there is no need to fear you have become a 'horrible old man'. I will be the first to tell you when you become like Ed., Randolph or other old friends who have become sadly insensitive to their effect upon others. As far as I know no one shouts '*Cave*, Waugh coming.'

The Gaitskell gold table will soon oust the Ghana gold bed from the headlines.[2] Mrs Gaitskell since seeing the embassies of Belgravia has grown weary of her homely furniture, so they have purchased a table which they think is of the Louis Seize epoch, in fact it is the top of a gigantic Victorian washstand, muddy marble precariously balanced on worm-eaten gilded wood, ornately garlanded with stucco. It looks very rum in Hampstead.

I have crucified myself this Easter by inviting my ailing ancient father and stepmother to the neighbouring hotel: he became faint looking for larks' nests on the golf course so I had to drive my car amongst the golfers; describing swift non-U turns to the accompaniment of angry shouts I rescued him. Thunderbird is on the golf committee and is awfully cross. The evenings seem very long for Thunderbird can think of nothing to say to my stepmother except 'Suppose you had a bathe before breakfast.'

Saw Cyril last weekend, very chubby and well; he says old age is a permanent Lent, always giving up something – drink, food, smoking – in order to survive.

Miss Judy was pursued by the press at the Roman airport at the start of her marriage journey to New York,[3] she took to her heels, fell on her knees, and went to the altar with legs sticking-plastered and bandaged.

Lady Dunn bought Willie Maugham's favourite painting in order to give it to him as an Easter present. Willie is convinced he is bankrupt. He wrote to me saying to hire a steam yacht and take him on a cruise, he says he would provide agreeable conversation which Winston tells him is so sadly lacking on the Onassis ship.

Thunderbird is in a decline because of the bad reviews he has received, accusing him of sadism and pornography;[4] he has told his publishers to stop all further editions (secret), I am doing my best to reverse this foolish gesture because of the yellow silk for the drawing-room walls.

When shall I see you?

Love

A

1 Waugh had written, 'You have totally misunderstood the cause of my consternation at the Hailes revelation. It is not that I especially value their opinion – though I like them both very much. Everyone bores somebody. The essence of my discomfort is that I was confident I was making myself unusually agreeable and amusing. When one has reached the age of illusion to such a degree, one must confine oneself to solitude. I have seen other horrible old men and women who became bores and did not know it. I am glad to have learned, if not in time, at least before the very end.' And to Nancy Mitford, '. . . it has been what young people call traumatic. . . You do see that it means that I can never go out again.'

2 There had been much publicity about a gold-embossed bed bought at Harrods by Mr Krobo Edusei, Ghana's Minister for Industry, for £3000. He was sacked.

3 Judy Montagu married that year Milton Gendel (1918–   ), the art historian.

4 For *The Spy Who Loved Me*. After the bad reviews for this more experimental book, Fleming reverted to formula.

From Evelyn Waugh

Combe Florey House, Nr Taunton   24 April [1962]

My Dear Ann

Thank you for writing. Did I tell you of the other blow to my self-esteem? I was sitting alone in White's when a man, older & dressier than I, known to me by sight but not by name, accosted me & said: 'Why are you sitting alone?' 'Because no one wants to talk to me.' 'And I can tell you why. Because you sit there on your arse looking like a stuck pig.' Also I had a letter from Gaston [Palewski] saying: '*Rome s'ennuie de vous*' but scholars tell me this does not mean what it seems to.[1] Debo started self-doubts when she turned on television during dinner. They have grown ever since to certainty. It is kind of you to try & reassure me but I recognise that I am in the John Fox [Strangways] class.

I noticed that Ian's latest book was being badly received by the critics. I am very sorry that this should upset him. He should know too much of journalism to mind what the papers say. He should also know that reviews have a negligible effect on sales once a writer has established a body of readers.

Tell Ian that reviewers live by saying either: 'Why doesn't he write as he used to?' or 'Why does he always write in the same way?' They cannot in that way fail to annoy.

I have been reading A. Powell's new book.[2] They will say: 'Why does he write in the same way?' A very good way.

The lawns are like hayfields & no one cuts them. Only the chestnuts are in bud. Meg is on the quays of Dublin. Bron kept Palm Sunday here with his wife – she very gravid, he as stout as she. Laura was tripped on Paddington platform and is going lame.

Yesterday I went to bore the Colytons[3] & told them that they should not speak of 'human dignity'.

I hope that Quennell, Freud & Forbes are proving serviceable.
                    Yours ever affec.
                    E.W.

1 It means in fact 'Rome misses you'.
2 *The Kindly Ones.*
3 As Henry Hopkinson, Lord Colyton had been Conservative MP for Taunton 1950–6.

To Evelyn Waugh

Hotel Bauer Grünwald, Venezia   10 June [1962]

Dearest Evelyn

Never get involved in a speedboat world, they usually belong to very dull people; we were awfully happy here till Ian got involved with Paul Münster[1] and golf on the Lido, now it is ceaseless speedboat dashes between the Giudecca, the canal, the Lido, overloaded with café society persons, hitting the water at a vicious rate of knots and inspiring fear and boredom.

The headmaster of Caspar's school told me that when you went to lunch *re* Ronny Knox, and took your deaf aid to the high table, a boy said 'Look, Evelyn Wuff has brought his own soup spoon.'

A jolly weekend at Chatsworth concluded on an electric note with the arrival for Sunday dinner of Mr and Mrs Aidan Crawley and Lady Pamela Berry. It had come to Andrew's ears that Lady P. had recently insulted Lady Elizabeth Cavendish, telling her that her uncle the PM [Macmillan] was a wicked senile old man. Andrew longed for a fight but Lady P. likes dukes and being anxious to please, a fight was not possible; but Debo's blue eyes froze and cold hostility pervaded the dinner table. Later, at the billiard table, it was clear that a great deal of wine had been imbibed by Andrew and the candidate now Member for West Derby; we started with Freda's game,[2] Andrew constantly saying to Lady P. 'Here's the black ball for you.' It ended with a violent game of billiard fives, me and Andrew playing Aidan and Robert Kee, feelings and tempers on edge – happily we won, but I shall probably have to have my thumb amputated. Upstairs the ladies made frigid conversation, I realised subsequently that Lady P. had given Debo a lecture on Derbyshire, the unpopularity of the Cavendishes, and the orders from Central Office that they were to play no part in the election. I enjoyed it all very much.

It freezes and rains here. Home on the 19th. Please come and bore me again. I want to hire Italian plasterers to finish our home.

With love

A

1 Count Paul Münster, son of Prince Alexander Münster of Derneburg, married in 1929 Margaret Ward.

2 A comparatively gentle game played without cues on the billiard table. Named after Freda Dudley Ward.

Note from Evelyn Waugh

Pixton Park, Dulverton   23 June [1962]

I stayed with Pam. She said: 'The most extraordinary evening at Chatsworth. Andrew had been working enthusiastically for Aidan and I brought him there to celebrate. Ann would not speak to us and scowled throughout the evening.'

To Evelyn Waugh

16 Victoria Square   29 June [1962]

Dearest Evelyn

I woke this morning with puffed and swelled eyelids, after the initial horror it was nice to stay in bed instead of the social life at Petworth – I find people very tiring these days. I could not bother to prevent the doctor rolling up the eyelids to look for foreign bodies for I was aware it was the culmination of Caspar's half term, Maurice Bowra, Charlie Chaplin, carbon monoxidal drives between Oxford and Sandwich, and visits to Dreamland at Margate.

Maurice's *soirée* for Charlie Chaplin[1] had its moments; it was a coldish darkish summer evening and ushered into the sub-aqueous light of the dining-room it was difficult to identify persons. After the guest of honour Maurice introduced in ringing tones 'Le Commandant Vallié', I was amazed to recognise Paul Louis Weiller, I could not believe it was true and Isaiah insisted that the resemblance was superficial, but it was indeed Paul Louis who is apparently Charlie Chaplin's best friend[2] and was also staying with Maurice. We dined in the college dining-room and Mr Chaplin sat between me and Elizabeth Bowen,[3] he made the mistake of thinking Oxford a serious place and was not funny at all, he was bitter about the workhouse childhood and half-baked politics – friendly but silly. After dinner Paul Louis approached and asked me about my villa in the south of France and my castle in Kent – a little out of date.

We terminated our holiday on a mountain pass in the Dolomites; alternate storms of snow and thunder, nothing growing except heather and pines. It was to be one night to see my father who was searching for Alpine birds and plants with a serious naturalist, Mr Mackworth-Praed, grandson of the poet: unluckily Ian fell in love with Mackworth-Praed and refused to leave this horror resort, he said Mr M.P. knew many interesting facts and should be protected from Charteris jokes. Certainly M.P. never smiled, least of all when cross-examined by Ian about the Loch Ness Monster – 'A very real animal,' he said, 'Macmillan has seen it often.' I thought this worrying for the Conservative Party, but was contemptuously assured that it was not the Prime Minister, but '*the* Macmillan' – now who can that be?

I do hope poor Auberon [Herbert] has not lost the Portofino money. There was an alarming story in the *Daily Express*.

Please write to me about the Pixton Ball.[4]

Love

A

1 Chaplin was in Oxford to receive an honorary degree. He was knighted in 1975.

2 Paul Louis Weiller is only mentioned in Chaplin's autobiography as being among 'an affluent *potpourri*' of guests lunching at Versailles.

3 The novelist was then living in Oxford, at work on *The Little Girls*.

4 Harriet Waugh's coming-out party, given at the house of her grandmother, Mary Herbert.

From Evelyn Waugh[1]

Combe Florey House, Nr Taunton   2 July 1962

Dearest Ann

Thank you for your letter.

I think your new friend (like so many of them) must be an impostor. Praed died in 1839 leaving 2 daughters (from one of whom Douglas Woodruff descends). It is possible, I suppose, that the younger daughter bore a son at the age of 45 and that he took his mother's name for reasons of social advantage and is now botanizing in Switzerland at the age of 78 – but it sounds fishy. Whatever his origin he is correct on the subject of the Loch Ness Monster. It was seen by the late Abbot of Fort Augustus.

Oddly enough I knew that poor Louis [Weiller] had tacked himself on to Chaplin. I was smoked out of my hole last week by the Pixton junketings & heard the news in London from Diana who was proud that her loyal boy should have made so good. We (Diana

& I) went to the theatre & saw a brilliant (to me) actress named
Maggie Smith.[2] We couldn't get seats & then said 'How about a
box?' 'Oh, yes, of course there's always a box. Do you really want
one?' So we sat cheek by jowl with Maggie Smith & admired her
feverishly. A stage box is the ideal place for a party of two. The
trouble is that people think that when they have paid four or five
guineas they must pack it & then no one can see or stretch his legs.
Well Miss Smith is a fair treat & the two little plays she is in give her
a chance to show it. She will become famous. Perhaps she is already
and it is like my saying: 'Keep an eye on a clever young American
called T. S. Eliot.'

From London I went to visit Pam Berry. She had an American
picture dealer there and socialists came to dinner. No sign of
Michael. Pam complained a great deal that everyone was dull, dirty,
drunk. She wishes to overturn the monarchy and set Lady Harewood up as First Lady. Her condemnations, so vehement as to be
scarcely rational, ranged from the Knights of the Garter to the
Marylebone Cricket Club. I said 'You are like Philip Egalité.' 'My
favourite man', but I found that all she knew of him was his portrait
as a child at Waddesdon. Have you been there? Very oppressive. It
is like being Alice, after she shrank, in the Wallace Collection.
Everything superb but twice its proper size. Pam: 'We ought to give
all these back to Versailles.' E: 'If the frogs have no king, they have
no right to have a palace.' P: 'Oh, how can you be so reactionary?'
From there to Claydon where the English Rococo seemed light as
down.

From Pam to Penelope Betjeman.[3] A sharp contrast. All the time
I was with her Penelope never said a disagreeable thing about
anyone. We went with the Woodruffs to Lyford (the house where
Campion was taken prisoner). It belonged to the Woodruffs for 30
years but always let to a farmer. Now two rich pious spinsters have
bought it, laid parquet flooring, exposed old beams, smothered the
place with white paint and attempting to make a Popish pilgrimage
centre have made a Maidenhead villa. But all the time Mia was
saying 'Just what Douglas & I always wanted to do if we could have
afforded it.' When the spinsters rebuilt the roof they found a unique
relic, an Agnus Dei (wax medallions cast and blessed by the Pope) of
Campion's date still wrapped in the paper in which it had been
tucked away when the pursuivants searched the house. An object,
to me, of greater interest than anything at Waddesdon. It was sad

for the Woodruffs to know that they had owned it for 30 years unawares.

Paul Betjeman is in a third-class jazz band touring American bases in France. His great ambition is to become a second-class bandsman. This can only be attained by a three-year course of study in USA. A strange grandson for the Field Marshal.

Penelope drove me home, stopping often for ginger beer on the road, and charged at once into the kitchen & began preparing dinner. A great boon to Laura who was worn down by her house party & her mother's ball. That seems to have been a success. They danced until six. The 'young men' were all 30-year-old alcoholics – Meg's set.

Penelope takes catechism classes at 9 in the morning 5 days a week. An edifying example to us all. She says the boys in the 'Secondary Modern' have not a clear grasp of the truths of religion.

Bron is the father of a daughter.[4] Grandfathers prefer grand-sons. I went to see Teresa. She was in a public hospital, uncomplaining and surrounded by flowers like a coffin. The woman in the next bed was herself a midwife.

There is an inexcusable fault in grammar in my review of Tony Powell in the *Spectator*[5] that will haunt me to my death. I may bore Hailes, I thought, but at least I can write grammatical English. Now this small prop to my self-respect is gone.

Your affec. coz.

E.W.

1 This is a complete text of the letter conflated with half that of 13 September 1961 in *The Letters of Evelyn Waugh*, pp. 569–71.

2 In *The Private Eye* and *The Public Ear* by Peter Schaffer with Kenneth Williams. Maggie Smith was known but not famous, having succeeded in revue but been unnoticed by Waugh when he saw Ionesco's *Rhinoceros*.

3 Penelope Chetwode (1910–). Writer, traveller and horsewoman. Daughter of Field Marshal Lord Chetwode, she married John Betjeman in 1933.

4 Margaret Sophia Laura Waugh (1962–). Publisher.

5 Waugh had written, 'The multitude of characters have been our companions. . .'

To Evelyn Waugh

16 Victoria Square   Friday
                                                                                 6 July [1962]

Dearest Coz.

Thanks for shedding light on the Praed family. The impostor's
B.F. [best friend] is Colonel Meinertzhagen of whom you have
doubtless heard, the latter has bidden us to a 'Mau Mau' party, this
is more exciting than meeting U Thant so we have accepted; amidst
the awful rites I will tax Praed with his ancestry.

A happy week to receive two letters from you.

Assuredly the paragraph in the *Sunday Telegraph* was Lady
Pamela's revenge,[1] probably only the first shot in a campaign to
hound you from the country; it has reached my ears that you forced
her to her knees on some Oxford pavement to apologise to Mr
Woodruff and yourself for maliciously causing you both to be late
for Penelope Betjeman's lunch party, she probably regards Penelope
as a dangerous rival hostess. I was told not to repeat this information, so in any further correspondence on this matter be discreet. To
be serious, Pam returned distressed and cross from the expedition to
Oxford: she said her watch was wrong and you had been *extremely*
disagreeable to her.

My reactions to visiting first Waddesdon and then Claydon
were the same as yours, Claydon remains an image of great beauty. I
visit it again on Sunday in the vain hope that some village craftsman
could emulate [it] for our folly.

I was accompanied to the two houses by Lady Rosebery[2] and the
Duke of Devonshire. Lady Rosebery was anxious to demonstrate
her relationship to the Rothschilds by skipping over the red ropes
and showing us secret drawers in French cabinets, she was sharply
reprimanded by a member of the women's institute who guard this
stifling treasure trove: Andrew's reaction was 'not a gentleman's
house'.

Lady Bridget Parsons is acting as broker for the mobile maker
'Calder'[3] whose works you may see at the Tate, some people think
he is exploiting her, her rooms are a mass of revolving objects in
primary colours; she is finding them difficult to dispose of, it would
be a kindness if you were to purchase one, it might serve to frighten
the window cleaner from peering at you.[4]

You should read *Catch 22*.[5] I enjoyed Powell.
With love
A

PS. What is the grammatical error that keeps you awake?

1 Waugh had told Lady Pamela Berry that he had been invited to dine with U Thant by the Prime Minister but had refused. A paragraph with this information appeared in the Albany column of the *Sunday Telegraph* and Waugh, wrongly assuming that Lady Pamela had passed on the information, described her as a 'sneak hostess' and added, 'If I ever see her again (which heaven forfend) I shall address her as Lady Randolph Grubstreet.'

2 Eva Strutt (b.1892). Married in 1924 Lord Primrose, whose mother was a Rothschild and who succeeded as Earl of Rosebery in 1929. DBE.

3 Alexander Calder (1898–1974). Sculptor.

4 Waugh had interjected in a letter, 'Window cleaners at work keep popping their faces up in a most disconcerting manner', and 'God, there's that window cleaner again.'

5 Waugh had been sent it by the publisher, to whom he replied: 'You are mistaken in calling it a novel. It is a collection of sketches – often repetitious – totally without structure. Much of the dialogue is funny.'

To Evelyn Waugh

16 Victoria Square   2 August [1962]

Dearest Evelyn

Our pornography fund has spent £300 on Augustus John's drawing of Cyril, Ian thinks it an investment for old Caspar and Cyril is to write a book on the back of it to make it more valuable.

A very jolly letter from Mr Somerset Maugham, the downfall of Lord John Hope fills him with joy, he says he looks forward to the future with animation and zest. Have you seen the magazine *Show* and Mr Maugham's memoirs?[1] It is not a pretty piece of writing; I had not realised that Mrs Maugham was married to Mr Wellcome of Wellcome and Burroughs when Liza was born.[2]

We had a noisy evening with Avons and Devonshires. Nigel Birch came to tell Anthony the gossip, and Andrew was very loyal to his uncle [Harold Macmillan]; it was civilised till Lord Avon's bedtime, then there was great uproar between Andrew and Nigel and lots of four-letter words; Debo said to Roy Jenkins[3] 'Can't you stop them by saying something Labour?' but this is something Roy has never been able to do. I had asked Clarissa if Anthony would like to see Selwyn Lloyd,[4] she replied he was a useful stick to beat Harold with but she would sooner not meet him socially.

Yesterday I lunched with the Devonshires before their departure to celebrate the Independence of Jamaica. They and Hugh and Lady Antonia Fraser were flying with Princess Margaret and Lord Snowdon. Their flying time was to be nineteen hours via the Azores – a curious route, it only takes the common man nine hours. Andrew was very peevish because Armstrong-Jones had twelve attendants and he was not allowed a valet: also the Jones's had two thirds of the aeroplane private and he only a seat between the hairdresser and the maid: bunks in the Jones's kitchen for Debo and Lady Antonia but they had to rise when the Joneses wanted breakfast. Five white tie occasions in the hurricane season will not be much fun, but I cheered with dazzling descriptions of Charles da Costa and Ian's black wife. Andrew has a spending allowance of £5 a day, so he will be able to buy lots of prickly fish with pink felt tongues like the one you bought me.

Wednesday last a preview of Ian's film *Dr No*. We were invited to dinner by the director – a private room at the Travellers' Club and co-guests the Duke and Duchess of Bedford,[5] Lord and Lady Bessborough,[6] John Sutro[7] and Peter Quennell: it was an abominable occasion. When we arrived very late at the private cinema our personal guests Mr and Mrs Crickmere, Nanny, old Caspar and all the Miss Lambtons were very restive, and I feared Mrs Crickmere might give notice and no more coconut soup; luckily she found the film 'quite gripping'. I wish I had, for our fortune depends upon it. There were howls of laughter when the tarantula walks up James Bond's body, it was a close-up of a spider on a piece of anatomy too small to be an arm. The heroine could not be eaten by crabs, for though they imported huge land crabs from Guernsey they died the minute they were placed on the heroine's body.

Diana came to tea before departure for Venice, possibly her summer holidays go wrong for lack of food; she very pale from ten days' starvation and a dozen colonic irrigations.

Yesterday sheets spread upon the lawns of Sandwich Garden City, markers for private helicopters bringing rich persons from Goodwood to golf. The noise was awful and Caspar missed them all with his catapult. The Wiltshire houseboat will at least be peaceful. With love to you and Laura,

A

1 Maugham's autobiography *Looking Back* was described by his publishers, Heinemann, who rejected it, as 'the ravings of a lunatic', but it was further serialized in the *Sunday Express* in September and October. It has never appeared as a book.

2 True. Syrie Maugham married in 1901 Henry Wellcome from Wisconsin, whose pharmaceutical company prospered when they began to dispense compressed drugs under the name 'tabloids'. Liza was born in 1915, their divorce was not final until 1917. Maugham never doubted that she was his child but wished she had been a boy.

3 Roy Jenkins (1920–). Labour MP 1948–76, President of the European Commission 1977–81, first Leader of the Social Democratic Party 1982–3. *See* Appendix of Names.

4 Selwyn Lloyd (1902–78). Conservative MP 1945–70 (when he became Speaker), Chancellor of the Exchequer 1956–60 and Lord Privy Seal 1960–2.

5 Nicole Schneider of Paris married in 1960 the Duke of Bedford (1917–).

6 Mary Munn of New York and Paris married in 1948 the Earl of Bessborough (1913–).

7 John Sutro (1904–85). Brilliant mimic and Oxford friend of Waugh. Worked in films.

To Evelyn Waugh

Portofino   28 August [1962]

Dear Evelyn
    I condole with you on Margaret's engagement not because of her choice but because you will miss her dreadfully. Surely the name 'FitzHerbert'[1] denotes ancient lineage, Norman blood? Did she meet him on a scoffing party? I imagine you will give her a splendid wedding, the Brompton Oratory followed by a ball at the Ritz.
    We are now twenty souls under one beach umbrella on the Parragi beach. Lady Rothschild[2] has arrived with Miss Emma Rothschild,[3] a dusky silent beauty; a history don named Chivers with a wife who feeds the pregnant cats of Portofino – I have known many people feed cats but never one who observed and selected pregnant cats – also a Jewish don called Beloff[4] and an Italian conductor named Julini [*sic*],[5] and Mr and Mrs Hugh Gaitskell. It is like being in the centre of a pack of hounds in full cry. I attempted to break the party into small units for dinner but the Gaitskells were

forgotten, I had chosen Maurice and the philosopher Hampshire (neither bastard nor peer) for my companions, but there is little *lebensraum* on the Portofino piazza, and Lady Berlin's sons, old Caspar and my nephew Francis seemed over-conscious of the Gaitskells' predicament – in turn the boys thrust their heads through the protective hedge where we had taken cover and yelled reproachfully 'The Gaitskells are alone on the piazza', Caspar adding 'and they're dreadfully lonely because they're not even being photographed.'

The Chairman of W. H. Smith and Son is now under the next beach umbrella and is charmed at his proximity to intellectuals, socialists and Jews.

There are constant rumours that your brother-in-law may materialise but, alas, no.

See you on Friday the 14th.

Love,

A

1 Margaret Waugh married Giles FitzHerbert (1935–) in October. Waugh described him as 'an Irish stock-broker's clerk, 27, penniless, rather raffish in looks, small, a Catholic (thank God)'. In 1966 he joined the Foreign Office.

2 Teresa Mayor married Lord Rothschild in 1946.

3 Emma Rothschild (1948–). Writer, now living in America. Married Alexander Cockburn.

4 Professor Max Beloff (1913–). Historian. Fellow of Nuffield College, Oxford, 1947–58; Principal of University College, Buckingham, 1974. Life Peer 1981.

5 Carlo Maria Giulini (1914–). Principal conductor at La Scala, Milan, 1953–5; closely associated with the New Philharmonic Orchestra.

To Evelyn Waugh

16 Victoria Square   1 December 1962

Dearest Evelyn

Would you care to take the underground to Croydon on Dec. 17th and see Ibsen's *Master Builder*? I consulted Diana who is better versed than I in current productions, and she seemed very dubious that you would enjoy any of them. I don't think justice triumphs in *King Lear*, but possibly it does in Noël Coward's *Sail Away*. If there is a Marx Brothers on at the Classic, Baker Street, should we settle for that?

It seems sad you should waste away money on marble halls,

though we may have to because the domestic situation is most uncertain: how much do you enjoy Spanish food? Your postcard has remained long unanswered because of relations, property and domestics. The last 'property' disaster was the installation in all bathrooms of a cheap metal fitting of not inconsiderable size announcing 'for electric shavers only' – when I complained the architect, who is seventy years of age, told me I was out of touch with the younger generation; have you had to install such objects for your sons and sons-in-law? Ali Forbes goes to his car each morning to perform this function, but I regarded his use of an electric razor as eccentric; what do you use?

Mrs Crickmere is very lonely without me, she came to cook dinner between Italy and Spain and insisted on remaining the night to frighten the Spaniards in the morning; she darkly warned me of the length of their siesta and their squalid habits, and as the poor peasants arrived by chance with Ian from Japan and the polar 'Galbraith' route, she sent them to the basement while she crooned over Ian.[1] Ian was more than pleased to have coconut soup after a diet of turtle blood and live lobster. Did you know that in the Kyoto Islands the Japanese female pearl divers ate live lobster with chopsticks?

I visited Chatsworth for a high society pheasant shoot. Debo was sucking up to the President's sister-in-law, Princess Radziwill,[2] and Andrew was sucking up to Duncan Sandys and his wife;[3] it was a *terrible* failure; Sandyses and Radziwills fled to their bedchambers alarmed by Mitford and Cecil wit – a confusing language to the uninitiated anyway, but to a Pole, an American, a French woman and a humourless politician it was the crackle of machine gun fire; worse was to follow for Duncan contracted an obscure disease, 'the devil's grip', doubtless from the dusty drapes of his stateroom bed; so I expect Devonshire will be one of the White's unemployed soon.

Of course if you were to accompany me to Oxford on Tuesday the 18th you would see Summerfields VIth form perform *Jonah and the Whale*, I doubt if we could get a box but it's a very high standard of acting, last year June Osborn's Christopher was a very jolly little Cleopatra.

With love

A.

1 Fleming had gone for a twelve-day tour of Japan with Richard Hughes, the journalist, and Torao 'Tiger' Saito, architect and former war correspondent. It was

a success but he returned exhausted, though still refusing to cut down on drink or cigarettes.

2 Lee Bouvier, sister of Jacqueline Kennedy, was married to Prince Stanislaus ('Stash') Radziwill.

3 Marie-Claire Schmitt of Paris married Duncan Sandys in 1962. He was Secretary of State for Commonwealth Relations and for the Colonies, that is to say, the Duke of Devonshire's boss.

From Evelyn Waugh

Combe Florey House, Nr Taunton   5 December 1962

Dear Ann

No, not Croydon by tube to *The Master Builder*. I am not dead set on entertainment. You are as good as a play. Why not a quiet evening *à deux* at the Hyde Park Hotel or in your house since you are so good as to suggest it? But I tremble to go there for fear of the kind of person I might have to meet.

Fr Caraman[1] has been recuperating here pruning apple trees & clandestinely saying Mass in the dining room. Almost certainly the first time Mass has been said in the parish for 400 years.

No, of course I don't use an electric razor. How can you suggest anything so absurd? Cyril Connolly had one in 1934 when they were a novelty. It left his dear face very blue & furry. Pauper Balfour had a cottage then in Hertfordshire. No electric current. So Cyril drove to the University Arms, Cambridge and collected an admiring audience as he shaved in the bar. A year or two ago some sinister little electric holes appeared in the bathrooms at the Hyde Park Hotel. I complained to the management who said Americans are afraid of cutting themselves with razors. A. Forbes is an American. Sir Robert Laycock uses a cut-throat razor.

Damn Summer Fields [*sic*]. I am being persecuted by a man who is writing its history and wants copies of Ronald Knox's Greek exercises.

I find my appetite for Laura's simple food greatly stimulated by a book called *The Great Hunger*. It is a very monotonous compilation of official correspondence, but taken a page at a time before meals it acts like Campari bitters.

I read in the paper that you are all choking to death in darkness in London. Here it is brilliant sunshine.

There was brisk bidding between *Sunday Times* & *Telegraph* for that story I told you about. *Telegraph* won at a price beyond the means of Fuddy-duddy Spender.[2]

> Ever your affec. coz.
>
> E. Waugh

1 Father Philip Caraman (1911–). Jesuit author, editor of *The Month* throughout the 1950s and close friend of Waugh.
2 Ann had suggested to Stephen Spender that he publish Waugh's story *Basil Seal Rides Again* in *Encounter*.

To Evelyn Waugh

16 Victoria Square   1 January 1963

Dearest Evelyn

I am seriously in need of gratification – never more so, and it would indeed gratify, please and flatter if your new story were to be dedicated to me, so pray don't change your mind and thankyou kindly. I arrived from Ireland this morning, an unpleasant journey, but relieved by Mrs Crickmere returned to her post and seeing your handwriting and subsequent agreeable surprising gratification.

My spirits have been sadly low, for poor sister Mary Rose died two days before Christmas. I lunched with her the day of our shopping jaunt, a sorry occasion. Nanny took the children to a cinema while she alternately slept or talked of Cynthia and James Barrie – she had no contact with the present and death was a merciful relief. She was found dead by the child [Francis Grey] and it was grisly depressing getting him on an aeroplane to Ireland, rescuing him from the senile father and the horrors of coroners and doctors. I took old Caspar to meet him at the airport and hoped old C. would shed some light on the degree of affection the poor child felt towards his mother, old C. said he did know but it was a secret he would never divulge and then said wistfully 'Do you think his spirits will be high enough for fighting?'

You were right to laugh at poor O'Neill entertaining the Thunderbird and the Fuddy-duddies [Peter and Spider Quennell], Thunderbird got terrible claustrophobia and continuously tried to escape to Dublin but was thwarted by the weather. The piercing giggles of Spider Quennell provoked an outburst of temper and she said she would never spend another night under the same roof as

Thunderbird, but the closing of London airport made this inevitable, so dinner that evening was not very gay and O'Neill, not for the first time, remarked that it was a very long Christmas. Mr, Mrs and Miss Morgan were a totally happy self-contained unit, Fionn has strong family feelings and was determined that all the O'Neill relations should see her child so they motored with the tot over many miles of sheet ice, she was suckled in snow drifts and parked in draughty halls, and now Fionn is amazed that she has lost weight.

The hypergamist has only one desire before exile to Brazil[1] and that is to meet you, is there any chance you will be in London before Jan. 27th? it would give Fionn a last gloat.

With love and gratification,

Ann

PS. O'Neill has no idea how much old people drink, the whisky and vodka were gone on Boxing Day.

1 John Morgan was Head of Chancery in Rio de Janeiro 1963–4. A hypergamist is one who marries a person of superior caste.

To Clarissa Avon

Goldeneye, Jamaica   30 January [1963]

Dearest Clarissa

It was so nice of you to write to me about Ian, and with hideous foresight to send Caspar a toboggan: he did write to you but I left the letter in London. It's been a drear drear Christmas and New Year, I have been too totally depressed to write before. My poor drunken sister was found dead in bed by her child, and there was a horrific inquest – three quarters of a bottle of brandy on an empty stomach. Poor brother Hugo had his gall bladder removed only to discover it was an abscess on the pancreas, so he is in a Glasgow hospital ward and will be for another six weeks; all this *grand guignol* coincided with poor Hugh [Gaitskell's] death. I mind very much more than I could have imagined, and I am sure it need not have happened. Two days before he died I felt impelled to go to the Middlesex Hospital and with much courage demanded to see Dora: she said she had complete faith in all the ten doctors – how can one like ten doctors? I last saw him in the Manor House Hospital on the

21st Dec. where they did a complete check-up and said he was perfectly alright.

When we arrived here I was far from cheerful but sharply rebuked by Ian who said he married me because I had the heart of a drum majorette!

The new High Commissioner's sister came to interview Ian for a magazine called *Home*: she wished to record the interviews and said to Ian: 'Could we say one, two, three, one, two, three, to see if our little box is working?'

I was glad to read in *The Times* that Judy [Gendel] had given birth to a daughter, the doctor had told her the child had ceased to grow, but further investigations suggested it might weigh 6lbs which, as Diana to console remarked, was 'ample, darling'!

With much love to you both, and thankyou for the so useful toboggan and your letter about Ian – who is far better here, but, alas, unable to prowl the reef.

A

To Evelyn Waugh

16 Victoria Square   12 March [1963]

Dearest Evelyn

I have some form of influenza: so though it's only 11 a.m. I am drinking whisky to give me strength to entertain the Donaldsons who come to lunch. Jack wrote to me so optimistically about the afterlife that I wish to ask him searching questions – he says it is easy for him to contemplate death because he knows we shall all be together again – I would love to believe we shall all be together again – recognisable, jolly, eating, drinking and talking hearty – does your religion hold any hope of such reunions? I believe – but not quite so certainly.

Thankyou kindly for your letters. I very much miss Hugh G., he was most lovable, loving and reliable, a Christian who refused to believe in God. I am very cross that they cremated him. It took me a week to prevent the cremation of Mary Rose. My father insisted that the gravediggers were perforce going as slow as the electricians, but I was resolute. So you see the breath has been on my neck. I am sorry that it is always on yours, or did you mean to convey that it was a pleasurable anticipation?[1]

I am gallantly reading brother Hugo's new novel,[2] alas, despite the good reviews I find it tedious. I shall send it to you.

Poor Hugo has been three months in the public ward of a Glasgow hospital,[3] according to sister Laura he suffered rotten medical attention and starvation, she went to visit him and nearly killed him by undermining his faith in doctors and nurses. 'No one' she declared loudly to the doctor 'has been allowed to swallow their own vomit on the operating table for fifty years.' This statement enraged the medico and profoundly alarmed all the other patients within earshot. Apparently the overcrowded ward was garnished with a small grill for making invalid toast, Laura claims to have fried several soles on it and fed Hugo unobserved, she also states that gangrene smells stronger than fish which helped her salvation activities.

Old Caspar took the news of Raymond's engagement[4] very badly, he said he had so hoped to be of royal blood; we were to lunch with the young couple in Oxford so I suggested he should put a cheerful face on the situation, which he did by announcing loudly in the dining-room of the Randolph that he would never marry because he was not so oversexed as James Bond – should I take him to a psychiatrist?

Loving Coz.

A

1 Waugh had written: 'I always feel the breath on my neck; you don't normally, I think; you will lose someone you love every year now for the rest of your life.'
2 *Pictures on the Wall.*
3 Hugo Charteris had been operated on for pancreatitis.
4 Lord O'Neill was engaged to Georgina Scott, daughter of Lord George Montagu-Douglas-Scott, the brother of the Duke of Buccleuch.

To Evelyn Waugh

Forest Mere Hydro, Hants   5 May [1963]

Dearest Evelyn

I am abed in a modern square box of a room, one wall is glass, I have always abominated these new dwellings but it is very agreeable to gaze at so much tree and verdure. The disadvantage is waking at six for though the curtains are thick there are no blinds.

Mr Sanderson, the boss, made friends with Cyril, or claims this honour. I have told Mr S. that you too might patronise if dark blinds are instituted.

Very lucky you did not come with me, so much poison to come out that I have a soufflé on my tongue, egg yolk eyes and feebleness of limb. I should have been no companion for you.

It was kind of you to entertain me and Thunderbird for dinner. Next time let me know well in advance so we may dine at home, Mrs C.'s summer fare is good but she needs long rests these days.

Poor Thunderbird suffered greatly in Monte Carlo, he went to collect his mother who is too old to travel alone. He had not travelled with her since he was twelve, she appears to think him still that age for the morning of departure he discovered that he was to share a sleeper with her and a picnic dinner – a dead partridge and half a bottle of *vin de pays*. He eluded these horrors but had to carry her jewel case (very heavy) and the x-rays of her gall bladder, also oversee fourteen cabin trunks. She is convinced that she is bankrupt and all her sons millionaires, they live in terror of disinheritance. She hired a room for Ian in the basement of the annexe of the Metropole Hotel, no daylight and much traffic, and such daylight as penetrated was obliterated at 8 a.m. by the parking of his mother's Rolls-Royce outside his basement window, it stood there all day in case she felt like a breath of air. T-B did not dare improve his living conditions in case Mama thought he was rich. His greatest embarrassment was her illusion that a cocktail party given by the Rolls-Royce company was a *concours d'elegance* which she would win. Her car being ten years old and herself ninety this seemed improbable, however he had to accompany the bedizened old lady, and as he suspected they merely wanted to sell her a new model. He is now resting in Istanbul, on location with the cast of *From Russia with Love*.

I lunched with Lady Grubstreet Berry and sat in uncomfortable proximity to Anthony Powell and George Weidenveldt. Anthony Powell complained that only politics were discussed these days, and seldom or never the arts, it transpired that he knows naught of music and I would surmise has never glanced at a painting. I suppose he reads books?[1]

Your beautiful Evangeline[2] and her mate dined with us without other company. I talked to her till pudding, then asked David from good manners a simple political question, he took forty-five minutes to answer, the boredom was acute and Evangeline most of all, she did little to hide it – the same terrible tension as seen on Clarissa's face when Anthony speaks.

Very shaming dinner at the Swedish Embassy, the guests distributed at small tables. My table consisted of the hostess,[3] then Greek Ambassador,[4] then self, then Harold Nicolson, then Soviet Ambassadress,[5] then John Wyndham, then Moura Budberg,[6] circle completed by Boofy, Lord Arran. Harold Nicolson is now deaf and slightly senile, he turned to the Soviet Ambassadress and asked how long she was staying in this country. I intervened with a formal introduction in a very loud voice, Harold apologised, rose to his feet and gave her a little mock curtsey. Presently, only too soon, Boofy and John Wyndham held the table with noisy private English jokes, leaving the Russian lady and the Greek gentleman in bewildered isolation. I was shocked.

Love,
Ann

1 Waugh replied: 'Tony Powell knows a lot about painting. In youth he drew Lovat-Fraser-like decorations of military subjects. He slept with Nina Hamnett [a painter] and attended the LCC School of Arts and Crafts in Southampton Row [Holborn Polytechnic]. I cannot judge his musical tastes. . . I don't think you appreciate Tony as you should. Of course everyone is at their worst at Grubstreet's table.'

2 Evangeline Bell married in 1945 David Bruce, American Ambassador in London 1961–9.

3 Anna Folchi-Vici was married to Günnar Hägglöf, Swedish Ambassador in London 1948–67.

4 Mikhail Melias.

5 Rufina Soldatov, whose husband Alexander was Soviet Ambassador 1960–6.

6 Maria [Moura] Budberg (1892–1974). Author, translator and costume designer. A Russian aristocrat, she married in 1911 John Benckendorff, lived with H. G. Wells, Maxim Gorky and Sir Robert Bruce Lockhart.

To Evelyn Waugh

16 Victoria Square   16 July [1963]

Dearest Evelyn

Weary though I am, I shall have to write to you, so you will have to answer – your jokes might cheer me.

I go to bed for dinner every night, it's so exhausting spending Ian's trust money. I squander a £1000 per afternoon and envy the poor.

Last weekend to Petworth where I anticipated the Bolshoi but not the Prime Minister: observing the PM from Saturday to Monday I concluded he was a crashing bore; it's not uncommon to love lords but it's rare to be besotted about dukes; suppose that's why he was never around with Oliver Stanley, Duff Cooper etc. in the pre-war days? Was Ronnie Knox his only friend?

Co-guests at Petworth were the Berlins, Fred Warner[1] and your old friend Quennell. Isaiah cheered the PM one evening, and Quennell didn't do too badly, but otherwise the PM was glum unless anecdoting on 1914, 15, 16, or merry tales of dukes in clubs, at home, on grouse moors etc. I think the poor PM should be analysed; sense of humour limited and facetious, terror of women, worship of the aristocracy. Perhaps he should join your church.

The Bolshoi arrived in three Green Line buses with three interpreters, and controlled by a whiskered fool. If he is not a fool then he's a competent saboteur paid by some foreign power, for firstly he told them it was a forty-minute drive, in fact it was three hours among motorists jostling to the south coast, secondly Russians never lunch before two so leaving London at one they anticipated an Elizabethan feast on arrival, and thirdly he was unperturbed by the hysteria of the prima ballerina[2] when they were offered raspberries, lemonade and sponge fingers. Do you know the vast terrace at Petworth? In one corner the PM was reading, then an interval, then the ballerinas on garden chairs, and in front Warner and Quennell playing football with the male dancers philistine while indoors Isaiah played chess with male dancers intellectual. The prima had angrily demanded soup, but when a Dresden plate full of tinned mulligatawny was placed on a dainty tray beside her, she rose as one stung by a wasp and dashed into the park with interpreter in pursuit. Isaiah explained that it was unprecedented preferential treatment and her strange behaviour was inevitable. It was the prima's first visit to England, she did not come last time because she was in disgrace for being John Morgan's mistress when he was in Moscow, I suggested Isaiah should introduce us and that might mend matters, but Isaiah did not think it would help. Luckily Rory McEwan[3] arrived with guitar, vodka was handed round and it ended on a happy note – or a fairly happy note, for the Green Line buses could not get out of the drive into the stream of traffic returning from the coast and they were going to be very late for a vital rehearsal with only a few raspberries in their stomachs.

Debo complains that touring Chatsworth with Rab Butler,[4] he collected dressing-table paraphernalia of all guests and put it in their beds, rocking all the while with mad laughter.

On July 28th I retreat to Sevenhampton. Would you and Laura come and visit?

With love

Ann

1 Frederick Warner (1918–84). Diplomat, then Head of South East Asia Department, Ambassador to Japan 1972–5. Member of the European Parliament since 1979. Knighted in 1972.

2 Maria Plisetskaya (1926–   ). Prima ballerina of the Bolshoi, described as 'dionysiac'.

3 Roderick ('Rory') McEwen (1932–83). Painter and singer.

4 Then First Secretary of State and Deputy Prime Minister.

From Evelyn Waugh

Combe Florey House, Nr Taunton   5 September 63

Dear Ann

Laura & I long to visit your expensive edifice but I think it would be better if we waited until old Kaspar and our own younger sons are back at school.[1] Whenever I pay their bills I write 'The holidays are inordinately long.' The headmasters chuckle & pocket the cash & know every day added is so much money saved them.

One of the exercises at Meg's pre-natal clinic is to sit in an armchair & repeat with a hypnotist: 'I am growing heavier &

heavier.' This is my experience. It must be checked. But Enton Hall is a stopped earth since my odious brother-in-law [Auberon Herbert] has made it his habitual London residence. Do you know of a similar institution? I am told there is one in the Italian Alps. Failing that, could I live at E.H. without ever seeing Auberon? Please tell me the correct form of engaging rooms. I think you told me it could be done as though at an hotel without medical introductions. Whom does one write to? Are there suites with sitting-rooms?

For four years I have been investigating a series of forgeries of my name at the London Library. I suspected Silchester [Thomas Pakenham]. I have now identified the culprit – Sweet Alice Chancellor. A rude shock. Damnit a friend of her great-grandmother's . . .[2]

Mrs Betjeman has published a log-book of her defecations in Spain.[3]

My revolting brother, Alec, is marrying a Mormon.[4] He announced his intention by writing (at the age of 65): 'For the first time in my life I am about to do something which I consider wrong.' Do you remember the passage in *Trivia*: 'I spell it with a W'?[5]

The book of which you kindly accepted the dedication is going to be jolly handsome. You will get a copy next month.

Did you know Fuddy-duddy MacNeice who kicked the bucket? I didn't nor did I read anything he wrote but those I respect e.g. Fr D'Arcy speak very highly of him.

I had to get my hair cut & try on some clothes so I took Fr D'Arcy to luncheon at White's. My word, the members were excited. After he left man after man came up & asked who that extraordinary fellow was. He had sat quietly in a corner in sober black but he put the fear of Hell into them.

Now don't forget; I want your instructions about thinning clinics. The 50s are a dreary decade. I have a pathetic belief that life begins at 60. But it must begin for me 2 stone lighter.

No good asking you here? I suppose not, but you would be *very* welcome.

Ever your affec. coz.

E.W.

---

1 Ann had just written, 'It would be nice to see you both, you will find me greatly aged. Caspar calls me Granny. It is a combination of T-B's permanent angry misery and the terrible expenditure on this folly. The tame ducks and the silence give pleasure so perhaps it is worth it.'

2 True. 'I have a cloudy memory of thinking it was good fun to pass oneself as Evelyn at the London Library. I think I only did it once.' Alice Chancellor.

3 *Two Middle-Aged Ladies in Andalusia*.

4 Alec Waugh did marry in 1969 Virginia Sorenson from Utah, a novelist and indeed a Mormon whom he had first met in 1954.

5 From 'The Spelling Lesson' in *More Trivia* by Logan Pearsall Smith. He says it for emphasis when some young people seem unacquainted with the concept.

To Evelyn Waugh

Sevenhampton Place, Wilts.   8 September 1963

Dearest Evelyn

Write immediately to Dr Sanderson, Forest Mere, Liphook, Hampshire – say you are a friend of mine and Cyril's, and ask for a balcony room facing south. The room is furnished with a comf. armchair, a television, private bath and loo – better go before they read your book. If you get bored you can have a face massage, a pedicure and your hair waved by Mr 'Teasy Weasy' Raymond. With luck Auberon [Herbert] (who *I* love) will not have discovered that it's a great deal more cosy than Enton Hall. You collect your light diet from the barmaid (lemon water or gruel) and carry it on a light tray to your bedroom and sip slowly gazing at geese on mere, you will then glance at your watch and realise it is much earlier than Mr Pinfold ever thought – 12.45. On the third day you will have golden eyes, a white soufflé on the tongue and a crashing headache, on the fourth you will be reborn. Write at once for they are very popular, and please believe that the results are startling, you will feel *so* happy. I sent Nanny before the move to the new house, she was getting fat, garrulous and crotchety and resentful of thirty years of slavery, she returned obliging and merry, able to carry sofas, cook, scrub, nurse Caspar and T-B and carry little trays to me.

Meg's pre-natal experiences sound crankier than Fionn's. Has poor Giles been dragged into it all? The hypergamist had to attend coloured films of childbirth in every country, France was the only funny one, the doctor dashed about shrieking '*J'ai perdu mon stethescope*.' Fionn knew I would disapprove and when she and John went to pre-natal orgies she told me she was at diplomatic cocktail parties.

I did not know you could forge names at the London Library, you and Sweet Alice do not look very alike.

Do you suppose Fr D'Arcy is the first priest to cross the threshold of White's?

The ducks have become too tame, I like the noise of their webbed feet slithering over the sill when they arrive to share breakfast, but the mess is appalling.

I worried about you at the literary feast, your vitality seemed low and you were breathless. Speaking of breath, do you intend to tell Dr S. of the paraldehyde? If a strong smell issues from your bedroom there may be an inquiry.

The Donaldsons came to lunch, very agreeable.

With love and in haste

A

PS. The haste is still the house, there are small huts all over the property where men who are being paid £15 a day sit sheltering from the rain, it is agony to watch. Lady Avon tells me some gardeners work in the rain and some don't but they can't be forced, ours don't. I set an example by weeding in the cloudbursts but it has no effect. Do Laura's serfs work in the rain?

From Evelyn Waugh

Forest Mere Hydro, Hants.   [October 1963]

Dear Ann

You did not prepare me for the great ugliness of house, furniture & scenery here. But my 50 guinea suite is spacious & the attendants civil.

You are not one of their prize patients. They said: 'You were recommended by Mr Ian Fleming.' 'By *Mrs* Fleming.' 'Oh. *Mrs* Fleming. Well . . . but we have had Mr Fleming here. Also Godfrey Winn.'[1]

In the last 24 hours I have had two glasses of hot lemon juice. I have sat in a 'sweat-bath' & been severely massaged. I have gained ½ pound in weight. Time hangs heavy.

Your affec. coz.

E. W.

We had the Donaldsons to stay. He broke my Brigg cane.

1 Godfrey Winn (1908–71). Whimsical journalist who earned a lot of money. Called 'God' by some of his friends.

To Evelyn Waugh

16 Victoria Square   6 December [1963]

My dear Coz.

The *Spectator* has become a haunted house, staffed by Randolph and his ghosts. Mrs Crickmere was cross with me and revengefully allowed him to talk to me on the telephone, first time for several years, so I had to be civil and expressed a wish to write upon the masculine dominated English motor car, by the next post I received a grovelling letter from Iain Macleod[1] saying he eagerly anticipated my contribution and would publish it forthwith.

Goodness, I miss the Old Bailey, the case did Ian a power of good, no smoking in court and one hour for a simple lunch; alas, reaction has set in, he misses the routine and it was sad for him having to settle. Our solicitors say we're alright, but one can never tell, so maybe we will have to sell up.[2]

We have acquired a marvellous painting, an unfinished picture of the young Queen Victoria in top hat and scarlet riding habit, by Sir David Wilkie.[3] K. Clark told me of it, and despite our uncertain future I snapped it up.

I am in a frenzy preparing for family Christmas, filling the bookshelves and the stockings, I got a job lot of secondhand books from Blackwells, forgetting my spectacles I could not read the titles, great mistake to choose books by touch. Great improvement since you were here are stuffed owls in the hall and a pair of palm trees.[4] I found your criticisms most helpful, though there is little I can do about noise, Sir Kenneth Clark told me that you cannot get builders to put fibreglass in the walls as it gives them silicosis – true?

The benignity of Cyril is alarming, I am totally relaxed with him, he has become warm, comfortable and cosy – like you have – though you *never* frightened me. The only little storm in Cyril's life was caused by him dedicating his book to 'Baby' and causing pain to Deirdre, who refused to accompany him to Jamie Hamilton's celebration publication dinner.[5]

Icy cold cheerful Christmas shopping spree in Oxford today, unfortunately returned rather gay and told Ian of holly, turkeys and Christmas trees, he has not spoken to me since.

Will you be in London before the festive season? So many plays to see – why not?

With love to Laura and yourself,

A

PS. I visited 'Forestmere' when Ian was in retreat. Dr Sanderson told me 'literary gents were very cussed', it will never be forgotten that when Dr Lord said to you 'Let's see, how long have we been here?' you replied 'It is not your business to know that.'

PPS. One woman patient had always thought you were a woman.

1 Ian Macleod (1913–70). Conservative MP from 1950, Editor of the *Spectator* 1963–5. Chancellor of the Exchequer for the last month of his life.

2 Fleming had spent 19–29 November at the Old Bailey. He had collaborated with the film director and writer Kevin McClory to produce a film script; when the film fell through he used bits of the script in *Thunderball*. Now Kevin McClory was suing him and his film partner Ivar Bryce for plagiarism. The case was settled out of court; McClory was awarded the 'film property known as Thunderball', and a large sum of money. All costs were paid in the end by Bryce; Fleming paid nothing.

3 Sir David Wilkie (1785–1841). Distinguished Scottish genre painter.

4 Waugh stayed at Sevenhampton and wrote that Laura had said he was too critical: 'What you have achieved is a house exactly suited to your and Ian's needs. If you had bought an old house it would have imposed its habits on you. You have made something where there is no predecessor breathing down your neck and you have ensured a happy twenty years in watching it mature and filling it with treasures.' To Nancy Mitford he wrote: 'She [Ann] has spent as much as the government have on the reconstruction of Downing Street, pulled down a large commodious house and put up a cottage. . . the few bedrooms are tiny cubicles with paper thin walls through which every cough and snore is audible.'

5 *Previous Convictions*, a collection of reviews, is dedicated 'To B. S. Oak before ash, look out for a splash', that is to say his previous wife, Barbara Skelton. His next collection, *The Evening Colonnade*, 1973, was dedicated to Deirdre Craig, whom he married in 1959.

Ann had been too ill to accompany Fleming to Jamaica in early January, describing herself to Waugh as having 'bronchitis and mysterious packets of liquid about the face – not pretty'. He suggested she recuperate with his wife Laura and himself in Menton: 'Your presence would be a great joy to us (unless you try to insinuate Muggeridge who sometimes lurks there. . . the clientèle of the Westminster, his hotel, are arthritic widows of Midland knights).' However Ann had written to Hugo Charteris the year before: 'Once the doctor had said five years about Ian I thought I should and indeed terribly wanted to be with him, for provided we are quite alone, and I'm sitting around scribbling, he becomes much calmer; he only goes mad if he sees my relations and friends!' She still felt she should be with Ian as much as possible, and left for Jamaica on 30 January.

To Evelyn Waugh

Goldeneye, Jamaica   4 February [1964]

Dearest E.

There are great grey bags of cloud overhead, no oxygen, dreadful humidity inducing even more dreadful lethargy, I yearn for knights' widows and Menton. These conditions made Thunderbird very ill; he discovered he could spend some of his dollars on a marvellous clear telephone line to Victoria Square, so coughing and spitting I reluctantly left London Airport on a perfect spring day, and after fourteen jet hours landed at Kingston in a tropical rainstorm. Independence has not improved the island, they have cancelled all porters at airports, instead fascist black police rock with laughter while elderly exhausted white tourists feebly try to move their baggage to the customs table where aggressive Negro customs officials enjoy themselves hugely by a minute examination of underclothes, displaying the curiosity of the savage in clocks or trinkets; this behaviour produced a welcome rush of adrenalin, in a trice I was behaving like Randolph, got instant slavish service and was united with T-B in the abominable hot deluge. I doubt the several hundred thousand the Jamaica Tourist Board is spending on advertising will counteract the discomfort and expense of life here.

Hilary Bray and his wife[1] were charged £20 for bed and breakfast at Montego for one night.

It was kind of you to send the details of delectable life at Menton, and promise to welcome me, and I had much looked forward to Muggeridge whom I knew to be lurking, but it was necessary to come here. At least I have persuaded Bond to give his public a rest, so he is only writing for one hour a day[2] and we have a black secretary for the fan mail. Canada broadcasting and television arrive this afternoon for a special interview, and I am supposed to look after them until Bond is strong enough to appear, luckily we have Hilary Bray, I shall take advantage of his virtue and boy scoutiness and put the Canadians in his charge.

Nothing on sale at Kennedy Airport bookshop except *Fanny Hill*, so I bought it and can find nothing of historical interest except the girl is attired for flagellation in white stockings – in the 20th century I believe they are always black.[3]

Cyril Connolly has gone to his dying mother in Africa after a further rumpus with his wife for telling him he was too old to wear shorts.

If you have a moment do write to me. It would be an excitement.

I hope Laura does well at roulette.

Love to you both

from an exiled Coz.

1 Hilary Bray (1908–   ). At Eton with Fleming and in the same stockbrokers, Rowe and Pitman. *On His Majesty's Secret Service* is dedicated to him and has Bond impersonate Sir Hilary Bray, who had 'a good war record and sounds a reliable sort of chap. He lives in some remote glen in the Highlands, watching birds and climbing the hills with bare feet. Never sees a soul.' Of all Fleming's friends perhaps the one Ann liked best.

2 He was at work on *The Man With the Golden Gun*.

3 *Fanny Hill* had been on trial for indecency and Waugh had written, 'I was delighted to hear Quennell claim that as an historian of the eighteenth century he found *Fanny Hill* an essential text.'

To Frances Donaldson

Goldeneye, Jamaica   16 February [1964]

Dearest Frankie

It was decent of you to keep in touch during my ambivalent illness. Had I stayed to enjoy the early spring, and every burgeoning nuance of leaf and bulb at Rutherford Pools,[1] I should have been wracked by guilt. Ian needs some kind of background to banging out Bond, he can no longer a-wooing go, and with alarming expansiveness said I was a 'solace', so I presume I must remain in this gilded prison until March 14th. He demands *silent* companionship and *civility* to his horrible friends. It's being an epic year for bores, mostly retired naval officers with letters of introduction from an old friend of his named 'Quacker' Drake. Even Ian could not endure the last couple, so he announced he had to rest at 1.45, they had a shortish lunch hour!

The Hilary Brays are with us, he is as good as Jack [Donaldson]; without his virtue it would not work so well as last year. I am a great deal more 'uppish' and she is a great deal more 'downish', owing to permanent bronchitis. It's quite difficult to plan for two fit and two unfit people, especially if the two fit ones have a strongly developed sense of irony, want to walk miles and play scrabble all night. It's easier now I have joined the walking wounded by falling off a table chasing a bug, and am temporarily lame.[2]

I hope eggboards and opera boards flourish, and the early flowers compensate for the cold weather – Mrs Crickmere complains of it.

Noël Coward is known as 'Chinese Nell' in this island – rather sinister?

Wishing you 'abundant wealth and boundless health', not Tennyson's best line, but an enviable state of affairs.

Much love to both,

A

1 A nickname for Sevenhampton since a swimming pool had been built.
2 Ann wrote to Lady Diana Cooper, 'Great bags of unexploded cloud and no oxygen, also twisted my fetlock, so I'm walking like a parrot and breathing like a grampus.'

To Clarissa Avon

Goldeneye, Jamaica   16 February [1964]

Dearest Clarissa

I *loathe* the tropics, can only think of this glorious early English spring and burgeoning bulbs at Sevenhampton.

I dined with the Bruces [David and Evangeline] and was placed next to Bobby Kennedy, whom I did not like at all. He either has a neck injury or suffers from furtive guilt, for he seemed unable to hold his head straight or look one in the eye. He seemed humourless and aggressive with the nasty American desire for facts, not my strong point, but he is obsessed by Ian's books which made it easier, as I do know one or two [things] about them; it was a pleasure to turn to Roy Jenkins, but when I turned again things had gone wrong, for Andrew Devonshire had given him the government line on Indonesia which so exaggerated his neck twist that he was only able to gaze into the eyes of Evangeline's spaniel. The embassy salmon gave ptomaine poisoning to all, but worst to Kennedy, so when the Bruces took him to Chequers the following day he could only sip Bovril, and Sir Alec [Douglas-Home] bowled him over easily.

Rumour has reached here that Lady Antonia Fraser has run down Lady Lambton on the Niarchos playground. Lady L. has a broken leg.

A new garage at end of garden has a juke box which plays from 6 p.m. to 3 a.m., especially a loud syncopated version of 'Three Blind Mice'.

Much love,
A

To Hugo Charteris

Goldeneye, Jamaica   17 February [1964]

Darling Hugo

It is fearfully humid here, but I feel I must sit it out till March 14th, and return with Ian. I *pine* for the crocuses and snowdrops, and the first spring at Sevenhampton, and for a few human beings. It is painful to see Ian struggle to give birth to Bond, and manage but half the typewriter banging of last year. At home 'Bond' life is conducted from the office, but here I witness the fan mail and hysterical success story. René MacColl, who I think was in Paris with you, arrives tomorrow for a special interview and pics: the Jamaica newspaper gives a lunch party for him – it never stops.[1]

We have Edward Rice's first cousin Hilary Bray and wife with us: he is a solace, a spare handsome man of religious habit and literary tastes, salmon fisher and stag grallocher; all Edward's irony under stern restraint till provoked by me! It was a quartet that worked splendidly last year, but this year an occasional breeze. For instance Hilary with gentle persistence tries to bring reason to bear on Ian's wilder evening statements, 'Ann only talks of who sleeps with who.' 'But,' says Hilary, 'she is the only woman I know who doesn't.'

Two brothers Blackwell arrive for lunch today. Crosse and Blackwell millionaires, the elder in the jockey club, the younger a private schoolmaster. Ian wanted a tropical repeat of their weekly golf lunches and said I was to take Mrs B. [Bray] out to lunch, she is an ill woman and it is a long way in the midday sun to find an eating hole. Hilary was surprisingly stern and firm, told Ian he would go with us, that he would not tolerate the imputation that his wife was 'uppity' nor that he could not count upon her manners, and knew that Ian must feel the same of me. The Blackwells have large stomachs and are reported to be in sharkskin shorts, their jokes are gross. To Hilary this is an exercise in behaviour, and clever though he is he has not grasped the extent of Ian's desire to be his alter ego in this company, and Ian's profound disappointment that women are to be present.

Forgive this egotistical scribble, it is engendered by heat and circumstances. I will give thought for Mary Rose's stone. Why not tell me the 'Blake'? It must be worth quoting if it suits us all! Innocence would apply to Mary Rose, and if it is from Songs of – why not?

Frances [Charteris] writes marvellous natural vital letters.

Do hope you all flourish, and pancreas progresses.

　　　　　　　　With much love

　　　　　　　　　　A

---

1 René MacColl (1905–). Celebrated journalist on Lord Beaverbrook's *Daily Express*.

To Evelyn Waugh

Goldeneye, Jamaica   22 February [1964]

Oh, dear Evelyn, *please* get well. If Laura still worries she should take you to Sir Daniel Davies, a consulting physician of great cleverness and awfully good company.

The missing passport is a nightmare story;[1] how lucky I did not add to your burdens with my guilt. It's far wiser not to travel but to enjoy the English spring. The Hilary Brays departed this morning, and only my wish to be sufficiently good and unworldly and go to Caraman parties prevented me escaping with them. You might tell little Margaret that I am sufficiently in a state of grace to be put on the holy father's guest list.

The Brownlows are very unpopular. He in permanent sulk: the Government want to run a teeny road over a small corner of his property, and are not interested in his threats to leave the island. The input of human monsters have prevented my telephoning to Wimborne, whom I usually visit, and would have Brownlow details; also Bray is better company than the peers who winter here.

The *Gleaner* newspaper gave a luncheon party for Beatle Bond,[2] and Beatle B. reports Charles da Costa told very funny stories but he don't remember them.

An effort to boost deservedly failing tourist traffic is the inauguration by an obscene American publication called *Playboy* of a Bunny Club. The Bunnies are girls wearing Bunny headresses, but unlike Mrs A.'s angels are untouchable.[3] A vulgar Western version of geishas. There is going to be a V.I.P. Bunny dining room, where for a vast sum you can sit next to an untouchable Bunny and are waited on by footmen. Perhaps the footmen are touchable, more appealing to Chinese Nell.

A new 'gas station' at garden gate possessed of infernal machine called a 'sound system'. It relays calypso from 9 p.m. to 3 a.m. Special favourite being a syncopated version of 'Three Blind Mice'. It would defeat vast doses of that smelly white stuff you drink. Poor Mrs Bray was so disturbed that the good Hilary walked on the midnight hour to the gas station to implore silence, but there was not a human being to be seen, only a relentless illuminated machine behind a vast plate glass window. The Beatle bedroom is the least noisy, 'Three Blind Mice' being offset by crashing waves or banging tropical rain, plus frogs and crickets.

God has sent me a toad, the only creature I wish to draw: so I must take him from my shower bath and get to work.

Could you write me one more letter? They are manna from heaven.

The editor of *The Sunday Times* and his wife [Denis and Olive Hamilton] arrive today. I doubt if he will be much assistance in feeding a toad.

With sympathy for the spoiled treat,

love to you both,

from an exile.

1 Waugh had hired a car and driven 150 miles to retrieve a forgotten passport, 'then in the dark with a London chauffeur unused to such excursions a hunt from cottage to cottage, pub to pub, to find the village woman who had the keys'.
2 So called by Ann because his fame equalled that of the Beatles whose 'I Want to Hold your Hand' was at that time in the Top Twenty.
3 Mrs Ape looked after a troupe of angels in *Vile Bodies*.

To Peter Quennell

Frenchman's Cove, Jamaica   [Thursday]
                                      5 March [1964]

Darling Peter – It was great joy to return from the Frenchman's Cove, the scene of our most recent tragi-comic episode, and find your most flattering, cheering, entertaining letter.[1]

We had a bad evening when the poor Commander took his sledgehammer to me. The burden of the blows being that he and old C. [Caspar] were badly housed and ill fed! and only you and assorted dons given priority of comfort and affection. This was followed by the arrival of 'Parkinson' and wife.[2] 'Parkinson' (whose initials I cannot remember) is a fellow best-selling author introduced by Peter Janson-Smith; he wrote a book called *'Parkinson's Law'*, swiftly followed by *'The Law and the Profits'*. Neither book had I read, nor did the titles ring bells though they seemed to smack of the facetious and dubious. My doubts were ill received and I was told that it would do me much credit with Crosland and Jenkins to have met such an important economist. This *so* wrong an approach to me, Crosland and Jenkins planted a tiny little seed of resentment in the garden of my heart; at lunch Ian was as bored as me, and retreated to his siesta at 2.25. Unhappily the Parkinsons' native chauffeur had a pal in Oracabessa and could not be traced till 4 p.m. I was therefore surprised to learn as they drove away that Ian had accepted their invitation to spend the following night as their guests at Frenchman's Cove and attend a 'Jamaican Beach Barbecue'. During that endless afternoon I had learned all the details of Mrs P's pregnancies, and also that Mr P. was both an economist and a naval historian. The boiling hot trade wind had been briskly blowing, the head was aching, so the mistake was made of an effort at logical conversation with the Commander as to the advisability of motoring three hours to spend a Jamaican evening with the economist. By post-whisky and mid-dinner logic was routed by statements causing great grief – 'Fuck off', 'Go home at once', 'You spoil everything', 'Do you expect me to look at your face every evening?', 'You're a monumental bore'. The scene produced hypertension, tears, and screaming claustrophobia – how does one leave Goldeneye at midnight? No friends to go to, not enough money. How soon can one get an air passage? I packed clothes, put out winter coat, found ticket and passport, then perforce anticlimactically to whisky flask and tranquillisers and sleeping pills: simultaneously Oracabessa was becoming riotously gay, the giant volume of canned music was accompanied by screams, shouts, and volleys of musketry, some ganja-happy Negroes had revolvers. Ian then appeared naked and furious, shouting, 'Come into my bedroom and go to sleep or else lock yourself in – there's too much shooting' – a James Bond situation? So towards dawn after hours of obstinacy and doubt, and doped, and to escape the noise, I collapsed in his bedroom. The pills worked by breakfast time, and in a stunned condition I was persuaded to drive through the trade winds to the 'Jamaican evening'. Our luxury cottage overhung a precipice above tumultuous waves but the bedroom faced the garden and was blessedly quiet. Each cottage has a gramophone, a kitchen and a well-stocked larder. In the blessedly quiet bedroom I slept, and was awakened at dusk by the strains of Strauss waltzes: feeling vastly better, I rose and joined Ian on the balcony, and with arms outstretched and leaning over the precipice said 'this is the end of your next book, girl hurls herself to death sooner than succumb to old virile philistine Bond. He has made a fearful bloomer in playing "Blue Danube", it reminds her of Europe, of great civilisations, of men with wit and gentle manners' – at this point in burst the Parkinsons who were amazed by my dramatic pose, untidy hair and lack of clothing. They came to welcome us and announce a cocktail party to precede the Beach Beano. I announced a fever, and settled for a cosy evening with *Shakespeare* by Quennell and eggs and bacon. It was delicious solitude, but the eyes grew tired at 9.30, so I went exploring. Frenchman's Cove has been cunningly designed, the cottages alike but very far apart, and after catching one or two toads I found with some dismay that I was lost, no shoes and in a night dress. It was a little bit alarming, and the alarm was not lessened by some master switch being pressed so that the network of grass paths was suddenly illuminated by fairy lights hidden in the grass verges; but at last after much rambling to wrong cottages I got home and decided to dress and do some spying on the beach. Prepared for this foray I heard the noise of a millionaire devil cart and it was Mrs Parkinson briskly driving the Commander home – he was in no condition to drive himself. He was a poor broken Commander, who had not enjoyed himself, in a very slurred voice he repetitively complained of the impossibility of getting a drink; he had also been very shocked by the cabaret, a naked three-year-old girl child doing a stomach dance, and a Negro impersonating a woman. Finally he fell into noisy drunken sleep, and I was left to ponder on his eccentric nature – what else could he have expected save dullness and vulgarity at such an occasion?

Sorry for this demented whine, but with no one to talk to, no expeditions, and permanent raging sea and wind the nerve strain is great. If safely returned home possibly the neurosis will cease. I enjoyed all the light you shed on this state of mind, I have always suspected that you can only love neurotics and possibly Spider is too well-balanced for you!

I am pleased you have become a Summerfield parent.[3] You might adopt Caspar for next summer's sports day, and we can run against the Peeks in the parents' races – think of Sir Francis's face when Spoonbill [Marilyn] does an Atalanta and drops a golden apple.[4]

I am much enjoying *Shakespeare*, no arithmetic has been scribbled on it, but numerous corners turned down for future reference when we meet.

The poor old blowfish look dusty and musty. I have a piece of cabbage coral like Valenciennes lace, but it is too fragile to pack.

Thankyou for writing such long wonderful letters, they have been the greatest help.

Come post Easter weekend if you are free. Ian will be at Sandwich.

With much love, darling Peter,

A

1 Peter Quennell had written that 'no one, I do flatter myself, has had more experience of depression in all its different shapes' and that Ann's had perfectly good reasons – 'the Commander's illness and ill temper, Jamaican humidity and tropic *cafard*' – and was therefore not neurotic. She had a duty to her friends 'who expect you to provide an example of ceaseless gaiety and tireless energy'.

2 Cyril Northcote Parkinson (1909–   ). Married Elizabeth Fry in 1952; they have two sons and a daughter. Parkinson's Law states that work expands so as to fill the time available for its completion.

3 Charles Peek (1957–1977), son of Marilyn Quennell and her first husband Sir Francis Peek, was at Summer Fields.

4 Atalanta would marry no one who could not outrun her, so Milanion got three golden apples from Aphrodite and cast them in her path, delaying her. .

To Evelyn Waugh

[Sevenhampton]   19 June [1964] (my birthday – 51st)

Dear Evelyn

It was ever so nice to get a letter from you. Nothing nice or funny is happening. Poor Thunderbird has been at home with a nurse these last two weeks, she is called Sister Forbes and I suspect it is Ali in disguise. Three days ago she took him to Brighton, he could not face his country home; and now he is not so well, and is distressed by the wet sea front, and wants his country home but is not allowed to travel. I visited him yesterday, we lunched at English's and he would not take a taxi home, and we stood in the rain in a bus queue, and that increased his pulse rate. Now I have returned to Sevenhampton for old Caspar's centenary Summer Fields' sports day, and the doctors think we had better leave Thunderbeatle alone with Sister Ali, as old C. might prove too exciting for him.

I was so haunted by this that I drove slap into a taxi in Eaton Square, oblivious of the red lights. I am convinced we both drove when the lights were amber, but the taxi driver nipped out and got a witness, while I foolishly did nothing, and when the police arrived it was too late. A very great bore. First incident in thirty years.

Thunderbeatle has won nine Pan Book Oscars, each book selling over a million copies. The Oscars are copies of a Graeco-Roman satyr in the British Museum, cast in bronze and gilded in eighteen-carat gold. I did not know there was any object so hideous in the museum, and sadder still, the first cost £1200 and the others £350 apiece. We would so have liked a cheque, it was hard to conceal our dismay when the Pan man proudly displayed them.

Diana and Paddy were here last weekend, which was very nice. Paddy spent much time carrying a card table and a chair to write below the weeping willow, arranging manuscripts, cigarettes and alcohol, then carrying it in again when it rained, it was good exercise but not many words were added to the opus.[1] Diana left at 6.30 Monday morning, refusing all nourishment save a bunch of bananas.

I enclose the consequences of a dinner party at Lord Gladwyn's in honour of Lady Avon. Lady A. has suffered earache for several months, but Lord Lambton's leg pulling of Lady G. reduced her to such ill-mannered and prolonged laughter that she was miraculously cured, I suppose she don't unclench her jaw at home very frequent. To save the situation I told Gladwyn he should be the next editor of *The Times*, and it provoked this letter to Tony who presented it to me; and pray return it [lost].

There is much gossip here as to who will replace Haley who retires in a year's time;[2] apparently he summoned Iain Macleod, and said he would do his best to get him appointed, as he approved of his views. This rumour reached the ears of Gavin Astor[3] via Lord Arran. Gavin did not care for the idea and suggested Frank Giles,[4] which to my mind would be a disaster. It is also said that Edward Heath[5] would like the job – very rum.

Each week the *Gardener's Chronicle* advertises a multitude of gardeners with 'wives prepared to help in house'; interviewing them is a dismal process, the first came from the passport office, a photostat recommendation signed 'Selwyn Lloyd'. He wanted to 'get away from it all', the second desired a dwelling for a vast quantity of children, and liked 'tinkering with cars': today a strapping youth appeared who shamefacedly admitted he enjoyed digging and getting his hands into the earth, alas, he knew it was nothing to boast of – perhaps I have been lucky.

Randolph is an awful pest about tulip trees, I have sent him to

Stanway where there is a very tall tulip tree struck by lightning and held together by putty applied at regular intervals by Lord Wemyss or Guy Benson – that should give Lord Snowdon a very good picture.[6]

I do hope that you are well – better than when we met. It would be a joy to stay with you and furnish Sevenhampton from the asphyxiated aunt's junk shop,[7] but I can make no plans.

I admire the new writing paper and would like to copy – who drew it? The porch looks most successful – does it really look so elegant?

Love to Laura and yourself

A

1 *Roumeli*, 1966.

2 Sir William Haley (1901–). Editor of *The Times* 1952–66, when William Rees-Mogg took over.

3 Lord Astor (1918–). Chairman of the Times Publishing Group 1959–66, when it was sold. President of Times Newspapers Limited since 1967.

4 Frank Giles was then Foreign Editor of *The Sunday Times* and became its Editor 1981–3.

5 Edward Heath (1916–) was then President of the Board of Trade, until the Labour Party won the election in October. Prime Minister 1970–4.

6 Waugh, the owner of a tulip tree, had written of 'the dangers of reconciliation with Randolph', who wanted to bring Lord Snowdon to photograph it. 'I think if you went from Tewkesbury to Exeter you would find one every five miles. The poor booby thinks them a great rarity.'

7 An aunt of Waugh's had indeed asphyxiated herself and he had said that as a result of storing her possessions Combe Florey was like a junk shop.

Patrick Leigh Fermor remembers:

I loved staying there [Sevenhampton] and went as often as I could, and often took work there, even managed to get some done. There were passionate games of croquet and I can remember every bump, hollow and hazard as we crept round glass in hand, often until it was too dark to see. All the vols. of the Greater *Oxford Dictionary* were in the dining-room and enthralling evenings of the Game stick in the memory. They reached an extraordinary pitch of elaboration and abstruseness, especially in the fabrication of illustrative quotations from real or imaginary authors. Few joys could surpass it.

And there were marvellous times with Diana Cooper. Apart

from being in a sort of way aunt and niece, they were very close friends. I went to Stanway once with both of them. I had never seen this marvellous place I'd heard of so long, but great wafts of reminiscences came from both of them, Diana's from the earliest days of her sister Letty's incumbency, Ann's from the whole of her childhood.

To people who only saw her in London, it came as a surprise how very much more deeply Ann really belonged to the country. She knew a lot about birds, animals, plants and trees from her father, she had loved hunting and still enjoyed stories about the odd events that invariably accompany it, and above all, she was a devoted, an untireable walker, unflinching in a sou'wester and a kind of groundsheet with a hole in it, through the most determined rain. Sometimes the start would be by car, then overland to the White Horse at Uffington, to the Bull's Tail, to Kelmscott Manor or that extraordinary Craven house isolated on the downs (whose name escapes me) or some other chosen point, often embracing a halt at a pub for the sake of the thirsty. I've mentioned earlier how fond Ann was of reading aloud; this was perfect for people who can enjoy doing it, like John Sparrow, Peter Quennell and me. Once, motoring back to London via Hazeleigh, I remember reading out the whole of the siege of Castel Sant'Angelo from the life of Benvenuto Cellini.

I once stayed there a long time after some disagreeable ray-treatment severe enough to make me feel weak and hopeless and incapable of uttering all but a word or two. Ann was wonderfully kind and consoling. I spent a lot of time playing paper games or sitting in her bedroom – which, as that was where the TV was, would fill up as populously as a drawing-room with Ann presiding from among pillows and books, and gazing at *Les Rois Maudits*. A quiet time with, I think, Peter Q. staying for some of it, and also Fionn.

To Evelyn Waugh

16 Victoria Square   26 June [1964]

Dear Evelyn

There is a hedgehog on the lawn. Have you any hedgehogs? They are a great joy.

May I copy your writing paper heading and lettering? How did you discover the names of all the craftsmen involved?

It is indeed a bore to be friends with Randolph, he telephoned last night and I think he called me 'bitch' because I showed some reluctance to leap from my bed, and watch a television programme giving some prominence to his attack on the *Daily Sketch*.

Today our gardener left; it has been bitter warfare – he never sprayed the roses. I sought revenge, but his new employer is old and totally blind and will never know he has no flowers; it's unkind to distress the aged, but goodness I hated the victorious smile of the gardener when he told me the state of his employer's eyes.

John Sutro [brought] Deborah Devonshire to the Encaenia luncheon at Oxford and seemed very over-excited, so over-excited that at the end of the meal he threw a great deal of coffee over her and an eminent physician in his new honour's robes had to hustle her off to the gents' cloaks and wash her down.

Maurice Bowra gave a very noisy dinner for an eminent Greek poet[1] on the previous evening. The poor poet was ancient and ill with ulcers: buckets of milk had to be sent to his room, and he was in no condition for Leigh Fermor.

I had been wondering since Max died[2] how to couch a letter of sympathy to his widow, when the enclosed arrived.[3] Do you think I can now forget the whole matter?

There was a nasty incident at Max's birthday party when the sword was put in his hand to cut the cake. He mistook Lord Rosebery's capacious white waistcoated stomach for icing sugar and lunged at him. Esmond claims to have diverted disaster.

With love

A

1 George Seferis (1900–71). Greek Ambassador to Britain 1957–61. Won the Nobel Prize for Literature 1963.

2 Lord Beaverbrook had died on 9 June. His eighty-fifth birthday on 25 May had been celebrated with a dinner for 600 at the Dorchester organised by Lord Thomson. After being urged not to go 'he ate heartily and outshone all others in gaiety' and contrived to refer to his own death 'so gaily that we hardly noticed [the] implication'. *Beaverbrook* by A. J. P. Taylor, 1972.

3 *Telegram*, 13 June 1964: TO HEAR FROM YOU WHILE THE DARKENING SHADOWS ARE ALL AROUND BRINGS A RAY OF COMFORTING LIGHT CHRISTOFOR BEAVERBROOK.

To Evelyn Waugh

16 Victoria Square   19 July [1964]

Dearest Evelyn,

I suppose 'Preters' is Christopher Hollis.[1] Who is the fat Conservative who you tortured? Today's instalment is still better. John Sparrow was here for this sunny day, and we pondered on Cyril's reactions – especially being a 'dandy' in Barcelona.[2] Did Bowra not take you up till you were famous? I must ask him.

I do enjoy it very much.

Patsy [Ward] made a marvellous 'chute'. She was lately reconciled with her brother [Eric Dudley], and the day before the 'chute' she returned from a happy yachting trip with him; she spent an evening in her garden, slept well, telephoned her serenity to sister Laura, and died. Laura is very sad.

Kingsley Amis came to dinner; his anger was well concealed, or has perhaps gone in middle age.[3] I suspected he wrote of Ian to further his own sales, but it seemed a genuine admiration, he thinks Ian should write a straight novel.

I believe the future Mrs Amis[4] interviewed you? She complained to Robin Ironside that you had been allowed to choose the questions she should ask you, this did not please her. The Croslands and Amises left at 3 a.m. after much drunken conversation; Tony insisting the classics were useless education, Amis putting forward your theory. Amis did not care for Tony, though he still says he will vote Labour, he was very shaken.

Sir Alec Home is much praised for holding the Commonwealth together. The government weekend party at Dorneywood was not without anxiety for Andrew, he was ordered to play golf with various black prime ministers, a game he has not played since he was ten; happily the hospitality committee ordained 11.30 for the match, and the Africans said it was always too hot to play after 8 a.m.

Diana, Evangeline and I went to hear Rowse[5] on 'The Sonnets', I had returned from Thunderbeatle and Brighton that afternoon and noted with sorrow we were a man short for dinner, and no time to contact hungry Freud and starving Forbes. But during the lecture I noticed that the Cornish professor addressed Evangeline and Diana in particular, and looked as if no one ever asked him out, so at the end I leapt upon the rostrum and said 'Oh, Professor Rowse, please come home with us and tell us more.' He accepted with pathetic alacrity and had a perfectly happy time with D. and E. but when the women left the dining room he was set upon by A. Powell, A. Ross[6] and S. Spender. He fled up the stairs sobbing 'Ladies, Ladies', squeezed Diana, hugged Evangeline, archly put an arm round each of their waists — and they *adored* it — then dashed from the house before the men could shout 'Yoicks, tally ho, gone to ground.' *Wish you had been there . . .*

Was decent of you to share the Bromo.

Love,

A

1 No, 'Preters', who appears in Waugh's autobiography, *A Little Learning*, is Lord Molson. When asked if he was interested in politics he had replied 'Preternaturally so', and lived up to his nickname by being a Conservative MP for twenty years. Extracts from Waugh's book were appearing in *The Sunday Times*.

2 Waugh wrote that Connolly was suffering from poverty: '. . . Cyril was haunted by an Anglo-Irish ghost of dandyism which he finally exorcised some years later by briefly identifying himself with Montparnasse and Barcelona. . . . When he comes to give his own account I may find myself quite at fault. As I have said, I did not know him well. He and Maurice Bowra were both acquaintances who became friends after I attracted some attention as a novelist.'

3 Kingsley Amis had been labelled as an 'Angry Young Man' in the late 1950s.

4 Elizabeth Jane Howard (1923–). Novelist. Married to Amis 1965–82.

5 A. L. Rowse (1903–). Historian. Among many books on Shakespeare he has published *William Shakespeare: A Biography*, 1963, and *Shakespeare's Sonnets: a modern edition*, 1973.

6 Alan Ross (1922–). Writer and Editor of the *London Magazine* since 1965.

On 24 July Evelyn Fleming died. Fleming insisted on attending her funeral at Nettlebed, near Henley. Ann left a note, 'When his mother died he said it was an unlucky time for Flemings. He said this often and fussed whenever I drove the car. He also developed a fear of the number thirteen and a horror of the colour black, so his bedroom carpet at Sevenhampton was changed to red. He insisted on going to his favourite hotel, the Guildford at Sandwich Bay, for August. He frequently repeated that he must now live as he wished or not at all.

To John Morgan

Sandwich   8 August [1964]

Dear John
   I am very grateful for a marvellously reassuring letter; in fact a model letter to a Ma-in-law! If one is in distress about one thing, one inclines to fuss unduly about all others.
   Ian's life from now on hangs on a thread. Such recovery as he could make depends on his self-control with cigarettes and alcohol. The doctor spent Bank Holiday with us, and was able to witness the sad change that ill health and drugs can bring. Poor Ian nags at me specially and then Caspar all the time. It ends all fun and is anguish to be with one one loves who is very mentally changed and fearfully unhappy – poor old tiger.
   It's quite impossible to make any plans at the moment about houses. But do count on Sevenhampton till you are fixed.
   Nothing funny except the funeral of Ian's mother – I call it 'operation granite' – it was tearless, musicless, and practically wreathless; they are a very Scottish family, the wreaths were the diameter of soup plates, and my sheaf of arum lilies shockingly conspicuous! The sons held a conference before the service to decide the sum to be given to the old lady's nurse; very bad taste!
   This letter is of course for both; I long for you all.
   Very grateful for your cheerful news.[1]
   With much love to all,

                              Ann

1 John Morgan (1964–   ), Fionn's son, had been born in Brazil.

   On 11 August Fleming attended a committee meeting of the Royal St George's Golf Club and stayed on to lunch but that evening Ann is reported as saying, 'He was in great despair.' The next day was Caspar's birthday and there was a tradition that the two of them dined together. However he had a severe haemorrhage and had to be taken to Canterbury Hospital, where he died at one in the morning.

WIDOW

1964-81

It is hard to exaggerate the importance of the death of Ian Fleming to Ann. He was the love of her life and now he was gone. As the years passed she came to forget, or at least to minimise, how difficult his last years had been, to remember how much he had meant to her. She had in effect been married ever since she was nineteen and although there had always been much beside domesticity to fill her time, there was now a gap at the centre. 'I am amazed you did not know how unhappy I was, what else could I be?' she writes to Hugo Charteris.

Waugh had written the year before, during which Ann's sister Mary Rose and Hugh Gaitskell had died, 'You will lose someone you love every year now for the rest of your life. It is a position you have to accept and prepare for.' This might seem premature gloom, for Ann was only fifty, but Waugh was justified by events. In 1966 he contributed to the melancholy list, the year after Ann's father died and she wrote with practised self-knowledge, 'I am only a bit recovered for the first time today. . . I get a pain in the throat and stomach but cannot cry till much later.' Hugo Charteris died of cancer in 1970 at the age of forty-eight, and less immediate but still valued friends followed, Cyril Connolly in 1971, Judy Gendel in 1972 and James Pope-Hennessy, horribly murdered, in 1974. The years immediately after Fleming's death were also beset with uncertainties about money, and Ann's health, always poor, deteriorated. All this was only the background to her great concern, Fleming's only child, Caspar. Charming, handsome and brilliant, he was twelve on the day his father died and some think he never recovered. Certainly he developed fits of depression and a precocious interest in guns and drugs, which caused Ann intense and increasing anxiety. Eleven years later, in 1975, her anxiety was proved to be well founded when he killed himself.

This was a blow so stunning that some of her friends thought that Ann, in her turn, might never recover. She had for some time been using alcohol as a calculated weapon in her struggle against the blacker side of her life and she continued to do so. Her looks, her wit, her style inevitably reflected this. Then, with a remarkable effort of will, she gave it up and took full control of her life once more. The strain must have been considerable and she was often tired or ill. She was relieved if a weekend came to a natural close after lunch on Sunday and she might spend Monday in bed; but once more she filled the lives of her friends with gaiety and laughter.

Ann consciously sought vitality in others. She prized it in contemporaries, and a party she held to celebrate Robert Kee's success with his book and television series on Ireland was notable for the abandoned dancing of the middle-aged (Ann herself was not well enough to attend). She made new friends among the young and became closer to old ones, such as her niece Sara Morrison. Nicholas Henderson replaced Evelyn Waugh as her chief correspondent. Though she travelled slightly less, Patrick Leigh Fermor's house in the Peloponnese was a haven of friends and pleasure for her, as Sevenhampton was for others. Above all she came to know Lord Goodman. 'A very *large* Jew' was how Ann described him to Waugh, accurately, and one who had lived in a world apart from hers. A negotiator of genius, his ability to solve, smother or evaporate problems, whether for governments or orphans, was just beginning to bring him a discreet fame. He was solicitor to the Prime Minister, Harold Wilson, which certainly helped but did not explain his power. Presumably prime ministers always have a solicitor but he does not usually emerge as the key figure in disputes between newspapers, theatre boards and rebellious colonies. Arnold Goodman's influence was always out of all proportion to the positions he held. For Ann he first banished financial problems, a feat made easier by the unstoppable success of James Bond. Then he became the central figure of her life. There was much speculation as to whether they would marry. As this surprising and happy relationship was conducted in person or by telephone, there is little among these letters of the man who warmed her last years. Ann's last illness was not too cruel or extended and she met it with the courage that had come to be expected of her; perhaps it is because she was so sharply defined a character, so much herself, that she is missed and remembered by acquaintances as well as those closer.

If there are fewer letters in these years it is because Ann, who would not complain, sometimes found herself with less material that would interest or amuse. Less important but still a significant factor is that recent gossip has lost less of its power to harm, hurt or embarrass. Time passes swiftly, therefore, and the sadder side of her life is told in less detail. This was forced by circumstances but does not seem regrettable. It would be a pity to remember Ann as a sadder, frailer person than in fact she was.

To Michael Astor

16 Victoria Square   Monday
                                               [August 1964]

Dearest Michael,
    You know, I was in despair that Caspar should see his father
carried from the hotel; it was miraculous that you should be there
and be so sensitive, loving and competent.
    It was a happiness to me that we both dined with you, and he
enjoyed himself as far as his physical condition allowed him to
enjoy. He liked Astors and Moffats, but was rarely prepared to
chance dining out like I do! but I did love being with him when he
would allow. He was a solitary, melancholy, and not illusioned by
his strange success. All of these things I think you can understand.
    For you and Pandora[1] to travel so far on Saturday I find nothing
to say except it puts you both in a rare class of humanity.
    Thank you for your most understanding letter and for all you
have done for me.
    With much love,

                        Ann

PS. You said kind things of my being a giver – thankyou – I need a
build-up.

1 Pandora Clifford was married 1961–8 to Michael Astor.

From Cyril Connolly

Provence, France   [undated]

Dearest Annie
    Thank you so much for your letter. I am so sorry you are so
unhappy and I wish I could say something to console you but, like

Ian, I am too melancholy myself. Only those with faith can console and then only those with faith can be consoled. It seems to me you have suffered in a particularly personal and traumatic form, in one fell swoop if you like, the process which is spun out for most of us in getting old – the awareness of being less and less wanted, desired, tolerated, and the being less able to want, desire or tolerate although one's faculties of mind and heart are in their prime – and you have lost your husband, the half of yourself as it were while most of us have to watch the loss inch by inch and cut by cut of all the warmth and intimacy on which we depend, to lie awake night after night waiting for someone to come to bed who will then be merely irritable, to see their eyes light up at sillier things said by younger people or glaze when one tries to interest them – old age is being flayed alive as the Frenchman said – and the area of interests gradually restricted like being on a melting iceberg – and at the end nothing but death – 'What's new?' being only death.

Quand une fois le coeur a fait son vendange vivre est un mal, c'est un secret de tous connu . . . I think if you consider your unhappiness you will see that it is only an acute form of the general human unhappiness which attacks everyone over twenty-five who is not totally immersed in his work (immersed beyond feeling disappointment or energy).

I should have thought that however unhappy you both were yours was a happy marriage, the bickering was on the same wavelength and its ending is an act of fate for which no one was responsible; marriage cannot remove neurotic conditions like melancholy, or cure loneliness, though it can palliate them – yet you gave Ian an enormous amount of emotional security which included the freedom to roam and grumble. Imagine his life if he had not been married, a clubman killing time, switching from girl to girl. At least you have many fascinating and devoted friends – Maurice, Evelyn etc. – you can express yourself and communicate and make a foyer for them (as you did for me) – but of course the feeling of personal loss is irreparable and nothing has any effect on it but time but that is absolutely bound to – don't tell yourself that intellectuals are more '*dans le vrai*' and have mysterious resources: in the crisis they have none and nothing abandons one faster than all the '*chers collègues*', the Montaignes and Pascals and Prousts and Valérys – they are none of them more than fair-weather friends just as James Bond could not have existed without you to provide the fair weather. . .

We are all on the rack except those who are already broken. Since you have the gift of conferring warmth and happiness perhaps your own happiness will come back to you through being free to bestow them on your friends without having to canalise so much of it away on one person. At least that is how I began to feel between my marriages so that I really dreaded giving up my freedom. It is not as if you can ever forget Ian – after all, he was (is) someone, a personality whose views and feelings and possessions will continue to reverberate many a long day. '*Il faut tenter de vivre*'! – and besides, he will go on living in Caspar, just as you will. So you must abandon yourself to your unhappiness while you can for you will not always have it with you and one day your friends will want you for themselves and you will have to give it up. I think of you continually.

Much love,

Cyril

To Jack and Frances Donaldson

16 Victoria Square   25 August [1964]

Darling Frankie and Jack

I am overcome with alarming physical exhaustion and zestless misery – when I telephoned I was on some kind of nervous energy – now I do not know how to face the Lambtons – but it's not good for C. to sit at Sevenhampton with me.

I love both of you, count upon your friendship and company, and thank you for your letters, and know you will not mind my answering them as one – you are more as one than any other couple I know.

In some degree I share Jack's faith, and have found letters from believers helpful. These last months have been terribly unhappy, more unhappy even than the last eighteen months, and now it's over I am more conscious of the strain than I was at the time. It was ages and ages since Ian really enjoyed anything.

I would love to see you both when I return – early September. With so much love and thankyou,

A

To Evelyn Waugh

Biddick Hall, Lambton Park, Co. Durham[1]   [August 1964]

Dearest Evelyn

I have been awfully ill. The doctor gave me a sedative which dried up tear ducts and saliva; this at first seemed an admirable plan, but on the fourth day the stiff upper lip became painful, and on the fifth the tongue would not wag, by the 6th I had a high fever and dry white fur in the mouth. Miss Judy diagnosed belladonna poisoning – she was right. I am now cured and blessedly tearful.

We came here so that Caspar should have youthful companions and shooting, and I Miss Judy for a companion. Lady Lambton plans horrible treats every day; there is nothing I dislike more than motoring through miles of factory towns in company of children and nannies. Yesterday we processed in three cars to an abominable fun fair, taking the ferry between North and South Shields; my consignment was Miss Judy, her baby [Anna Venetia] and Italian nurse: the baby used its pot on the ferry and Miss J. threw the contents into the Tyne. I thought Anna Venetia young for Seaton Delaval or for big dippers, and more likely to put on weight if left at home in a pram. Contending with these daily horrors keeps sorrow at bay.

It was extremely thoughtful of you to send me *A Little Learning*; stepfather Quennell was in residence, he snatched it and whiffled through the index – pining for insults, he is profoundly disappointed you did not write more of him.[2] I searched for Cecil Beaton, was also disappointed, but joyfully discovered him in the text[3] – shall I tell him of it? I read all the book with great pleasure, and have many questions to ask when we meet.

It is very kind of you to suggest I should go to Spain with you and Laura. I very much want to go to Madrid and the Prado – will you be going there? Do enlarge on dates and places. I am involved with local Conservatives but would sooner travel.

On Tuesday I take Caspar to Amiens to collect my nephew from his senile father, who is to attend a 1914 regimental dinner there. It is a prospect I view with little enthusiasm, but it has to be done. We shall be home on the 11th and then I must make some plans. Sorrow in middle age seems to destroy all energy and willpower, but perhaps it will return.

With much love to you both

Ann

1 Home of Lord Lambton.
2 Peter Quennell is mentioned as not enjoying Oxford, as attending the Ruskin School of Art though 'Peter, who had decorated his first book of verse, drew worse than I and realised the sooner where his talent lay' and again as being clearly destined to be a writer.
3 Cecil Beaton is not named: 'There is a professional photographer (and theatrical designer) who sometimes crosses my path when I go to London. His hair is sparse and his smile wry; his clothes rather flashy.'

To Evelyn Waugh

Sevenhampton Place, Wilts.   15 November [1964]

Dearest Evelyn

I was with David Cecil when he read your review,[1] he did not mind a bit, he said he rejoiced in his drawing-room grammar; and neither of us perceived the howler,[2] but it has since been pointed out to him and he's awfully pleased at your school-room French.

I have not been well and I am as poor as a church rat.[3] Fionn is here with two children and the upstart, so I am leading a quiet life and trying to replace whisky and sleeping pills with fresh air and vitamins. Present custom despises joy and sorrow, did you read Philip Toynbee's condemnation of Max Beerbohm's innocent and happy life?[4] I think a period of mourning is essential to the nervous system, London life seems pointless to me and is an added depressant.

What do you know of solicitors? The word 'to solicit' is not pleasant. Owing to my inability to understand legal gibberish and my folly in not taking the will to be translated when it was shown to me some years back, I am in the power of three solicitors and O'Neill. Peter and Richard Fleming are doing all they can for me, and poor O'Neill spends hours with the solicitors; 'Bleak', the solicitors say – 'the outlook is bleak.' When a few shillings appear anywhere they say we must think of the remainder; the 'remainder' is apparently Caspar, they wish to store up for him and give me an annual pittance which won't buy sufficient Portuguese chianti for stepfathers Freud and Quennell.[5]

The widower Lancaster is deeply involved with a tall beautiful lady-journalist called Anne Scott-James;[6] post-obsequies he wished to take her to Cornwall to join J. Betjeman and E. Cavendish, but E. Cavendish did not feel up to it.

Cyril Connolly is being very kind to me – he still hopes for a first edition. I am unfair to him, he is still being very kind and he knows there will be no first edition. The Connollys were supposed to come for the weekend, but Mrs Connolly had a nervous breakdown in Highworth: Cyril telephoned at intervals to ask what there was for dinner and report the situation: he groaned when told there was grouse and gaspacho soup, but it was little use, Deirdre refused the last mile and the prospect of M. Bowra and E. Rice. So Cyril took her to Burford to the hotel in the Good Food book, and they ate good food till the proprietress told them she had no good beds, and they wandered round Gloucestershire for many miles before they could find the most simple accommodation.

Now to play Scrabble with the remainder, who's enjoying a half-term holiday.

Please write often, nothing on the breakfast tray but people who think they are James Bond, or want to be James Bond, or legals telling me to sell everything. I sleep less than you and have no paraldehyde.

Do your grandchildren disorganise the household? The upstart forces Fionn to breastfeed her child by Brazilian hours, and soon to prepare him for Pekin by Chinese hours, so the house is like London airport.

With love to you and Laura

Ann

1 Waugh's review in *The Sunday Times*, 8 November, of David Cecil's *Max*, a biography of Max Beerbohm, says, 'Lord David has an easy, Whiggish negligence of grammar which gives the happy illusion that he is reading aloud in the drawing room and occasionally pausing to comment colloquially on the entertainment.'

2 *Marriage blanche* for *marriage blanc*.

3 Fleming left £289,170 and Ann was the principal beneficiary but there was still considerable confusion about tax. Income from James Bond went to Caspar.

4 Philip Toynbee (1916–81). Novelist and reviewer on the staff of the *Observer* from 1950. He had written, 'A typical sentence from the biography begins, depressingly for both writer and reader, with the words "Even less happened to Max in 1927 than in 1926. . ."'

5 Waugh had written: 'It would be disastrous for Caspar, now, if you produced Ali Forbes or Quennell as a stepfather. You will suffer the particular loneliness which only widows know. But half the most admirable women I have known have been widows.'

6 Anne Scott-James (1913–   ). Married Osbert Lancaster in 1967. She had edited *Harper's Bazaar* 1945–51 and had a column in the *Daily Mail* 1960–8.

To Evelyn Waugh

16 Victoria Square   31 November [1964]

Dear Evelyn

Very jolly day with the Flemings, first to Tooth's to share out the Augustus Johns, then to the solicitors for the jewels. Wicked Mrs Fleming willed that the children should choose by seniority, solicitors decreed that my right was forfeited, but the good brothers-in-law insisted, so I chose after Peter, Richard, Amaryllis,[1] and Michael's widow.[2] Alas, though they feigned ignorance of the arts, and Peter said he had never before been in a picture gallery, and Richard shouted 'Tally ho' and other hunting noises, they were quite sharp at choosing the best pictures. We then went to the solicitors for the jewels, and sat in a circle round a big desk, and the solicitor said 'We are awfully sorry we have made a mistake, Mrs Ian had the right of second choice, so will Mrs Ian say if she is satisfied' – in such a situation what would you have done? Of course I had to say I was satisfied, though I hankered for a painting of a magnolia that would have looked well on yellow walls of Seven-hampton. Then the solicitor could not open the lid of a large japanned box, and a hammer was sent for; all it contained was the Marquess of Winchester's seal and a small revolver. The jewellery and furs were left to Amaryllis with a proviso that the daughters-in-law could buy anything from her that she did not need. Throughout these rum proceedings Peter Fleming gazed as one on a mountain in Tibet, puffing his pipe and nary a glance at his relations.

Love

A

1 Amaryllis Fleming (1926–   ). Cellist. Daughter of Augustus John and Evelyn Fleming, at first referred to as adopted.

2 Letitia ('Tish') Borthwick married Michael Fleming (1919–40), who died of wounds after Dunkirk.

To Evelyn Waugh

Sevenhampton Place, Wilts.   1 February [1965]

My dear cousin

The obsequies of Sir Winston[1] prevented my replying to your letter immediately. I am amazed that 'serving soldiers' despised his orations, this was surely not a widely held opinion; General Laycock would be shocked by your views.

One can see that your health has improved by renewed vigour of address, and the returned beauty of your handwriting. Your last letter was almost as ungrammatical and ill-written as my own.

Do come and mumble at me between teeth, there will certainly be a day or two of bleeding gums – we could go to a theatre.

I hope you have chosen a good dentist. I go to Alistair MacDonald, recommended by the late face-lifter, Sir Archibald Macindoe. Mr MacDonald crowned all my back teeth in gold to prevent my nose meeting my chin. I had developed an overbite and awoke each morning with my top teeth sunk into lower jaw gums: it was most painful.

Lord Lambton took me to view the catafalque in Westminster Hall, the sorrow and beauty of the occasion was marred because he arrived in a murderous bad temper, the explosion was caused by the insistence of Lady Lambton that she should accompany us with four daughters, an infant son, an ancient nurse, crutches, and an invalid chair. Officialdom refused to lever the chair down the steps, but when Tony and I paused reverently beside the coffin, a vast mediaeval door upon our right swung open and various sergeants-at-arms and police constables towed in all the Lambton progeny, the infant heir wailing on its mother's knee.

Muggeridge has shat upon Ian, very surprising, I thought his venom glands reserved for statesmen. It happened in the December number of *Esquire* and only lately seen by me: if sooner, I would have written ignoring venom but denying pipe smoking, Bentleys and the statement that Ian had discussed his first book with Mugg. and declared he was going to give people 'snobbery, sex and sadism'. Ian met Malcolm for the first time after the publication of the book, and his public appeal was most certainly not calculated.

Please come to Egypt in the Easter holidays with Laura and Septimus. Your new snappers will crunch sheep's eyes and other

Arabian delicacies – while we take the children round the tombs. Caspar insists on going – and I don't want us to go alone and be cheated by guides.

Love

A

1 Sir Winston Churchill had died on 24 January and Waugh commented: 'He is not a man for whom I ever had esteem. Always in the wrong, always surrounded by crooks, a most unsuccessful father, simply a "radio personality" who outlived his prime. Rallied the nation indeed! I was a serving soldier in 1940. How we despised his orations.'

To Evelyn Waugh

Sevenhampton Place, Wilts.   28 March 1965

Dearest Evelyn

You chose a bad week to have your snappers extracted, it must have been a mighty cold journey home, hope you kept a scarf round your face and the express was not delayed by snowdrifts.[1]

My life is no longer a bowl of cherries, and personal correspondence was inspired by exuberance, not spelling, nor grammer, nor a gift for the English language. The little vitality left is absorbed in grubbing for money; I am too old to be poor, and it don't seem necessary.

The Sunday Times are being most kind to me for helping an unknown called John Pearson[2] to write Ian's life. Alas, cautious speech is not for me, Mr Pearson thrives on nervous giggles and floods of indiscretion, he leaves me to tears and dreadful exhaustion and goes home well pleased. Great bouquets of flowers arrive from Leonard Russell[3] thanking me for my cooperation, and I wake in the night with screams of guilt.

It's rather nice to talk of the happy past, in the late thirties Ian was known as 'Glamour Boy' and in the war as 'the Chocolate Sailor', but how can this poor young man understand that jokes were prompted by hopeless love? I don't understand myself. Have you known such a situation yourself? You are not always very kind about 'Baby'. I mean Jungman,[4] not Cooper.

Cyril has inherited a bran tub of silver. Something to do with an aunt who deceased in Spain. He is fearfully excited, though it is likely to be Victorian and not Paul Storr.

Brother Hugo's brother-in-law gave up broad acres to become a parson, he has lost his faith and is at an institution in Nottingham for faithless parsons;[5] Hugo is to write about it for the *Sunday Telegraph*. Sixty % of the children of C. of E. clergy are delinquent, and this seriously affects the faith of the father. One child took the collection money because he wished to 'communicate'. Hugo is very much enjoying Nottingham, and is sending me the pamphlet they issue on nervous diseases of the bereaved. I was mad enough to tell him I suffered from an over-active bowel, there is a great deal about this unpleasant affliction in the pamphlet. Does your Church have a school for the faithless?

I go to Egypt next Friday, but do not let this prevent you from writing to me. It would be a joy to see your handwriting at the Winter Palace, Luxor.

Egyptian religion seems based on the fallacy that you can take it with you – wish I had not read books on it, I thought a little knowledge would stimulate my interest, but my worst fears are confirmed, none of it appeals. The trustees regard the journey as extravagance, in fact it is a sacrifice to please Caspar who has learned so much of this uncivilisation that I am impressed.

Went to the United Arab Republic for a visa, two sinister trunks in the hall, and beyond a vast colour photograph of Nasser provoking jingo thoughts.

The Lady Antonia Fraser cancelled a dinner-party when Laura Lovat died at dawn, Diana thought it was Lady Longford who had died and she and Antonia were at cross purposes for some minutes. I dined with Diana as a result, far more nice than an Antonia evening, though I would have talked to her more and seen less television for choice. Diana was not eating for she was flying to Paris the following day for a fitting at Balmain, but she was occasionally drinking. A small cottage pie was procured for me from a neighbouring pub for 2/6 and herring paste from the local delicatessen, both were delicious. I ate them off a tray at the foot of Diana's bed. She was looking very beautiful and occasional huge tears, provoked by Iris Tree's[7] cancer, and drinking my wine and bit of grapefruit juice and gin with no food foundation. We watched a torture film and she was surprised I did not want to stay for the late news. I do love her.

God willing, will be home for Easter and hope to see you.

Tell me the latest snapper news, and if mastication has renewed your interest in life, and when we may meet.

Love

A

1 Waugh had his teeth extracted without anaesthetic. 'His son Auberon has told me that in his opinion he never got over the operation.' *Evelyn Waugh* by Christopher Sykes.

2 John Pearson (1930–   ). Worked on the Atticus column of *The Sunday Times*, as did Fleming. He had written a novel and a book about Donald Campbell breaking the world speed record before *The Life of Ian Fleming*, 1966.

3 Leonard Russell (1906–74) was Literary Editor of *The Sunday Times* and married to its film critic Dilys Powell.

4 Teresa Jungman (1907–   ). In the early 1930s between his marriages Waugh was in love with her, as were many others, but she did not return his affection.

5 Timothy Forbes Adam did have treatment but is still a parson.

6 Iris Tree (1897–1968). Daughter of Sir Herbert Tree, she toured as the nun in *The Miracle* with Lady Diana, whom she had known from childhood. Her condition was critical after much of her colon had been removed but she objected to transfusions: 'Bourgeois blood. I would have preferred horse or tiger to fiercen me.'

To Evelyn Waugh

New Winter Palace, Luxor   Thursday [April 1965]

Dearest Evelyn

I should like to purchase the Victorian furniture, parquet floors and elegantly draped bedsteads of brass and white-painted iron in this hotel. If the management was not Egyptian it might be most agreeable. It is ruined by disgusting food and surly service. Last night thirty-five minutes after we had ordered, not a morsel to eat – I strode the length of the dining-room, collected a dish of black olives, white sheep cheese, butter, bread and tomatoes – the waiters gathered in fury but did not interfere. Caspar said I looked awfully silly.

The Valley of the Kings is a nightmare of glare, heat and tourists, and the tombs smell awful. I do not like Egyptian art, it seems monotonous. Neither youth, nor age, nor love, nor fun is depicted. It's a necrophile materialistic religion.

Happily our companion, Fred Warner, takes Caspar out at dawn. I know him no better than when we left England and cannot conceive why he should wish to be with us. He is a super tutor and dragoman, and pumps out knowledge ruthlessly; he likes to talk of the miserable economic circumstances of Arab countries with American intensity. He has American blood – I should have been warned: Caspar thinks him a marvel, and there are only six more days! Do not tell Diana I complained of Warner, she, Nose Wyndham[1] and most people dote on him.

I was *grateful* for your letter, you don't sound very gay. Pray for my safe and speedy return, and I will visit you with a basket of oysters.[2]

This afternoon we drive two hours into the desert to see a temple. I bet it's as dull and ugly as the others.

Nasser has closed all brothels in Cairo. All imports have been stopped – no razor blades, no scissors, no watches and clocks. No nail varnish, no hair shampoo, no sunburn lotion. Whisky £5 a bottle, no English cigarettes. I am an improvident traveller and need cosmetics against the terrible heat and dust, my skin is like the crocodile's.

Caspar is awfully happy. He spends his evening bargaining in the antique shops, and enjoys walking the streets alone followed by starving Arab children yelling for baksheesh. At dinner he returns triumphant with a bundle of fake scarabs and amulets.

Thinking of you and your snappers.

With love

A

1 Violet Wyndham (1890–1979). Author and the second wife of Ann's great-uncle, Guy Wyndham.
2 Waugh had written that with his new false teeth he could not bite meat and so lived on a diet of omelettes and oysters. Later he added, 'My snappers are a failure.'

To Evelyn Waugh

Sevenhampton Place, Wilts   17 May [1965]

Dear Cousin

Yesterday Robert Heber-Percy awarded first prize at his fête to the James Bond float – eight dairy maids in black leather on a farm cart. I missed this spectacle because 'Cecily' Beaton came to lunch with his 'friend' and secretary and refused to visit Faringdon because he hates Robert.

Cecil now travels like Jean Cocteau with a healthy young American male and a buxom plain young woman. I believe Cocteau was always accompanied by a retinue of this nature.

Darling Maurice Bowra's poetry grows senile, his last verses were to sorrow for Sparrow and the creation of a hut in his garden to accommodate new Fellow of All Souls; it has verses describing the departure of Lady Pam and Lady Ann, and an atmosphere of desertion and loneliness; it was misunderstood by Miss Kelly Clark[1] who promptly wrote to Maurice and said 'We all love you, you must not feel like this.' I fear she caused pain.

Lord Longford persuaded me to the House of Lords to hear Boofy Arran speak in favour of 'consenting adults'.[2] Dear old Frank, who has convinced so many imprisoned 'consenting adults' that they were victims of an unjust society, was most pompously pretending to be unpartisan and toeing the Wilson line – I don't think I love Lord Longford.

Swindon is now a town of one hundred thousand souls, and W.H. Smith and Sons are to build a further factory. The mayor and councillors have money galore, forty thousand was spent on an art gallery, but no one contemplated exhibiting painting or sculpture or anything but the horrific untutored results of the amateur sketching club, they were amazed when I suggested a travelling show from London, and I hope grateful that I shall organise it.

A brief encounter with Lady Pamberry was rewarding – 'I am lunching on a tray with Tommy Balogh' . . .[3]

Cyril dines on Wednesday, he has ordered the guests and the food – Lady Diana Cooper, Sir Frederick Ashton, James Pope-Hennessy, gaspacho, *chaudfroid* of sole, asparagus, melon *charentaise*.[4]

Deborah Mitford has a special train for her son's[5] midsummer crowning: all have accepted and the carriages will be filled with the old important and flowering youth; Deborah wonders if there will be a greater train robbery or lumps of concrete on the line.

Have you changed your snapperman so you can lunch on June 1st?
Eat more,
Drink less,
Love

A

1 Colette (Kelly) Clark (1932–). Daughter of Kenneth Clark, goddaughter of Sir Maurice Bowra. Member of the Board of the Royal Opera House since 1974.

2 The Earl of Arran introduced a bill for homosexual law reform. On another occasion he led a campaign for the protection of badgers, which his wife kept. These successes were described as 'teaching people not to bugger badgers and not to badger buggers'.

3 Lord Balogh (1905–85). Hungarian economist. Fellow of Balliol 1945–73, Minister of the Department of Energy, 1974. Life Peer 1968.

4 Ann reported to Patrick Leigh Fermor, 'We ate melons the size of tennis balls and tasting of nectarines, they come from Israel and can only be procured for two weeks of the year, costing 7/6 each, doubtless the trustees could think of cheaper fare but not so delectable. Cyril enjoyed the evening least for he wished to see himself and John Betjeman doing a quiz programme on BBC2. BBC2 is still a capricious station and alack, mine did not work. We all said the right things but somehow there was a bitter aftertaste that got mixed up with the melon.'

5 The Marquess of Hartington celebrated his twenty-first birthday that summer.

To Hugo Charteris

Sevenhampton Place   25 June [1965]

Darling Hugo

I am amazed that you did not know I was unhappy, what else could I be! I mind nothing about myself, but surely you see that I cannot let you write about Ian.[1] There was the diamond episode,[2] then not one of my family offered to come to the funeral or sent a flower.[3] Since funerals are for the living, it looked rotten to the Flemings, though it made for conversation that the Astors were representing the Charterises! It was with a wry smile that I read your diatribe against the Astors at Ba's[4] funeral. I keep up guerilla warfare against the Bond parasites, and was amazed you did not see in how ugly a light you would appear if you had cashed in on my griefs.

I am very sorry that I was so remote at half term, I did not know how bad it was going to be, there is nothing I can do when I freeze – so far only two other beings have produced this ice, Granma Tennant being one, and Eric Dudley the other!

Should have written sooner, but liver returned owing to surfeit of honey – easier to give up than alcohol.

Just off on Pangbourne Eton circuit.
Will telephone,
Love
Ann

1 Charteris wished to write a biography of Ann and Ian Fleming. She absolutely refused and threatened to bring an injunction. He had not written much but had to pay back the advance.

2 After his travels in West Africa in 1957 Charteris told Fleming a story which he thought Fleming used without permission. He resented it deeply.

3 Charteris and his family were leaving for a holiday the day they heard of Fleming's death, but he personally had had time to send flowers and had not done so.

4 Barbara Chase, who had died that year, had been married to the Marquess of Lansdowne.

To Evelyn Waugh

Sevenhampton Place, Wilts.   14 September 1965

Dearest Evelyn

Two months driving Caspar on Scottish visits have proved exhausting. Caspar hates me and talks of little but matricide. What shall I do? He is too old and strong to hit.[1]

The Flemings are very hearty on their grouse moor, eight Flemings walking in line, five of them females in knickerbockers: we walked for three hours in the morning and three in the afternoon, the lunch interval was brief, nasty dry sandwiches and NOTHING to drink – no alcohol, no liquid, and far from a mountain stream. Did you know one walked faster and further if parched with thirst? You should consider it.

I long to see you and trust your health has improved.
Love
A

1 Waugh replied, 'It is very wrong of Caspar to plot your murder. Do you think those terrible modern pictures have unsettled the boy? I don't mean films of course but the paintings you have lately acquired? ... Could you deflect Caspar's homicidal tendencies from yourself to fuddy-duddies such as Beaton, Quennell, Forbes etc.? I suffer far more than you can understand by the present degradation of the Church. I will pay Caspar's single fare (first class) if he will go to New York to assassinate the Pope.'

To Nicholas Henderson[1]

Sevenhampton Place   17 September [1965]

Dearest Head Boy

Come home and have some lessons in handwriting from E. Waugh, yours is hard to read and I don't want to miss a word.

Even if you did know your boys were smoking after lights out, you wouldn't tell me – so we can skip all that!

Roy[2] blew in for dinner, he was house hunting at East Hendred. He says all political leaders are as identical as Hilton Hotels – the Hilton Wilson, the Hilton Johnson, the Hilton Heath etc. He was very funny about drive from Stafford to Short Bros. with French Sec. of Aviation – the bus was specially upholstered for occasion and staffed with out of work air hostesses, a four-course meal was served with claret and champagne corks popping, only hitch a mini got in way of bus and violence of brakes caused custard pies and alcohol to fly through air, Roy was holding expensive specially printed brochure on knee so got less wet and dirty than frogs. Roy reports Hilton Wilson as euphoric, I wonder why?

People trickle home from hols., have seen a few, only talked to Mark [Bonham Carter] on telephone plotting to prevent publication of Hugo's next book.

Love,
A

1 Nicholas Henderson (1919–   ). Diplomat, at that time Minister in Madrid. *See* Appendix of Names.
2 Roy Jenkins was Minister of Aviation at the time.

To Evelyn Waugh

Sevenhampton Place, Wilts.   4 October [1965]

Dearest Evelyn

Great confusion here; I decided to sell, mend, cut, drain all the same time – result – chaos; the road is soft tar and the furniture van cannot approach to bring me twelve Augustus John drawings, to remove furniture for sale and the invalid chair to you. The lake was drained to mend the sluice gate, but no sluice gate menders have appeared and the ducks languish.

Such is the avarice of Sir Jock Campbell who garners the 'Bond' royalties, that he has hired at a vast price Kingsley Amis to impersonate Ian and continue the series. Peter Fleming was party to the transaction – they have not yet agreed to a pseudonym for Amis.[1] No one understands why I am distressed; though I do not admire 'Bond' he was Ian's creation and should not be commercialised to this extent. Is there any parallel in literature? Should not Kingsley Amis be ashamed? It's all a left-wing plot.

I am very sorry about the absurd democratising of your Church, it was grand and splendid and strong, and now it will be weak and futile, like everything else. Alas, much I have not read and would probably not understand, but I do sympathise. Old Caspar wants to kill all Jews, but perhaps he should assassinate the Pope for forgiving the Jews.

Aunt Cynthia's diary[2] is with me, it would appear your mother-in-law's habit of saying 'What?' at the end of every sentence began in 1915. The diary is wonderful family reading. I cannot judge what it would be for the public. Cynthia comments on Mary's engagement to Uncle Tom Strickland[3] as: 'Perhaps it would be an adventure to marry quite outside one's *milieu*.' Simon Asquith has found purpose and power in possessing this manuscript, and many people see him who would not otherwise, including myself.

I hear from Diana you come to London soon. *PLEASE* see me. I will come to you but not till the planting season is over.

Your loving Coz.,

A

1 The royalties on James Bond books were paid to Glidrose Productions Ltd, a company owned partly by Booker McConnell Ltd and partly by Ian Fleming's will trust, the income from which was received by Ann or by Caspar. Peter Fleming was a director of Glidrose. Sir Jock Campbell was chairman of Booker and derived no personal financial benefit from the Bond royalties.

Ann later agreed to the publication of *Colonel Sun* (1968), the James Bond novel written by Kingsley Amis under the name of Robert Markham, though not without regret.

2 Lady Cynthia Asquith's *Diaries 1915–18* also appeared in 1968. There is a foreword by L. P. Hartley but no mention of an editor.

3 Algernon ('Tom') Strickland (1891–1938) married Lady Mary Charteris in 1915.

From Evelyn Waugh

Combe Florey House, Nr Taunton   15 October 1965

Dear Octopussy

I hope you have recovered from your pill. It was very nice seeing you in London, but I thought you definitely under the influence.

I was sick at 11 p.m. that evening – not the result of drink or of Diana's tasty supper. Just exhaustion. I have felt stronger since but it was touch or go whether I reached the privacy of the Hyde Park Hotel in time. Please explain this to Diana as the reason for my leaving her so abruptly.

The film she took me to had two characters (one insane) & lasted two hours.[1] It was a sort of gala performance. Your dear little boy would have found many victims for his racial passions. Bob Boothby & his wife[2] left after an hour. I longed to go but felt it would be impolite to Diana who had taken such trouble to get me in. She dozed intermittently so suffered less. Coming out I met P. Lindsay[3] whom I have never regarded as a wit, and said: 'I am not clear what the heroine died of.' 'Boredom, presumably?' I see the film extravagantly advertised. Keep away. It is called *The Collector*.

My boy Bron's book is better than the last.[4] All he knows much about is hospital life, which he describes excellently.

Vomiting is a great exhilaration. One feels so ghastly just before & so rejuvenated immediately after. I read that all the schoolgirls in Lancashire have taken to it.

Ever your affec. coz.,

E

1 Terence Stamp and Samantha Eggar appeared in William Wyler's film of John Fowles's novel, *The Collector*.
2 Wanda Sanna of Sardinia married Lord Boothby in 1967.
3 Patrick Lindsay (1928–   ). Director of Christies since 1955.
4 *Who Are the Violets Now?*

To Evelyn Waugh

Sevenhampton Place, Wilts.   21 January [1966]

Dearest Evelyn

Carnage round the bird table, robin slays robin and blackbird fights blackbird; the more food, the more birds, the more bloodshed – a sort of birds' eye view of Nigeria[1] – you should read *Birds and their Territories* and give them Hyde Park Hotel feasts, it might temporarily allay your misery and take your foot out of the cradle. I am sad that you suffer so much, it is so unfair – the different temperaments – I am unhappy but awfully easily excited and you have ceased to be excited by anything. Fuddy-duddy Beaton is awfully unhappy – he has shingles and they have affected his sciatic nerve, but his condition improved when he went to the 'Boudin Ball' at Christies and painted a portrait of a Rolling Stone.[2]

A youthful scholastic person[3] wants to marry me, he is not yet forty-five and his profession may take him to Leeds, Manchester or Nottingham – would I be happy with a 'chéri' in the Midlands?

A great todo at Oxford, Sir Isaiah contemplates becoming Master of a post-graduate college at Oxford,[4] or rather Iffley, he will only do so if he is given a million, he is to find it himself – so presumably it is Jewish money, and an American architect called 'Johnstone'[5] is considered – all very foreign. Maurice and Sparrow are against Isaiah being an administrator, they think he should not waste his genius in this fashion. This is TOP SECRET, so do *not* make mischief – though I doubt if it is of any interest to you.

Why do you not do a television programme on the horrid new Mass? One must fight for one's beliefs. It's much easier for me who believes there is a God but the approach to him don't signify, I call it mysticism, but I do not know what I am talking about. Where could I learn most easily the facts of your present predicament? Is it *much more* than the Mass being rendered in English?

I find it rum that the University of East Anglia is to build a vast prayer room for all denominations, there are beautiful churches in Norwich and if 'pink bricks' are not denominational surely the students can walk a few yards?

Rillington Place [Sevenhampton] is very warm, inside hyacinths and outside snow dogs, pharaohs, mermaids and other creations of Caspar and his pals, since there has been no thaw these ten days.

Do go to my dentist Mr Alistair MacDonald – he's a great genius and would fit your snappers at once, it's *quite* unnecessary to suffer as you do.

Please stay alive, and answer this letter.

With love

A

1 The civil war in Nigeria was being fought. Auberon Waugh's third child is named Biafra in memory.

2 Mick Jagger. 'I saw him on television and he inspired me,' said Beaton. 'He looks like someone who has sprung out of the woods.'

3 Professor Marcus Dick (1920–71). Philosopher. He had been a Scholar and taken a first at Balliol, Oxford where he became a lecturer in 1947. In 1963 he became Professor of Philosophy at the University of East Anglia. He had been married before, and married again in 1968.

4 Sir Isaiah Berlin became President of the new Wolfson College 1966–75.

5 Philip Johnson (1906–   ). Powell and Moia built the college.

From Evelyn Waugh

[Combe Florey House]   26 January 1966

Dear Ann

Trembling hand can't write. Not drink or drugs. Just old age.

It is kind of you to ask me to Rillington. I am not up to it. Come here and rough it. The population explosion has struck Combe Florey. The two women who worked for us are both pregnant so you would have to make your own bed.

Do you think you would really be happy in red-brick academic society? I am full of curiosity about your suitor. A provincial don is better than a London aesthete. But why not remain a widow? Many of the most admirable women I know have had long and happy widowhoods. Mary Herbert has been ill and causes anxiety. Like you she cannot repose.[1]

Laura's life is pretty dreary. She would like it awfully if you came to visit her.

I read in this morning's paper that there is a financial misdemeanour called 'Bond washing'.

Ever your affec. coz.

E

1 Waugh's mother-in-law did not die until 1970.

To Nicholas and Mary Henderson

Sevenhampton Place   12 February [1966]

Dearest Nico and Mary

Tomorrow will be the third week in bed with afternoon fever and no other symptoms till this morning, when common cold in head developed. Thursday and Friday I tried mind over matter by walking towards the Academy and Bonnard, but ended clinging to a lamp post with sweat pouring down spine.

Last night I would have put my head in gas oven, if I was not too frightened of the cook to go into the kitchen. I wonder if other suicides have been prevented by cook fear?

Lady Diana Cooper has had a *coup de jeunesse* since trussed up and robbed. She was once more the centre of the stage and enjoyed calming all the shrieking Italians, finding a belt for them to tie her hands and telling where the jewellery and fur coat was. A telegram from Paul Louis Weiller read '*Je n'aime pas que tu sois froide, cherie, allez vous chez Dior et achetez vous un mink*' – very nice to be kept in this manner at 72.

This horrible malady coincided with the manuscript of Ian's life. Sedatives, *Sunday Times* pressure and the agreement of Colonel P. Fleming account for a very wrong decision; if written it had to be, it should have been by a reputable author or someone who knew Ian. This MSS when not vulgar is dull, and in my present condition reduced me to floods of tears, total recall of the past perfect, the past imperfect and the author's totally false deductions. Despite fever I summoned Quennell and after several whiskies we blue-pencilled at least half. There has been no news from the author, and I imagine he and the *Sunday Times* apparat are considering the next move.

P.M. (Temp. gone up, HELL)

Since Clarissa writes from Barbados to ask if I am to marry Prof. Marcus Dick, I feel this rumour may have reached Madrid. I am old enough to be his mother, and he is married for two more years – but a friendly soul to have around the place, which is otherwise a bit empty.

Clarissa was complaining at having to give a bite of lunch to the Queen, but consoled that since it was only the Queen there was no need to hire a butler. I guess it was one of those occasions when she might have made a few friends by asking some folk to come around.

With much love

A

To Evelyn Waugh

Sevenhampton Place, Wilts.   18 March 1966

Dearest Evelyn

I was very happy to hear your health is improved, and receive a letter from you: this is the first moment I am strong enough to answer your kind enquiry. I have been ill for nine weeks; my doctor should be a Master of Fox Hounds, I was running a fever for which he could find no cause – he daily examined me and said 'drawn blank again', he did not appear to have heard of X-rays so it was not till the fourth week I made the suggestion and my sinuses proved full of pus in the pretty pictures, so into hospital and an uncomfortable tube in each nostril. Alas, the MFH had been feeding me with pills the price of early plover's eggs, and it is from them I am recovering on a lowering diet of Vichy water and Epsom salts.

There is a very good paperback called *Disease, Drugs and Doctors*, I will send it to you in case you are tempted by the plover's egg pills.

The only person who can save your trust is Lord Goodman, 79 Portland Place, W1, he admires your works and is clever and funny, he has done much for me and never sends a bill. He has saved me from the solicitors, found me a doctor to replace the M.F.H. and can get tickets for the National Theatre. I *seriously* suggest you should seek his advice, would you come to lunch with him one day? He is a very *large* Jew.[1]

As you know the guest rooms at Sevenhampton are far from comfortable, you and Laura slept in the best ones, and if the Quennells are here they have the same treatment, but I did think Fuddy-duddy Q. should move out for Lady Egremont; he refused, so she had a mean apartment with a small stained mirror, she could not paint or powder without placing it on the floor and sitting cross-legged before it. Q. happened to pass the door and said 'Darling Pamela, when you are not at Petworth you give the impression of someone on safari' – she was awfully cross. Now Easter looms, also the Quennells, and self-invited Mr Home Secretary Jenkins,[2] I explained the bedroom problem to Mr J. who has arranged to have Fuddy-duddy arrested at Swindon station. I fear this will kill Q. who is awfully frightened of *authority* but what can I do?

Cyril Connolly much enjoyed a visit to your friend Charles da Costa. I lunched with Cyril to discuss his West Indian trip, he took me to Wiltons and the bill was £10 without wine, unluckily we observed others eating aspargus and did not resist – it cost sixty shillings for five stalks each.

I am pleased your mother-in-law is better, in Cynthia's diaries she emerges well – better than any other, male or female – does she know this?

Old Caspar did the scenery for *Caesar and Cleopatra* at Eton; *The Times* said unkindly it might have been done from the drawings any Roman soldier sent home to his family. Old C. loves Eton and takes the Archeological Society to Sotheby sales. Does old Septimus [Waugh] interest you?

No visiting till after holidays and dull election.

Wish I liked peacocks, I am sure they are unlucky and will not have them here.

Are you writing?

R.S.V.P.

Love

A

PS. Hugo telephoned from Scotland to ask if he might write a biography of me for George Weidenfeld – a very furtive way to climb on the Bond wagon – our conversation was brief and not happy.

1 Arnold Goodman (1913–) had been created a peer the year before. Worked for Harold Wilson, who had become Prime Minister in 1964, and seemed to have a finger in every pie, among them the National Theatre, the *Observer*, Rhodesia, and the Newspaper Publishers' Association. Became Ann's closest friend in her later years. Among Ann's papers was a remnant from an after-dinner game of anagrams, a place card for John Sparrow who had written 'Arnold Goodman – An old Roman God' and improved it to 'A Man? No, Lord God'. (He had also written Asa Briggs – Sir Gasbag.) *See* Appendix of Names.

2 Roy Jenkins was Home Secretary 1965–7. The Labour Party had won the election with a greatly increased majority. Ann foresaw this threat: 'If these guys get back with a majority of sixty or so, it won't be tiptoe through the tulips with Tony and Roy, but Harold may put Foot on the pedal and an old reactionary like me should hang around, although totally impotent.' She therefore supported Charles Morrison, who had married in 1954 Ann's niece Sara and in 1964 became MP for Devizes, which he still is.

To Nicholas Henderson

Sevenhampton Place   13 May [1966]

Dearest Nico

I have thought of you a great deal, but no pen to paper. I find without alcohol there is no tiger in my tank.

I recovered from black spots and wondering if the foot would meet the ground on Easter Saturday, which was just as well for apart from Caspar and cousin there were Diana C., Quennells and Roy, also much tennis and coming and going with the Astors.

Roy had two detectives because of the Easter rebellion, marvellous at moving furniture for the Roys and a boon and blessing for children because of revolvers in holsters under armpits and more than ready to give demonstrations. Nothing was seen of the Jellicoes.[1] Roy has a pretty imagery that without the Hendersons they are isolated – an island in a vast ocean.

Have written insulting letter to Editor of *Spectator* about Evelyn's obituaries,[2] and demanding review [of] Beverley Nichols' book on Willie Maugham;[3] the illustrous dead are badly treated these days by lesser jealous mortals, it reflects ill on periodicals and newspapers. Deserted by Evelyn and permitted a sip of whisky you may hear *much* more from me. I had been writing to him to cheer but could no longer expect dazzling answers, now all my correspondents are dead except you.

Last Monday made fool of myself on the Kee-Levin[4] show. It goes on the air without rehearsal at 11.30 p.m. on Monday nights, interviews and so-called 'natural' conversation is introduced, ended and interrupted by a gentleman playing a harpsichord; everything is against it being a success, it has had awful notices as knockabout turn. I, of course, went hoping to be sadistically interviewed by Robert – alas, they were both alarmingly kind. The co-guests were Hitchcock[5] and Ned Sherrin of T.W.T.W.[6] Alfred Hitchcock just returned from a guided tour of the vice houses of Paris, he described rooms full of dog-masks, collars, leads, and how the girls wear different coloured heels to their shoes to denote if they are proffered to beat or be beaten, and other little foibles. Hitchcock says the colour chart saves a lot of time. Oh, by the way, this was after the show: in fact he was such good company that I did not return home till very late.

Tuesday I had a dinner party for darling Lord Goodman; the women were a total flop, me from post-tele exhaustion, Diana Cooper very drunk, Susan Mary Alsop, silent. Crosland[7] had telephoned before dinner to say he must come round to see Goodman on business – as it smelled nostalgically of intrigue and I can't say no to Tony they were put in the ante-chamber while Diana lit the fire next door, making it like the black hole of Calcutta, and I refused to let anyone out. Andrew [Devonshire] escaped to get a drink and reported that the intriguers were discussing the vital importance of the immediate rape of Barbara Castle[8] to soften her up about the speed limit. I know she's adamant about 70 m.p.h., which irks Jenks and Cros. in cabinet.

Last night the guests mostly on crutches, I had dug up Stanley Morison[9] to complain of the ugly new *Times*, the poor man is old and ill and has some kind of contract with the newspaper that prevents him writing what he feels.

Today is magic beauty, only known to England, small sailing clouds and bright pale green trees. I did my cowslip and kingcup walk to the foot of the downs; plenty of cuckoos, birdsong and mud.

The Jenkins have a party Monday night. Will report on behaviour of your old pals, who should all be present.

With much love and thankyou for the plaintive postcard.

Hope the greenhouse Mary took to Spain is packed with flora, and Madrid has compensations.

A

1 Philippa Dunne married Earl Jellicoe in 1966. He became leader of the Conservative Party in the House of Lords 1970–3 but resigned over a scandal about prostitutes at the same time as Lord Lambton.

2 Evelyn Waugh had died suddenly of a heart attack on 12 April.

3 *A Case of Human Bondage*, 1966, by Beverley Nichols was little more than a bitchy anecdote.

4 The programme chaired by Robert Kee and Bernard Levin was called *Comment and Conversation*.

5 Alfred Hitchcock (1899–1980). Film director, whose *Torn Curtain* was released that year. Knighted 1980.

6 Edward ('Ned') Sherrin (1931–). Producer and director of *That Was The Week That Was*, a topical television revue. Also writer and performer, frequently connected with musicals.

7 Anthony Crosland (1918–77). Labour MP 1950–5 and 1959–77. Secretary of State for Education and Science 1965–7. Had just been made Foreign Secretary when he died. Among his books is *The Future of Socialism*, 1956. Ann thought him

very attractive; he disapproved of much about her but used to come to parties at Victoria Square.

8 Barbara Castle (1910–   ). Labour MP 1945–79, Member of European Parliament since then. Minister of Transport 1965–8.

9 Stanley Morison (1889–1967) had designed the typeface for *The Times* in 1932.

To Nicholas Henderson

Sevenhampton Place   24 October 1966

Dearest Nico

It's delectably blighty this evening, a day of what the 'Met. men' call 'hazy sunshine', followed by a pink sunset enhanced by sear and yellow leafage, a pleasure after the black greens of July and August.

I am glad you liked E. Waugh's autobiography,[1] most people were disappointed, expecting many more jokes, I presume; sad that there will be no second volume which was to be called *A Little Hope* from the French '*Un peu d'espoir, et puis bonsoir*'. Evelyn could not find the poem or the author, only this one sentence in *Trilby*, Connolly and Mortimer[2] were no help, and then I discovered it as a competition set by Ian for the best third verse in the *Spectator*, it was written by a not very obscure author – Alfred de Musset.

Subsequent to the Labour Party Conference there arose an amazing scandal, the source of which is still far from clear, it seems that Mr H. Wilson imagined or was wrongfully informed that the July weekend you spent here with old pals, I was entertaining Callaghan,[3] Crossman[4] (some say Crosland) and Jenkins, hatching a plot to uncrown Wilson and crown Callaghan. Though there is a certain reticence in the voices of Jenkins and Mrs Crosland, in that no one will tell me *all*, it is an astonishing bit of Russian scandal. I was first told by Arnold Goodman on condition I did not mention it to a soul, and that he had been asked by a Wilson go-between if it could be true, but a week later Jennifer [Jenkins] telephoned because the *Sunday Telegraph* was on to them and threatened to telephone me. Jennifer said Roy had arrived at the Brighton Conference exhausted by his American trip plus antibiotics, and H. Wilson gave him frozen stares, which reading between lines caused alarm and despondency, however he has since seen Wilson and exonerated himself. The press got on to it because of chatterings of Wilson and his entourage, and in the last ten days most of the newspapers have telephoned me asking if I was the 'July plot hostess', it became a great temptation to say yes! Now what do you and Mary make of that? Malice or a germ of truth somewhere? R.S.V.P. Doubtless it will creep into letters from your other pen pals in varied fashion.

Spider [Quennell] has departed for America to seek her fortune, and Peter mistakenly hopes she will find it – very odd, because in many ways they suit each other.

The Hendersons are sadly missed, specially by me since I find them more sympathetic than many of the friends, can I come to Spain for Christmas holidays?

J. Pearson's book revolts me, and I am distressed that I played any part in it – but it will soon be over and forgotten, though one day I would like a very short appraisal of Ian to be written, though heaven knows who by – the truth is immediately forgotten. I am grateful for letters from Alan Ross and Frankie Donaldson saying the letters to me were not a breach of taste but added [they] proved Ian capable of real feeling, and not a bit like the rest of the book, a bit of Bond fantasy. I have had guilt in showing them to the rabbit Pearson, who became a ferret.[5]

What of you and Mary, and the Spanish problems? I do not read details – there is too much of everything – but whenever I see a headline I think of what part you are playing – handicapped by a dumb ambassador, and in my opinion NOT where you ought to be. I hope it is tolerable and you do not pine too much for Beagle and the downs.

With love and do write again,

A

1 A Little Learning, 1964.

2 Raymond Mortimer (1895–1980). Literary critic.

3 James Callaghan (1912–   ) was Chancellor of the Exchequer 1964–7, Prime Minister 1976–9.

4 Richard Crossman (1907–74). Diarist and Labour MP 1945–74, Leader of the House of Commons 1966–8, Editor of the New Statesman 1970–4.

5 John Pearson writes: 'I'm sorry Ann found me such a "ferret" although I suppose it's what a biographer has to be, and sorrier still to have been the cause of such distress of which I was genuinely ignorant. Odd I was so "unknown" to her, as I was originally hired by Ian for The Sunday Times and worked as his assistant there for several years. As for my Life of Ian Fleming, the reader will soon discover that far from being just 'a bit of Bond fantasy' it was a solidly researched account of the whole of his extraordinary life and career. Re-reading my references to Ann I find it quite incomprehensible why she found them so objectionable. Presumably remorse, which I hadn't thought afflicted her. And of course she found everything to do with poor old Bond vulgar and more or less contemptible.'

To Lord Campbell

16 Victoria Square   13 April [1967]

Dear Lord Campbell

Since Peter Fleming agrees to the counterfeit Bond, I am prepared to accept his judgement. Though my distaste for the project is in no way altered.

I think Amis should publish under his own name and show the world that his left-wing intellectual pretensions were easily turned to money grubbing – like everyone else.

Yours sincerely,

Ann Fleming

1 Lord Campbell pointed out that he was no longer Chairman of Booker McConnell which had bought Bond and passed the 'unfriendly' letter on to Charles Tyrrell, who was.

The James Bond novel *Colonel Sun* by Robert Markham (Kingsley Amis) was published in 1968. Ann was asked to review it for the *Sunday Telegraph* but they refused to publish her review for fear of libel. An unfinished draft survives in which she accuses Amis of trying to cash in and finds the title, villain and jacket inferior to those of Fleming's novels. Errors are noted. Her theme is that Bond is humourless and non-political but that Amis is capable of being neither: 'Since the exploiters hope *Colonel Sun* will be the first of a new and successful series, they may find themselves exploited. Amis will slip "Lucky Jim" into Bond's clothing, we shall have a petit bourgeois red-brick Bond, he will resent the authority of M, then the discipline of the Secret Service, and end as a Philby Bond selling his country to SPECTRE. James to Jim to Kim.'

Amis answered the questions about his motives in an essay, 'A New James Bond', written in 1968 and collected in *What became of Jane Austen*, 1970: 'Why do it? . . . well, yes, I do indeed expect to make quite a lot of money out of the venture and jolly good luck to me . . . What at the outset was an unimportant motive but has since developed into a major fringe benefit, is the thought of how cross with me the intellectual left will get . . . Enough of negatives: I consider it an honour to have been selected.'

To Nicholas Henderson

Sevenhampton Place   5 May [1967]

Dearest Nico

There's an awful fuss going on about *Encounter*, it appears that Stephen Spender did not know it was financed by CIA, very rum for everyone else did.

Natasha [Spender] telephoned hysterically that Stephen's honour was at stake, I skipped the gist and said 'I'm sure you want Stephen and Frank Kermode[1] to see Lord Goodman', and having arranged this was unprepared for Stephen's condition when he flew over for a showdown meeting with Lasky[2] and A. Schlesinger[3] and came here for the night. It all seems to me mountains out of molehills, but everyone is excited. Cecil King who now owns the whole show, with no CIA money, wants to retain Lasky and Spender, but Spender is going unless Lasky resigns.[4] Considering the CIA is supposed to be a semi-secret service they get an awful lot of publicity – including the Greek revolution, which must be distressing to M.[5]

With much love to you both,

A

1 Professor Frank Kermode (1919–). Winterstoke Professor of English at Bristol 1965–7, Lord Northcliffe Professor of Modern English Literature at UCL 1967–74. Fellow of King's, Cambridge since then.

2 Melvin Lasky (1920–), co-editor of *Encounter*, remained.

3 Arthur Schlesinger (1917–). Writer. Schweitzer Professor of the Humanities at New York University since 1966.

4 Spender resigned as Editor in 1967.

5 Mary Henderson is Greek. The Colonels staged their coup in April 1967 and remained in power until 1974.

Ann took a villa in Sardinia for a holiday, 'an extravagance and a folly'.

To the Duchess of Devonshire

Liscia di Vacca (Smooth Cow), Sardinia   26 August [1967]

Darling Deborah,

No air and no rest here, pining for pals and the English climate. Though there has been much comedy. First morning two *Express* reporters up garden path and into bedroom, I was in bed sipping coffee but no make-up and curlers, very handicapping for they were brazen and beastly, and hunting for Jenkins; did not want to make matters worse for Roy, so coldly advised a search for front door.

Jenks arrived following day and we had an agreeable time with cheerful children, but next morn a flotilla anchored below our windows, the Snowdons and the Aga, better than the Derby through the field glasses but grisly for Roy, for reporters and police swarmed. Gloom set in and the Jenks fled, leaving older boy and bossy female friend. Temporary lull shattered by arrival of M. Bowra and further shattered by C. Connolly. Cyril made fearfully restless by vicinity of Snowdons, saying not to meet them was like being in Garden of Eden without seeing God! Local tycoon then called and invited me to dine with 'Margaret and Tony'. Cyril distraught! I corner tycoon and explain situation who invites all three of us. Dinner wholly successful owing to Maurice singing first world war songs and Lord S. being ill. Social scene grows tense on Highness's departure, she tells tycoon she has no plans for the morrow, he is filled with despair for the poor brute is lunching with me. I ask all to lunch, Cyril beams. Next morning Cyril rises at 11.30 and asks what I have ordered special for lunch, I say nothing since I can only communicate with Italians in deaf and dumb language, he scowls, and says did I notice what the Princess drank last night, I say no, he says it was white wine and martinis and may he go to hotel for the right stuff. I say yes, and have to pay enormous bill. Illustrious guests arrive, and since it is buffet I am the parlour maid; they stay till 3.30 and ask if they may return at 6.30 to record Maurice singing 1914 songs, I go to bed, they return at 5.30 from the sea and walk straight into my bedroom while I am struggling into skirt, they then have acrimonious discussion because she does not want to be alone while he water skis, finally he departs and we all talk daintily, then repair to her hotel swimming pool, where Maurice and I can watch Caspar kissing his first love in the distance,

Tony and R. O'Neill water ski-ing and best of all princess and Cyril in pool, Cyril looking like blissful hippo! She seems to have been marooned by the Aga who is gone to collect a new yacht.

Very mistral and hand slips, it was folly to come here because of finance, an impossible party to 'gel', and only have small car with no brakes. It would be OK without Cyril who complains of mosquitoes, food and climate, and only wants royalty and money; now he has met the Snowdons he dreams of being invited on the Aga's yacht saying wistfully 'but if I was, I might be expected to act charades on water skis'!

Do communicate – return on Sept 2nd.

Hope the grouse season was fun – oh, for lovely bracing moor weather.

Lots of love

A

To Hugo Charteris

16 Victoria Square   5 October [1967]

Darling Hugo

I am so very pleased that *The Times* published your appreciation of Papa.[1] I find it faultless, evocative of his unique personality and very moving. Aside from personal response, it is rare that there is anything in the obituary column except arid recapitulations of public service: so much so that I feared they would not print it. Lord Brownlow had to buy four square inches for Sachie Sitwell's appreciation of the late Lady B! So someone must have appreciated the uniqueness of the subject and the merit of the writing!

The reaction has indeed been awful, I guessed it would happen to you and I am only a bit recovered for the first time today – total inertia – it usually comes with sorrow – so insensible that mourning is no longer – it's a necessity for the nervous system. I get a pain in the throat and stomach but cannot cry till much later.

Enclosed Papa's last letter, which I would like returned, thought you would like to see it.

With much love and I am so pleased that you wrote it,

A

1 Guy Charteris had died on 21 September.

To Joan Rayner

Sevenhampton Place   26 October [1967]

Dearest Joan

Thankyou so much for writing to me – an insoluble depression set in, only lifting this week. Papa was mourned as you only can be if you have lived eighty-two years in a small community; the last days of schoolchildren bringing flowers to the door and general young neighbourliness was very touching.

Happily for my sanity the horror of the funeral was saved by Aunt Letty Benson refusing to allow her fifty-seven year old son[1] to read the lesson chosen by my stepmother and Papa's favourite: Ecclesiastes – 'and the silver cord shall be loosened and the golden bowl be broken'[2] – there is some line about the 'grinding ceasing', and Letty said it was the grinding of old men's teeth and very ugly and depressing; so by the time the Charterises and Bensons were through with wrangling the atmosphere was much more tolerable.

We had a Fred Warner beano at Victoria Sq., much confusion caused by Fred having to bring the Foreign Secretary and Financial Minister of Laos, he was here on an official visit but though the government arranged two lunch parties for him, they had left him to his own devices in the evening. He proved a minute coffee-coloured gentleman and more or less sat on my knee. He was very imperturbable considering the conversation ranged between much argument on jockey club law between Andrew and Col. Wigg,[3] and much Philby talk from the Editor of *The Sunday Times* and Raymond Carr. Colonel Wigg was a new guest, and seemed delighted when Debo asked him to tap her telephone.

This weekend the Quennells come, baby [Alexander] and all. The angel nurse from Laverton who appeared like a miracle to care for Papa is now with Quennell baby, I have to keep her in circulation till I feel like dying, it should not be difficult since someone is always in need of such a person. I turn a blind ear to Hugo's notion, that her loving kindness is due to sex starvation and it would be kinder to find her a lover – heaven forfend.

Much time is taken by friends requiring legal advice *gratis* from the patient Lord Goodman, Stephen is nearly set up with a counter-*Encounter*, James P.H. has been saved from some buggery scandal to do with soldiers not being consenting adults; and now Bill

Deakin seeks redress for the newspapers saying St Antony's College is a training ground for spies.

I struggle with Angus Wilson's novel,[4] and enjoy James's slave trade book,[5] it's amazing how well he writes considering he gets sillier and sillier.

The Quennells have now arrived, and Peter *totally* domesticated – when he is not feeding the dog he is feeding the baby!

With much love to you both and thankyou,

Ann

1 David, Earl of Wemyss, was in fact fifty-five.

2 'In the day when the keepers of the house shall tremble, and the strong men shall bow themselves, and the grinders cease because they are few, and those that look out of the windows be darkened. . . Or ever the silver cord be loosed, or the golden bowl be broken, or the pitcher be broken at the fountain, or the wheel broken at the cistern.' Ecclesiastes 12, 3–6.

3 George Wigg (1900–83). Labour MP 1945–67, Paymaster General 1964–7, life peer 1967. Lord Goodman had written in September 1966: 'George Wigg is fascinated by you but is not in love with you. It will take another meeting at least, but he spoke of you three times without prompting. . . He is not in the least sinister but hugely kind, gentle and dedicated and will – if allowed – become your slave.'

4 *No Laughing Matter*.

5 *Verandah*, 1964. Ann wrote to the Countess of Avon six weeks later, 'James Pope-Hennessy also shows signs of senility, he spends much time with Princess Alice, and told me she laughs exactly like Queen Victoria, how does he know?' Earlier she had reported that he had 'fallen in love with the Duke of Gloucester – thinks he should be made king at once, and insists he has the brains of Einstein and the wit of Voltaire'.

To Nicholas Henderson

Sevenhampton Place   4 November 1967

Dearest Nico

How's this for service? I have had a nice shuffly walk in the autumn leaves, and taken endless pains to endear myself to the shovellers and crested duck. It is long leave, Caspar and cousin are footling with fireworks and sawn-off shot guns, and no social life till Raymond and Sara Carr with four junior Carrs arrive tomorrow – so why not answer your marvellous letter?

Lord G. told me he was having a spot of trouble with Brer Brown[1] this week for sitting on the floor at the Spanish Embassy, which Brown's P.R.O. did not wish to get in the newspapers. It's an understatement of the saloon version, for it transpires that Princess Snowdon was giving her views on Gibraltar to her host Santa Cruz, but was so noisily and frequently interrupted by Brown that she finally said to him, 'Shut up', at which he was led away and placed on a chair but his balance being impaired by alcohol he slithered to the floor and remained horizontal until removed.

Personally I think whatever the provocation, princesses should not say 'Shut up' to foreign secretaries, had I been in her tiny shoes I would have had him thrown down the stairs by the footmen.

. . . Collecting my nephew from the nautical college made one think about our dear old English traditions, an old sea captain who seemed in control risked bereaving parents and orphaning boys by exposing all parties to a bitter east wind for some mumbo jumbo called 'parade', it consisted of standing at attention with behinds stuck out until we were all blue with cold and someone blew a whistle. I had long since been tempted to yell 'Dismiss' but was prevented by Caspar.

With love,
A

1 George Brown (1914–85). Labour MP 1945–70, Foreign Secretary 1966–8, during which time his social exploits were much remarked. Created a life peer in 1970.

To Nicholas Henderson

Sevenhampton Place   12 May [1968]

Dearest Nico

Naples was best, and I should dearly have loved to continue with you and Mary to her native Greece. Rome was a bit lonely: Milton [Gendel] was entertaining an old army friend not seen for twenty years, a squat blonde moustached American of great dullness; he proved to be the Lieutenant Pinkerton who did not get away, for he had married his Japanese mistress, subsequently tried to escape, and she making a bosh shot at suicide was partially paralysed in speech and limb; they were a claustrophobic couple and, plus Caspar, filled Milton's ear so I avoided expeditions and did much botanising on the forum.

Seeing in a trice other company was necessary I boldly wrote to Nancy Shuckburgh[1] with your postcard. They were entertaining all Italian consuls, but we lunched with them the last day, and I found Evelyn delightful but was just as frightened of Nancy as I am of Pinky B. [Beckett]![2] Evelyn's enthusiasm for gardening is of course very sympathetic, and he let Caspar have a good grub for tiles under Nero's aquaduct.

I have been long in writing, because constantly on the move. Paris fun, then drove with J. Craxton[3] across Wales and ferried to Ireland and the Devonshires' romantic Lismore – very agreeable. Then a second trip to Paris to try on a frock or two; and was plunged into the student riots. It was icy cold, pouring rain, a taxi strike, and impossible to approach the metro without stinging eyes from pervading tear gas. Barricades seem a national French inheritance – great black police vans blocking all avenues to the Arc de Triomphe, fences that appear to be gold (they have a lot of it!) and on wheels drawn across smaller streets, great numbers of formidable hostile police with plastic shields guarding *Figaro* and *Match* offices. One night it was impossible to return to base at the Avenue d'Iéna, and I had to go back to the Seine, and saw the student procession at the end of their 35-kilometre march – they looked tired, young, and beautiful.

But what of the London scene, and dear Enoch Powell, and poor Heath, and in the future a Conservative majority with a most alarming lack of leaders, at least no one we can love let alone revere!

Paddy's 'I Tatti'[4] sounds less comfortable than Berenson's, the Quennells were very happy there but Peter did say the water was hot only once a week, and his towel was never changed or wastepaper basket emptied. The bated breath is correct since the architectural amenities continue, Paddy's latest ploy being an Alma Tadema marble gazebo.

Love to you both,

A

---

1 Nancy Brett (1918–) married in 1937 Evelyn Shuckburgh (1909–) who was knighted in 1959 and appointed Ambassador to Italy 1966–9.
2 Her sister, Priscilla Beckett (1921–) who married in 1941 the architect Martyn Beckett.
3 John Craxton (1922–). Painter, now living in Crete.
4 Leigh Fermor was building himself a house in the Mani in southern Greece.

To Nicholas Henderson

[Sevenhampton Place?]   27 October [1968]

Dearest Nico

Friday was a purification day with Lucian round the galleries –
especially the delights of Balthus at the Tate. Purification was
necessary, because of 'Keeping up with the Goodmans' – perhaps I
should look out for a retired M.F.H. Anyway, the last event in my
new set was dining at the Bank of England, without Goodman,
since it was me the Governor[1] had fallen for – sensible man.
Unluckily the occasion coincided with Peter Q.'s cocktail party to
launch *Alexander Pope*[2] which left me but ten minutes to drive
down the foggy foggy embankment to the Old Lady of Thread-
needle Street. This seemed an impregnable fortress markedly lacking in friendly open doors, and no place to circle in a long evening
dress; just as it assumed a Kafkaesque situation a porthole was
opened and flunkey peered out, then with caution opened a slice of
the street wall from which emerged a sad clerk with briefcase. He
proved friendly and said the Governor's flat was in the new building
and he would walk me there, he did not say it would take fifteen
minutes, so I arrived among the higher echelons of financial power
in a bedraggled and apologetic condition.

Only the British could have spent so much money on such bad
taste as was revealed by the Governor's apartments, ill-propor-
tioned rooms, thick stucco pillars, dirty cream walls and cretonne
covers. Between the pillars a philistine from the Ministry of Works
had chopped exquisite Chinese wallpapers and pasted at random;
the dining-room had horrific modern paintings, at least I think they
were horrific, but the brilliance of the spotlighting made it difficult
to judge.

On my left was Lord Thomson of Fleet Street. Knowing Roy
Thomson detests Arnold because he acted for the *Observer* in the
Times deal, I said to him 'Do say something bad about Lord
Goodman'; this he was cagily loath to do, but under pressure he
warmed to the theme. Alack, he took this frivolous conversation
seriously and next day sought Arnold out at a horrid public lunch
and besought him not to believe anything I recounted. Arnold took
this equally seriously and was quite put out. Oh, dear, these
ambitious establishment people are grisly.[3]

Leslie O'Brien I like very much, and intend to get him to Vic. Square, though he must grow up a bit more and not shake like a leaf when I tell Roy Thomson he should have married Jackie Kennedy.

Freddy Ashton's new ballet, *Enigmas*,[4] must be seen by you and Mary. Freddy has most perfectly evoked the tranquillity of late summer, a touch of Chekhov, a touch of mystery, a little magic. I was entranced, and think the critics carping who infer one cannot dance in a bustle, for somehow this did not detract from a small work of art. Robin Fedden and I left *Hair*[5] after the first act, it should be called *Noise* or *Dirt*, the youthful cast can neither dance, nor sing, nor act, they are neither shocking, nor obscene, nor beautiful. Caspar and co. have no wish to see it. A better night was *The Relapse*,[6] real wit, Mark [Bonham] Carter laughing one side and Martyn Beckett[7] the other.

Fionn is with me, and the leaves fall. Much bulb planting but I cannot remember the pattern from last spring.

With much love to you both

A

1 Leslie O'Brien (1908–   ). Governor of the Bank of England 1966–73. Made a life peer in 1973.

2 *Alexander Pope: the Education of a Genius 1688–1728* by Peter Quennell, 1968.

3 Lord Goodman, unaware of any detestation by Roy Thomson, is confident that no recognisable version of this conversation took place.

4 *Enigma Variations* with music by Elgar had its first night on 25 October.

5 The American 'tribal love-rock musical' had opened in September and ran for almost two thousand performances.

6 *The Relapse* by John Vanbrugh had been a great personal success for Donald Sinden as Lord Foppington.

7 Sir Martyn Beckett (1918–   ). Architect, painter, pianist, remarkable shot. Chairman of the Wallace Collection and Trustee of the British Museum.

To Clarissa Avon

Sevenhampton Place, Wilts.   27 February [1969]

Dearest Clarissa

Your letter cheered – very necessary since the world turned upside down when ten days ago your godson terminated his career at Eton and vanished for twelve unbearably long hours. The housemaster found a revolver in his room, told C. he would say nothing about it this time, subsequently got cold feet and reported it to Chenevix-Trench [the headmaster]. The latter had flu' and, being unable to beat, reported it to the police without telling me. I was livid with rage, for I think it monstrous not to tell or consult the parent before invoking the law. The authorities were very surprised that C. refused to divulge the name of the boy who had sold him the gun, but with the aid of Peter Fleming the incident was closed; next night Caspar vanished. . . . Anyway he was retrieved, and is now recovered from the shock – but what do we do next? He was never sacked because not minding about leaving books, like Lord John Hope, I merely telephoned the housemaster and said 'Caspar has returned and that will be that', banging down the receiver. Last holidays he was white and in tears a great deal of the time, and dreading 'A' levels, though his report was wonderful and he was expected to do very well: somehow he felt under pressure, and is now talking all the trendy nonsense of his generation, anti-materialism and all sorts of nonsense.

Worse has followed, C. sold another gun to —, who was arrested last Saturday for having cannabis and firearms and promptly told the police that C. had other weapons. These weapons had been given over to Peter Fleming and I had thought no more of them. Two days ago I was lying here with a temp. of 102, when in stalked two detective sergeants acting on the information, so now it looks as if Peter, Caspar and me will all be in Wormwood Scrubs when you return.[1] [unfinished]

1 Peter Fleming locked up the weapons except for a Browning automatic which he curiously chose to drop down a well at his house. He then told the police it was there and was fined £30 for illegally possessing firearms and ammunition. Ann told Nicholas Henderson that when Caspar came before the juvenile court and was fined £25 'he was tried by three olive-skinned hook-nosed men with ugly ears and missing teeth, they looked like Bond villains'.

To Nicholas Henderson

Sevenhampton Place   11 May [1969]

Dearest Nico

London is recovering from an invasion of provincial Texan etc. American millionaires who call themselves the 'International Members of the Museum of Modern Art'. We started with a not wholly swinging party given by Lord Goodman at the Arts Council, and ended on a draughty river steamer heading for Tower Bridge, hired by 'Fifty-seven Varieties' Heinz;[1] when we disembarked ten charabancs were waiting to drive us fifty yards to an ancient hall approached by fifteen steps, and a fiddler fiddling on each step. The edifice seemed part of a students' hostel, and there was a furious female student face at every window, or else contorted with laughter, as the middle-aged wended their way up the stairs to the fiddling, all blue with cold or pink with drink. 'Is this not a trifle ridiculous?' said Lord G., panting more than slightly.

In fact it was great fun because there was a nucleus of jolly English souls, Antrim, Alan Ross, Robin Fedden etc., who much enjoyed themselves and paid scant attention to the wealthy foreigners. My neighbour at dinner said he had 600 paintings, 'mainly pop and minimal art'.

This is dashed off amidst birdsong and the hideous prospect of London tomorrow. I dislike it more and more, but might grow very eccentric alone here.

Old peer on Lady Chatterley debate: 'I don't care if me wife and daughters read it, it's me gamekeeper I don't want to get 'old of it.'
Much love to you both

A

1 Henry John (Jack) Heinz II (1908–   ). Chairman of H. J. Heinz Company since 1959.

Charles Ritchie, a Canadian diplomat, provides a contemporary account of one of Ann's parties in *Storm Signals*, 1983.

5 June 1969

... Home, and a quick change, and to Ann Fleming's party. Literary figures, a don or two, and Andrew Devonshire. Our hostess, Ann, looks sadder and more human since her husband Ian Fleming's death. Diana Cooper, in a pyjama suit, greeted me in joke tones of thrilling sincerity. In the next room Elizabeth and Stuart Hampshire stood murmuring by the bar. The writer Leslie Hartley sat on a sofa like a giant panda, being patted and petted, making mumbling and inconclusive sounds. He is loved by all. Our hostess, in grey and diamonds, was alternately pert and pensive. Of herself she said: 'In my youth I did what I wanted and never knew guilt. Women's frustrations are different and simpler than those of men, and come from not getting what they want, usually something quite uncomplicated – a husband, a lover, a home, children – but men suffer from not knowing what or whom they want.'

To Nicholas Henderson

Kardamyli, Messenia   [Summer 1969]

Dearest Nico

Land travel is so demoded and degraded that all strength has been needed to survive.

Mary's country makes Italy a painted old Harridan. We motored from Patras to Olympia, thence here. The Greek Colonels are working like mad on the roads, and it took half the anticipated time. We should have a yacht one year. I could spend many a day gazing at chrome-coloured mountain peaks melding with the pale sky. To me, the Greek mountains seem without threat and all legends credible.

Our journey to Rome was companioned by four *jeune filles en fleur americaines*, they painted their toenails with nasty-smelling varnish, never looked from the window; one said 'The round trip to Capri was value for money, and we had a really scary bus drive.' A further busload of them at Olympia talked throughout lunch of their salaries.

Paddy has melded cloistered passages, long cool rooms, paved garden round olive trees, quite perfectly with the landscape. He has achieved his plethora of stone tables in shady nooks for authors, at one of which yours truly is sitting sipping thick sweet coffee and staring at the unpolluted sea. The author himself has not time to write at his stone tables, for he is building his private Belvedere where he will wield the pen in privacy and shade. Joan is doubtful.

We dine on the terrace above the sea where Paddy's experiments with lighting coincide with peasants bearing food, and we are all suddenly plunged in Stygian dark, and Joan's shrieks of 'Oh, Paddy' grow more doleful.

Portofino bathing was horrible, the day after my arrival all beaches closed between us and Genoa because of pollution, the day after opened again, such outcry from those who make a living from cabinos and giving people a chance to contract typhoid. Stormy weather cleared the Portofino beach of crawling foul humanity, but my solitary swim was rewarded by an untimely wave wafting an old French letter into my mouth.

Do hope so much, dearest Nico, you are better. God willing, home on Aug. 2nd – see you soonest.

Much love to you both

A

To Lady Berlin

Sevenhampton Place   5 August 1969

Dearest Aline,

Greece was not propitious for writing letters, hence the long delay in thanking you for a holiday which was really a holiday. The first for ten years without tension. Other moments at Portofino have been memorable and fun, but not since the original visit have I been relaxed. This in no way reflects on the Berlins, who for many years now have been the greatest solace, but on other persons imported, or being responsible for nieces etc.

The rest of the travel was successful, Caspar a wonderful companion: we both enjoyed the Brindisi ferry and the drive across Greece, though Greece was marred for me by the extreme heat and dining out of doors every night. It's a disagreeable sensation to be very hot and very damp. Isaiah would not have enjoyed it.

The Leigh Fermors' house is a triumph. Paddy is a much better architect than writer. The stone, the wood, the water, and the marble came from vast distances and a mini Xanadu constructed. It includes stone tables under shady olives designed to inspire a spate of writing, but Paddy is only inspired to further vistas and fountains, and Joan wails at approaching bankruptcy.

I hope Abano does Isaiah much good, and you have a tranquil happy time in no way marred by You Know Who.[1] You Know Who will never go to the Leigh Fermors, not, I think, because of the Colonels, but because he has no longer the physical health for so arduous a journey, the last half mile being on foot through impenetrable scrub, the descent to the beach 24 uneven stone steps and though the bathing is perfect I suspect he prefers a table where he can shout *'Vino subito'*.

With love to you both and thankyou very much.

Ann

PS. Laura now says she does not mind the Duke of Marlborough but cannot stand the *Son et Lumière* at Blenheim. I have advised her to marry and make it her life's work to close the place to the public.

1 Sir Maurice Bowra.

To Nicholas Henderson

Sevenhampton Place   25 October [1969]

Dearest Nico

Dusk falls, and I prepare to have a strong drink and depart for Swindon town Hall to hear Paul Channon[1] speak: only seven days to polling day.

The civic sense (mostly dormant) that took me to the Brighton Conference did not deter me from making the most of the weather and spending much time in the Pavilion, on the pier or in the antique shops. The Gilmours and [Sara and Charles] Morrisons kindly invited me to lunch. Ian G. was white and strained and released from hospitalisation for ulcers. Both Gilmours and Morrisons seem far to the left of our Labour pals, indeed Robin Day[2] had to point out to Ian G. that if he attended Conservative conferences he must expect to find one Conservative, this being me. It took me some time to soothe and calm the luckless candidate for Swindon, whose nerve was entirely broken by encounters with Katie Macmillan[3] and Sara Morrison.

Last Sunday, I *very very* mildly and for the first time criticised the CHANCELLOR [Roy Jenkins], I *only* said that if they brought in a wealth tax then everything I loved and to which he was not averse would end – e.g. country houses and large tracts of unspoiled countryside; that Squire Eyston probably protected much of the beauty of East Hendred. I had hoped Jennifer was out of earshot, but no, she interceded with alarming vehemence; naturally I retreated since I have always recognised the sea green incorruptibility of the female of the species! She is far more formidable than Roy, not handicapped by the wish to please.

The attack was provoked by the poverty of 'Quonnolly', Quennell and their ilk, who cannot pay such high income tax and are also allowed no overdraught [*sic*], but Jennifer's interruption prevented a further onslaught.

Much love to you both, it's more fun when you are at home – missing you.

Love

A

1 Paul Channon (1935–   ). Conservative MP since 1959. Opposition Spokesman on the Arts 1967–70, Minister for the Arts 1981–3, Minister for Trade since 1983.
2 Robin Day (1923–   ). Television and radio journalist. Knighted 1981.
3 Katharine Ormsby-Gore (1921–   ). Married in 1942 Maurice Macmillan, son of the Prime Minister and Conservative MP.

To Patrick Leigh Fermor

Sevenhampton Place   7 November [1969]

Darling Paddy

It's awfully rum having a house full of teenagers. I had anticipated a joyful period but the age gap is too great, and it's permanent stress organising meals, transport, and trying to offset their modish gloom. I worship Caspar but nothing he does adds to peace of mind. Last weekend we had Dick Wyndham's granddaughter, Catherine Guinness,[1] who I feared might be shocked by permissiveness, but she was studying the Marquis de Sade for her 'A' level in philosophy and was well up to the level of conversation – or down, whichever way you look at it!

Mark Bonham Carter is preventing Judy from publishing those

letters [from Asquith to Venetia Stanley] – very beastly of him, and becoming a '*cause célèbre*'; the blow has had a curiously enlivening effect on Judy, who has been suffering a period of ten-minute delay between words, and now seems all brisked up and ready for battle.

I have seen nobody nice since Joan left, and have spent much time winning Swindon for the Conservatives,[2] for Jenkins's threat of a wealth tax would mean the end of country-house life, though these were not the words I used on the doorsteps of council house estates.

It was an experience driving old persons to the poll, who are fated to live in faceless houses miles from shop, pub – *sans* anything. It's strange the planners don't plant a pub here and there.

'Berlioz and the Romantic Tradition' is the best exhibition ever – a corner devoted to a bloodstained tricolour and burning buildings, plus revolutionary noises; marvellous portraits of Byron, Chateaubriand, paintings by Turner and Géricault, Berlioz background music, and the whole depicting just the age for us.

I am very out of touch, and will write a better bulletin soon: depression is in the ascendant, induced by having to pass what Kingsley Amis has written about Ian for the *Dictionary of National Biography*, and being assailed by the BBC for material for the *Omnibus* programme they are doing on Ian – I want to kick them all and burst into tears. Improbably, the Beatles have put my quandary into words – a song that goes

> I want to be at the bottom
> of the sea
> In an octopus's garden in the shade[3]

How do the Beatles know octopuses have gardens? I thought only I knew that, there must be more to them than meets the ear.

With much much love and a better bulletin soon

A

1 Catherine Guinness (1952–) was to marry in 1983 Ann's cousin Lord Neidpath and live at Stanway. Her mother Ingrid Wyndham was married 1951–63 to Jonathan Guinness and in 1963 to Paul Channon.

2 The Conservatives won the bye-election at Swindon and the election next year, which brought in Edward Heath as Prime Minister.

3 'I'd like to be
   Under the sea,
   In an octopus's garden in the shade.'
'Octopus's Garden' on the record *Abbey Road*.

To Lord Campbell

16 Victoria Square   19 November [1969]

Dear Lord Campbell

I am in a quandary about the *Omnibus* programme, which I understand you are taking part in. I had very much hoped it would be confined to Ian's old friends: those whom he met after his first illness were of a different category.

It makes it difficult for me to give Mr Cordern photographs etc. unless you are going to tell the truth – how much money you made out of him.[1]

Ann Fleming

1 For Booker McConnell, who bought half of Ian Fleming. *See* notes on pp. 372, 383.

To Nicholas Henderson

Sevenhampton Place   24 December [1969]

Dearest Nico

We had a very drunken *soirée* at Victoria Sq., F. Bacon, Sonia Orwell,[1] R. Fedden very abusive to each other about 'Pinkville':[2] I tried awfully hard to change topic and never before realised how cross drunks get if you do this thing to them – like taking a bone from mad alsatians. French lady, unknown to me and imported by Francis; she is organising a retrospective exhibition of his paintings at the Grand Palais; he is the first English painter to have such an honour bestowed upon him, tho' I should think the occasion is in some jeopardy now.

Elizabeth Longford was suddenly totally lovable and very pathetic at the Weidenfeld Wellington Beano.[3] She looked frail and was clearly in considerable pain from her motor accident. George had been horribly successful in collecting military figures to grace the occasion. I got Field Marshal Sir Gerald Templer who was sadly unlike the great Duke of Wellington, and did not seem to appreciate me or Lady Hartwell, and seemed to fear us more than a German tank regiment.

The real depression is because Hugo has cancer, operable but beastly. I have been in Yorkshire with V. and the children, she was with Hugo in hospital all day and since they have no domestic help and no central heating, it was indeed an ordeal. I was so tired that the dread news is only now realised. Hugo had a permanent jaundice for six weeks, they operated in York, and now he has been moved to London and another op. as soon as he is strong enough.

Not to end on a grim note I dined with Gay and Martin [Charteris] for the Annenberg ball.[4] First to arrive, they apologetically said 'it's only "household"', not cheering news, but it seemed I was to get the husband of Lady S. Hussey.[5] This suited since he is Managing Director of the *Daily Mail*, but we were swept asunder because, as Gay told me afterwards, she thought it would be embarrassing for me to meet anyone to do with that newspaper!

The Annenbergs' idea of an English supper was curried prawns, steak and kidney pud., cherries in brandy. Lord Goodman did it justice.

I do miss you, why not come and cheer the winter solstice?

Much love and best wishes for the next decade

A

1 Sonia Brownell had worked on *New Writing* for John Lehmann and on *Horizon* for Cyril Connolly. She married George Orwell, whom she described as the only intellectual she knew who could mend a fuse, in October 1949, three months before his death. She died in 1980.

2 There had been allegations of a massacre of Vietnamese by the American army for some time and Lieutenant Calley had been charged with 109 murders in November.

3 For *Wellington; Years of the Sword* by Elizabeth Longford, 1969.

4 Leonore Colm married in 1951 Walter Annenberg (1908–). He was American Ambassador in London 1969–74 and popularised the word 'refurbish'.

5 Lady Susan Waldegrave married in 1959 Marmaduke Hussey (1923–). He was Managing Director of Harmsworth Publications 1967–70, joined the Thomson Organisation in 1971 and has been a director of *The Times* since 1982.

To Nicholas Henderson

Sevenhampton Place   9 August 1971

Dearest Nico

I have hesitated to write because since early June I am infested with microbes, and have mainly lain abed with a low fever. The local doc. says no antibiotic is absorbed by the system if one takes any alcohol at all; this is (as you know better than me) the *last* straw. Gloom drove me to swilling down the pills with more and more alc., even a spot of brandy for elevenses, to help slight nausea.

It is just 6 o'clock so, sober as a judge and wholly suicidal, I write to you. It's impossible not to write in the mood, tho' one can put on an act for an hour or two with friends actually present, hence the long silence.

Roy and Jennifer came to lunch ten days ago. He is so popular a hero that neighbours came from all round to touch the hem of his robe. They brought a young Labour MP[1] who was in a depression, supposed to be an ace tennis player he took to the woods and by 5.30 his wife feared he was drowned. Roy can ill afford to lose any of his team, so it was a relief when he was discovered sitting mournfully behind one of the urns.

I dined with Caroline [Somerset][2] for the Northumberland hop. The Duke's sitting room was furnished with half a bottle of Haig so he, Paddy L. F. and myself fared well, and it was after midnight when the terrifying noise of the upper class baying for drink reached our ears, and the Duchess appeared white and frightened and implored Hughie to do something about it. He did singularly little, two bottles of whisky were produced, and later when Caroline tried to take one from Peter Coats[3] he gave a low masculine growl of rage. There was nothing to eat but cold plastic sausages.

I rarely see Hughie [Northumberland], but he is clearly a most eccentric nobleman these days. As the night progressed he unlocked various elegant pieces of furniture, and there stowed away were bottles, or half-bottles or half-empty bottles of whisky, these were shared with me, Paddy, and W. Douglas-Home;[4] they all sang Harry Lauder songs, and as we were several drawing rooms and galleries away from the starving thirsty masses, we had a most agreeable evening.

I took my germ to Chatsworth, thinking it would cheer to be with Robin Fedden and Paddy, and watch the start of the practise walk for the Andes. Now that Andrew has given up drink he can't stop walking, and was taking the journey so seriously that he said he thought an orange each was all they should take on the Derby Dales. Robin and Paddy looked awfully downcast, they had anticipated a ducal picnic. Bacon sandwiches was a compromise.

The last news of the expedition was that Renée Fedden had felt the height most and had to return to Lima to acclimatise. I had expected her to be nursing them all.

How lovely it will be to see you all in September. It's much nicer when you are at home. I have heard no news for ages. Roy was delighted with your telegram. Are you well? Can you drink? Or shall we take one orange on a picnic?

With much love to you both,

A

1 Michael Barnes (1932–). Labour MP 1966–74, helped form SDP 1981, rejoined Labour Party 1983.

2 Lady Caroline Thynne (1928–) married in 1950 David Somerset who succeeded as Duke of Beaufort in 1984.

3 Peter Coats (1910–). Gardener and journalist; published his autobiography *Of Generals and Gardens* in 1976.

4 William Douglas-Home (1912–). Playwright. *The Reluctant Debutante*, 1955; *Lloyd George Knew My Father*, 1972.

To Nicholas Henderson

Sevenhampton Place   11 December [1971]

Dearest Nico

Sir Edward and Lady Hulton were reincarnated, giving an astonishing party at the Ambassadors' Club, Park Lane. A band was playing most excellent charlestons and other tunes recalling the glorious past, by luck I happened upon George [Jellicoe] and the years seemed to slide away – or anyway for me!

The Hultons are clients of Arnold's, hence my presence, usually their invites go straight to the wastepaper basket. I was driven from his side by maggots – to whit a host of flatterers and power-loving snobs who don't know Rhodesia from a hole in the ground, e.g. R. von Hofmannsthal, Whitney Straight and other beasts pawing Arnold.[1]

Invited to dine out of the blue at Downing Street, I put off old friends, and putting on my best evening frock toddled off to the hub of power. It was a great feast for the P.M. of Singapore and his better half. I hope you will be very sympathetic when you hear that all efforts to 'identify' with Margaret Thatcher[2] and John Davies[3] were frustrated by the Croslands attaching themselves to me like limpets on a rock.

There were some forty persons present, but not enough to deafen Tony announcing that he understood all the evenings at Downing Street were musical, so could it be arranged he could watch 'Miss World' on television. After dinner I engaged Mrs Singapore in polite conversation, joined by Susan;[4] on the departure of the Singapores Mr Heath joined us, and we were all three fascinated by the interior decorating of Chequers and Downing St when Susan turned white and said 'Something terrible has happened to my husband', and there was Tony, swaying more than slightly, and breaking into complaint of the misty vision of the television, and dinner lasting so long he had missed 'Miss World'. I did not blame Ted for an abrupt departure to more conventional groups of guests!

It seems Jellicoe and John Fowler are decorating Chequers, which is a very good thing.

Why, oh why, did I not write before? I have a cold and Christmas looms. Nanny is too old for so much cooking, and in black sulks because a male Cambridge undergraduate is coming to help.

This comes with much love and wishes to you all, and hope for news.

Ann

1 Lord Goodman had been to Rhodesia in November with Sir Alec Douglas-Home, who had reached an agreement with Ian Smith which was later found unacceptable to the mass of Rhodesians.

2 Margaret Thatcher (1925–) was Secretary of State for Education and Science at the time.

3 John Davies (1916–). Conservative MP from 1970, President of the Board of Trade 1970–2.

4 Susan Barnes, an American journalist, married Anthony Crosland in 1963 and published his biography in 1982.

To Patrick Leigh Fermor

Sevenhampton Place   4 March 1972

Darling Paddy

I did enjoy your letter, do stick to the new handwriting – it's such a joy to read easily.

Thankyou very very much for the strangely indecent duck caller, it looks like an instrument found in a brothel or torture chamber. It's the cry of the female for the male, they will be awfully disappointed when they find me. 'He ducks' are silent, female ducks 'quack'. So far it has been used mostly indoors for the sake of the soothing noise, but when the weather grows clement and the mating season starts, it will be a still greater joy.

The power cuts induced sleep, one can read with four candles but not flounder around in the chill for writing materials. This is the first Saturday eve with heat and light. I am told people were enraged when the television went off, but in my limited circle of antique retainers a crisis seems to boost winter morale.

The Connollys came to dinner in company with Robert and Lady Caroline deed poll Lowell,[1] P. Quennell, C. Sykes and after dinner three Miss Toynbees and escorts, two Miss Charterises and escorts. It was supposed to be cunningly arranged that the ancients would leave early and the young disport themselves, but at midnight Robert Lowell was lying on one of the beds in my room, Peter Q. on the other, a plentiful supply of claret and a tremendous exchange of Baudelaire quotes, Lady Caroline and Deirdre [Connolly] hanging around them. It was happy downstairs with Mortimer and Sykes, but, alas, it was all no good to Cyril who had desired Conservative ministers and smart people, he was also the only sober person and left alone very early.

Only other social effort was Lord Carrington[2] coming to dinner, and only minutes before he arrived did I realise that it was impossible to ask him if the 'Paras' had lost their heads in Derry. I had anticipated asking him for weeks! Despite this he was such a combination of wit, charm and information that it was quite difficult to turn two thirds through dinner to Michael Stewart[3] – so you see what a standard he set! He don't seem to care for the Stormont Government, and said that when he went to talk to them – early evening – they were all drunk and their behaviour very unlovable; until then he was not anti. He also told me that Mrs Mintoff was born Cavendish-Bentinck,[4] daughter of admiral commanding the Mediterranean fleet, but now estranged. His first visit to Heath at Chequers he invited the estranged Cavendish-Bentinck to a reconciliation tea without warning his host, who, though he has many qualities, is not experienced in 'pouring out' and being a marriage guide.

Oh dear, too much to say, and have just said sad farewells to Francis Grey, who has been posted to the Bogside. Nine months in the ranks ahead of him, and no leave or wandering around. Nil but riot drill and barrack life. I feel guilty although the army was his choice. His loneliness very apparent tonight.

Feeling against exposing the army to IRA hardening in all political parties, but no one has a solution. Raymond's garage blown up – no loss of life, also Antrim bus stop and two bombs in Randalstown. I wish he would send the children over here. I only don't fuss when I am there.

Robin Fedden ruined the Carrington evening by being far too drunk far too soon. I love him but he has an ancient mariner quality, and long before the men left the dining-room he had prevented any sensible talk by howling like a banshee about 18th-century architecture; I understand that Michael Stewart got quite cross, for all would have sooner talked to Peter Carrington but Robin *would* interrupt. Only comedy was Andrew proudly sober, and for *once* captain of the team who helped Susan[5] take him home.

Will really try to write a sober news bulletin soon.

Could we really come to Greece, to Mani, at earliest August? Will seek advice on getting car for Rachel [Toynbee] to drive Caspar about and long to loll with Joan and you.

Much love to both

A

1 Lady Caroline Blackwood married the poet Robert Lowell (1917–77) in October 1972 when his divorce from Elizabeth Hardwicke was finalised.

2 Lord Carrington (1919–   ) was Secretary of State for Defence at the time.

3 Michael Stewart (1911–   ). Ambassador to Greece 1967–71, Director of Ditchley Foundation 1971–6, director of Sotheby's since 1976. Knighted 1966.

4 Moyra de Vere Bentinck married in 1947 Dom Mintoff, Prime Minister of Malta from 1971.

5 Susan Bligh married William (Bill) Stirling in 1940 and died in 1983.

To Nicholas Henderson

Sevenhampton Place   16 March [1972]

Dearest Nico

I am really sad you are not to be in England, sad for you and selfishly sad.[1]

Tomorrow I go to Bruern,[2] it's Lord Goodman's ideal country outing; the Carters and Jenkins also there. So I turned down the long drive to Chequers and the Pompidou, but think it a bad sign of advancing years to dread the long drive, solitary in evening wear.

Wednesday was the Marlborough funeral,[3] Thursday I opened the Goldfinger Tavern in Highworth. The Highworth Mummers were dressed as Oddjob etc., stills from the film on the wall, and all the theme songs played loud on tape! I had imagined a more simple ceremony, and was so unnerved I unveiled the inn sign too hurriedly, and pulled the veiling all over my head.

My sister had taken to being a duchess and living in a palace, and to be deposed after six weeks is not to her liking. The new Duke will have great difficulty in deposing her. She gazes towards Woodstock and murmurs about 'my people'!

Mr and Mrs Charles Morrison drove me in the slow motorcade from Woodstock Church to Bladon Churchyard, Mrs M. reviling the aristocracy all the way. At the subsequent baked meats she was in a huddle with Ian Gilmour, finding a seat for him etc., and I talked to Charlie. The baked meats were mercifully short because the majority of mourners were on their way to Cheltenham races.

With much love

A

1 Henderson's next appointment was as Ambassador to the Federal Republic of Germany 1972–5.

2 Michael Astor's house near Burford. Patrick Leigh Fermor remembers one occasion there:

Annie drove over to luncheon to spend the day. Rain came down in buckets and the afternoon offered so bleak a prospect that Pandora barred the shutters, drew the curtains, piled logs high in the hearth, lay us all out on cushions round the flames, turned out the lights and put on the overture of a Mozart opera. Then she flung blankets over us and we lay listening in the healing firelight. Hours later rain was still pouring down but we had all recovered, and, resurrecting at drink and lamplighting time, Annie said, 'That's the coziest *Fan Tutti* I've ever heard.'

3 The Duke of Marlborough had died shortly after Laura Charteris married him.

Leigh Fermor recalls Ann's next visit to the Mani:

In August 1972 Ann and Casper they came again, with Rachel Toynbee this time, a charming girl Caspar was attached to, the most serious attachment in his short life. Xan and Daphne Fielding were here, and we explored the Mani and visited the ruins of ancient Messenia. 'I long to pinch all the bits of marble lying about,' Caspar said, pretending to linger with intent to put the wind up Ann and us. 'Just look at that lion's head! *Asking* for it!' I hurried him on. . . he had a passion for archaeology in all sorts of abstruse branches, and knew a great deal about it. The passion had followed his previous Bond-like craze for weapons, swordsticks, daggers, pistols, guns and even steel crossbows that sent glittering arrows whizzing at high speed across the croquet lawn at Sevenhampton and thudding into tree trunks. He had extraordinary adventures and scrapes chaffering over guns and artefacts, and heaven knows what else, with shady dealers in the attics and cellars of Soho. Was he nineteen or twenty then? He looked younger and rather frail and slender and pale with a few scattered freckles and thick dark curls, rather like an angry and vulnerable faun. He got very excited cleaning a Graeco-Roman funerary slab (which I had unearthed in one of the hill villages) with a solution of *aquaforte*, and made friends with a very nice American couple called Pomeroy, who were constantly hunting for fossils and remains; the wild-eyed husband had a theory that the Nile rose in Lake Chad.

We sat up late into the hot August nights playing the dictionary game; there was exciting rivalry and a lot of cheering in victory and tearing of hair in defeat. Caspar was wildly competitive and very good at it, which gave us a feeling of success and made Ann enjoy it too. (She *always* enjoyed things normally, but when Caspar was there, her anxiety about his pleasure dictated hers. It reminded me of the aria '*Dalla sua pace il mio dipende*' in *Don Giovanni*). He was deep in Egyptology and when he left, signed his name in the book in Egyptian hieroglyphics: beautifully drawn cartouches filled with sphinxes, palm leaves, ibises and galleys.

To Patrick Leigh Fermor

10 Holland Park   [21 March 1973]

Darling Paddy

This should be a 'Grovel' but it's a 'Wail'.

I can't get abreast of events, dull personal ones, like flu', Christmas, and a serious under-estimate of leaving Vic. Square.[1]

Some people take a year to move. After twenty years I gave a party and left in a week. Finally sitting on the floor beside a telephone, not even an ashtray! Cyril was a consoling presence among the books; Caspar's junior pals from Christies a bit alarming, since I had no notion of what they were stuffing in great brown paper bags for obscure sales.

This all leads to how bestial not to acknowledge thanks, and express true and due regard that you wrote so well of Judy.[2] Only you and Mark B.C. managed. All that were published were wrong, specially Colin Tennant.

Please forgive, but it arrived when I was submerged, with among other problems getting Arnold to take on the crumbs of Judy's inheritance and make them into mountains for Anna [her daughter]. It all already seems far away, a nasty time trick as one grows older.

I am here till June 1st, when I go to live on the top floor of Pamela Egremont's house, and am going to give parties in a huge bathroom! It was such a relief when she suggested it, for I hate London more and more, and this means no housekeeping and a stuffed owl in the hall.

Dont miss *Last Tango in Paris*.[3] I went to the first performance with Aline Berlin, who got last-minute nerves about being accosted by journalists when we came out: happily there was a woman of ninety who was plastered all over the *Evening Standard* saying she would sooner see *South Pacific*. The critics have stressed serious and not erotic. I found it very erotic because it was serious.

Forgive scrawl, it was a wish to Kommunicate with Kardamyli.

Much love to you and Joan

A

1 It had been sold for £50,000.

2 Judy Gendel had died on 8 November 1972.

3 *Last Tango in Paris*, directed by Bertolucci and starring Marlon Brando, was a *succès de scandale*.

To *Patrick and Joan Leigh Fermor*

Shane's Castle   6 February [1974]

Darling Paddy and Joan

Thanks awfully for the welcome contribution to the Gloom Book,[1] and a newsy letter.

Dignified and beautiful gloom you sent me – poetry gloom. Here at the moment in public life there seems little dignity (perhaps there never is!), chaos approacheth, and friend circles *shocked* by James's death.[2]

Though I had not seen much of James in recent years, because he was so drunken, we had tried to re-establish the old friendship in the last six months, mainly because Len Adams[3] was decorating and painting here, and James was the go-between. It was not a very successful effort, for poor James would switch off or start trembling, all the old fun and communication gone.

None the less the manner of his death induced in me a mood never suffered before, horrors, tensions and headaches. Of all Len's assistants the one I liked and talked to was Sean Seamus O'Brien; he adored the country, seemed a beautiful woodland creature, found birds' nests by instinct, shinned up tree trunks, was shy and good-mannered. *How* could he have murdered James?[4]

James met him in Ireland three years ago and I imagine brought him to London, apparently he was a frequent visitor to Ladbroke Grove, and that's why James let them in, the other two men are unknown to the heartbroken Len, and we presume to James. It's no good old Caspar saying that he is sure that when my back was turned Sean jumped up and down on the ducks' eggy-weggies, I simply don't believe he was like that. After much pondering I think I shall ask Jack Donaldson to visit Sean in prison, it would give Lord Longford too much pleasure! Anyway I can't let it rest. Doubtless there are many stories in circulation now, but I have been away from London. I don't want the underworld to get mixed up with C. because it is too too frightening.

John Pope-Hennessy[5] has gone to Italy. He looked very white and frozen at the Requiem Mass. I had never been to a Requiem Mass before, it was strange that James was not mentioned by name, the priest was most briefly in the pulpit speaking of 'a baby christened in the name of God – a life giving pleasure to many –

today we rejoice that he is united with God' – all a bit remote and impersonal.

A

1 The Gloom Book was started in 1963. Friends were invited to enter a favourite piece of gloomy prose or verse. The first entry is from Ian Fleming:
    Solitude becomes a lover,
    Loneliness a darling thing.
Patrick Leigh Fermor contributed two in Greek with translations: 'For there is nought more miserable than man of all the things that breathe or crawl upon the earth' from the *Iliad* and 'Alas, what are mortals but phantoms and insubstantial shadows?' from Sophocles' *Ajax*. Other contributors include Peter Quennell, John Sparrow, Robin Ironside, Lady Diana Cooper, Sir Stephen Spender, Leslie Hartley, Stuart Hampshire, James Pope-Hennessy, Edward Hussey, Noël Annan, John Gere and Mark Bonham Carter.

2 James Pope-Hennessy had been stabbed in his own house after being tied up.

3 Len Adams. 'Companionship, fortunately, James would never lack; he had many staunch friends. Of these the best, staunchest and most resolutely patient was that Homeric figure Len Adams, a native of Sheffield, one-time paratrooper and prisoner of war, whom he had happened to meet in a lift at Holland Park underground station in the early months of 1948 ... [he] became James's confidant, travelling companion, aide de camp, bodyguard, household help and general nanny, even in times of crisis, a limited privy purse.' Peter Quennell in the introduction to *A Lonely Business; A Self-Portrait* by James Pope-Hennessy.

4 Sean Seamus (later called John James) O'Brien had been charged with the murder on 28 January and was found guilty and sentenced to seventeen years in prison.

5 John Pope-Hennessy (1913–). Brother of James. Author and administrator. Director and Secretary of the Victoria and Albert Museum 1963–73, Director of the British Museum 1974–6. Knighted 1971.

To the Countess of Avon

Chatsworth   16 February [1974]

Dearest Clarissa
    John Pope-Hennessy said 'If only it had been an Agatha Christie, and not the Duchess of Malfi.' Arnold said I could have John to dine in his flat; it did not seem an occasion for a restaurant, and I feared John's inhibitedness, and that we might need television. Would that he had been more inhibited, for it started my nightmares again: an unusual state of horror-gloom since I heard the news. Much enhanced by the fact that Sean O'Brien painted the new spare room last summer, was gentle and charming and found bird's nests like a water diviner finds water.

Cristina Cholmondeley[1] has not eaten or slept since it happened, and Sybil[2] has asked me to lunch for a gossip. This I have declined by *pretending* to canvass in Swindon.

Oh dear, unlike everyone else and all the polls, I have a horrid hunch the Labour will win. Those beastly housewives and shopping-baskets, they put Heath in and I fear they will put him out.[3] When today's *Times* arrives in Portugal, you will see that this week the price of 'Carnation condensed milk', 'St Ivel Cheese Wedges' and 'Miracle Whip' has gone up – I am sure it *all* depends on that.

If, as I am vaguely led to believe, the election had been three weeks earlier, when Lord Carrington, Mrs C. Morrison, and Ian Gilmour etc. wanted, victory would have been certain. The Dunkirk spirit prevailed, no one exceeded 50 m.p.h., now on M4 it is *totally* disregarded, Negroes and Pakistanis pass one regardless, and lorries thunder. . .

Incoherent scribble but sent with love, and hope Anthony well. Tel. on return. Thanks p.c.

A

1 Cristina Solari married in 1957 Lord John Cholmondeley. She had been a great friend of James Pope-Hennessy.

2 Sybil Sassoon married the Marquess of Cholmondeley in 1913 and so is Lady John's mother-in-law.

3 Ann was correct and Harold Wilson became Prime Minister.

To *Patrick Leigh Fermor*

Sevenhampton Place   16 January [1975]

Darling Paddy

The earliest spring for fifty years, I glare at the primroses, and have missed frost and snow and exhilarating weather.

It seems tremendously strange that Cyril [Connolly] is no longer alive,[1] now that Caspar is a bit better I have realised the dread loss to Joan,[2] and considerable to me. At the time everything was minimal except the Swindon psychiatric ward, and from there to swallow brandy in the nearest pub.

Good news that Marilyn Quennell goes to the Bahamas for a holiday, I look forward to seeing much of Peter, tho' I wish the nipper [Alexander, his son, now six] kept earlier hours; they come next weekend and will be sharing a room!

Robert H. P. [Heber-Percy] says Daphne is being very brave and good about Xan and Magouche.[3] I hope Xan will be alright, I never could love Magouche like you do, she's a bit like the wolf in Red Riding Hood and might suddenly gobble one up.

Devastation at the end of the lake, an out-of-work bulldozer gave a cheap estimate for dredging reeds round the island, it sank in the slime and its insurance company sent a larger bulldozer to rescue it – alas, that also sank, and they looked like two sad dinosaurs. We all climbed over them and staggered about in the mud, and it was momentary winter entertainment. Then the army was called in, and produced a monumental piece of machinery with excessive horsepower and vast steel cables, and the dinosaurs were dragged over shrubs, box bushes, trees – and I am left with a First World War battlefield. Nothing for it but to build a bridge, as the holes left by the dinosaurs permit access to island. An engineer was summoned who built all the bridges over the M4. He was not very interested, and left saying 'It's a sort of willow pattern plate you want'. I doubt hearing from him again.

Do draw me a bridge, it's awfully good for people building bridges, and I need that kind of therapy.

A

1 Connolly had died on 26 November 1974.
2 Joan Leigh Fermor had known Cyril Connolly since the mid-1930s.
3 Alexander Fielding had left his wife Daphne for Magouche Phillips.

Caspar Fleming's involvement with drugs had become increasingly serious. Ann had first been aware of this late in 1973, but could not bring herself to take a very firm line. She nevertheless tried to prevent him being out of her sight for long. In August 1974 Caspar went out to Jamaica; while there he took an overdose, swam out to sea, and was only saved by luck and by the swift action of friends who summoned a helicopter from Kingston Hospital. Back in England he spent the next year in and out of institutions, and was never well for long. On 2 October 1975 he killed himself with another overdose. Ann was in the country, and so heard the news by telephone.

To Lady Diana Cooper

Sevenhampton Place   30 October [1975]

My darling Diana

We will never abandon each other. The last fifteen months have been nightmare. The best of the 'shrinks' described C's condition as 'malignant depression'. For my sake C. made efforts to come to terms with life, but lately he has never been other than despondent.

Do bring Nigel[1] for any weekend. I would love it.

You are always associated with the happiest times in my life.

Much love

Annie

1 Nigel Ryan (1929–). Then Editor and Chief Executive of Independent Television News. Lady Diana described him as 'the last attachment' but he was succeeded by Sir Robert Mayer who was 100 to her 86, enabling her to complain that he was too old for her. Ryan married in 1984 Susan Cavendish, who had been married to Quentin Crewe.

To Noël Annan[1]

6 November 1975

Darling Noël,

Thank you for your affection and your love, and the friendship I have enjoyed with you and Gaby for many years now. I particularly remember last summer's party that the girls gave for you, it was an oasis in a miserable time, though then I had not quite given up hope.

Caspar tried to come to terms with life, for my sake, and then suddenly could not try any more. The note he left said 'If it is not this time it will be next.' It was an act of will and the best analyst wrote to me what you did – at the moment there is no cure. I shall miss him forever, until a year ago he was a marvellous companion and more recently one's heart was anguished for there was no help one could give.

I wish you would both come and stay, and I will telephone.

Love to you both and gratitude.

Anne

1 Gabriele Ullstein of Berlin married in 1952 Noël Annan (1916–), writer and Provost of King's College, Cambridge 1956–66. He was made a life peer in 1965, and was to deliver the address at Ann's memorial service.

Ann's attempt to defend herself against the strain and her unhappiness included a calculated indulgence in alcohol. Friends worried as to whether she would recover from Caspar's death and its effects; perhaps she never did completely. She had been drinking in the months before it, particularly when she had been to see him in his various nursing homes; also she often felt ill and said that whisky made her feel better 'at once'. However as soon as she felt able to she showed exceptional courage and willpower in breaking her reliance on alcohol and recovered much of her old dash and style, though she tired quickly and was often less than well.

To Patrick Leigh Fermor

Sevenhampton Place   26 July [1976]

Darling Paddy

Its always a joy when you are in England, you never cease to 'enhance' during your darkest hours – incredible courage.[1]

Here I am gazing wistfully at the drink tray and whining that it is forbidden. Had a week in a nursing home to kill desire for the lovely stuff. Diana telephoned and said 'Hear you're in a home for inebriates': she then came along, seduced all and sundry and left after booking a bed to die in; my prestige *much* improved by the visitation.

Alas, I either go to Sicily or Corfu – tho' you, Joan, and Warners are awfully tempting – but too late alas for such drastic changes.

Heat and humidity continues – going to Scotland for rain.

Forgive scribble,

Masses of love to you both

xxxx

A

1 Leigh Fermor had been seriously ill but recovered completely.

To *Patrick Leigh Fermor*

Sevenhampton Place   24 October [1976]

Darling Paddy

Very sad to miss you in London, but was locked in nursing home with Robert Lowell. Nothing wrong with liver but permanent nervous gastritis from misery of last years. In fact became auxiliary nurse to the Lowell poet who arrived with early morning tea at 7.30 a.m. bearing volumes of Ezra Pound and T. S. Eliot and inexorably read aloud till 8 p.m. He possessed one torn shirt and never washed; as the anti-depressive drug began to work, his gait became unsteady and the chain smoking lost its aim so the day was spent extinguishing small bonfires, until Caroline [Blackwood] and the psychiatrist called in a special nurse and he was led away, frustrated, sad and distinguished.

He also read a great deal of his own poetry, one called 'Porcupine' about Cyril,[1] and much else *very* good: it was infectious, that non-rhyming blank sonnet verse, and impossible not to imitate in thought and words. . . . It's Robert's third collapse this year.

Debo a little bit overdid outrage of D. Pryce-Jones's 'Unity' book,[2] but *don't* breathe a word. Furious letters to Weidenfeld have reacted to being called the 'Devonshire House' set, and Tony Lambton unluckily wrote to Weidenfeld calling Pryce-Jones a pornographic writer – unlucky coming from him.

Much love

A

1 In fact 'Hedgehog' in *History*, 1973.
2 David Pryce-Jones had written a biography of the Duchess of Devonshire's sister called *Unity Mitford: A Quest*, which Weidenfeld published in the autumn.

Raymond Mortimer sent an elaborate thankyou letter for a house party that included Peggy Munster, Midi Gascoigne and Mark Boxer with a visit to Robert Heber[-]Percy at Faringdon:

Festival of Light   22 November 1977

Dear Lady Fleming,

Having had my life saved by penicillin, gratitude urges me to send you a warning about the company you *inadvertently* keep. The Faringdon representative of our Festival of Light has just addressed to me a painful report. She says nothing against Princess Munster, who sounds a very nice lady, or about the American Mr Who. But Sir Robert Percy, I am told, is very cruel to his pigeons, which he plunges into coloured dyes, and there are other stories about him which I dare not specify to your refined ears. Again, the Honble Mrs Gascoyne has a son who is an ATHEIST, judging from his TV programme attacking the Christians, which ought never to have passed the censor; and Mr Mark Boxer makes disgusting jokes in his drawings for *The Times*, which obviously you have never seen. Worse still, Raymond Mortimer in *The Sunday Times* pokes fun at devout clergymen, and is allowed also to make indecent insinuendoes.

It will be my painful duty to denounce all these deplorable characters, but I don't want to do so before enlightening you about them, so that you can escape further contamination.

Yours very sincerely

Mary Whitehouse [Raymond Mortimer]

Dearest Ann,

Staying with you is one of the greatest treats that I still enjoy; everything from your lake to your wit is delicious; and you make every allowance for my feebleness both of body and of talk. I do hope that your Nanny recovered from her shock, and that your car is not badly injured. The angelic Midi [Gascoigne] drove me all the way to my club, which was ill-heated, but my room here can be kept warm. I loved the walk with the glorious views, and all the bridge; you are my favourite partner.

That book you lent me about Mrs Mandelbaum impresses me hugely; and the pieces in *My Oxford* which I found in my room amused me, not least by a revelation about Robert's venerable ancestor, Bishop Heber, whose grave I once piously visited in southern India, and who, the book says, could not be trusted among choirboys.

Fondest love,

Your ever most grateful and affectionate

Raymond

To Michael Astor

Sevenhampton Place   10 July 1978

Dearest Michael,

Judy said to write you a funny letter, I find it would be easier to write you a love letter.

You see I do love you, for being perceptive, aware, witty, unique jokes and laughter.

Many feel like me and are wretched for you to be having so beastly an experience. GET WELL. The more intelligent the male, the more impatient and miserable in adversity.[1]

Take Hemeneverin; when you bit one and your eyes watered, and you did not like the taste, I was far from honest and did not admit that I have been hooked for years. The slightest approach of gloom and I reach for that very strong optimistic-making pill.

Nancy Lancaster to Diana Cooper at the Phipps ball:[2] 'You're so remarkable, when you die you will get stuffed'; Diana C. to me: 'I don't think Nancy knows what getting stuffed means.'

Tried to prevent Paddy overtipping parlour maid 'but look here, darling, I went to the ball in her tights, and they're most frightfully laddered, swine that I am.'

Poor Paddy hates his visits here more and more, no circle of friends in London, and somehow out of things, although still life and soul of. . . . .

To Portland Place tonight, if you would care for a very brief visit, do send a message, I will come round at once.

This is not a funny letter, but I don't feel funny, but it is sent with great affection.

Ann

1 Michael Astor knew he was dying of cancer.
2 Diana Phipps gave a ball to which the guests came as characters from opera. It was a great success and has been celebrated in fiction by Clive James in *Dazzling Creatures*, 1983.

Patrick Leigh Fermor recalls the Phipps ball:

The most crowded moment at Sevenhampton, for me, was a few years ago when all those in the bursting house and many others from round about gathered for drinks before Diana Phipps' ball at Buscot for the coming-out of her daughter Elizabeth. The place was suddenly overflowing with people dressed up as operatic figures. Diana Cooper as a nun – a time-honoured disguise of hers (the other, if the head only was called into play, being a Highlander's feather bonnet), Robert Heber-Percy in scarlet as Mephistopheles, Lord Goodman as Friar Tuck, Evangeline Bruce in something splendid; Jellicoes, Hendersons, Zana and Nicky Johnson, Coote Lygon, Rupert and beautiful Candida Lycett-Green, Jessica and Charles Douglas-Home, Jacob and Serena Rothschild, Fionn and, unless I'm getting it muddled with some other occasion, Raymond Carr dressed as a lion with his tail looped over his arm exactly like the Tenniel illustration; though if it *was* this time, I can't think of the operatic pretext. Not that one was really needed: Ann, dazzling in a splendid gold and peach-coloured dress, wore a headdress of ostrich feathers spreading from her brow in a fan of heralding plumes; when asked what she was she said, 'The Spirit of Carnival – no, the Ghost of the Opera.' She had a knock-out combination of looking simultaneously beautiful, gay, comic and self-mocking. My outfit was André Chenier. (I notice that however dim one is about other people's rig, one always remembers one's own.) I'd got the knee-breeches, but the stockings had been forgotten. The two chief people in command at Sevenhampton were Ann's marvellously kind nanny – who I think had been with Ann for 50 years – and a very nice, and nice-looking, and amazingly competent Mrs Durbridge (?) with beautifully done grey hair with a black bow. I told her my plight and she lent me a pair of her own stockings, and when they would not stay up, vanished and came back with a black suspender belt discreetly wrapped in tissue paper. I had it on in a moment, and all was well. I told Ann about this just as we were all leaving. She stopped dead halfway along the book passage. 'You mean,' she said, 'you've got Mrs Durbridge's suspender belt on?' I said yes, and she exploded with laughter and made a gesture of blindly reaching for support.

We found, on arrival, that Diana Phipps' American in-laws had flown a vast marquee from Long Island: it was more like an entire mansion in canvas, with subdivisions, corridors, striped poles and tufts of feathers, and garlanded now with swags of flowers – a mixture of the Field of the Cloth of Gold and *The Great Gatsby*, with, thanks to Diana's decorative Austrian relations, a dash of the Congress of Vienna. The tent was just as well as it poured, with occasional breaks of watery moonlight and clouds rushing across – no strolls across the river's bank – but all was radiant within. About 3 or 4 a.m. it was getting a bit out of hand and I found myself dancing in a ring with several others in an improvised Balkan *horo* with hands on each other's shoulders. I rashly reversed and George Jellicoe came down with a bang on my left foot – no featherweight, as Ann said next day – and split a small bone, as an X-ray later showed. But as often happens when spirits of both kinds are at work, I felt nothing till next day, when I hobbled back to Greece with a walking stick and a bedroom slipper. A fortnight later George came to stay, promptly trod on a sea-urchin and was bristling with spines which Joan winkled out with a needle and olive oil. A local submarine revenge for my still convalescent foot, it was thought.

To Patrick Leigh Fermor

Sevenhampton Place   15 January [1979]

Darling Paddy
    There's a perfectly frightful thaw in progress: days ago one of the twin dead giant elms fell into the lake through the ice, it froze some more and became a splendid icicled adventure to walk down or gaze upon; now all the beauty is gone, the sluice gate clogged with rotting wood, and it's a sorry scene.
    I left you at the Becketts without a fond farewell, driven home by thirst, since neither orange or champagne suits and I loathe the famous mixture.
    There is masses of food and petrol here, and the road's a joy with no tankers or lorries to get in the way or obscure the view. Travelling far not too jolly, no aeroplanes from Ulster, so a slow train journey from Scotland, though the stations where we lingered were gloriously snowclad and romantic.
    The National Gallery is far worse than any of you said, I have

attacked Isaiah and will proceed to Annan, Isaiah says that the N.G. architect wants to lower the ceilings to make the rooms seem smaller, I pointed out that many masterpieces are now at foot level and perhaps heightening them would be cheaper than lowering ceilings. Oh dear.

Now I must work, send a news bulletin soon.

Much much love and wishes to you and Joan for this year,

Annie

To Joan and Patrick Leigh Fermor

Sevenhampton Place   6 March [1979]

Dearest Joan and Paddy

Your letters were harbingers of spring and arrived over the week that proved the snowdrops and the aconites had been doing their homework beneath the snow; there they were plus blue sky and Greek stamps.

I immediately most terribly missed you at Stephen [Spender's] 70th. Stepping from the lift at the College of Art was a serried row of Janetta, Magouche, Xan, Robert [Kee], the Glenconners,[1] the Becketts – oh it was lovely, but you should have come home for it, you really should.

Stephen, Natasha and Lizzie[2] looked like Rheingold, splendidly Valhalla – alas, I wrote that in my thankyou letter, forgetting how deeply horrible Wotan and Frieka are – never mind, can't get it out of the post.

Wooing youth, which is my new design for living, I made for Mark Boxer and Tony Snowdon, who were gazing at a buxom woman of late middle age, brightly tinted gold hair, ever so pink and white complexion, erect carriage and balcony breasted, and aware that she was *someone*. Tony said three questions, high marks if you get it right – Does she own Madame Tussauds, is she an actress dame from the thirties, or is she Mrs T. S. Eliot? I spoilt it all because I knew it was Mrs T. S. and apparently the courtiers surrounding her were all hoping to get at the papers and be first in with a Biog.

Tony's new wife[3] is elegant, tall, funny, and pretty; I took a great fancy to her. Then Frank Longford butted in, and scarcely listening I thought he said he sent flowers to Myra Hindley once a week, and asked rapidly 'How much do you spend? Lilies of languor, roses of vice?' He was fearfully cross for he was lengthily explaining efforts to get apology from *Daily Mirror* for publishing that bouquets to prison cells were frequent.

Pen changed, and writing worse after day in London, and umbrella blown inside out by a March wind: but to continue with Stephen's 70th, Angus Wilson told me next novel dedicated to me and called '*Setting the World on Fire*' – alas, title nothing to do with dedicatee; then exciting return journey from Knightsbridge to Marylebone, Pat T. R. [Trevor-Roper] driving at red lights with same zest he had shown for red Mouton Rothschild – Philippe's birthday present.

Going Orkney and Grimond end of May, then West Ireland, wild flowers at beginning of June, so disclose plans for home so I may not miss you.

Peter Q. had forty-eight hours' leave here, decided that he needed young women, so dialled tycoon Keswick[4] who obligingly produced Hon. Charlotte Greville (18) and Lady Caroline Cholmondeley (19). P. grew all pink and lecherous and the beastly highland terrier lifted its leg on Lady Caro's new suede boots.

Oh, for your freesias and flower carpets and thanks for the descrip. of the '*Prieto*'.[5]

With much haste and very much love to J. and P.

A

1 Elizabeth Powell married in 1935 Christopher, Lord Glenconner (1899–1984).

2 Elizabeth Spender, an actress.

3 Lucy Davis married the Earl of Snowdon in December 1978. She had previously been married to Michael Lindsay-Hogg, the director.

4 Henry Keswick (1938–). Chairman of Jardine Matheson and Co. since 1975. Proprietor of the *Spectator* 1975–81.

5 'I found my bed looking like a tent, lifted the corner to reason with the incumbent to find a strange framework in which a glowing brazier full of charcoal was precariously balanced. I managed to get the whole boiling thing out onto the floor – another *grappa* and the *albergo* would have gone up in flames – and crept in. This mad Italian answer to the warming pan is called, it seems, a *prieto* . . .'

To the Duchess of Devonshire

Sevenhampton Place   1 June 1979

Darling Deborah

Your letters should be published – lovely description of Toynbees.

Orkney was wonderfully sunny, full advantage taken by pilot of twin engined old plane who scared the sea birds flying below cliff level, and took a few slates off the chimneys of the Castle of Mey before a bumpy landing at Aberdeen. Aberdeen airport full of sturdy oil rig men wearing T-shirts embroidered 'I'm not a dead diver, I just smell like one.'

Jo Grimond shares your view of festivals, he says that Orcadians like dancing reels and looking at local pottery, and he can't imagine why they are forced to have Barbara Hepworth sculpts and modern Maxwell Fry music – it's upon him, poor soul, at any minute.

The sun set at midnight, shocking pink sea and sky. Very jolly life with Grimonds, picnics, flowers and birds nests. Highly recommended to you for rest cure.

Do ask me any time in July. It's been too long since a talk. Paddy might appear then – can't read a word of his descrip. of the Rose Red City.

Raymond Mortimer is quite young enough to find letters, let me know if you want me to prod, he should keep an interest in life other than cards.[1]

Much love

A

1 Raymond Mortimer, 84, had said that he was too old to look for his letters from Nancy Mitford.

To Patrick Leigh Fermor

Sevenhampton Place   9 March 1980

Darling Paddy

It's a spring Sunday evening, sunshine, wood pigeons, rooks, blackbirds all making appropriate seasonal noises.

A month ago I returned from Israel, bubbling to talk of Jews and deserts: Michael Astor came over at once, we had lunch and giggled all the afternoon. He was looking marvellous and very funny. Three days later he had a stroke from cancer of the brain, and now, unbelievably, he is dead. I had become very dependent on him for neighbourhood companionship and evening telephone calls. It's a dreadful dreadful blank. Judy is a sad child but will recover.

With the Grim Reaper reaping away like anything, a lunch with Peter Q. was entirely devoted to reassurance of the jauntiness and health of his demeanour – indeed happily true, but I could have done with a change of subject.

You can imagine that in this woeful scene, your adventures in Barcelona have proved a sovereign remedy – I dine out on your misadventures all the time: it was a wonderful bonus of a letter – thanks for the cheer.

Though in fact, I have had lovely travels, just returned from a week in Morocco with Patrick Trevor-Roper. Forty-eight hours in Rabat and then belted down to Marrakesh; had we gone over the Atlas we would have belted too much, so we lotused there. I fear he should have had a younger, less timorous companion: there was a lot of screaming to stop the car to explore fields pale orange with marigolds beside patches of dark purple linaria. So last Sunday morning he was swimming in the Atlantic at El Dadija, and me in unheated empty swimming pool – I mean empty of people. No rooms at Mogador – damn. And now home to the cold and Cecil's memorial service.[1] In the future I am determined to pursue youth, and have attended a party for Andy Warhol;[2] no one over thirty – goody. They were all over him like a swarm of flies, but I was told not to leave without a peep because he looked like a transparent scorpion. Quite true; the result of being shot in the stomach by a woman libber and losing all his hair, so now it's a sandy wig and long eyelashes to match.

Masses of love to you both

Annie

1 Cecil Beaton had died.
2 Andy Warhol, painter, film director and self promoter.

Patrick Leigh Fermor again:

Other expeditions. About two years ago – how recent it is! I kept
Ann company on the Newcastle train to stay with Tony Lambton.
The other guests – Debo, Hugh Fraser, a very nice Frog called Paul
de Ganay and several deadeye magnates of the north – had come for
the pheasants. A wet summer had left the trees thick with leaves that
were only just beginning to change colour; and, in spite of a legion
of Geordie beaters, the birds were invisible until they actually flew
across clearings. We found all the others assembled after the last
drive in a walled, half-ruined farmyard in the woods. Dusk was
falling, but all was lit by a bonfire on which half a tree was ablaze
and showers of sparks leaped out when intrepid beaters stoked it
with long staves. Well-behaved dogs were lying or standing about,
steaks were sizzling and spitting on hot iron, vodka was thrown
down gullets out of vermeil-lined noggins, followed by the mulled
wine that Tony, on leave from Tuscany, poured into silver goblets
for the new arrivals. He was looking extraordinary, and rather
splendid in what sticks in my mind as a sort of tattered hauberk
caught in with a belt. Ann thought there was something of Uccello's
Nocturnal Hunt about the scene; there was, and a suggestion, too,
thanks to the flames and the dogs and the falling night, of similar
gatherings in Poland or Lithuania. It was an extraordinary place.
We walked back through the dark woods – enormous trees, deep
ravines, a river, ploughed fields, uninhabited Lambton Castle
soaring into the shadows, a garden descending through elaborate
feats of pollarding, topiary and espalier work and cunningly inter-
woven branches, until we saw the bright windows of the charming
house. (It seemed more remarkable still when somebody said that
all this wilderness and cultivation was entirely surrounded by
millions of lights; it was the insatiable urban spread of Durham and,
seen from the air, a sudden oval of darkness expanded in the middle
like a black hole in the solar system.) When breaking-up time came,
the return journey was a long drive, with Debo at the wheel,
through bleak, Buchan-like and border ballad regions, and finally
across wind-grieved hillsides to Cold Comfort Farm where Emma
and Toby live. Their pretty daughter Stella seized all whom she
could lay on, to lead them, in a state of near ecstasy, into a barn
where a speckled black-and-white Prussian hen which she'd been
given under the illusion that it was a cock, had all of a sudden laid

five eggs. They had just hatched out, and there the chickens were, to her joy and acclaim.

To Lord Lambton

Shane's Castle   17 January [1981]

Dearest Tony

I delayed answering your very funny news bulletin too long, and was overcome by twisted intestines and a horrible time in a Swindon hospital. It happened on a Friday, my party for Paddy, and judging from their thankyou letters they enjoyed themselves far more than if I had been there. While they were playing paper games I was removed unconscious by ambulance men and attendant doctor but no one noticed the disturbance!

Only outing to the opera, where Arnold and George Harewood[1] had lured the Thatchers, hoping that a horrible rendering of *Tosca* sung in English would increase the government subsidy; the first interval the private room guests were John Julius, Lady Diana, Artemis, Jason, and Mrs T. had to spend thirty-five minutes talking to them. When the performance was mercifully over we had supper in Arnold's flat, the Harewoods, the conductor and silent wife,[2] the Chairman of the Stock Exchange and silent wife[3] and Mr and Mrs T.

They were all strangers to me and it seemed a glum affair; but not boring to study the improbable P.M. She seems *totally* humourless, and with a nervous system usually attributed to fishes, surely she has never read a book or looked at a picture? Do you know her well?

Saw something of Quennell while in Sister Agnes, it was a change from White's Club . . . The Levers[4] and Joe Alsop came the same weekend; Joe and Harold seemed to enjoy boring each other, they breakfasted in dressing gowns from nine o'clock till one but they tip so munificently there were no complaints from the staff.

There are now more peers than robes, and since Diane was determined to go to the opening of parliament, I borrowed Raymond's to adorn Harold, assuring the O'Neills they would receive caviar or *paté de foie gras* but not at all, only a note from Diane to say Harold had looked so beautiful she had fallen in love with him again.

It's an Ulster Sunday, and has rained continuously for days, all dripping evergreens and gloom. So this is a dull letter. But lots of love to you and Clare

Annie

1 Earl of Harewood (1923–   ). Managing Director English National Opera since 1972. Married Patricia Tuckwell of Australia in 1967.
2 Amanda Stein married in 1980 Mark Elder (1947–   ) who has been Musical Director of the English National Opera since 1979.
3 Judith Abel Smith married in 1960 Nicholas Goodison, Chairman of the Stock Exchange since 1976. He was knighted in 1982.
4 Diane Bashi married in 1962 Harold Lever (1914–   ) Labour MP 1945–79, Chancellor of the Duchy of Lancaster 1974–9. He was made a life peer in 1979.

To Peter Quennell

79 Portland Place   [?April 1981]

Darling Peter
    Belated wishes for your birthday
    I have laryngitis and cancer – no voice to complain!
    DAMN. Home tomorrow, and here next week. I will telephone when not speechless.
    The pills I have to take cause nausea, dizziness and despair, but no surgery and apparently side effects lessen with time.
                        With much love to you
                                A

To the Duchess of Devonshire

79 Portland Place   [?April 1981]

Darling Deborah
    I have laryngitis and cancer, the former is the most immediately depressing – voiceless.
    Will telephone when speech returns. Home tomorrow and here next Tuesday and Wednesday. Hope you flourish, it would do me good to see you.
                        Much love
                                A

Ann returned to Sevenhampton, and was not to leave again. The doctors accurately predicted that she had three months to live but she was not told and, though she noticed that she was becoming weaker, not stronger, she did not care to have it put into words. Sometimes she would rally in the evenings and occasionally friends would gather round her bed for talk and laughter. Fionn was with her, sometimes Raymond could come down. Always pale, she grew paler and looked not well but beautiful. She did not like becoming too feeble to look after herself but did not complain. The end came swiftly when it came, and she died on Sunday 12 July 1981.

APPENDIX OF NAMES

ARRAN, EARL OF (1910–84). Journalist and broadcaster, Arthur 'Boofy' Gore married in 1937 Ann's cousin Fiona Colquhoun and succeeded his brother in 1958. Once described as 'a poor man's Duke of Bedford and a rich man's Godfrey Winn', he made a reputation for himself by expressing opinions in his column in the *Evening News* that were calculated to shock. He played the role of eccentric peer so skilfully that it was difficult to tell to what extent he actually was one.

ASHTON, SIR FREDERICK (1904–). Founder-choreographer of the Royal Ballet, of which he was Principal Choreographer 1933–70 and director 1963–70. He was also an accomplished dancer, 'of very light build and medium height. He had small feet and hands but a very impressive head, well-shaped with a long face and a long nose that I thought "aristocratic" without quite knowing why. His manner was at first diffident.' (*Margot Fonteyn*, 1975) A brilliant mimic, he enjoyed Ann's parties in spite of 'finding the politicians rather frightening'. He was knighted in 1962, CH 1970, OM 1977.

AVON, COUNTESS OF (1920–). Clarissa Churchill is the daughter of Lady Gwendoline ('Goonie') Spencer-Churchill and Jack Churchill, Sir Winston's brother, and so a cousin of Randolph (*q.v.*). Attractive and vivacious, she moved in aesthetic and intellectual circles in her youth, not in political ones, so her marriage in 1952 to Sir Anthony Eden came as a surprise to her friends. He was then Foreign Secretary, became Prime Minister in 1955, and was created Earl of Avon in 1961.

BACON, FRANCIS (1909–). Widely acclaimed as the greatest living painter. Descended from the Elizabethan Francis Bacon, born in Dublin. Having received little formal education or instruction in painting, he trained race-horses in his youth, travelled in London, Paris and Berlin and made a living decorating. A small exhibition in 1934 failed and he has said that nothing he painted before 1944 is of any worth. In 1945 a triptych based on the crucifixion caused a sensation, largely of revulsion, which his raw meat and screaming popes have continued to excite. His first portrait was of Lucian Freud and he has painted Lord Goodman.

BEATON, SIR CECIL (1904–80). Photographer, theatre designer, diarist and social figure, less successful as painter and playwright. In September 1953 in a passage possibly rewritten for publication, his diary records 'Ann deserves high marks: ten for general intelligence, eight for intuition, seven for sensitivity, and at least five for commonsense. Very good marks, too, for gaiety, courage and humour. Less than one mark for looking after herself and keeping friends or relations away when she is ill or utterly exhausted.' Knighted in 1972.

BONHAM CARTER, MARK (1922–). Publisher and politician. Grandson of Herbert Asquith, and so connected with Ann through his second wife, Margot Asquith, her great-aunt. Also nephew of Cynthia Charteris who married Herbert Asquith. Married in 1955 Leslie Nast. Director of William Collins Ltd 1955–8, Liberal MP 1958–9, first Chairman of the Race Relations Board 1966–70. Vice Chairman of the BBC 1975–81.

BRYCE, IVAR (1906–). Built a sandcastle with the Fleming boys in 1914, and remained a lifelong friend of Ian. As attractive young bachelors they pursued girls together. A spy in South America during World War II, he lived for a time in Jamaica and later arranged the purchase of Goldeneye for Fleming. Married to Vera de Sa Sottomaior of Brazil 1930–8 (she then married Lord Dunsany), to Sheila Taylor-Pearse Byrne 1939–50, and to Marie-Josephine Hartford in 1950. He and Fleming struggled together to launch James Bond in the cinema and were sued together for plagiarism. Bryce wrote an admiring memoir of Fleming, *You Only Live Once*, 1975 and 1984. He now manages a stud and owns racehorses.

CHARTERIS, HUGO (1922–70). Novelist. Ann's only brother, educated at Eton and Oxford, served as an infantry officer 1943–4 in Italy, where he was twice wounded. From 1945–7 he was a public relations officer in Java and Malaya. In 1948 he married Virginia Forbes Adam and became a journalist for the *Daily Mail* in London and Paris before retiring to Sutherland to write novels. These frequently contained portraits of his family and friends, including Ann and Laura, and this led to trouble.

CHARTERIS, LAURA (1915–). Two years younger than Ann, Laura's life and marriages form a curious parallel with her elder sister's. Just as Ann was married young to a respectable peer, Laura married Viscount Long in 1933 when she was eighteen. Ann would in all probability have got a divorce after the war had Lord O'Neill not been killed in action in 1944; Laura did obtain a divorce in 1943, but Lord Long was also killed in action in 1944. Each remarried a rich and powerful figure, Viscount Rothermere in Ann's case, the Earl of Dudley in Laura's. Each was the second wife and each was to leave her husband, Ann to marry Ian Fleming and Laura, after a few years with another man, to marry Michael Canfield, the love of her life. In each case the third husband died, and in 1972 Laura married the Duke of Marlborough, only weeks before he died. By her first husband Laura had a daughter, Sara, who married a Conservative MP, Charles Morrison, in 1954 and became an intimate of Ann's. Laura's auto-biography, *Laughter from a Cloud*, was published in 1980.

CHURCHILL, RANDOLPH (1911–68). Son of Sir Winston. Extremely good-looking in his youth; journalist, then Conservative MP 1940–5. Married 1939–45 to Pamela Digby and 1948–61 to June Osborne; he was also in love with Ann's sister Laura. An impossible guest, rude to servants and often to everyone else too, he was a generous host and frequently, but not quite always, forgiven his excesses. 'Randolph animates me, repeats what I say with relish, makes me feel jolly.' Evelyn Waugh in 1947 (*Diaries*, 1976).

CONNOLLY, CYRIL (1903–74). Critic and writer. Married to Jean Bakewell, an American, 1930–45; to Barbara Skelton, a writer who then married Lord Weidenfeld, 1950–4; and to Deirdre Craig, who is now married to Peter Levi, 1959–74. Connolly felt that he never lived up to his early gifts and wrote a book about this predicament, *Enemies of Promise*, 1938. He was co-founder and Editor of *Horizon*, and then the leading reviewer for *The Sunday Times*. His friend Evelyn Waugh named various fictional characters after him: some evacuee children in *Put Out More Flags* and an African general (in *Black Mischief*), as well as using him as the model for Everard Spruce, Editor of *Survival*, in *Sword of Honour*. More Fleming's friend than Ann's, he invented 'Gold Prick', which was changed to Goldfinger, and his parody, *Bond Strikes Camp*, was enjoyed by both the Flemings.

COOPER, LADY DIANA (1892–). Indestructible beauty, actress, and a lifelong friend of Ann, with whom she was connected through her brother, the Duke of Rutland (who married Ann's aunt) and her sister, Lady Violet Manners (who married Ann's uncle and became 'Aunt Letty'). When Ann had an affair with a married man in the 1960s Lady Diana was the only person to whom she wrote about it. Married in 1919 to Duff Cooper, who was Ambassador in Paris 1944–7, she retained her title when he was created Viscount Norwich in 1952. Her autobiography was published in three volumes: *The Rainbow Comes and Goes*, 1958; *The Light of Common Day*, 1959; and *Trumpets from the Steep*, 1960. All were reissued in one volume in 1984.

COWARD, NOËL (1899–1973). Playwright, performer and composer. When Ann first got to know him after the war, he was already known as The Master after his successes in plays, musicals and revues. A neighbour on the north coast of Jamaica, Coward sold the remainder of the lease on his house near Dover, White Cliffs, to the Flemings shortly after they were married. He became godfather to Caspar. Ann sometimes found his veneration for the royal family and his assumption that he should be the centre of attention tiresome; always witty, he could be a witty bore. Knighted in 1970.

DEVONSHIRE, DUCHESS OF (1920–). Deborah ('Debo') Mitford, younger sister of Nancy, Pamela, Tom, Unity and Jessica, married in 1941 Lord Andrew Cavendish, who succeeded as Duke of Devonshire in 1950.

A lasting friend of Ann and Evelyn Waugh, who, on seeing her in the same dress twice, wrote to her sister Nancy, 'Should not a girl with her beauty, wit and high position make a bit more of herself?' Though claiming never to have read a book, she wrote a highly successful one, *The House: A Portrait of Chatsworth*, 1982.

DONALDSON, LORD AND LADY. Frances Lonsdale (1907–) married in 1935 John ('Jack') Donaldson (1907–) who was created a life peer in 1967. She is the biographer of her father Freddy Lonsdale (1957) and author of *Evelyn Waugh: portrait of a country neighbour*, 1967; *Edward VIII*, 1974; and *P. G. Wodehouse*, 1982. A closer friend than might be imagined from these letters, she preferred Ann in quieter mood, finding her social manner and sometimes her writing style, particularly to Evelyn Waugh, a little forced. Jack Donaldson has been a farmer, director of the Royal Opera House 1963–74, Under-Secretary of State in Northern Ireland and Labour Minister for the Arts 1976–9. He joined the SDP in 1981.

DUDLEY, COUNTESS OF. *See* Charteris, Laura.

FERMOR, PATRICK LEIGH (1915–). Writer, traveller, war hero and linguist. Of Anglo-Irish descent, he left King's School, Canterbury prematurely and set off to walk to Constantinople at the age of eighteen. After several years of travelling, largely in the Balkans, he joined the Irish Guards and was liaison officer to Greek Headquarters in Albania. In the battle of Crete, he returned to hide in the hills, dressed as a shepherd, for two years while commanding guerilla operations, including the kidnap of the German commander, General Kreipe. He became a major and was awarded the OBE in 1943, the DSO in 1944. Has twenty Cretan godchildren. He married Joan Rayner in 1968 and lives in a house he designed in the south of the Peloponnese. His books include *The Violins of St Jacques*, 1953; *Mani*, 1958; *Roumeli*, 1973 and *A Time of Gifts*, 1977.

ALASTAIR FORBES (1918–). Well-born American journalist, described by James Lees-Milne in 1943 as 'a deb's delight of classic beauty, with fair, unblemished skin. Very young and a little portentous. . . ambitious for a parliamentary career, witty, mischievous, censorious and bright'. Although he has worked for many papers and has known 'everyone', he has not become as famous as might have been expected, perhaps because his natural labyrinthine style is unsuited to a swift perusal.

FREUD, LUCIAN (1922–). Painter. Grandson of Sigmund Freud, whom he liked, son of Ernst Freud, an architect. Born in Berlin, he came to Britain when he was nine, became a British subject in 1939 and spent six months as an ordinary seaman in the Merchant Marines in 1941, before being invalided out. Held his first one-man show in New York in 1944. Married 1948–52 to Kathleen Epstein, daughter of Jacob Epstein, and 1953–7 to

Lady Caroline Blackwood. 'Lucian is, in fact, an anomalous figure, a socially sought-after solitary with a seemingly facile mind to whom the pursuit of his vocation is a sombre ordeal daily renewed, a seemingly material temperament, who, like Francis Bacon, beyond needing ready cash in his pocket, is without the acquisitive urge and whose successive studios would be rejected as unfit to live in by the student of today.' *Modern English Painters* by John Rothenstein, 1974. Among his subjects for portraits have been Francis Bacon, several members of the Devonshire family and Ann. CH, 1983.

GENDEL, JUDY (1923–72). Daughter of Venetia Montagu, the close friend and correspondent of Asquith. Plain, exuberant, she had a wide circle of friends which included Ann, Mary Churchill and Princess Margaret. 'She wasn't remotely like anyone else . . . intelligence and flair and an innate competence at almost everything . . . she loved friends and lived for company . . . she lived at full tilt.' (Patrick Leigh Fermor in *H. H. Asquith's Letters to Venetia Stanley*, ed. Michael and Eleanor Brock, 1982). In 1962 she married Milton Gendel, an art historian, and they moved to Rome.

GOODMAN, ARNOLD (1913–). Solicitor, *éminence grise*. After the death of Fleming, Sir Henry d'Avigdor-Goldsmid told Ann that if she was involved in financial complications, he knew just the man to help her. Arnold Goodman's astonishing career was taking off: he was solicitor and friend of the new Prime Minister, Harold Wilson. Soon he was the most important negotiator in the country, with a finger in every pie. He was created a peer in 1965 and among his particular interests were the Arts Council, the Royal Opera House and the English National Opera, the Royal Shakespeare Company, the National Theatre, the Observer and the Newspaper Publishers Association. He received the CH in 1972 and became Master of University College, Oxford in 1976. He first met Ann in 1964, and his affection for her was immediate; hers for him grew steadily and there was much speculation as to whether they would get married; certainly he was the greatest friend of her last years.

GORE, ARTHUR 'BOOFY', *See* Arran, Earl of.

HENDERSON, SIR NICHOLAS (1919–). Son of Sir Hubert Henderson, Warden of All Souls. Diplomat who, after being Ambassador to Poland, the Federal Republic of Germany and France, was brought out of retirement to represent his country in Washington 1979–82. Married Mary Cawadias in 1951, after being at the embassy in Athens 1949–50. Knighted 1977.

JENKINS, ROY (1920–). Married in 1945 Jennifer Morris. Labour MP 1948–76 (Chancellor of the Exchequer 1967–70, Deputy Leader 1970–2, Home Secretary for the second time 1974–6) when he resigned in order to become President of the Commission of the EEC. He was the first Leader of the SDP and became an MP once more in 1982. Biographer of, among others, Asquith (1964). Hugh Gaitskell said of him in 1959: 'He is very much in the social swim these days and I am sometimes anxious about him and young Tony [Crosland].' (*The Backbench Diaries of Richard Crossman*, ed. Janet Morgan) Although a connection with Ann's circle was of no help to any Labour politician, he never made any secret of his friendship with her. A competitive croquet player.

LINDSAY, LADY, *see* Westminster, Loelia, Duchess of.

MARLBOROUGH, LAURA, DUCHESS OF, *see* Charteris, Laura.

MAUGHAM, SOMERSET (1874–1965). Among the most successful storytellers of the century, Maugham was a friend and correspondent to whom Ann remained faithful. When she knew him in the 1950s, his literary status was high and the Villa Mauresque in the South of France a desirable place to stay. Ann kept the letters of no one else with such care and respect. As he grew from being old to being very old, Maugham became deafer and more difficult, his reputation waned, but Ann maintained their relationship and, after his death she wrote: 'I loved Willie Maugham and associate the Villa Mauresque with fun and happiness . . . Willie's sardonic humour made him an excellent companion . . . the Mauresque was a haven of comfort, good food, beauty and entertaining talk.' (*Spectator*, 17 May 1980)

QUENNELL, PETER (1905–). Writer and among Ann's oldest friends. Good-looking, and a published poet before he left Oxford, Quennell seemed so certain of the most brilliant literary and social career that it is not surprising if he excited a certain amount of envy. He has edited *The Cornhill Magazine* 1944–51 and *History Today* 1951–79, published many biographical works both historical and literary and won from his life-long enemy Evelyn Waugh the grudging admission that he 'has in his dry vacuous way a mastery of language'. His autobiography (*The Marble Foot*, 1976 and *The Wanton Chase*, 1980) describes Ann as 'the stimulating inspiratrice'.

ROTHERMERE, VISCOUNT (1898–1978). Married 1920–38 to Margaret Redhead, and had one son and two daughters. Married to Ann 1945–52 and in 1966 to Mary Ohrstrom of Texas. He accompanied Lloyd George to the Peace Conference in Paris, 1919 and became a Conservative MP that year, when he was 21. Extremely good-looking and an excellent squash and tennis player, he was always attractive to women and wished to be agreeable to all. He had not expected to succeed to his father's position running the *Daily Mail* and gave the impression that he rather wished he had not, though shrewd about money. He was a kind stepfather to Ann's children but she found him lacking in dash and even accused him of physical cowardice when, for instance, he refused to climb down a ladder.

WAUGH, EVELYN (1903–66). Became well-known as a novelist in the 1920s and had an international success with *Brideshead Revisited* before he made friends with Ann after the war. Though she struck his ear trumpet with a fork because she thought it an affectation and he frightened her son by pulling faces, they remained close friends until his death.

WESTMINSTER, LOELIA, DUCHESS OF (1902–   ). Loelia Ponsonby was married 1930–47 to the enormously rich second Duke of Westminster and 1969–81 to Sir Martin Lindsay, MP. A great friend of Ann's, she acted as chaperone at Goldeneye while Ann was still Lady Rothermere, a role which left her 'drugged with boredom and lethargy'. Fleming called her 'Lil', as *loelia* is the Russian for 'lily'.

INDEX

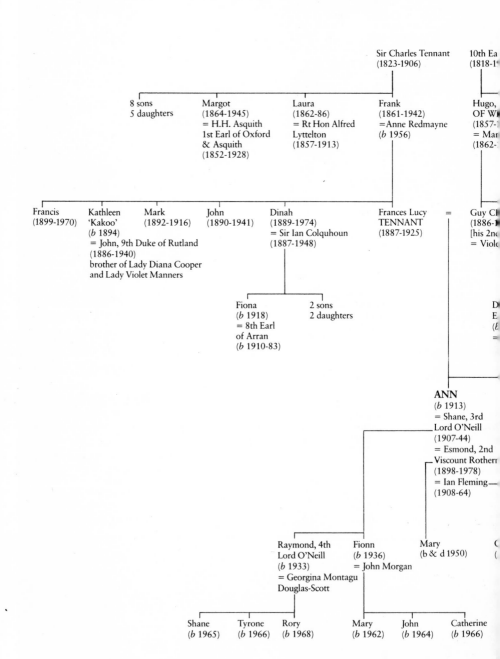

Sir Charles Tennant
(1823-1906)

10th Ea
(1818-1

8 sons
5 daughters

Margot
(1864-1945)
= H.H. Asquith
1st Earl of Oxford
& Asquith
(1852-1928)

Laura
(1862-86)
= Rt Hon Alfred
Lyttelton
(1857-1913)

Frank
(1861-1942)
=Anne Redmayne
(b 1956)

Hugo,
OF W
(1857-
= Mar
(1862-

Francis
(1899-1970)

Kathleen
'Kakoo'
(b 1894)
= John, 9th Duke of Rutland
(1886-1940)
brother of Lady Diana Cooper
and Lady Violet Manners

Mark
(1892-1916)

John
(1890-1941)

Dinah
(1889-1974)
= Sir Ian Colquhoun
(1887-1948)

Frances Lucy
TENNANT
(1887-1925)

=

Guy Cl
(1886-
[his 2n
= Viole

Fiona
(b 1918)
= 8th Earl
of Arran
(b 1910-83)

2 sons
2 daughters

D
E
(b
=

ANN
(b 1913)
= Shane, 3rd
Lord O'Neill
(1907-44)
= Esmond, 2nd
Viscount Rotherr
(1898-1978)
= Ian Fleming
(1908-64)

Raymond, 4th
Lord O'Neill
(b 1933)
= Georgina Montagu
Douglas-Scott

Fionn
(b 1936)
= John Morgan

Mary
(b & d 1950)

C
(

Shane
(b 1965)

Tyrone
(b 1966)

Rory
(b 1968)

Mary
(b 1962)

John
(b 1964)

Catherine
(b 1966)